THE HISTORICAL
ATLAS OF THE
CONGRESSES
OF THE
CONFEDERATE
STATES OF AMERICA
1861–1865

THE HISTORICAL ATLAS OF THE CONGRESSES OF THE CONFEDERATE STATES OF AMERICA 1861–1865

Kenneth C. Martis

Cartographer
Gyula Pauer

Research Assistant
B. Reed Durbin

Simon & Schuster
A Paramount Communications Company

New York   London   Toronto   Sydney   Tokyo   Singapore

Academic Reference Division
Simon & Schuster
15 Columbus Circle
New York, NY 10023

Printed in the United States of America

printing number

1 2 3 4 5 6 7 8 9 10

Library of Congress Cataloging-in-Publication data

Martis, Kenneth C.
        The historical atlas of the Congresses of the Confederate
    States of America: 1861–1865 / Kenneth C. Martis: Gyula Pauer,
    cartographer
                p.   cm.
        Includes bibliographical references and index.
        ISBN 0-13-389115-1
        1. Confederate States of America. Congress—Maps.   2. Confederate
    States of America. Politics and government—Maps.   3. United
    States—History—Civil War, 1861–1865—Politics and government—
    Maps.   4. United States—Historical geography—Maps.
    G1281.F8M3   1994 <G&M>
    973.7'022'3—dc20   93-46478
                                                            CIP
                                                            MAP

To all my teachers

Thank you for your knowledge, patience, and inspiration.

CONTENTS

MAPS

TABLES

PREFACE

The Civil War is the most written about subject in American history. *The Historical Atlas of the Congresses of the Confederate States of America: 1861–1865* examines the Civil War in a way never before attempted. It is the first political atlas of the Civil War; indeed, it is the first Civil War atlas that does not have a military or battlefield theme. It maps and analyzes the political geography of the Civil War South by focusing on the legislative branch of the Confederate States of America. The core of this book is forty-five multicolor maps that illustrate a wide variety of phenomena. These maps, and accompanying data and text, bring Civil War history alive in a new and unique fashion.

A Congress constituting the legislative branch of government existed during the entire history of the Confederacy. A unicameral Provisional Congress legislated in the first year; a bicameral Congress consisting of a House of Representatives and a Senate modeled after the U.S. Congress existed from February 18, 1862, to March 18, 1865. One of the objectives of the maps, data, discussion, and analysis in this atlas is to enhance the understanding of the Confederate Congress's role in the South during the Civil War, thereby enlarging the understanding of the war itself.

Organization

The Historical Atlas of the Congresses of the Confederate States of America: 1861–1865 is organized to facilitate its use both as a general reference book on the Confederate Congresses, the Confederate States of America, and the American Civil War, and as a research atlas and cartographic tool.

Chapter 1 introduces the Confederate Congresses and their importance in the organization and governance of the Confederacy. All legislative bodies have inherent geographical-regional characteristics. Chapter 1 discusses the contributions of the geographical study of the U.S. Congress and other legislatures and how it is applied to the Civil War and the Confederate Congresses.

Chapter 2 examines the Provisional Congress and its role in establishing the Confederacy and organizing the permanent Confederate government. In addition, this chapter introduces one of the most important ideas in understanding the Confederate Congresses: the consequences of Union occupation of states and districts and the continued participation of these representatives in wartime policy-making. Four maps in Chapter 2 and twelve maps in Chapter 3 illustrate this phenomenon.

Chapter 3 discusses the establishment and characteristics of Confederate congressional districts. In the permanent Confederate House of Representatives the South continued the United States' tradition of geographically based elections. Because this atlas maps congressional boundaries, matches districts with their representatives, and provides legal descriptions of the counties making up the districts, it can be used not only as a general information reference, but as an active tool of research, analysis, and illustration. The congressional district base maps and accompanying membership lists allow students, teachers, and researchers in history, geography, and political science to map and study any congressional roll-call vote and a wide variety of other phenomena. Chapter 3 uses the congressional district base maps to illustrate five important variables that reveal critical physical and human geographical differences and political divisions in the South. The geographical pattern of these district variables not only suggests significant differences between the upper and lower South, but also aids in interpreting subsequent election results and individual representative roll-call voting behavior.

The chapter on Confederate congressional elections, Chapter 4, is the longest in the book. The information and maps in this chapter are based on the first comprehensive compilation and aggregation of Confederate congressional election statistics in American history. These statistics are used to analyze ballot competition, method of election, and voter turnout, and the former political party, secession stance, and incumbency of those elected. Each state is analyzed with respect to the above characteristics and national results are mapped, interpreted, and discussed. The eleven election maps in Chapter 4 show regional differences and noteworthy changes from the First to Second Congress.

Chapter 5 maps, discusses, and analyzes roll-call voting in the Confederate Senate and House. The factors influencing roll-call voting are enumerated, especially with respect to the major policy issues addressed in the Confederacy. One of the major influencing factors was the continuation in the Confederacy of the United States' tradition of political representation in which congressmen respond to and defend local, district, and state concerns. The ten congressional roll-call voting maps in this chapter were produced using the district boundary base maps and yea-and-nay votes from the *Journal of the Congress of the Confederate States of America, 1861–1865*. Research on roll-call voting behavior reveals noticeable regional concentrations of support and resistance on many individual ballots. The general geographic pattern of roll-call voting is even more strikingly revealed in maps of multiple votes on one issue and multidimensional behavior. Local, district, and state concerns many times overrode national concerns, even in time of war.

Chapter 6 summarizes the major findings and conclusions. This and the introductory chapter suggest that understanding the Confederate Congresses is important for the full understanding of the Confederacy. Consequential regional differences in the South were manifested in political sentiments, which were in turn reflected in the Confederate Congress. Congress and the Jefferson Davis Administration shared national Confederate policy-making. Within Congress the great debate over the Civil War and the national issues of the day were played out. This atlas maps for the first time many of the significant political aspects of the Civil War South. These maps enhance and expand the understanding of the Civil War and the causes, issues, inner conflicts, and prolongation of the most important single event in American history.

Background

The Historical Atlas of the Congresses of the Confederate States of America: 1861–1865 is part of a series of books whose objective is to expand the geographic understanding of American history. Over the last fifteen years my research on United States historical political geography has been supported in part by the National Endowment for the Humanities, the National Science Foundation, the Association of American Geographers, the Newberry Library, and the Huntington Library. The initial work in this series, *The Historical Atlas of United States Congressional Districts: 1789–1983* (1982) was the first to map all congressional districts for all states and congresses in American history. It was designated a Selected Reference Book by the journal *College and Research Libraries* and won the American Historical Association's Waldo G. Leland Prize for the best reference book in all fields of history for the period 1981–1986. In 1989 *The Historical Atlas of Political Parties in the United States Congress: 1789–1989* was the first book to identify and map the political party affiliation of every member to serve in

the House and Senate. The Library of Congress selected the political cartography from this work as the centerpiece of its main exhibition in celebration of the 1989 bicentennial of the United States Congress, "Tides of Party Politics: Two Centuries of Congressional Elections." *Library Journal* designated the political party atlas as one of the Best Reference Books of 1989 and *College and Research Libraries* named it a Selected Reference Book of 1989–90. In the congressional district and political party atlases the South is, of course, conspicuously missing for the 1861–1865 period. One of the objectives of this atlas is to fill this gap in American history.

In 1993 *The Historical Atlas of State Power in Congress: 1790–1990* was the first to map the changes in decennial apportionment in the United States House of Representatives throughout American history. One of the four major demographic-political shifts discussed in this work is the decline in the number of members in Congress from the southern slave states in the decades leading up to the Civil War. Several months after its publication, the Washington Book Publishers presented this work its Best Book Design Award. The intellectual history and theoretical foundation for all the above publications is delineated in a spring 1984 article in *Prologue—Journal of the National Archives*, "Mapping Congress—Developing a Geographic Understanding of American Political History." This article won the Organization of American Historian's Charles Thomson Prize for the best article on American history based on archival research. This atlas further expands the general theme of the atlases and article by mapping the Confederate Congresses and developing a geographic understanding of political history in the Civil War South.

Acknowledgments

The Confederate atlas project was conducted over a four-year period with the cooperation of numerous individuals and researchers. The Department of Geology and Geography at West Virginia University led by Chairman Alan C. Donaldson continued to provide a model research atmosphere. As he as done in the past, John Luchok, an editor at West Virginia University, read the entire first draft of the manuscript and made salient comments that added to the clarity of the text.

Over the last four years I have corresponded with many Civil War historians, archivists, librarians, and private researchers and they have helped immensely in the compilation of this work. These individuals are referenced by name in the chapter footnotes and especially in the footnotes in Appendix IV dealing with the primary source research regarding Confederate congressional election candidates and vote totals. I especially thank the staff of the West Virginia University library for the many hours they have given in reference and

interlibrary loan. Three historians gave me an especially large amount of help: Thomas B. Alexander (University of Missouri, Columbia), Paul D. Escott (Wake Forest University), and Dale Baum (Texas A&M University). Wayne C. Moore, archivist with the Tennessee State Library and Archives, was notably generous in assembling and microfilming copies of the original returns for the second Tennessee election, the compilation appearing in Appendix V and Map 30. I used the information from all cited individuals and references in the final selection and interpretation of the atlas maps and take responsibility for these interpretations and any factual errors.

Several undergraduate students at West Virginia University helped in the research of this work, including Greg Lieving, Shauntell Freeman, Dominic D'Eramo, and Amy Morris. They participated in many tasks such as compiling dozens of draft roll-call vote maps, photocopying material, rereading hundreds of pages of Civil War newspapers in search of references to Confederate elections, and double- and triple-checking tables and appendixes. Through a program developed by the West Virginia University Regional Research Institute, one undergraduate honors student, Reed Durbin, was selected to participate in an undergraduate research experience. Reed quickly became a trusted research assistant and his help was invaluable in almost all phases of the project. His original nine-month appointment became over two years of work, extending into his graduate program in history. The compilation of Confederate congressional election candidates and vote returns in Appendix IV is largely due to his efforts. This atlas is better because of his involvement and perseverance.

The multicolor maps are the centerpiece of this work. I am proud to work again with my cartographer, Gyula Pauer, Director of the University of Kentucky Cartographic Laboratory. His cartographic expertise and Old World diligence transformed my original sketches into an attractive and revealing series of political maps.

The final manuscript, tables, and appendixes, and four-color map negatives were assembled into book form by Simon & Schuster's Academic Reference Division, headed by Charles E. Smith. Charlie encouraged me to select the Confederate atlas as the next project in the historical political atlas series and his support for cartography and research made this book possible. My editor at Simon & Schuster, Stephen Wagley, and I worked over one year on this project, and his congenial style, coupled with his vast professional expertise, made the final product not only a joy to work on but a polished reference book.

Kenneth C. Martis
Morgantown, West Virginia
January 8, 1994

THE HISTORICAL
ATLAS OF THE
CONGRESSES
OF THE
CONFEDERATE
STATES OF AMERICA
1861–1865

1

INTRODUCTION

The Confederate Congresses

The Civil War is the single most significant and pivotal event in American history. It has been described as an occurrence even more defining than the American Revolution itself and the founding of the nation.[1] This significance, plus the military losses and destruction, and the political and social legacy of the Civil War, has spawned over fifty thousand academic and popular works, more than any other subject in American history.[2] The quality of recent scholarship has not only enhanced understanding of the Civil War but also enlarged the already formidable literature and broadened its spirited and controversial historiography. This work examines the American Civil War in a way never before attempted. *The Historical Atlas of the Congresses of the Confederate States of America: 1861–1865* is the first atlas on the American Civil War that does not have a military or battlefield theme.[3] Specifically, it examines the organization, proceedings, and actions of the Confederate Congresses by way of an inquiry into its political geography.

During the entire history of the Confederate States of America a Congress constituting the legislative branch of government existed. In fact, the Confederacy was formed at a convention in Montgomery, Alabama, by means of a Provisional Congress. The Montgomery convention met on February 4, 1861, and drafted and then approved a Provisional Constitution on February 8, 1861. The Provisional Con-

stitution established a unicameral Provisional Congress and the Montgomery convention became that Congress. The Provisional Congress drafted and then approved on February 28, 1861, a Permanent Confederate Constitution, which provided for a bicameral Congress of a House of Representatives and Senate modeled after the United States Congress. The Permanent Confederate Congress was elected in late 1861 and convened on February 18, 1862, as the legislative branch and first assembly of the Permanent Confederate government. The Permanent Congress met in two Congresses with six sessions, adjourning March 18, 1865, a few days before the end of the Civil War. Table 1-1 gives the dates and sessions of the three Confederate Congresses. Map 1 illustrates the thirteen states admitted to the Confederate States of America and participating in the Confederate Congresses. These states meeting on these dates under the organization of the Confederate Congresses are the only consistent and central assembly of representatives of the far-flung Confederacy during the Civil War. The Confederate Congresses and the Jefferson Davis Administration are the only two formal, national, functioning, civilian administrative bodies in the Civil War South.

Although the Confederate Congress was pivotal in the organization of the Confederate government, and therefore the direction of the war itself, it receives scant coverage in the general Civil War literature. Only two book-length works have been written on this subject, *The Confederate Congress* by Wilfred Buck Years (1960)

and *The Anatomy of the Confederate Congress* by Thomas B. Alexander and Richard E. Beringer (1972).[4] In addition, there is one book-length biographical directory of members, the *Biographical Register of the Confederate Congress* by Ezra J. Warner and W. Buck Yearns (1975).[5] These three pathfinding works make the geographical analysis and mapping of the Confederate Congress in this atlas a more achievable undertaking.[6]

The objective of this atlas is the geographical analysis and mapping of critical aspects of the legislative branch of the Confederate government. This atlas focuses on the civilian political geography of the South during the Civil War as seen through the Provisional Congress and the First and Second Permanent Congresses. This nonmilitary, nonbattlefield approach focuses upon the inner Civil War: the feelings, issues, and political influences of the civilian Confederate population as expressed through their national elected representatives. The political geography of these feelings, issues, and influences had regional differences within the Civil War South, and these differences changed over the course of the war. The geographical study of the Confederate Congress is essential not only to understanding this assembly, but also the operation of the Confederate government and the issues within the Civil War South. *The Historical Atlas of the Congresses of the Confederate States of America* is derived from a long tradition of legislative behavior studies and the contributions of geographical studies of political systems.

TABLE 1-1

**Congresses and Sessions
Confederate States of America**

Provisional Congress – February 4, 1861, to February 17, 1862

First Session – February 4, 1861, to March 16, 1861
Second Session – April 29, 1861, to May 21, 1861
Third Session – July 20, 1861, to August 31, 1861
Fourth Session – Called for September 3, 1861
Fifth Session – November 18, 1861, to February 17, 1862

First Congress – February 18, 1862, to February 17, 1864

First Session – February 18, 1862, to April 21, 1862
Second Session – August 18, 1862, to October 13, 1862
Third Session – January 12, 1862, to May 1, 1863
Fourth Session – December 7, 1863, to February 17, 1864

Second Congress – May 2, 1864, to March 18, 1865

First Session – May 2, 1864, to June 14, 1864
Second Session – November 7, 1864, to March 18, 1865

Geographical Study of Legislative Assemblies and Legislative Behavior

Democratically elected legislative assemblies have a wide variety of sizes, levels, and forms. In the United States representative assemblies range from city councils, county commissions, state legislatures, and the U.S. Congress. Internationally, elected assemblies also range from village councils and provincial governments to national parliaments. All democratic representative bodies, irrespective of size, scale, or form have at least these three things in common: members are chosen by some sort of free election process; elected members assemble and vote on legislation, resolutions, and laws; and virtually all members are elected from some sort of geographical unit, precinct, ward, city, county, district, state, or province.

The study of representative assemblies is mostly the domain of political science. Indeed, a large and significant subfield of political science is legislative behavior, which attempts to understand all aspects of the election-representation-legislation process.[7] In addition, economists, sociologists, historians, and even physiologists have brought their expertise to understanding legislative behavior. Those who have studied legislative bodies have implicitly or explicitly recognized that a geographical component exists in many aspects of the election-representation-legislation system. Since all three characteristics have a geographical component, geographers, particularly political geographers, with their unique interests, training, and expertise also have made contributions to the understanding of legislative assemblies. Indeed, if the election-representation system is geographically based and has additional strong geographic components, the geography of the system must be understood for

a complete comprehension of the total system. The contributions of geographers in understanding legislative behavior has covered a wide variety of topics, but the focus is on three natural areas of inquiry: drawing the boundaries and subsequent characteristics of representative districts; the spatial differences in political party support in elections; and regional-sectional differences in voting patterns on legislation within representative assemblies.

Districts and District Characteristics

The drawing of election districts—in its essence an act of political cartography—affects who is elected and therefore the entire democratic process. Gerrymandering, the drawing of odd or erratically shaped district boundaries to favor a particular group, goes back to the very first U.S. congressional elections.[8] Some form of gerrymandering has been practiced in virtually all nations where districts are used for elections.[9] In the United States, partisan gerrymandering, the drawing of districts favoring a particular political party, and racial gerrymandering, the drawing of districts favoring a particular racial or ethnic group, are the most common forms. Geographers bring special expertise to the study of district boundaries and gerrymandering, as well as prescriptions for the better construction of these geographic areas.[10]

After the creation of a district system, each district or election unit becomes its own realm or political domain. Each election unit has its own individual physical, cultural, and demographic characteristics, and these shape the character of its own particular election. These constituent characteristics are important for understanding, and possibly even predicting, subsequent elections and representative behavior. Within a city some wards can be very wealthy and some very poor. Within a county some commission districts can be suburban and some can be urban. Within a state some assembly districts can be mountainous with poor soils and some flat with rich alluvial soils. Within a nation some districts can be agricultural and others industrial. All these characteristics bring certain "district interests" to bear, and understanding the geographic distribution of these characteristics and interests makes possible a better understanding of the legislative body itself.[11]

Elections

Elections have a variety of geographical components.[12] One of the most obvious and most studied is the distribution of political parties. In northern England the political party support is different from southern England, northern Italy is different from southern Italy, and eastern Austria is different from western Austria.[13] A map of the location of political party members in these parliaments reflects regional and sectional differences within these nations. In the United States similar geographical differences in party strength are found: suburban wards are different from urban wards, rural agricultural state assembly districts are different from urban industrial districts.

For example, within the U.S. Congress for over a century after the Civil War the Republican party dominated rural northern congressional districts and the Democratic party southern congressional districts.[14]

The final numbers and geographic distribution of political parties are significant since they determine the general outcome of an election. However, a vast array of other noteworthy phenomena is salient to understanding the electoral process, both in its politics and geography. For example, in some areas the electoral competition between parties is weak, while in other areas competition is strong with very close races. In some regions the voter turnout is very high and in other areas consistently low. In some sections the voters consistently elect new members, while other sections have a high incumbent return rate. Geographical differences in the election process extend far beyond the distribution of political parties but can include almost any political, historical, economic, sociological, cultural, or demographic variable.[15]

Roll-Call Voting

The study of the geography of roll-call voting in legislative bodies is relevant if certain circumstances are present: most importantly, if the election of representatives is from districts, and if the elected representatives have some freedom of roll-call voting decisions independent of political party. In the European-style parliamentary systems political party bloc voting is strict and consistent. Geographical studies of parliamentary roll-call voting is relevant in only a small number of cases when a rare "free vote" is allowed. In U.S. state legislatures roll-call voting is also closely related to political party membership, and a geographical study of voting is relevant only in some states and in some voting situations. However, in the U.S. Congress the representatives and senators have a greater freedom of roll-call voting behavior than in any other national legislature in the world. A geographical examination of roll-call voting therefore is relevant in a large number of cases.[16]

One other important phenomenon that distinguishes members of the U.S. Congress from members of European-style national legislatures is the philosophy of representation. In the European tradition members of parliament are primarily representatives of a political party and political ideology and are concerned with the interests of the nation as a whole. In the American tradition members of Congress are primarily representatives of local and state interests. This mix of party freedom mentioned above and representation of local interests creates a geography of roll-call voting behavior unlike any other legislative assembly.

Patterns of roll-call voting in the U.S. Congress is the phenomenon that first alerted historians, then political scientists, to the imperative of studying and understanding the geographical aspects of the American House of Representatives and Senate. In the 1890s the prominent American historian Frederick Jackson Turner and his student Orin G. Libby were the first openly to call for the geographical study of votes in Congress.[17] Turner's famous frontier and sectional theories of American history are based, in part, on the first formal mapping of critical votes in Congress.[18] The Turner school of history not only promoted macrolevel studies and explanations of the American experience, but also used such quantitative techniques as the matching of data, in this case roll-call votes from the *Congressional Record*, and maps, in this case past congressional district boundaries.[19] Early roll-call voting studies confirmed four obvious facts: regional-section voting is stronger in some eras—the antebellum era, for example; regional-sectional voting is stronger in some issues; party voting is stronger in some eras; and regional-section voting is found in all periods.[20] The factors influencing roll-call voting in general, and regional-sectional voting in particular, are numerous, multifarious, and interactive. The fact remains that regional-sectional voting patterns can be found in all historical eras and virtually all issues, and the geographic study of Congress and other legislative bodies is important for their total understanding.

The Geography of the Confederate Congresses

The Congresses of the Confederate States of America are perfect candidates for a relevant and fruitful legislative-geographical study. First, the members of Congress were elected from geographical areas. In the Provisional Congress the election and roll-call voting was by state with each state having one vote. In the Permanent Congress members of the House of Representatives were elected by districts, and there were 106 total districts. This is a large number of representatives and districts, and detailed maps analyzing and illustrating elections, roll calls, and constituency attributes are able to be drawn. In the Senate each state had two senators, and various senatorial characteristics can be mapped by state. Since political parties did not exist in the Civil War South, members of the Confederate Congress had a freedom of roll-call voting unprecedented in American legislative history.

The Historical Atlas of the Congresses of the Confederate States of America: 1861–1865 explores the major geographical aspects of the Confederate Congresses. Chapter 2 introduces the Provisional Congress, including discussions of the representation of states and an introduction to the concept of Confederate territory under Union control. Chapter 3 describes the organization of Confederate congressional districts in the Permanent Congresses, including apportionment, district boundary laws, and resultant district/constituent characteristics.

In the Permanent Confederate Congress there were two national elections. The First House election took place November 6, 1861, and the second at various times in 1863 according to state law. The results of these congressional elections are studied in a number of ways. Chapter 4 focuses on Confederate congressional elections, both House and Senate, by first examining the context of the election system in the Civil War South. Each state is surveyed with respect to the results of the First and Second Congress elections. The national results are then summarized, focusing on the former political party of the those elected, their secession stance, method of election, and incumbency. Voter participation in Confederate congressional elections is also discussed using the election results from the first systematic research and compilation of Confederate congressional vote returns in American history.

In the Confederate Congress there were 1,956 roll-call votes taken in a four-year period. Each of these roll calls was a statement of an individual, district, state, or region about an aspect of the Confederacy and Civil War. These votes have been studied with respect to the issues and factors influencing final voting decisions. However, this atlas is the first work to focus upon the geographical aspects of Confederate roll-call voting. Chapter 5 discusses the context of roll-call voting in the Confederate Congresses and the issues and influences of this voting. Ten roll-call vote maps analyze and illustrate the dominant geographical patterns in congressional decision making.

Chapter 6 summarizes the findings of the geographical aspects of the Confederate Congresses and the role spatial analysis and mapping have in enhancing their understanding. The better understanding of the Confederate Congresses undoubtedly enhances the knowledge of the Confederacy and its governmental organization and general governance. This understanding adds to the larger assessment of the organization of the Confederate government, political life within the Civil War South, the conduct of the war, and the timing of its ending. In addition to enhancing the understanding of districts, elections, and roll-call voting, the atlas provides a tool, guide, and model for any individual, student, teacher, or researcher to use the congressional district base maps to map any roll-call vote, election result, or congressional characteristics in the history of the Confederate Congress. The atlas as a tool, as well as a reference book, will, it is hoped, provide a basis for knowledge about the Confederacy and the Civil War not yet envisioned.

[1] C. Vann Woodward, "What the War Made Us," in Geoffrey C. Ward, *The Civil War* (New York: Alfred A. Knopf, 1990), pp. 398–401.

[2] James M. McPherson, *Battle Cry of Freedom: The Civil War Era* (New York: Ballantine Books, 1988), pp. 865–882.

[3] Richard W. Stephenson, *Civil War Maps* (Washington, D.C.: Library of Congress, 1989). *A Guide to Civil War Maps in the National Archives* (Washington, D.C.: National Archives and Records Administration, 1986). John H. Wright, comp., *Compendium of the Confederacy An Annotated Bibliography*, 2 vols. (Wilmington, North Carolina: Broadfoot Publishing Company, 1989). Garold L. Cole, *Civil War Eyewitnesses: An Annotated Bibliography of Books and Articles, 1955–1986* (Columbia: University of South Carolina Press, 1988). Allan Nevins, James I. Robertson Jr., Bell I Wiley, eds., *Civil War Books: A Critical Bibliography* (Baton Rouge: Louisiana State University Press, 1967). Computer searches were conducted in March 1993 with the terms "Civil War Atlases" and "Civil War Maps" in two online data bases: *OLUC: Online Union Catalog* [Machine-readable data file] (Dublin, Ohio: OCLC, Online Computer Library Center—producer and distributor, March, 1993); and *America: History and Life* [Machine-readable data file] (Santa Barbara, California: ABC-CLIO, Inc.—producer, and Palo Alto, California: DIALOG Information Services, Inc.—distributor, March 1993).

Prior to this work every Civil War atlas focused on military/battlefield mapping, and most have as their basic reference the public domain maps in United States War Department, *Atlas to Accompany the Official Records of the Union and Confederate Armies* (Washington, D.C.: Government Printing Office, 1891–1895). For a listing of the major original Civil War atlases see the Bibliography. For a review of recent Civil War atlases and a discussion of modern cartographic techniques applied to battlefield maps see Kenneth H. Williams, review of John MacDonald, *Great Battles of the Civil War* (New York: Macmillan, 1992) and Craig L. Symonds, *Gettysburg: A Battlefield Atlas* (Baltimore: Nautical and Aviation Publishing, 1992), in *Journal of Southern History* 59 (February 1993): 143–145. Even the most recent atlas, David C. Bosse, *Civil War Newspaper Maps: A Historical Atlas* (Baltimore: Johns Hopkins University Press, 1993), focuses exclusively on battlefield maps taken from mostly northern newspapers of the day. Of course, some individual sheet maps exist illustrating several types of "nonmilitary" phenomena—for example, the railroad network of the North and South. A number of maps of phenomena from the 1860 census are found in several sources. One excellent antebellum atlas maps southern population (1790–1860) and agricultural characteristics (1840–1860): Sam Bowers Hilliard, *Atlas of Antebellum Southern Agriculture* (Baton Rouge: Louisiana State University Press, 1984).

[4] Wilfred Buck Yearns, *The Confederate Congress* (Athens: The University of Georgia Press, 1960). Thomas B. Alexander and Richard E. Beringer, *The Anatomy of the Confederate Congresses* (Nashville: Vanderbilt University Press, 1972).

[5] Ezra J. Warner and W. Buck Yearns, *Biographical Register of the Confederate Congress* (Baton Rouge: Louisiana State University Press, 1975).

[6] Several other works that focus on the Confederate Congress are used extensively in this atlas. John B. Robbins, "Confederate Nationalism: Politics and Government in the Confederate South, 1861-1865," (Ph.D. diss., Rice University, 1964). Richard Bensel, "Southern Leviathan: The Development of Central State Authority in the Confederate States of America," in *Studies in American Political Development*, Vol. 2, ed. Karen Orren and Stephen Skowronek (New Haven: Yale University Press, 1987). In most general histories of the Confederacy the Confederate Congress is given peripheral coverage with citations limited to specific issues—conscription, for example, or Congress as an irritant to President Davis, or Congress investigating a military operation or campaign. One general work that does highlight Congress is Chapter VII "The Confederate Congress," in *The Confederate States of America 1861–1865* by E. Merton Coulter, Volume VII, in *A History of the South*, ed. Wendell H. Stephenson and E. Merton Coulter (Baton Rouge: Louisiana State University Press, 1950). The bibliographies and works cited in footnote 3 reference hundreds of additional sources on the Confederate Congress in manuscript collections, official government publications, newspapers, journal articles, and other secondary sources focusing on individual Congress members, states, and issues. The specific sources used in this atlas are cited in the appropriate chapters and referenced in the Bibliography. In Bensel's extended essay focusing on the Confederate Congress he summarizes the practical reasons for the relatively small number of studies on this subject, which include the existence of secret sessions; the small number of official records because of war conditions; poor press relations and coverage; and the fast pace and conditions of wartime legislation. Bensel, "Southern Leviathan," p. 78.

[7] Gerhand Loewenberg, Samuel C. Patterson, and Malcolm E. Jewell, *Handbook of Legislative Research* (Cambridge: Harvard University Press, 1985). Philip Norton, *Legislatures* (New York: Oxford University Press, 1990). See also the journal *Legislative Studies Quarterly*.

[8] Elmer C. Griffith, *The Rise and Development of the Gerrymander* (Chicago: Scott Foresman, 1907), pp. 32-40.

[9] Peter J. Taylor, *Political Geography* (London: Longman, 1985), pp 150–152.

[10] Richard L. Morrill, *Political Redistricting and Geographic Theory* (Washington, D.C.: Association of American Geographers, 1981). Kenneth C. Martis, *The Historical Atlas of United States Congressional Districts 1789–1983* (New York: Free Press, 1982).

[11] See Table 11, Part III, Martis, *Congressional Districts*, p. 18.

[12] J. Clark Archer and Fred M. Shelley, *American Electoral Mosaics* (Washington, D.C.: Association of American Geographers, 1986). R. J. Johnston, *Political, Electoral, and Spatial Systems: An Essay in Political Geography* (New York: Oxford University Press, 1979). Peter J. Taylor, "The Geography of Elections," in M. Pacione,

ed., *Progress in Political Geography* (London: Croom Helm, 1985).

[13] T. T. Makie and R. Rose, *The International Almanac of Electoral History* (London: Macmillan, 1974). J. Sallnow, *An Electoral Atlas of Europe* (London: Butterworth Scientific, 1982).

[14] Kenneth C. Martis, *The Historical Atlas of Political Parties in the United States Congress 1789–1989* (New York: Macmillan, 1989), pp. 130–217. Kenneth C. Martis, "Sectionalism and the United States Congress," *Political Geography Quarterly* 7 (April 1988): 99–109.

[15] See Table 11, Part II, Martis, *Congressional Districts*, p. 18.

[16] Ruth Anderson Rowles and Kenneth C. Martis, "Mapping Congress: Developing a Geographic Understanding of American Political History," *Prologue: Journal of the National Archives* 16 (Spring 1984): 4–21.

[17] Orin G. Libby, "A Plea for the Study of Votes in Congress," *Annual Report of the American Historical Association* (Washington, D.C.: Government Printing Office, 1897).

[18] Ray Allan Billington, *Frederick Jackson Turner: Historian, Scholar, Teacher* (New Haven: Yale University Press, 1973). Ray Allan Billington, *The Genesis of the Frontier Thesis* (San Marino, California: The Huntington Library, 1971).

[19] Richard Jensen, "American Election Analysis," in *Politics and the Social Sciences*, ed., Seymour M. Lipset (New York: Oxford University Press, 1969).

[20] Clifford L. Lord, *A Description of the Atlas of Congressional Roll Calls: An Analysis of Yea-Nay Votes* (Newark, New Jersey: Work Projects Administration—Historical Records Survey, 1941). C. O. Paullin and John K. Wright, *Atlas of the Historical Geography of the United States* (New York: Carnegie Institution and American Geographical Society, 1932).

MAP 1

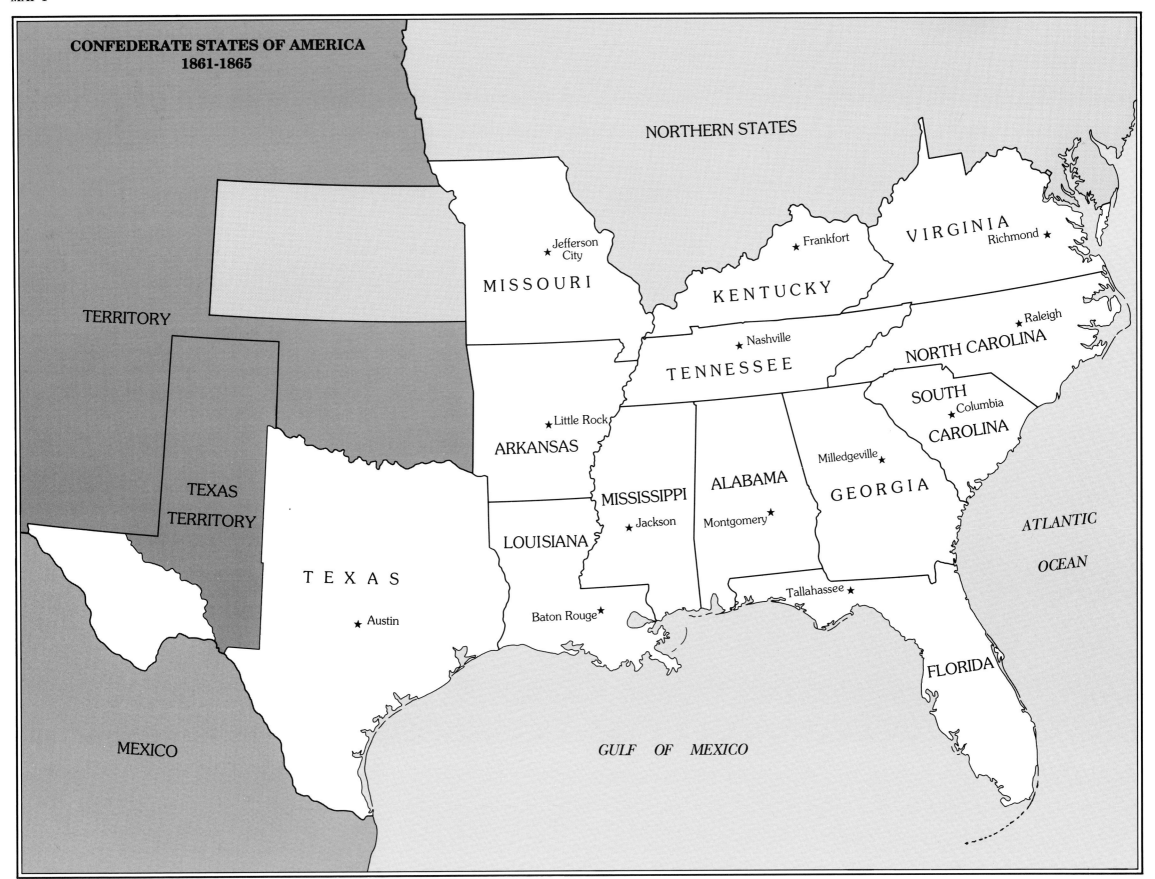

CONFEDERATE STATES OF AMERICA
1861-1865

NORTHERN STATES

TERRITORY

MEXICO

TEXAS
TERRITORY

T E X A S

★ Austin

MISSOURI

★ Jefferson
   City

ARKANSAS

★ Little Rock

LOUISIANA

Baton Rouge ★

KENTUCKY

★ Frankfort

★ Nashville

T E N N E S S E E

MISSISSIPPI

★ Jackson

ALABAMA

Montgomery ★

Tallahassee ★

V I R G I N I A
           Richmond ★

★ Raleigh

NORTH CAROLINA

SOUTH
★ Columbia
CAROLINA

Milledgeville ★

G E O R G I A

ATLANTIC

OCEAN

FLORIDA

GULF   OF   MEXICO

2

PROVISIONAL CONFEDERATE CONGRESS

Organization of the Provisional Confederate Government

Secession and the Montgomery Convention

The November 6, 1860, election of Northerner and Republican Abraham Lincoln as president of the United States was the culmination of decades of events that precipitated the secession of the lower South states. In anticipation of Lincoln's election, the legislatures of several Deep South states were prepared to meet in special session or authorized their governors to call state secession conventions. Four days after Lincoln's election South Carolina was the first to call a state secession convention. The election of members for this convention occurred December 6, 1860. The South Carolina convention convened eleven days later and on December 20, 1860, approved an ordinance of secession. South Carolina was not only the first to secede but also encouraged other southern states by way of interstate "commissioners" and personal correspondence. In addition, the South Carolina state convention called for a southern "Convention at Montgomery, in the State of Alabama" and outlined a program for its organization.[1] The purpose of this southern convention was to create a new and independent nation. Inspired by

the lead of South Carolina, a wave of secession hit the lower South in January 1861. As Table 2-1 indicates, six additional states called secession conventions, held statewide constituent elections for convention members, convened, and passed secession ordinances between January 9 and February 1, 1861.

The South Carolina plan for the Montgomery convention called for each state to have one vote, but to have an actual delegation size equal to the number of U.S. representatives and senators. For example, under the apportionment for the 1850s South Carolina had six representatives and two senators; hence, South Carolina was entitled to eight delegates. Table 2-2 lists the southern states in order of secession, the method of selection of the Montgomery convention–Provisional Congress delegates, the number of entitled delegates, and the actual number of delegates seated. Each of the original seven Confederate states, except Florida, elected its delegates by a majority vote in the secession convention. Appendix I gives a typical example of the convention delegate selection process, the election of the delegates from Texas. The method of determining delegation size prompted some states to select one delegate from each of the standing congressional districts and two at-large.[2]

The Montgomery convention convened February 3, 1861. The political institutions of the temporary and permanent southern government

were formulated in the subsequent six weeks. A committee of twelve was formed to write a Provisional Constitution. This daunting task was lessened because of the program put forward by the South Carolina secession convention, and because the South Carolina delegation brought substantial working drafts to Montgomery. Within five days the Provisional Constitution committee reported a final draft, and the document was debated, amended, and approved. The Provisional Constitution called for the establishment of a "Confederate States of America" with legislative, executive, and judicial branches.[3] The Provisional Constitution was modeled after the U.S. Constitution, but with strong references to the philosophy of state rights and state sovereignty and the recognition of slavery.[4] One manifestation of this philosophy was the organization of the legislative branch as a unicameral Congress with each state having one vote, with the actual size of the state delegation based upon its previous congressional representation as suggested by the original South Carolina plan and as the Montgomery convention was organized.

With the establishment of a Provisional government the Montgomery Convention became the Provisional Congress. The Provisional Congress completed the Provisional government by temporarily continuing the laws of the United States until amended and electing Jefferson Davis of Mississippi Provisional president. Davis

TABLE 2-1

Southern Secession Conventions
November, 1860 to November, 1861

State	Convention Called[1]	Selection of State Secession Convention Members	First Convened (Place and Date)	Seceded	Final Vote	Approved
South Carolina	November 10	December 6 Election	Columbia, December 17	December 20	169–0	
Mississippi	November 26	December 20 Election	Jackson, January 7	January 9	84–15	
Florida	December 7	December 22 Election	Tallahassee, January 3	January 10	62–7	
Alabama	December 5	December 24 Election	Montgomery, January 7	January 11	61–39	
Georgia	November 20	January 2 Election	Milledgeville, January 16	January 19	208–89	
Louisiana	December 11	January 7 Election	Baton Rouge, January 23	January 26	113–17	
Texas	December 3[2]	January 8[3] Election	Austin, January 28	February 1	166–8	[4]
Virginia	January 14	February 4 Election	Richmond, February 13	April 17	88–55	[5]
Arkansas	January 12	February 18 Election	Little Rock, March 4	May 6	65–5	
Tennessee				May 6		[6]
North Carolina	May 1	May 13 Election	Raleigh, May 20	May 20	unanimous	
Missouri	September 26[7]	Assembly of Pro-Confederate State Legislators	Neosho, October 21	October 28		
Kentucky	October 29-30[8]	Open Meeting of Pro-Confederate Citizens	Russellville, November 18	November 20		

[1] Date secession convention called is usually the day of authorization by the state legislature or call by governor under a preauthorization. In almost all cases both the legislature and governor were involved in the legal process of calling the conventions. Ralph A. Wooster, *The Secession Conventions of the South* (Princeton: Princeton University Press, 1962).

[2] Date of first call by secession leaders. *Journal of the Secession Convention of Texas* (Austin: Texas Library and Historical Commission, 1912), pp. 7–12.

[3] Date the majority of counties/districts held convention elections; however, some counties/districts held elections from December 3, 1860, through January 8, 1860. Wooster, *Secession Conventions*, p. 124. *Texas Journal*, p. 7.

[4] Statewide referendum approved Texas secession ordinance on February 23, 1861, by a vote of 46,153 to 14,747.

[5] Statewide referendum approved Virginia secession ordinance on May 23, 1861, by a vote of 125,950 to 20,373.

[6] There was no secession convention in Tennessee. The state legislature approved a secession ordinance on May 6, 1862, with the requirement of a statewide referendum on June 6, 1862. The referendum passed by a vote of 104,913 to 47,238. Governor Isham Harris officially announced results June 24, 1862.

[7] Called for by deposed pro-Confederate governor Claiborne F. Jackson.

[8] "Convention" called for by meeting of Confederate supporters.

was inaugurated on February 18, 1861, in Montgomery. Until the establishment of a permanent government, Congress and the president were the ruling authorities of the new nation.

Provisional Congress

State Representation

Six states voted for the establishment of the Provisional government of the Confederate States of America on February 8, 1861. Although Texas had already seceded, its delegation did not arrive in Montgomery by this date. When the Texas delegation did arrive in mid February, they were seated but not given full voting rights until after the February 23, 1861, statewide referendum and until the Texas secession ordinance went into legal effect on March 2,

1861.[5] Since the Texas delegation signed the original constitution and they were seated in the First Session of the Provisional Congress they are designated as an original member on Table 2-3.

The First Session of the Provisional Congress adjourned March 16, 1861. The Provisional Constitution stated that the provisional government should continue for a maximum of one year or until a permanent government is established. Four additional sessions of the Provisional Congress were eventually called, and three were held during this period. The Second Session was held in April and May, the Third in July and August, and the Fifth from November, 1861, to February, 1862. Table 2-3 gives the exact dates for each of these sessions. A Fourth Session, called for September 3, 1861, was never held.

The Provisional Constitution provided for the admission of additional states. Two groups of states, four from the upper South and

subsequently two from the border South, were admitted to the Confederacy at two distinct time intervals. First, four upper South states, Virginia, Arkansas, Tennessee, and North Carolina, seceded after the firing on Fort Sumter and the call by President Lincoln for troops to quell the southern rebellion. Virginia passed an ordinance of secession on April 17, just three days after the surrender of Fort Sumter. As Table 2-1 notes, the ordinance was approved by a statewide referendum on May 23, 1861. Arkansas reconvened its secession convention, which had previously rejected disunion, and passed a secession ordinance. Both state conventions sent delegates to the Provisional Congress, and they were seated in May during the Second Session (see Table 2-3). The Tennessee legislature passed a session ordinance on May 6, and since Tennessee did not convene and elect a state secession convention, it required a confirming statewide referendum. The June 6 popular vote overwhelmingly passed the ordinance, and on June 24 the governor officially proclaimed the results.[6] North Carolina was the last southern state to call and elect a secession convention. North Carolina passed a secession ordinance on May 20, one day before the end of the Second Session. Because of the timing, both Tennessee and North Carolina were not seated until the Third Session.

The founders of the Confederacy desired and ideally envisioned a peaceful creation of a new union of all slaveholding states, including the border states of Delaware, Maryland, Kentucky, and Missouri.[7] Because of the resistance of the North and its geographic position, Delaware was not given serious consideration in the Provisional Congress. Maryland had a large prosouthern population, but northern militia movements to secure Washington, D.C., in April, 1861, and virtual martial law prevented this possibility. In fact, much discussion was given in the Provisional Congress to the postwar status of Maryland and the Confederacy. However, extraordinary actions by prosouthern elements in Kentucky and Missouri brought about their admission late in 1861.[8] Although Kentucky and Missouri had substantial prosouthern populations, they were undoubtedly a minority in each state. Pro-Union elements eventually gained control of both state governments, and Confederate sympathizers established secessionist governments in the southern portion of each state. In both states insurgent assemblies passed secession declarations. In spite of the minority status and rump nature of these assemblies, the Provisional Congress unanimously admitted Kentucky and Missouri as a reward for establishing prosouthern governments and to extend the Confederacy to all slaveholding states.[9] Kentucky and Missouri were seated in December 1861, during the Fifth Session (see Table 2-3). They became officially the twelfth and thirteenth Confederate states. Table 2-4 is a membership list of all who served in the Provisional Congress, including their first date of seating, and any replacements.

Three months after the admission of Kentucky and Missouri, Union forces consolidated their hold on these states and permanently occupied them for the remainder of the war. The admission of Kentucky and Missouri had great significance for the politics of the Confederate Congress. In addition, the presence of Kentucky and Missouri established a political map of the Civil War South requiring the consideration of these areas in the study of the geography of the Confederate Congress.

State Representation and Territory under Union Occupation

Maps 2 to 5 illustrate the sequence of state representation over the course of the Provisional Congress (see also Table 2-3). There is one map for each session of the Provisional Congress. *The operative date for a state appearing on the session map is the day the first member(s) of the state delegation is seated and is eligible for participation in roll-call voting.* The seating date is used rather than the secession or admission date because the atlas maps are designed, in part, to illustrate which states were actually represented and participated in Congress during a particular session and to serve as base maps to allow the cartographic illustration of roll-call votes or other characteristics.[10] In addition to illustrating the states present in each session, Maps 2 to 5 identify territory within these states occupied by Union forces during that session. The specific criteria used to define and delimit "occupied territory" and "unoccupied territory" of the Confederate South are enumerated and explained in detail in Appendix II.

First Session—Montgomery, Alabama

  Intersession: None

  Session Dates: February 4, 1861–March 16, 1861

  Total Period: February 4, 1861–March 16, 1861   [41 days]

The First Session of the Provisional Congresses of the Confederate States of America convened in Montgomery, Alabama, on February 4, 1861. As Table 2-1 indicates, seven states passed secession resolutions by this date. Six states assembled on the first day of the Montgomery convention, and Texas was officially seated on March 2 (see Table 2-3, footnotes 4 and 5). As Map 2 shows, all of the original seven states of the Confederacy are located in the lower South.

Just before and after secession the southern states seized all federal property, fortifications, and armories within their territory. As Map 2 indicates, three places in Florida were not seized because of their size, strength, geographic location, and their ability to be resupplied by the Union. They include two installations in the Florida Keys, Fort Taylor (Key West) and an island/fort off the main Keys, Fort Jefferson, as well as one fort guarding Pensacola Bay, Fort Pickens. Following the rules outlined in Appendix II, these forts are identified in blue because they remain permanently occupied by Union forces throughout the Civil War.

TABLE 2-2

State Delegation Selection and Size
Provisional Congress

State	Method of Delegate Selection	Delegates Entitled	Delegates Seated	Replacements [1]	Total Participating
South Carolina	Secession Convention	8	8	1	9
Alabama	Secession Convention	9	9	3	12
Georgia	Secession Convention	10	10	2	12
Mississippi	Secession Convention	7	7	2	9
Louisiana	Secession Convention	6	6	0	6
Florida	Governor	3	3	2	5
Texas	Secession Convention	4	7 (+3)	0	7
Virginia	Secession Convention	15	16 (+1)	0	16
Arkansas	Secession Convention	4	5 (+1)	0	5
Tennessee	Regular State Congressional Elections [2]	12	7 (-5)	0	7
North Carolina	Secession Convention	10	10	0	10
Missouri	Assembly of Pro-Confederate State Legislators [3]	9	8 (-1)	0	8
Kentucky	Provisional Confederate Governor and Ten Councilmen [4]	12	10 (-2)	0	10
Total		109	106 (-3)	10	116

[1] All replacements and those replaced are listed with notes in Table 2-4.

[2] The Tennessee secession ordinance directed that the Provisional Congress delegates be selected at the regular congressional elections the first Thursday in August. Although Tennessee was entitled to twelve delegates, in August 1861 the state was still divided into ten districts. Pro-Union candidates won in the eastern portion of the state, and three eventually were seated in the U.S. Congress. Kenneth C. Martis, *The Historical Atlas of Political Parties in the United States Congress: 1789–1983* (New York: Macmillan, 1989), pp. 37, 114–115. Six pro-Confederate candidates won in the middle and western portions of the state, and one claimed victory in the eastern portion of the state; these seven were seated in the Provisional Confederate Congress. James W. Patton, *Unionism and Reconstruction in Tennessee, 1860–1869* (Chapel Hill: University of North Carolina Press, 1934), pp. 28–29.

[3] Selected/appointed by assembly of pro-Confederate legislators meeting in Cassville, Missouri, and approved by pro-Confederate governor. Two individuals were selected/appointed to serve as senators and seven as representatives in the First Permanent Congress and to serve as the Missouri delegates in the remaining portion of the Provisional Congress. See also section in Chapter 4 on Missouri First Election.

[4] The ten Kentucky delegates to the Provisional Congress were selected/appointed by the Kentucky Confederate Provisional government composed of a Provisional governor and ten councilmen who were selected by the Russellville secession convention. See the biographies of the ten delegates in Ezra J. Warner and W. Buck Yearns, *Biographical Register of the Confederate Congress* (Baton Rouge: Louisiana State University Press, 1975).

TABLE 2-3

Dates of Secession, Admission, and Seating
Provisional Congress
1860–1861

State	Secession[1]	Admission[2]	Seating[3]
First Session: February 4, 1861 – March 16, 1861			
South Carolina	December 20	original member	
Mississippi	January 9	original member	
Florida	January 10	original member	
Alabama	January 11	original member	
Georgia	January 19	original member	
Louisiana	January 26	original member	
Texas	February 1[4]	original member[5]	March 2, 1861[6]
Second Session: April 29, 1861 – May 21, 1861			
Virginia	April 17[7]	May 7	May 7
Arkansas	May 6	May 20	May 18[8]
Third Session: July 20, 1861 – August 31, 1861			
North Carolina	May 20	May 17[9]	July 20
Tennessee	May 6[10]	May 17[9]	August 12
Fifth Session: November 18, 1861 – February 17, 1862			
Missouri	October 28[11]	November 28	December 2
Kentucky	November 20[12]	December 10	December 16

[1] Secession date is the day the final ordinance of secession passed the state secession convention or other assembly.

[2] Admission date is the day the statute was approved, that is, signed by the president.

[3] Seating date is the day the first state delegate(s) "appeared, were qualified, and took their seats" and were eligible for roll-call voting. Maps 2 to 5 are drawn using this date.

[4] Statewide referendum approved the Texas secession ordinance on February 23, 1861.

[5] The law admitting Texas was approved March 2, 1861. *Statutes at Large of the Provisional Government of the Confederate States of America* (Richmond: R. M. Smith, 1864), p. 44.

[6] Texas delegation was seated on February 16, 1861, with all rights except roll-call voting since "the ordinance of the secession of Texas does not take effect until the 2d day of March." *Confederate Journal*, Vol. 1, p. 60.

[7] Statewide referendum approved Virginia secession ordinance on May 23, 1861.

[8] The law admitting Arkansas was approved May 20, 1861. *Statutes at Large,* p. 120. However, the Provisional Congress voted in favor of admitting Arkansas on May 18, 1861, and on that day seated Arkansas delegates, when they began participating in roll-call voting. *Confederate Journal*, Vol. 1, pp. 244–247.

[9] The Provisional Congress used the term *admit* "on certain conditions."

[10] Secession ordinance drafted and popular referendum called by state legislature on May 6, 1861. Referendum was held and ordinance passed June 6, 1861, and the governor "proclaimed" results June 24, 1861.

[11] Date secession ordinance passed assembly of pro-Confederate state legislators.

[12] Date pro-Confederate meeting passed ordinance of "independence."

The military and geographic situation of these forts, especially Fort Pickens, was similar to Fort Sumter, which guarded the Charleston, South Carolina, harbor. The federal garrison at Fort Sumter did not want to surrender to state Confederate authorities. During the entire time of the First Session of the Provisional Congress Fort Sumter remained in federal hands. However, it is not identified on Map 2 as a Union-occupied area because it did not remain in permanent federal control throughout the war (it surrendered on April 14).

Second Session—Montgomery, Alabama
Intersession: March 17, 1861–April 28, 1861
Session Dates: April 29, 1861–May 21, 1861
Total Period: March 17, 1861–May 21, 1861   [66 days]

Map 3 illustrates the states represented and territory occupied in the Second Session of the Provisional Congress. Three critical events swayed the upper South states to secede: federal forces attempted to resupply Fort Sumter; South Carolina forces fired upon the fort, whose garrison surrendered; and President Lincoln called for troops to quell the southern rebellion. Three days after Fort Sumter's surrender Virginia passed a secession resolution. On May 7, 1861, Virginia was officially admitted to the Confederacy and a delegation seated in the Provisional Congress. Arkansas passed a secession resolution May 6 and was seated on May 18, three days before the end of the session.

To the north Virginia bordered two free states, Ohio and Pennsylvania; one slave state, Maryland; and the District of Columbia. In May 1861, the situation in the portion of Virginia bordering the free states was ambiguous. The Appalachian Plateau portion of Virginia had very few slaves, in fact, by far the least percentage of any other large area of the Confederacy.[11] In addition, the economy of the northern panhandle and Ohio River cities was linked to the North. In a statewide referendum on secession on May 23, 1861, most of the counties in this area voted against secession. Although Unionists began to organize within days after secession, especially in the northern panhandle, no military forces from the North physically moved into western Virginia during this period. Following the criteria designating occupied territory, outlined in Appendix II, this area was not militarily in Union hands at this point.

During the Second Session the Union began implementing a naval blockade along the Confederate coast. James River/Hampton Roads, Virginia (May 2), and Charleston, South Carolina (May 18), were the first areas blockaded. The continued Union occupation of Fort Monroe, Virginia, at the mouth of the James River across from Norfolk, enabled the Union quickly to blockade the adjacent area. Fort Monroe is colored blue on the Second Session map, indicating permanent Union occupation throughout the war.

Third Session—Richmond, Virginia
Intersession: May 22, 1861–July 19, 1861
Session Dates: July 20, 1861–August 31, 1861
Total Period: May 22, 1861–August 31, 1861   [102 days]

North Carolina and Tennessee were given "conditional" admittance to the Confederacy on May 17, 1861. North Carolina actually seceded May 20, the day before the last day of the Second Session. However, because of the timing, the North Carolina delegation was not seated until June 20, the first day of the Third Session. Again, states are shown on the Provisional Congress map when they were actually seated and eligible to vote; therefore, North Carolina is displayed for the first time in the Third Session. The Tennessee voters approved a secession referendum on June 8, and on June 24, the governor announced the results. The Tennessee delegation arrived in Richmond on August 12, in the latter portion of the Third Session.

The main military movement in this short period came in northwestern Virginia. Ohio troops occupied several cities and points across the Ohio River. Federal troops advanced into western Virginia occupying Grafton (May 30), Philippi (June 3, perhaps the first land battle of the Civil War), Beverly (July 12), and Charleston (July 25). In northern Virginia, Alexandria, across the Potomac River from Washington, D.C., was occupied (May 24). This area became part of the defense line for the U.S. capital and staging area for Union troop movements south. On May 29 Newport News in Tidewater Virginia, near Fort Monroe, was occupied by Union troops. These regions appear blue on Map 4 since they are permanently occupied by the Union. In early July Union forces also occupied towns in northern Virginia near Maryland (for example, Martinsburg and Charles Town); after the First Battle of Manassas (July 21), however, they withdrew from this area. Following the rules established in Appendix II, these regions are not colored blue at this time since they were not permanently occupied by Union forces.

Fifth Session[12]—Richmond, Virginia
Intersession: September 1, 1861–November 17, 1861
Session Dates: November 18, 1861–February 17, 1862
Total Period: September 1, 1861–February 17, 1862
[170 days]

The five-and-a-half-month period of the Fifth Session and intersession is the longest span covered by a Provisional Congress map. During this period two of the most far-reaching decisions were made with respect to the Confederacy and the Confederate Congress, the admission of the border states of Missouri and Kentucky. The presence of occupied Missouri and Kentucky had a profound impact upon future roll-call voting and, therefore, a profound effect on the

TABLE 2-4
Delegates to the Provisional Confederate Congress [1]
February 4, 1861, to February 17, 1862

First Session – February 4, 1861, to March 16, 1861   Second Session – April 29, 1861, to May 21, 1861

Third Session – July 20, 1861, to August 31, 1861   Fourth Session – Called for September 3, 1861   Fifth Session – November 18, 1861, to February 17, 1862

Alabama – February 4
William Parish Chilton (February 4)
Jabez Lamar Monroe Curry (February 4)
Thomas Fearn [2] (February 8)
  Nicholas Davis [3] (April 29)
Stephen Fowler Hale (February 4)
David Peter Lewis [4] (February 8)
  Henry Cox Jones [5] (April 29)
Colin John McRae (February 4)
John Gill Shorter [6] (February 4)
  Cornelius Robinson [7] (November 30)
Robert Hardy Smith (February 4)
Richard Wilde Walker (February 4)

Arkansas – May 18
Augustus Hill Garland (May 18)
Robert Ward Johnson (May 18)
Albert Rust (May 18)
Hugh French Thomason (May 20) [8]
William Wirt Watkins (May 18)

Florida – February 4
James Patton Anderson [9] (February 4)
  George Taliaferro Ward [10] (May 2)
  John Philip Sanderson [11] (February 5, 1862)
Jackson Morton (February 6)
James Byeram Owens (February 4)

Georgia – February 4
Augustus Holmes Kenan (February 4)
Augustus Romaldus Wright (February 4)
Francis Stebbins Bartow [12] (February 4)
  Thomas Marsh Forman [13] (August 7)
Howell Cobb (February 4)
Thomas Reade Rootes Cobb (February 4)

Martin Jenkins Crawford (February 4)
Benjamin Harvey Hill (February 4)
Eugenius Aristides Nisbet [14] (February 4)
  Nathan Bass [15] (January 14, 1862)
Alexander Hamilton Stephens (February 4)
Robert Augustus Toombs (February 4)

Kentucky – December 16
George Washington Ewing (February 14, 1862)
Theodore L. Burnett (December 16)
George Baird Hodge (January 11, 1862)
John Milton Elliot (January 15, 1862)
Henry Cornelius Burnett (December 16)
Samuel Howard Ford (January 4, 1862)
Thomas Johnson (December 18)
Thomas Bell Monroe (December 16)
John J. Thomas (December 30)
Daniel Price White (January 2, 1862)

Louisiana – February 4
Charles Magill Conrad (February 7)
Duncan Farrar Kenner (February 4)
Henry Marshall (February 4)
John Perkins, Jr. (February 4)
Alexander De Clouet (February 4)
Edward Sparrow (February 4)

Mississippi – February 4
William Taylor Sullivan Barry (February 4)
Walker Brooke (February 4)
Josiah Abigal Patterson Campbell (February 12)
Alexander Mosby Clayton [16] (February 8)
  Alexander Blackburn Bradford [17] (December 5)
Wiley Pope Harris (February 4)
James Thomas Harrison (February 4)

William Sydney Wilson [18] (February 4)
  Jehu Amaziah Orr [19] (April 29)

Missouri – December 2
William Mordecai Cooke (December 5)
Thomas Alexander Harris (December 6)
Casper Wistar Bell (December 2)
John Bullock Clark (December 7)
Aaron H. Conrow (December 2)
George Graham Vest (December 2)
Thomas W. Freeman (December 5)
Robert Ludwell Yates Peyton (January 22, 1862)

North Carolina – July 20
William Nathan Harrell Smith (July 20)
Thomas David Smith McDowell (July 20)
Allen Turner Davidson (July 20)
William Waightstill Avery (July 20)
Francis Burton Craige (July 23)
George Davis (July 20)
John Motley Morehead (July 20)
Richard Clauselle Puryear (July 20)
Thomas Ruffin (July 25)
Abraham Watkins Venable (July 20)

South Carolina – February 4
William Porcher Miles (February 4)
William Waters Boyce (February 4)
Robert Woodward Barnwell (February 4)
James Chesnut, Jr. (February 4)
Lawrence Massillon Keitt (February 4)
Christopher Gustavus Memminger (February 4)
Robert Barnwell Rhett (February 4)
Thomas Jefferson Withers [20] (February 4)
  James Lawrence Orr [21] (February 17, 1862)

Tennessee – August 12
John De Witt Clinton Atkins (August 13)
David Maney Currin (August 16)
Robert Looney Caruthers (August 12)
William Henry De Witt (August 16)
John Ford House (August 12)
Thomas McKissick Jones (August 12)
James Houston Thomas (August 12)

Texas – March 2 [22]
John Gregg (March 2)
John Hemphill [23] (March 11)
William Beck Ochiltree (March 6)
Williamson Simpson Oldham (March 2)
John Henniger Reagan (March 2)
Thomas Neville Waul (March 2)
Louis Trezevant Wigfall (April 29)

Virginia – May 7
Thomas Stanley Bocock (July 23)
William Cabell Rives (May 13)
Waller Redd Staples (May 7)
John White Brockenbrough (May 7)
Robert Mercer Taliaferro Hunter (May 10)
William Hamilton Macfarland (July 20)
James Murray Mason (July 24)
Walter Preston (July 22)
William Ballard Preston (July 20)
Roger Atkinson Pryor (July 24)
Robert Eden Scott (July 22)
James Alexander Seddon (July 20)
John Tyler [24] (August 1)
Alexander Robinson Boteler (November 27)
Robert Johnston (July 20)
Charles Wells Russell (July 20)

---

[1] Membership and seating dates from the *Journal of the Confederate States of America* (Washington, D.C.: Government Printing Office, 1904). Confirmed by Ezra J. Warner and W. Buck Yearns, *Biographical Register of the Confederate Congress* (Baton Rouge: Louisiana State University Press, 1975), pp. 290–293.

[2] Resigned after First Session.

[3] Elected to fill vacancy caused by resignation of Thomas Fearn and took his seat April 29, 1861.

[4] Resigned after First Session.

[5] Elected to fill vacancy caused by resignation of David Lewis and took his seat April 29, 1861.

[6] Resigned in November of 1861, to become governor of Alabama.

[7] Elected to fill vacancy caused by resignation of John Gill Shorter and took his seat November 30, 1861. Resigned January 24, 1862.

[8] Date first mentioned in the Confederate Journal.

[9] Resigned April 8, 1861.

[10] Elected to fill vacancy caused by resignation of James Patton Anderson and took his seat May 2, 1861. Resigned February 5, 1862.

[11] Appointed to fill vacancy caused by resignation of George Taliaferro Ward and took his seat February 5, 1862.

[12] Killed at First Manassas on July 21, 1861.

[13] Appointed to fill vacancy caused by death of Francis Stebbins Bartow and took his seat August 7, 1861.

[14] Resigned in December 1861.

[15] Appointed to fill vacancy caused by resignation of Eugenius Aristides Nisbet and took his seat January 14, 1862.

[16] Resigned May 11, 1861.

[17] Elected to fill vacancy caused by resignation of Alexander Mosby Clayton and took his seat on December 5, 1861.

[18] Resigned after First Session.

[19] Elected to fill vacancy caused by resignation of William Sydney Wilson and took his seat April 29, 1861.

[20] Resigned after Second Session.

[21] Appointed to fill vacancy caused by resignation of Thomas Jefferson Withers and took his seat February 17, 1862.

[22] Official admittance date. John Gregg was seated without roll-call voting privileges on February 15 and Thomas Waul on February 19.

[23] Died January 4, 1862.

[24] Died January 18, 1862.

type of legislation passed, support of President Jefferson Davis's administration, and the general continuation and conduct of the war.

As a border state Missouri had the entire spectrum of options concerning slavery and secession. In the 1860 U.S. presidential election many northern counties, and areas along the Mississippi River across from Illinois, voted for northern Democrat Stephen Douglas (35 percent of the total Missouri vote). A large number of Missouri counties, many in the middle portion of the state, voted for Constitutional Unionist John Bell (35 percent). A large portion of the southern part of the state supported Southern Democrat John Breckinridge (20 percent). The above vote and the presence of over one hundred thousand slaves indicates significant southern sympathy. Even Republican Abraham Lincoln received a sizable vote (10 percent), concentrated in Saint Louis County. The 17,028 votes for Lincoln was the largest number he received in any slave state.[13]

In the early part of 1861 pro-Union and prosouthern elements in the legislature and state government maneuvered to support their side. On March 9 a state committee reported there was no cause to leave the Union. The split loyalties came to a head in mid-July when Confederate sympathizer Gov. Claiborne Jackson was ousted and federal sympathizer Hamilton Gamble declared governor. Both claimed to be the legal governor of Missouri. In mid-August the Provisional Congress recognized Governor Jackson and later offered aid to Missouri Confederates.[14] Governor Jackson called a special session of the pro-Confederate remnant of the state legislature to meet October 21, 1861, in Neosho in the southern part of the state. After reconvening in Cassville, Missouri, the rump legislature "officially" seceded Missouri on October 28 and requested to join the Confederacy. On November 28 Congress approved admission, and a delegation was seated in the Provisional Congress on December 2. However, federal troops and Missouri Union sympathizers controlled most of Missouri by February, 1862. The movement of Union troops into southern Missouri and the subsequent Battle of Elkhorn Tavern (March 7, 1862), just south of the border in Arkansas, secured Missouri for the North thereafter.[15]

The border state of Kentucky also had mixed sympathies regarding slavery and secession. In the 1860 U.S. presidential election, unionist candidates gained the majority of the vote, Constitutional Unionist John Bell receiving 45 percent and Northern Democrat Stephen Douglas 18 percent. However, Southern Democrat and Kentuckian John Breckinridge received a sizable 36 percent. In the first half of 1861, Kentucky tried to negotiate a neutral path. Its position between the North and South made it strategically and politically valuable for both sides. By September the majority unionists were in control of the government and most of the state. In western Kentucky neutrality ended when Confederate forces seized Columbus on the Mississippi River and then Union troops seized Paducah at the confluence of the Tennessee and Ohio rivers. Confederate sympathizers met in convention in Russellville in the southern part of

Kentucky, and on November 20 declared Kentucky free and independent and requested admission to the Confederacy. On December 10 Kentucky was approved as the last Confederate state, and a delegation was seated December 16, 1861. During this period Confederate and Union troops moved into the state. On January 19, 1862, the Union victory at Mill Springs, Kentucky, broke the Confederate defense line in southern Kentucky, and with the occupation of the Provisional Confederate capital at Bowling Green (February 14), the state was consolidated for the North.

Positions in western Kentucky allowed Gen. Ulysses Grant to move into the heart of a true southern state in early February, 1862. Moving south along the Tennessee and Cumberland rivers, Union forces captured Fort Henry (February 5) and Fort Donelson (February 16) in northern Tennessee. As the Fifth Session closed and the First Session of the Permanent Congress opened, Union forces were poised to strike deep into Tennessee and the South.

Strategic locations were also occupied by Union forces along the Confederate coastline during the Fifth Session. The first was Ship Island off the coast of Mississippi (see Map 5), occupied on September 16, 1861. This island was used as a staging area for the blockade of the Mississippi River and the future move on New Orleans. Three weeks later Port Royal-Beaufort, South Carolina was captured and held throughout the war. Port Royal was used as resupply area for the Charleston blockade and the blockade of other parts of the coast. Adjacent Hilton Head Island was also occupied and became a haven for runaway slaves. During the late summer and early fall of 1861 Virginia civil government on the two eastern shore counties ended and this area is colored blue for the remainder of the war. Just before the end of the Provisional Congress both Roanoke Island (February 9) and adjacent Edenton (February 12) along the North Carolina coast were occupied.

Organization of the Permanent Confederate Government

Provisional Congress as a Constitutional Convention

After the adoption of the Provisional Constitution on February 8, 1861, another committee of twelve delegates was appointed to draft the Permanent Constitution. The general attitude of most delegates and Southerners was that they were the actual defenders of the U.S. Constitution and that it should be the fundamental model for the new southern constitution. The goal of the committee was to restore and refine the U.S. Constitution using the experience of southerners in Congress and the nation for the last several decades. The "improvements" were to be made in at least three ways: first, by constitutionally recognizing the institution of slavery; second, by institutionalizing the philosophy of state rights and the concept of state sovereignty in a way so as to be explicit in the final document

and unambiguous to citizens and the courts; and third, by making several practical institutional innovations.

The constitution committee reported back to the Provisional Congress on February 28. For a dozen days the Provisional Congress met as the national legislature in the morning and as a constitutional convention in the afternoon. The Permanent Constitution draft was discussed, debated, and amended, with twenty recorded roll-call votes taken. Nevertheless, the final document was remarkably similar to the U.S. Constitution, with some significant changes.[16] Some of the word changes imbued the idea of state rights, such as in the preamble, "We, the people of the Confederate States of America, each State acting in its sovereign and independent character."[17] The structural changes include such elements as: the item or line-item presidential veto; executive branch/cabinet representation in congressional floor debate; exclusion of protectionism; restrictions on internal improvements; the single six-year presidential term; and other limitations on central government power and responsibilities.[18]

On March 12, 1861, the Provisional Congress constitutional convention unanimously adopted the Permanent Constitution. Four days later the First Session of the Provisional Congress adjourned, having set up a provisional government with a Congress, elected a Provisional president, drafted a Permanent Constitution, and passed a number of resolutions and laws with respect to such items as the continuance of the U.S. legal system and items dealing with trade and commerce. The Permanent Constitution required in its last Article, "The ratification of the conventions of five States shall be sufficient for the establishment of this Constitution between the States so ratifying the same."[19] Because of its location the Alabama state secession convention convened on March 12 and ratified the new Constitution the same day. Mississippi was the fifth state to ratify the document on March 26 and Florida the last of the original members on April 18. Interestingly, South Carolina was the least satisfied with the final document and had the only ratifying convention with some opposition.[20] As each additional southern state seceded, it was admitted to the Confederacy upon its acceptance of the Permanent Constitution.

Permanent Confederate Constitution and the Permanent Confederate Congress

Article I of the Permanent Confederate Constitution established a legislative branch with a bicameral Congress of a House of Representatives and Senate. Article I, Section 2, created a House of Representatives with virtually the same institutional structure as the U.S. House of Representatives.[21] Representatives continued to serve two-year terms and were allocated to the member states based upon population. Article I, Section 3, created a Senate. As in the U.S. Senate, senators served six-year terms and were elected by the state legislatures. The Permanent Constitution stipulated after its ratification the Provisional Congress should "prescribe the time for holding the first election of members of Congress under this Constitution, and time for assembling the same."[22] The Provisional Congress passed a law stipulating the first Wednesday in November 1861 (November 6) for the first national Confederate presidential and congressional elections.[23] February 18, 1862, was set for the beginning of the Permanent Confederate Congress. Setting the date for the first elections and Permanent government required the states to complete a number of tasks before these dates, including: redrawing congressional districts based on the new expanded number of Confederate representatives; reestablishing election laws under the Confederate banner, including the possibility of soldier and refugee voting; and electing two Confederate senators.

The following three chapters discuss the steps in the above process and the geographical aspects of the Confederate Congress. Chapter 3 elaborates on the apportionment of House members and the drawing of new congressional districts. The geographical aspects of these new districts are then analyzed with respect to selected characteristics and territory under Union occupation. Chapter 4 discusses the next step in the process, Confederate congressional elections in both the House and Senate. The electoral system of the Civil War South is introduced, and state and national results are mapped and analyzed for both the first and second elections. After congressional elections the behavior of congressmen is examined when they enter the House and Senate by way of roll-call voting

decisions. In Chapter 5 the major legislative issues and factors influencing voting are discussed and illustrative roll-call votes are mapped. In the roll-call vote chapter, Provisional Congress issues, voting influences, and votes are discussed, as they are in other chapters where appropriate. The objective in each of these chapters is to map and analyze the geographical aspects of the Confederate Congresses.

[1] *Journal of the People of the State of South Carolina* (Columbia: R. W. Gibbes, 1862).

[2] Wilfred Buck Yearns, *The Confederate Congress* (Athens: University of Georgia Press, 1960), p. 7.

[3] *Journal of the Congress of the Confederate States of America* (Washington, D.C.: Government Printing Office, 1904), Vol. 1, p. 899.

[4] Charles R. Lee, Jr., *The Confederate Constitutions* (Chapel Hill: University of North Carolina Press, 1963), pp. 61–81.

[5] *Confederate Journal*, Vol. 1, p. 60.

[6] See the section in Chapter 4 on the Tennessee First Congress elections.

[7] Wendell Holmes Stephenson and E. Merton Coulter, eds., *A History of the South*, 10 vols. (Baton Rouge: Louisiana State University Press, 1950), vol. 7: *The Confederate States of America 1861–1865*, by E. Merton Coulter, p. 3.

[8] See also the sections below on the Provisional Congress Fifth Session and the First Congress elections in Kentucky and Missouri in Chapter 4.

[9] All states voted in the affirmative. For Missouri there was one negative vote in the Georgia delegation, while for Kentucky the delegate vote was unanimous. *Confederate Journal*, Vol. 1, pp. 484 and 546.

[10] See, for example, the Provisional Congress multidimensional roll-call vote map in Chapter 5.

[11] See Map 10 and the section in Chapter 3 on the free and slave population of the South.

[12] A Fourth Session, called for September 3, 1861, was not held.

[13] Delaware had the largest slave state proportion of the vote for Lincoln with 23.7 percent; Missouri's proportion was 10.3 percent.

[14] The August 19, 1861, alliance with Missouri by the Provisional Congress is considered by some tantamount to admission. E. B. Long, *The Civil War Day By Day, An Almanac: 1861–1865* (Garden City, New York: Doubleday, 1971), p. 110. However, the official admission by the Congress on November 27, and approval on November 28, 1861, is used in this atlas.

[15] Missouri, Kentucky, and northwestern Virginia were also represented in the U.S. Congress during the Civil War and participated in U.S. congressional and presidential elections. Kenneth C. Martis, *The Historical Atlas of Political Parties in the United States Congress: 1789–1989* (New York: Macmillan, 1989), pp. 115–119.

[16] Many references align parallel copies of the two constitutions with the word differences highlighted, for example see, Lee, *Confederate Constitutions*, pp. 170–200.

[17] *Confederate Journal*, Vol. 1, p. 909.

[18] Marshall L. DeRosa, *The Confederate Constitution of 1861* (Columbia: University of Missouri Press, 1991), pp. 79–99.

[19] *Confederate Journal*, Vol. 1, p. 923.

[20] Lee, *Confederate Constitutions*, pp. 134–137.

[21] There were some important legal-political changes made regarding Congress in Article I. See the comparative constitutions and analysis in both the Lee and DeRosa books referenced in footnotes 4 and 18.

[22] *Confederate Journal*, Vol. 1, p. 923.

[23] *Statutes at Large of the Provisional Government of the Confederate States of America* (Richmond: R. M. Smith, 1864), Session II, Chapter 34, pp. 122–123.

MAP 2

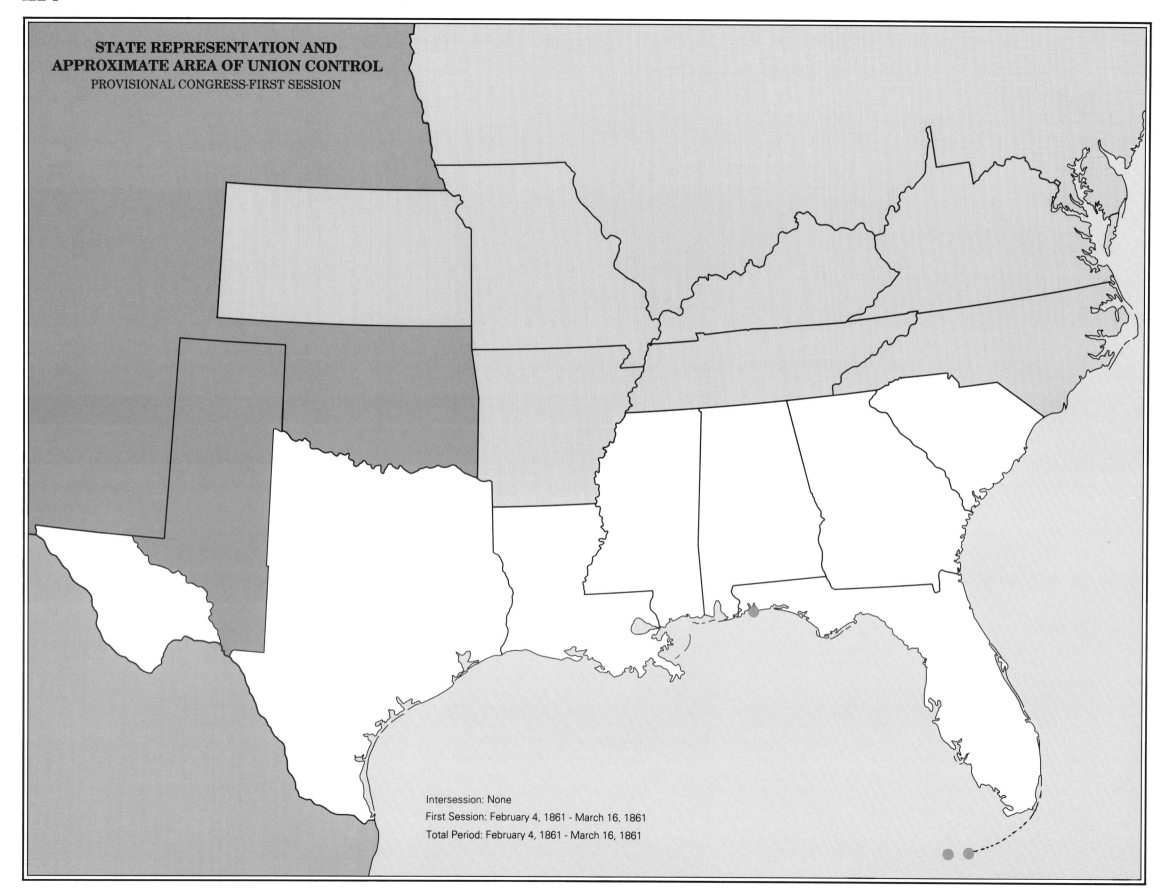

STATE REPRESENTATION AND APPROXIMATE AREA OF UNION CONTROL
PROVISIONAL CONGRESS-FIRST SESSION

Intersession: None

First Session: February 4, 1861 - March 16, 1861

Total Period: February 4, 1861 - March 16, 1861

MAP 3

STATE REPRESENTATION AND APPROXIMATE AREA OF UNION CONTROL
PROVISIONAL CONGRESS-SECOND SESSION

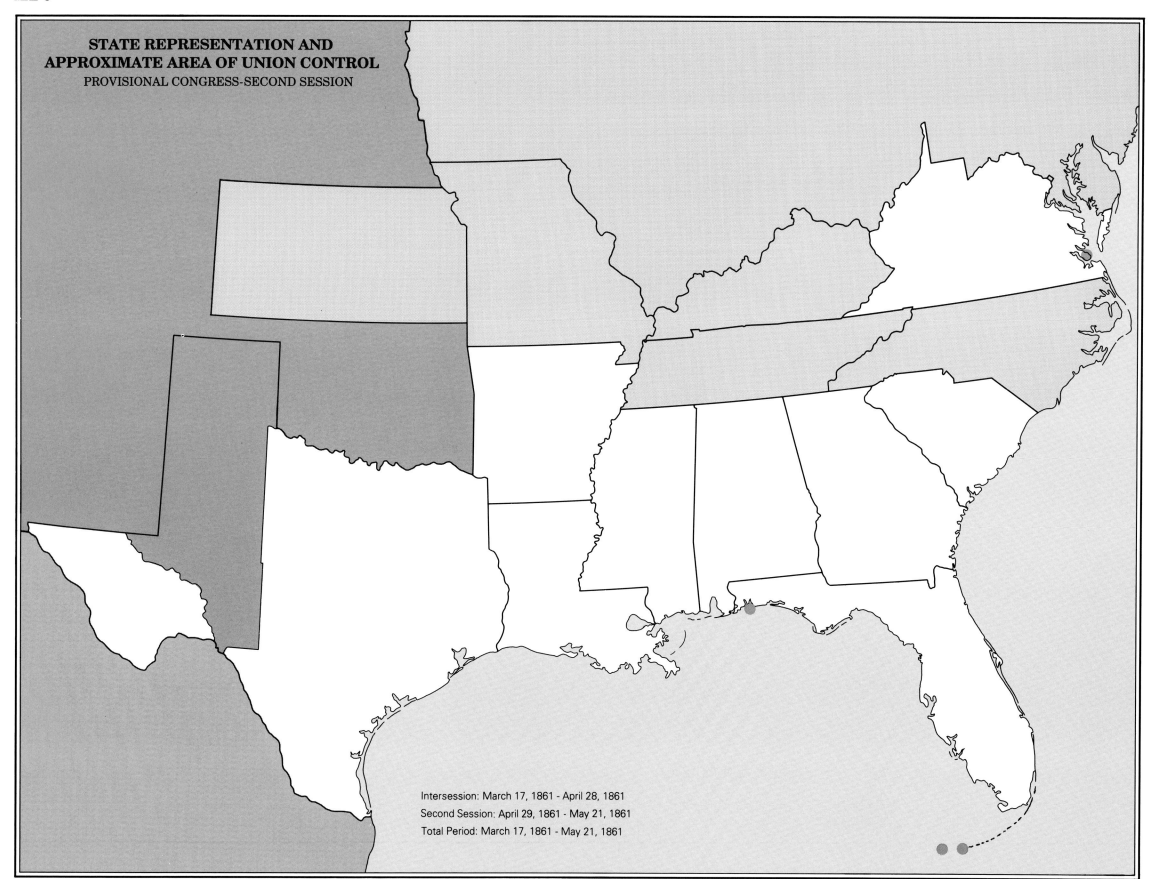

Intersession: March 17, 1861 - April 28, 1861

Second Session: April 29, 1861 - May 21, 1861

Total Period: March 17, 1861 - May 21, 1861

MAP 4

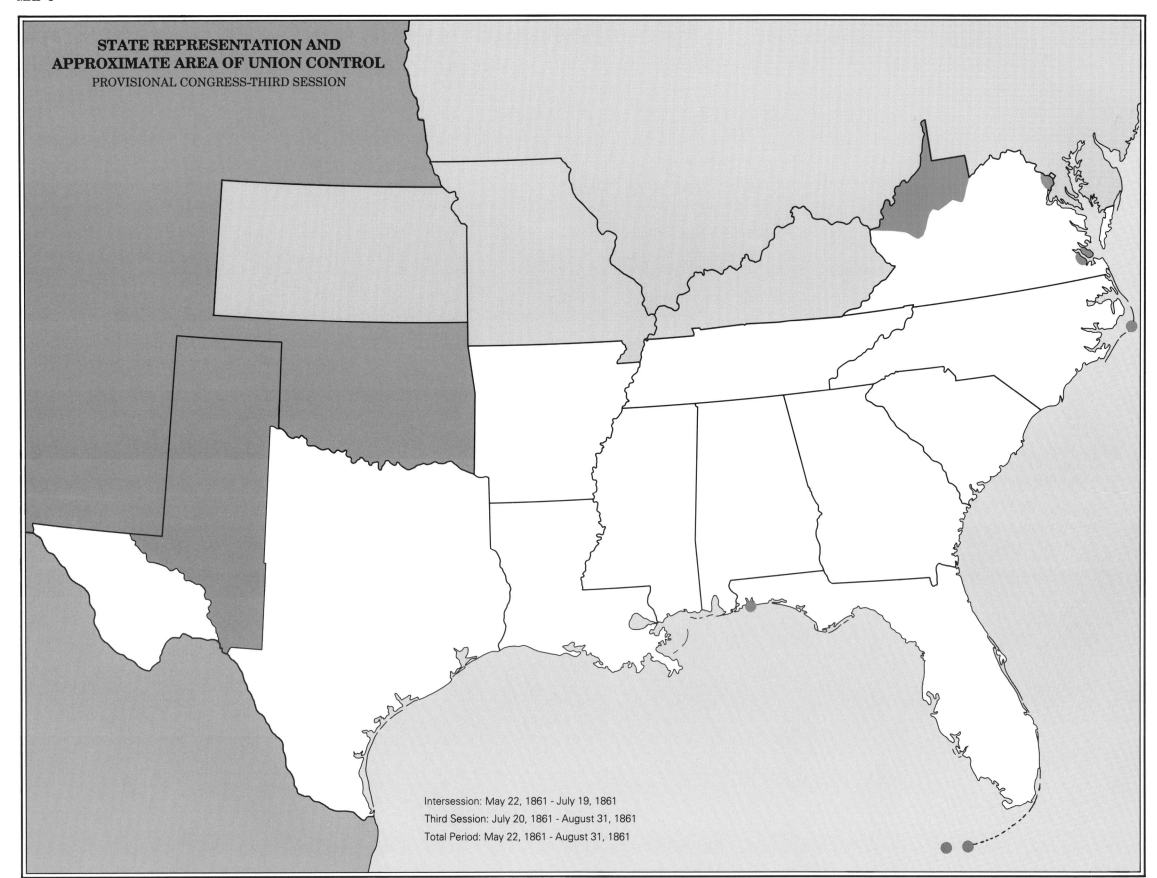

STATE REPRESENTATION AND
APPROXIMATE AREA OF UNION CONTROL
PROVISIONAL CONGRESS-THIRD SESSION

Intersession: May 22, 1861 - July 19, 1861

Third Session: July 20, 1861 - August 31, 1861

Total Period: May 22, 1861 - August 31, 1861

MAP 5

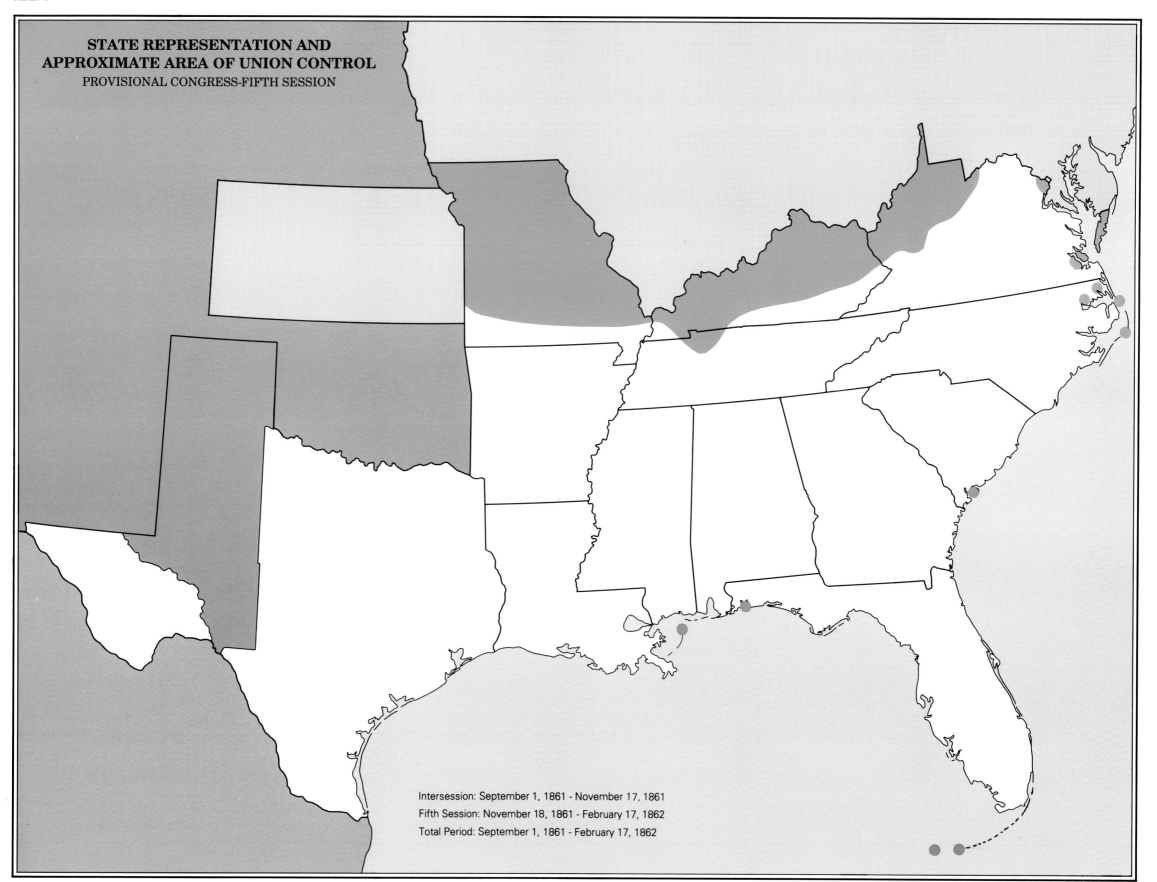

STATE REPRESENTATION AND APPROXIMATE AREA OF UNION CONTROL
PROVISIONAL CONGRESS-FIFTH SESSION

Intersession: September 1, 1861 - November 17, 1861

Fifth Session: November 18, 1861 - February 17, 1862

Total Period: September 1, 1861 - February 17, 1862

3

CONFEDERATE CONGRESSIONAL DISTRICTS

Apportionment of the House of Representatives

The Confederate Constitution created a Congress modeled after the United States Congress. In Article I, Section 3, each state is allotted two senators irrespective of population. Article I, Section 3, stipulates that a state's delegation in the House be apportioned on the basis of the size of its population. The calculation of the actual "apportionment population" retained the same formula as in the U.S. Constitution, that is, a count of free people and a calculation of three-fifths of the total "slave" population.[1] The numbers were based on the 1860 United States census. Table 3-1 gives the relevant population figures for the Confederate states. For example, Georgia was the most populous of the original seven states with a total population of 1,057,286. The Georgia population was composed of 595,088 free individuals (56.2 percent) and 462,198 slaves (43.7 percent). The apportionment population was calculated by multiplying the slave population by three-fifths and adding the free population.[2] Table 3-2, which gives the final apportionment population for each Confederate state, indicates Georgia has an apportionment population of 872,406.

The Confederacy allocated representatives to the states on the bases of one representative for every ninety thousand in the apportionment population, with an additional representative if the

remaining fraction was over one-half.[3] Georgia's apportionment population was divided by 90,000 to calculate the size of its delegation. This calculation is 9.69, entitling Georgia to ten representatives, nine plus an additional member for the fraction over one-half. The original seven states had their House allocation stipulated in the Permanent Confederate Constitution and the remaining states in subsequent laws.

Table 3-2 lists all the Confederate states in order of population size and gives the total and apportionment population, the calculated apportionment ratio, and final number of representatives. Also noted are the additional apportionment laws for the remaining states. Two states vary from the apportionment calculation. Florida was given two representatives in the Permanent Constitution rather than the one calculated. Missouri was allocated thirteen seats in their admittance law; however, the Confederate Missouri government-in-exile continued the same nine Provisional Congress representatives to the Permanent Congress, seven as representatives to the House and two to the Senate.[4]

A final House size of 106 representatives was reached after all thirteen states were admitted. The geographical distribution of population and congressional representatives in the Confederate South is noteworthy. Table 3-2 shows the four most populous states: Virginia, Missouri, Kentucky, and Tennessee, all in the upper South. Missouri and Kentucky were occupied by the North soon after the

war began, and large parts of northwestern Virginia and western Tennessee were occupied soon thereafter. On the other hand, six of the seven least populated states were in the lower South. The seven original Confederate states eventually had a combined total of forty-six representatives, only 43 percent of the total House.

State District Laws

The election of representatives by single-member geographical districts has a long precedent in American history. Election by area became the norm in the colonial legislatures. Districts were by far the dominant method of electing members to the United States House of Representatives from the very first elections in 1788 and 1789.[5] The single-member contiguous congressional district was finally made a federal law in 1842 and every southern state used districts from the 30th Congress (1847–1849) on. Because of the above precedents, when the Permanent Confederate Constitution established a House of Representatives it was understood that election of House members would be from single-member districts, even though the Confederate Constitution did not specifically stipulate this method, even as the U.S. Constitution did not stipulate this method.

After the House apportionment was enumerated in the constitution and various state admittance laws, the states began writing

TABLE 3-1

Population of the Confederate States 1860

State	Total Population	Free Population[1]	Percentage of Total Population	Slave Population	Percentage of Total Population
Virginia	1,596,318	1,105,435	69.2	490,865	30.7
Missouri	1,182,012	1,067,081	90.3	114,931	9.7
Kentucky	1,155,684	930,210	80.5	225,483	19.5
Tennessee	1,109,801	834,082	75.2	275,719	24.8
Georgia	1,057,286	595,088	56.3	462,198	43.7
North Carolina	992,622	661,563	66.6	331,059	33.4
Alabama	964,201	529,121	54.9	435,080	45.1
Mississippi	791,305	354,448	44.8	436,631	55.2
Louisiana	708,002	376,276	53.1	331,726	46.9
South Carolina	703,708	301,302	42.8	402,406	57.2
Texas	604,215	421,649	69.8	182,566	30.2
Arkansas	435,450	324,335	56.1	111,115	43.9
Florida	140,424	78,679	56.1	61,745	43.9
Total	11,441,028	7,579,269	66.2	3,861,524	33.8

Source: U.S. Census 1860

[1] Includes the free black population: Virginia 58,042; Missouri 3,572; Kentucky 10,684; Tennessee 7,300; Georgia 3,500; North Carolina 30,463; Alabama 2,690; Mississippi 773; Louisiana 18,647; South Carolina 9,914; Texas 355; Arkansas 144; Florida 932. Total 147,016.

TABLE 3-2

Apportionment of the Confederate House of Representatives

State	Total Population	Apportionment Population	Ratio	Representatives[1]
Virginia	1,596,318	1,399,318	15.55	16
Missouri	1,182,012	1,136,039	12.62	7 (13)[2]
Kentucky	1,155,684	1,065,490	11.84	12
Tennessee	1,109,801	999,513	11.11	11
Georgia*	1,057,286	872,406	9.69	10
North Carolina	992,622	860,197	9.56	10
Alabama*	964,201	790,169	8.78	9
Mississippi*	791,305	616,652	6.85	7
Louisiana*	708,002	575,311	6.39	6
South Carolina*	703,708	542,745	6.03	6
Texas*	604,215	531,188	5.90	6
Arkansas	435,450	391,004	4.34	4
Florida*	140,424	115,726	1.29	2
Total				106

[1] Congressional apportionment for the original seven Confederates states (*) was stipulated in the Confederate Constitution. Apportionment for Virginia, Tennessee, North Carolina, and Arkansas was stipulated in a law passed in the Second Session of the Provisional Congress, Chapter XXXIV, May 21, 1861. The apportionment for Kentucky was stipulated in a law passed in the Fifth Session of the Provisional Congress, Chapter XVI, December 21, 1861.

[2] The apportionment for Missouri was stipulated in a law passed in the Fifth Session of the Provisional Congress, Chapter II, November 29, 1861. This law allocated thirteen seats for Missouri; however, the pro-Confederate Missouri government only selected seven representatives for the House, the same number and districts as apportioned in the 1850s U.S. House.

their own internal state districting laws based upon the number allotted. The number of representatives allocated by the 1 to 90,000 ratio was significantly higher than the numbers allocated in the 1850s U.S. House apportionment. This necessitated that virtually all the Confederate states write new congressional district laws, ideally using the new 1860 census population figures.

Only one state, South Carolina, did not have its House membership increase. It retained six members, the same as in the 1850s U.S. House. This indicates a slow population growth relative to the rest of the South. Because the South Carolina delegation did not increase or decrease in the Confederate House, the state was not under great pressure to write a new congressional district law. Instead, South Carolina stipulated in their new Confederate state constitution that the old congressional districts be used until a new law was written. The November 6, 1861, South Carolina House elections were held using the same districts as in the 1850s U.S. House elections. When a new statute was written in September 1863 it simply codified again the use of the same 1850s districts.

The state of Missouri also used the 1850s U.S. congressional districts for its Confederate representation in spite of being given a substantial increase in membership from seven to thirteen. The Con-

federate state government in exile was in such disarray that it did not organize a new district plan and election. The nine delegates chosen by the pro-South legislature for the Provisional Congress were kept on as the two senators and seven representatives even though thirteen representatives were authorized. Seven representatives also continued to be used in the elections to the Second Congress.

Seven states, Arkansas, Alabama, Florida, Georgia, Kentucky, Louisiana, and Virginia, established new congressional districts by incorporating them into their new Confederate state constitutions or conventions. The remaining six states created new districting laws through the regular procedure of the state legislature.[6] All these laws had to be in place well before the constitutionally mandated November 6, 1861, national elections to the First Congress.

All the Confederate states continued the time-honored use of counties as the components for congressional districts.[7] For example, the First Congressional District of Alabama was composed of the counties of Lauderdale, Franklin, Lawrence, Limestone, Madison, and Morgan. Appendix III references each state law and enumerates the counties making up each congressional district for each Confederate state.

District Maps

Maps of Confederate congressional districts were compiled using the state district laws and the county boundary lines of the era. The state district laws are the primary source material referenced in Appendix III. The 1860–1861 county boundary lines were obtained from three sources: Lord Collection, RG-69, National Archives and Records Service, Washington, D.C.; *Map Guide to the U.S. Federal Censuses, 1790–1920*, by William Thorndale and William Dollarhide; and *Historical U.S. County Outline Map Collection 1840–1980*, by the Department of Geography, University of Maryland Baltimore County.[8] The maps produced with these sources were verified with those published in the dissertation "Confederate Nationalism: Politics and Government in the Confederate South, 1861–1865" by John B. Robbins.[9]

This procedure produced and verified a Confederate congressional district boundary map with district numbers. This map is the same for both the First and Second Congresses. However, because of deaths, resignations, and turnover in the second House election, the membership lists for the First and Second Congresses are significantly different. The members of both the First and Second

Congresses, both those initially elected and replacements, are matched with their proper district and area represented. This was primarily accomplished by the first comprehensive compilation of Confederate congressional election results in American history.[10] These results were obtained principally from primary source election documents from the various states and newspapers of the day. The results of this research are discussed in Chapter 4 and found in Appendix IV.[11]

Map 6 illustrates the congressional district boundaries for the First Confederate Congress. Opposite Map 6 is the membership list, by state and district, for the First Congress, both House and Senate. Map 7 illustrates the congressional district boundaries for the Second Confederate Congress. Opposite Map 7 is the membership list, by state and district, for the Second Congress, both House and Senate. Any replacements during the Congress are indented, footnoted, and placed beneath the appropriate congressional district and original occupant of the seat.

Chapter 1 introduces the importance of the geographical study of legislative bodies. The number of possible variables for analysis is extensive.[12] Maps 6 and 7 and their accompanying membership lists allow the mapping by congressional district of any phenomena in the history of the Confederate Congress. In the remaining portion of this chapter two categories of phenomena are discussed and mapped by district. First, the concept of mapping congressional district characteristics is discussed, and examples from physical geography, population geography, agricultural geography, economic geography, and political geography are discussed and mapped. Second, the critical concept of Union occupation of Confederate territory and congressional districts is discussed and mapped. In addition, Chapter 4 discusses and maps phenomena with respect to Confederate congressional elections, and Chapter 5 discusses and maps congressional roll-call voting behavior. These maps and discussions lead to the geographic understanding of the Confederate Congress, Confederate political history, and the conduct of the Civil War.

Geographical Aspects of Congressional Districts

Characteristics of Districts

The South is a large section of North America, stretching from Tidewater Virginia to west Texas, and, northern Missouri to south Florida; consequently, it has a wide range of physical and human geography. The congressional districts created by the southern states reflect these physical and human variations and, therefore, have a wide range of characteristics. This section of Chapter 3 examines the attributes of Confederate congressional districts as encompassed by their boundaries at the time of their creation. These character-

istics are helpful in understanding the differences within the South regarding secession, the congressional elections held within these districts, and, later, the roll-call voting of representatives from these districts. The first characteristic examined is physical geography, specifically physiography. Understanding the physical geography of the South sets the stage for, and is essential in interpreting, the other agricultural, demographic, economic, and political characteristics and patterns discussed below.

Physical Geography—Physiographic Regions

The wide variation of landscapes helps explain many of the differences within the South. The South is divided into seven physiographic regions; (1) Atlantic and Gulf Coastal Plain, (2) Mississippi River Alluvial Valley, (3) Appalachian Piedmont, (4) Appalachian Highlands and Plateau, (5) Interior Low Plateau, (6) Interior Highlands, and (7) Interior Central Lowlands.[13] Map 8 classifies each Confederate congressional district into one of these seven regions. Most districts are completely within one area. However, a number of districts, especially the large western ones and those near physiographic boundaries, have some counties in one topographic area and some in another.[14] These districts are classified based on the physiographic area that comprises at least one-half of the total territory of the district.

Coastal Plain. Map 8 shows that the largest physiographic region is the Atlantic and Gulf Coastal Plain, comprising forty-two districts (39.6 percent of all districts). The Coastal Plain spans the entire South from coastal Virginia through Texas, with districts in every state except Missouri, and even in Missouri the extreme southeast portion of the state along the Mississippi River is considered part of the plain. The plain is a flat low-lying warm, moist subtropical area ideal for large-scale plantation agriculture. However, soils vary within this very large area. Along the coast soils can be marshy and not well-drained, while other locations have sandy soils, which do not hold water well. However, in some locations rich local soils can be found. The low-lying districts along the Virginia Tidewater and the Carolina coast are good examples of Coastal Plain geography.

Mississippi River Alluvial Valley. Although this area appears physically similar to the Coastal Plain, it is a separate region since the alluvial soil deposited by river flooding is significantly richer than the leached subtropical soils of most of the Deep South Coastal Plain. The Mississippi River valley dominates eight districts (7.6 percent). Although only containing a small number of districts, this area has the flattest and most extensive high nutrient soil in the Confederacy. The elongated Fourth District of Mississippi, which follows the course of the river, is a perfect example of alluvial valley physiography.

Appalachian Piedmont. The major relief feature in the eastern part of North America is the Appalachian system. The Appalachians are divided here into two areas: Piedmont, and Highlands and

Plateau. As Map 8 indicates, the Piedmont runs south from central Virginia through to Georgia and Alabama just west of the Coastal Plain. The seventeen districts (16 percent) of the Piedmont have a subtropical climate similar to the Coastal Plain. The main difference is a more rolling hilly topography. This topography is gentle nearer the Coastal Plain and increases in relief westward toward the mountains. Because of the different underlying rock Piedmont soils are generally more fertile than those in the Coastal Plain.

Appalachian Highlands and Plateau. This region, which stretches from western Virginia southwest to northeast Alabama, is made up of two distinct subregions with the common factor of a rugged high-relief topography. The core of the Appalachians is the Blue Ridge and Ridge and Valley system with its narrow valleys and long sinuous folded mountains. The better soil, and obviously the flat land, is found in the valleys. Highland areas can reach four to five thousand feet above sea level with a peak in North Carolina of 6,684 feet. The climate of the highlands is much cooler than that of the Coastal Plain and, hence, the growing season is much shorter. The soils can be quite thin on the mountain slopes and acidic from the natural deciduous hardwood forest and the mixed softwoods and hardwoods in the higher elevations.

Just west of the mountains is the Appalachian Plateau. The plateau is lower in altitude, but its undisturbed sedimentary strata are dissected by numerous streams and rivers that give it an extremely complex rugged topography with steep canyons, high local relief, and little flat land. In the north the plateau has a more moist continental climate because of the distance from the ocean, the separation from the ocean by the highlands, and the westerly winds in North America. In the south a more subtropical climate is found, especially in lower elevations. The soils also tend to be acidic from the deciduous forest vegetation. All told the Appalachian Highlands and Plateau comprise seventeen districts (16 percent). The Tenth, Eleventh, and Twelfth districts of Virginia are good examples of a ridge and valley topography with the Great Valley of Virginia, including the Shenandoah Valley, traversing this area. The Cumberland Plateau of eastern Kentucky, centered around districts Ten and Eleven, is a perfect example of dissected plateau geography.

Interior Low Plateau. Just to the west of the Appalachian Plateau is an extension of the Interior Plain called the Interior Low Plateau. The fourteen districts (13.2 percent) of the Low Plateau stretch south from central Kentucky through Middle Tennessee. The general landscape of this region is gently rolling hills, although some parts have high local relief in dissected plateaus. This area is on the northern fringe of the subtropical climate, and the soils generally are not high in nutrients. However, two large important physiographic subprovinces are located here, the Nashville Basin, centered on District Six in Tennessee, and the Lexington Plain-Bluegrass region of Kentucky, centered on districts Eight, Nine, and Eleven. These areas are flatter basins that have good local limestone soils and are considered some of the best agricultural land in the upper South.

Interior Highlands. Two physiographic regions are located in the northwest periphery of the upper South. The Ozark-Ouachita Interior Highland area is much like the Appalachians, displaying both ridge and valley in the Ouachitas of northwest Arkansas, and a rugged dissected plateau in the Ozarks of southern Missouri. Like the Appalachians, the Interior Highlands have high local relief, little flat land and thin, low nutrient soils. The somewhat more northern location and altitude make this area's subtropical climate more severe than adjoining areas. Only three districts (2.8 percent) lie in the Interior Highlands.

Interior Central Lowlands. Just north of the Ozarks begins the core of the great Central Lowlands portion of the North American interior plains. This area is characterized by the flat topography, cool moist continental climate, and rich high nutrient soils that are also found in the adjacent Midwest-Great Plains states of Iowa, Kansas, and Nebraska. The Central Lowlands are mapped here since Missouri was admitted to the Confederacy and to illustrate the "non-southern" physical geography of this edge of the South. The five (4.7 percent) districts of northern Missouri, including St. Louis (District One), are in this region.

Agricultural Geography— Cotton and Tobacco Cultivation

Cotton. The location of cotton cultivation is dependent on climate, soil, and topography. The English initially settled the southeast coast of North America because it had a long growing season, moist subtropical climate, and large areas of flat land that could grow crops not easily cultivated in more northerly colonies or in Europe. The earliest crops were tobacco in Virginia and rice, indigo, and sea island cotton in South Carolina. Cotton was a relatively small crop until invigorated by the invention of the cotton gin and the opening of the first cotton mill in the United States in the late 1790s. However, it was exports to Britain that allowed the South to rise to become one of the world leaders in cotton production in the early 1800s. The first area of extensive cotton cultivation was central South Carolina and central Georgia.[15] The increasing demand for cotton and soil depletion on the eastern Atlantic Coastal Plain encouraged the spread of the cotton slave plantation system westward across the South during the first half of the nineteenth century.[16] In the first decade of the 1800s, cotton surpassed tobacco as America's most valuable export. On the eve of the Civil War cotton accounted for over one-half of all exports. In addition, cotton fabrication and textile manufacturing, mostly in the North, arose to become America's most important industrial enterprise, even though the United States never internally consumed more that one-seventh of the harvest.[17]

By 1860 an identifiable Cotton Belt had evolved in the southern United States. This belt was an geographic area of intensive cotton plantation stretching westward almost continuously from the Carolinas, up the Mississippi River Valley, and expanding rapidly into east Texas. The extent of the heavily cultivated portion of the Cotton Belt is vividly illustrated on Map 9, which identifies the thirty-six Confederate congressional districts (34 percent) in which intensive cotton cultivation took place.[18] By 1860 the most extensive area of cotton production was in the Mississippi River valley (see physiographic Map 8) in an area on both sides of the river north of Baton Rouge, Louisiana, to Greenville, Mississippi. The Fourth and Fifth Districts of Mississippi and the eastern river valley portion of the Sixth District of Louisiana were the most intensively cultivated areas of the South at the start of the Civil War. The rich flat alluvial soils and the subtropical position near the Gulf Coast made this area an ideal location for cotton cultivation. In addition, the transportation system of the river allowed for cheap and easy trade of this valuable commodity. Although the entire river valley was planted with cotton to the northern Arkansas border, a second particularly identifiable concentration was in the districts surrounding Memphis, Tennessee, especially the counties of the Eleventh District of Tennessee and the First District of Mississippi. The data in Table 3-3 shows that the state of Mississippi was by far the largest cotton producer in 1860 and the state of Louisiana third.[19]

The second largest area of intense cotton production was the so-called Alabama Black Belt. This region developed because of a unique physiographic subdivision of the Coastal Plain stretching in a band from northeast Mississippi through central Alabama.[20] The soils in this area are particularly dark and fertile because of the underlying chalk rock. District Three of Mississippi and particularly districts Five, Six, and Seven of Alabama are the core of this area. One other area of intensive cultivation in Alabama was in the Tennessee River Valley in the northwest part of the state (District One) and adjoining areas of southern Tennessee (District Seven). The Black Belt and Tennessee River valley cultivation enabled Alabama to become to the second largest cotton producing state by 1860.

Cotton Belt production, as enumerated in Table 3-3 and illustrated in Map 9, was found in the lower South. Cotton is a subtropical plant that needs a long growing season. Because of climatic restrictions cotton cultivation was virtually nonexistent in the three most northern Confederate states, Missouri, Kentucky and Virginia. In addition, because of topographic and/or climatic restrictions, large-scale plantation cotton agriculture was almost nonexistent in the higher elevation and mountainous Appalachian Highland and Plateau region, including Appalachian districts as far south as northern Georgia and northeast Alabama (compare Maps 8 and 9).

Tobacco. The establishment of the first permanent English colony at Jamestown, Virginia, was based upon the cultivation of tobacco. The first commercial cultivation in 1612 was an immediate success, and within fifteen years half a million pounds were exported. In the colonial period tobacco cultivation spread throughout Coastal Plain Virginia and adjacent areas of southern Maryland. Within seventy-five years of the first cultivation tobacco exports rose to twenty-eight million pounds and were the economic base of both Virginia and Maryland. Indeed, tobacco was America's most valuable export until the cotton boom of the 1790s; cotton eventually overtook it in the early 1800s.[21]

The rapid depletion of the soil caused by tobacco cultivation encouraged both large plantation holdings, so that crops could be rotated, and continual expansion westward for new fertile land. Tobacco production spread onto the Piedmont area of Virginia in the eighteenth century. After the American Revolution trans-Appalachian lands were opened for new Euro-American settlement. Tobacco cultivation began in Kentucky in 1783 and in Tennessee in 1789. The 1840 U.S. census, the first to record agricultural data, showed that Kentucky had grown to over two-thirds of the Virginia production, fifty-three million pounds versus Virginia's seventy-five million.

Map 9 identifies the twenty-four districts (22.6 percent) with a heavy concentration of tobacco cultivation.[22] On the eve of the Civil War there were three main geographic centers of tobacco production in the South. The premier area was still the original concentration in Coastal Plain-Piedmont Virginia. Table 3-3 indicates Virginia was by far the leading tobacco state. This area of cultivation extends into the southern counties of Maryland and a line of counties in north central North Carolina along the Virginia border. Indeed, North Carolina was the fourth-ranking southern tobacco state in this period.

The second concentration of tobacco planting was in the northern portion of the Interior Low Plateau (see Map 8) in Kentucky and

TABLE 3-3

Southern Cotton and Tobacco Production 1860

State	Cotton Production[1]	Rank	Tobacco Production[2]	Rank
Alabama	997,978	2	221,284	9
Arkansas	367,485	6	999,757	6
Florida	63,322	10	758,015	8
Georgia	701,840	4	919,316	7
Kentucky	4,092	12	108,102,433	2
Louisiana	722,218	3	40,610	13
Mississippi	1,195,699	1	127,736	11
Missouri	100	13	25,086,196	5
North Carolina	145,514	9	32,853,250	4
South Carolina	353,413	7	104,412	10
Tennessee	227,450	8	38,931,277	3
Texas	405,100	5	98,016	12
Virginia	12,727	11	123,967,757	1
Total South	5,196,938		332,210,059	
Total U.S. (1860)	5,198,077	99.9% South	429,390,771	77.4% South
Total U.S. (1850)	2,445,793		199,752,655	

Source: U.S., Department of Commerce, Bureau of the Census, *Eighth Census of the United States, 1860: Agriculture*, 2: 200-01.

[1] Bales of 400 pounds each

[2] Pounds

Tennessee. The core of this area was the western half of Kentucky and adjacent counties in northwestern Tennessee. Four counties in the Lexington Plain-Bluegrass region produced over one million pounds in 1860; therefore, three districts in this area are displayed on Map 9. Kentucky was by far the second leading tobacco state with the adjacent Tennessee areas making it a distant third.

One additional area of cultivation stands out in Map 9, the tobacco planting on the Interior Central Lowlands in northern Missouri. Tobacco is a hardy plant, and many strains tolerate a shorter growing season than subtropical crops. Although the subtropical climate type found in Virginia and the Carolinas is ideal for tobacco, the hardiness of the plant allows its cultivation outside the South. Indeed, the ability to grow tobacco and the value of the crop encouraged even northern farmers to grow this plant. Missouri's twenty-five million pounds made it the fifth largest producer of tobacco in the South in 1860, but it ranked nationally behind Maryland's thirty-eight million pounds and just behind Ohio's twenty-five-and-one-half million pounds.[23] Tobacco cultivation took place throughout the South, many times for personal and local consumption, and even many counties in the Appalachian Highlands and Plateau grew substantial quantities.

The geographic distribution of tobacco cultivation in the United States during the antebellum period was centered in the upper South, with Virginia and Kentucky far ahead of the other states. Tobacco cultivation has a pattern distinctly separate from cotton cultivation, and therefore both can be portrayed on Map 9. Both patterns are important in understanding the economic development and demographic structure of the South. Tobacco production more than doubled from 1850 to 1860, with the southern states growing a large percent of the national commercial crop. However, on the eve of the Civil War tobacco accounted for only 6 percent of the export total of the United States. Cotton production also more than doubled from 1850 to 1860, as it had in every decade since 1820, and virtually all U.S. production took place in the lower South. This was even more significant since cotton represented over 50 percent of the total U.S. exports.

Population Geography—Free and Slave Population

The introduction and wide use of African slaves in North America is primarily attributed to the large-scale commercial cultivation of tobacco and subtropical crops, especially cotton. These crops are labor-intensive, that is, they need care over much of the period of their growth, harvest, and commercial preparation. This care necessitates not only a large inexpensive labor force, but one that could be forced to work, in the case of cotton, in a hot, humid, subtropical climate. The invention of the cotton gin in the 1790s and the growing markets in the early 1800s revitalized and expanded both the small-scale and large-scale cotton plantation slavery systems.

The population of the thirteen states admitted to the Confederacy was 11,441,028 according to the 1860 census (see Table 3-1). As noted in the section on apportionment, the largest four states in population are all in the upper South; Virginia, Missouri, Kentucky and Tennessee. The densest concentrations of population were in Tidewater and Piedmont Virginia, the Bluegrass region of Kentucky, Middle Tennessee, the Mississippi River valley, and of course the large cities. Areas of low population density were the western frontier in Texas and Arkansas, south Georgia, Florida and the Gulf Coast up to the Mississippi River valley, and areas of the Appalachian Highland and Plateau in Virginia and Kentucky.[24]

Of course, the most significant aspect of antebellum southern population was the division between free and slave. Of the 11,441,028 people, 7,579,269 were free (66.2 percent) and 3,861,524 slave (33.8 percent). There were significant differences in the geographic distribution of free whites and African slaves. Table 3-1 gives the numbers and percentages of free and slave population for the thirteen Confederate states. While slaves participated in almost every conceivable type of work, the general explanation of the free and African slave population distribution in the South is largely accounted for by the distribution of tobacco and cotton cultivation as illustrated in Map 9. Understanding both these agriculture and demographic patterns and their relationship is critical for understanding the South and the Confederate Congresses.[25] For example, South Carolina's slave population made up 57.2 percent of its total population, the largest percentage of any state. Of course, South Carolina perhaps had the most to lose over eventual emancipation, and it was the first to secede and the first to begin military hostilities. The largest cotton-producing state, Mississippi, was the only other state to have over one-half the population (55.2 percent) slave.

Map 10 gives a more detailed look at the free-slave population geography by way of districts. This data was compiled by congressional district by John B. Robbins in his work, "Confederate Nationalism: Politics and Government in the Confederate South, 1861–1865." An additional source was used to verify, illustrate, and analyze this data, the slave population map in *Atlas of Antebellum Southern Agriculture* by Sam Bowers Hilliard.[26] The dark red color indicates Confederate congressional districts with a slave population of 50 percent or more. Twenty-seven of the 106 districts (25.5 percent) had a population of over one-half slave. Table 3-4 lists the ten districts with the highest percentage of slave population. The largest district was the Fourth of Mississippi, with 74 percent of the population made up of African slaves. The Third District of South Carolina had a 72 percent slave population and was the only other district over 70 percent.

The geographic area of the large slaveholding districts was somewhat contiguous. The main segment stretches along the Cotton Belt from South Carolina along the Coastal Plain and Piedmont west through central Georgia, Alabama, and Mississippi to the Mississippi River valley and into Louisiana. The one other heavy concentration of slaves was in the tobacco-growing districts of Piedmont Virginia.

The state with the largest proportion of free population, over 90 percent, was Missouri. Kentucky also had a large free population of

TABLE 3-4

Slaves as Percentage of Population in Confederate Congressional Districts

Ten Highest Percentage Slave Districts

Rank	State	District	Percentage Slave[1]	Number Slave
1	Mississippi	4	74	105,227
2	South Carolina	3	72	98,357
3	Louisiana	4	65	76,246
4	Mississippi	5	64	73,031
5	Alabama	5	62	87,963
6	South Carolina	6	62	80,650
7	Alabama	6	60	90,827
8	Virginia	5	60	65,167
9	South Carolina	4	59	80,596
10	Louisiana	3	58	69,616

Ten Lowest Percentage Slave Districts

Rank	State	District	Percentage Slave	Number Slave
97	Tennessee	2	9	8,521
98	Kentucky	5	9	7,406
99	Missouri[2]	7	8	13,082
100	Kentucky	12	8	9,244
101	Arkansas	1	8	7,638
102	Virginia	14	5	4,393
103	Missouri[2]	6	4	7,256
104	Missouri[2]	1	2	3,810
105	Virginia	15	2	1,849
106	Virginia	16	1	911

Sources: John B Robbins, "Confederate Nationalism: Politics and Government in the Confederate South, 1861–1865," (Ph.D. diss., Rice University, 1964), pp. 246–272. Sam Bowers Hilliard, *Atlas of Antebellum Southern Agriculture* (Baton Rouge: Louisiana State University Press, 1984), p. 34.

[1] When two districts have the same percentage the district with the greater number of slaves is ranked higher.

[2] Missouri has a somewhat higher number of slaves because it was apportioned thirteen districts based upon population, but only used seven districts (see section on apportionment in Chapter 2). The other state number differences reflect the final apportionment ratio (see Table 3-1) and intrastate district population differences.

80.5 percent. Although these were the only states with more than a 80 percent free population, thirty-three districts (31.1 percent) in ten states were over 80 percent free. The light red color on Map 10 indicates congressional districts with a free population of 80 percent or more. Table 3-4 also ranks the districts with smallest percentage of slaves. The district in the South with the lowest number of slaves was the Sixteenth District of Virginia, 1 percent of the total population. This district, made up of the northern panhandle of Virginia and other counties bordering Pennsylvania and Ohio, is on the Appalachian Plateau and is very northern in its climate, culture, economy, and economic ties. Two other districts had less than 2 percent slaves, one other northwestern Virginia district, Fifteen, and District One, St. Louis city and county, Missouri.

The districts with a very large free population are also geographically concentrated. These districts are located in two large areas in the upper South: the Appalachian Highland and Plateau region of Virginia, Kentucky, North Carolina, and Tennessee; and Missouri and the Kentucky districts bordering the North. Three districts are anomalies. Two districts in Louisiana, New Orleans (District Two—88 percent free) and delta of the Mississippi River (District One—83 percent) fell into this category as did the First District of Texas (85 percent) on the frontier of American settlement.

Forty-six Confederate congressional districts (43.4 percent) fell into the middle category. These districts are located in two geographical areas. First, a band of districts in the middle South from North Carolina west to Arkansas separating the two extremes of districts, that is, separating districts with a large white population found in the upper South and districts with a large black population found in the lower South. The other type of middle district is found on the frontier extremities of the South, Florida, and Texas.

The vast majority of seven and one-half million southern whites were not slaveholders.[27] Most Southerners were poor white yeoman farmers who sometimes grew tobacco and cotton but owned no slaves. This situation was more common, however, in Kentucky, Missouri, Tennessee, and the Appalachian Highland and Plateau, and less common in eastern Virginia or the Mississippi River valley. The concentration of slaves in the Cotton Belt is one of the most important geographic patterns in the antebellum South. While the Cotton Belt disintegrated in the latter half of the twentieth century, the high percentage of African Americans in the rural Deep South counties persists to the present.[28]

Economic Geography—Land Values

The antebellum South was a rural agricultural society. This was a legacy of the British colonial period sustained by the rejuvenation of the cotton plantation slavery system at the end of the eighteenth century. Why the South did not industrialize and establish manufacturing enterprises at the pace of the North has been analyzed at length.[29] The economic differences between the South and the North and within the South can be measured in a number of ways: average annual income; value of crops; number of manufacturing enterprises; urbanization; and industrial production.

Since the South was an agricultural society, one of the best and most available ways of measuring the intraregional economic structure is the value of land. Map 11 illustrates the average value of farm real estate per acre by congressional district according to county data

in the 1860 census.[30] The county land-value data was compiled by congressional district by Thomas B. Alexander and Richard E. Beringer in *The Anatomy of the Confederate Congress*.[31] They divided Confederate districts into three categories: high-value districts—those with the median county in the district having the average cost of land of twelve dollars per acre or more; middle-value districts—those with the median county in the district having the average cost of land of eight to twelve dollars per acre; and low-value districts— those with the median county in the district having the average cost of land below eight dollars per acre. This land-value division is used not only to illustrate and analyze which areas of the South were thriving and which lagging, but also to analyze, using a representative measurement, southern subregional economic differences. The objective, again, is the better understanding of the South in general and Confederate elections and congressional roll-call voting in particular.

Thirty-five of the 106 Confederate districts (33 percent) are in the high-land-value category. All of these districts except one are coterminous with at least one or more other districts. These concentrations indicate larger areas of significant economic development. Map 11 identifies six geographic conglomerations of high land values: the Mississippi River valley; northern Virginia; the Black Belt of Alabama; the Lexington Plain-Bluegrass region; Nashville Basin-Middle Tennessee; and northern Missouri. The largest of these areas, with eleven coterminous districts, is the Mississippi River valley of Louisiana, Mississippi, and western Tennessee. The quality of fertile river-bottom land and high-yield cotton production make this area one of the most valuable in the South. Table 3-5 lists the ten highest land value districts in the Confederacy. The second and fifth highest-ranking districts are in the Mississippi River valley. The Second District of Louisiana has a average land value of fifty-one dollars per acre, but this is explained by the city of New Orleans being within this small one-parish district. The fifth-ranked Third District of Louisiana encompasses the alluvial valley between New Orleans and Baton Rouge. This area was valuable because of its location near these large cities and the mouth of the river, but specifically because this was the one large sugar cane-growing area in the nation.[32] Since the four top ranking districts are small districts with large cities, the Third District of Louisiana had the most valuable rural agricultural land in the South in 1860. One other area of exceptionally valuable rural agricultural land in the Deep South was the Alabama Black Belt. The Fifth and Sixth Districts of Alabama are high-value areas because of their productivity and concentration of cotton cultivation.

The second largest concentration of valuable improved land was in Virginia with ten districts. The location of northern Virginia near the markets of the growing cities of the North partially explains the cost of land on this edge of the South. Of course, the Virginia Coastal Plain and Piedmont was the center of tobacco production in the nation. The farms of the Great Valley and northern Virginia were one of the centers of wheat, rye, and oats production in the South.[33] The northern panhandle Sixteenth District of Virginia is ranked the

TABLE 3-5

District Land Values in the Confederate Congress

Ten Highest Land Value Districts

Rank	State	District	Land Value per Acre in Dollars[1]
1	Missouri	1	72
2	Louisiana	2	51
3	Kentucky	7	43
4	Kentucky	11	42.5
5	Louisiana	3	33
6	Virginia	16	27.5
7	Kentucky	8	26
8	Tennessee	6	25.5
9	Kentucky	9	25
10	Kentucky	6	23

Ten Lowest Land Value Districts

Rank	State	District	Land Value per Acre in Dollars[1]
97	North Carolina	7	4
98	Georgia	9	4
99	Alabama	8	4
100	Texas	4	3.5
101	Texas	3	3
102	Texas	1	3
103	North Carolina	4	3
104	Alabama	2	3
105	Kentucky	12	2
106	Georgia	1	2

Source: Thomas B. Alexander and Richard E. Beringer, *The Anatomy of the Confederate Congresses* (Nashville: Vanderbilt University Press, 1972), pp. 354–389.

[1] Land values per acre in the median county in the district. When two districts have the same land value the alphabetical order of the state is used.

sixth most valuable because of its river cities, Ohio River location adjacent to the North, and a surprising agricultural sector in spite of having a plateau geography.

The Lexington Plain–Kentucky Bluegrass region stands out as the largest single concentration of top ten districts. All five Bluegrass districts are ranked in the top ten most valuable districts. The Seventh District is the highest within the Bluegrass region because Louisville is in the district, and the Eleventh District is next because Lexington is in this district and it was the heart of the Bluegrass region. Another part of the Interior Low Plateau with high-value land is Middle Tennessee, with three districts. This area is led by the eighth-ranked Sixth District in the heart of the Nashville Basin. Both the Bluegrass region and Nashville Basin had high-density population, grew a wide variety of crops, and were noted for their tobacco cultivation.[34]

The final high-land-value area is the Interior Central Lowlands of northern Missouri. The rich farmland of this region had land prices similar to the neighboring Midwest and Great Plains states. This area not only grew tobacco but was an emerging area of wheat and corn cultivation. The highest-value district in the South was here, the First District of Missouri, which comprises just one county and the city of St. Louis.

Forty-one districts (38.7 percent) are classified as having relatively low land values. They are scattered throughout the South and are found in every state. Nevertheless, three areas had a large number of coterminous districts: the frontier, the Gulf Coast, and Appalachia. The largest was made up of the ten coterminous districts of the frontier of Texas, including western Arkansas and southwestern Missouri. The low amount of improved land, especially in the western portion of the Texas districts, brought down the median land value in comparison with more developed areas. Three Texas districts are ranked in the lowest ten found in Table 3-5.

The second large undeveloped area is Florida and the Gulf Coast districts up to the Mississippi River valley, a sparsely settled area of poor soils. The First District of Georgia (rank 106) and the Eighth District of Alabama (rank 99) are in this region, the former having the lowest land values in the South. Both districts are in the Coastal Plain area with inferior soils and a southern pine forest.[35] The Georgia district has very poorly drained soils highlighted by the Okefenokee Swamp in the southern counties.

Eight of the seventeen Appalachian Highland and Plateau districts are in the lowest land value category. Two districts, the Twelfth of Kentucky and Ninth of Georgia, are in the bottom-ten ranking in Table 3-5. The high relief, poor soils, and isolation of these areas kept their economic development lagging.

The South is a large diverse region with areas in various stages of economic growth and development. Since the antebellum South was an agricultural society, Map 11 illustrates to a great extent areas blessed with high-amenity farmland. This farmland not only attracted commercial agriculture but also a dense settlement pattern with some urban development, all of which helped keep land values high. Three of the six concentrations of high land value border the North, while two out of the three low-value areas are in the extreme southernmost locations.

Political Geography—
The 1860 U.S. Presidential Election

The Civil War was the most traumatic and significant political event in American history. In the antebellum period political sentiment with respect to slavery, state rights, the Union, and secession varied across the South. The election of Abraham Lincoln in November 1860 set off a chain of events that led to the secession of seven Deep South states.

The upper South states did not commit to secession until after the firing on Fort Sumter in April 1861 and the call for Union troops. Political sentiment in the South was in turmoil before the 1860 election, during the 1860 election, after the results of the election were known, during the Montgomery convention, and after Fort Sumter fell.

Knowledge of the political geography of the immediate antebellum South gives insight into the elections and voting behavior in the Confederate South. Obviously there are a number of time periods and methods in which this sentiment can be analyzed. This section discusses the geographic variation of political party support in the South in the November 1860 U.S. presidential election. This was the last major election and complete set of voting data before the Civil War and gives an understanding about the South in general and particular subregional variations.

The 1850s were filled with political disarray and change. In the beginning of the decade there were two major national parties, the Democrats and Whigs. These were nonsectional parties, drawing voting strength from all regions of the country.[36] As abolitionist sentiment grew in the North, the South grew more adamant in the defense of slavery. Both political parties, but primarily the Whigs, split into two factions over this issue, even though they agreed on most other issues of the day. Most southern Whigs were conservative and proslavery, but also unionists, while most strong state rights-proslavery-prosecessionist Southerners were usually Democrats. Many times political party support took ironic twists; for example, many very large slaveholders and wealthy plantation owners were Whigs because of the Whig national economic policy and because they thought the Union was actually the best way to preserve and keep their human slave property. Most northern Democrats were tolerant of slavery, while most northern Whigs decried slavery. The Democratic party was able to hold together longer; however, the Whig party fell apart over abolition after the presidential election of 1852 and the U.S. congressional elections of 1852–1853.

The Democratic party grew in strength in the South and began to dominate the region after the demise of the Whigs. Nevertheless, for the remaining portion of the 1850s former Whigs, members of the American party (Know-Nothings), and various opposition parties and candidates ran and won in congressional districts throughout the South.[37] In the presidential election of 1856 Democrat James Buchanan swept the southern and border states, but again there was a significant anti-Democratic vote of one-third to almost one-half in this region.[38]

Vote by State. By the time of the 1860 presidential election the abolitionist-slavery sectional battlelines were drawn. Reflecting the turmoil of the times, four candidates ran for president. Each candidate represents a different position on the slavery-abolitionist/secession-Union political spectrum. In the North a sectional Republican party was solidifying after mobilizing former Whigs, Americans (Know-Nothings), some antislavery Democrats, and a growing abolitionist general population. The Republicans, representing the most

abolitionist party, especially as perceived by Southerners, nominated Abraham Lincoln of Illinois for president. In 1860 the national Democratic party finally broke into two wings over the presidential nomination. A southern proslavery wing nominated John C. Breckinridge of Kentucky. Southern Democrat Breckinridge generally represented a sentiment of a strong defense of slavery, including extension into the territories, and a strong state rights position. The Northern Democrat wing nominated Stephen A. Douglas of Illinois. Northern Democrat Douglas generally represented a sentiment tolerant of slavery, but strongly pro-Union. In an attempt to bring a moderating force to southern presidential politics former Whigs, former Americans (Know-Nothings), and Unionists nominated a fourth candidate, John Bell of Tennessee, under the banner of the Constitutional Unionist party. Unionist Bell generally represented a sentiment of allowing slavery to continue in the South as accepted in the Constitution, but rejecting secession and favoring the federal Union. In the November election the southern states basically split their vote between Breckinridge, the Southern Democrat, and Bell, the Constitutional Unionist. In the electoral college Breckinridge swept the Deep South; Bell captured three upper South states, Virginia, Kentucky, and Tennessee; and Douglas carried Missouri. Republican Lincoln swept the North, and because of its greater population Lincoln won in the electoral college and was elected president.

Table 3-6 lists the voting statistics for the 1860 U.S. presidential election for the thirteen states that were admitted to the Confederacy. The total vote and percentage for each candidate and state is given. A total of 1,168,240 votes were cast in the South. Southern Democrat Breckinridge won the highest number of votes at 44.6 percent. His support was strongest in the Deep South and weakest in the upper South. Unionist Bell was the second-largest vote getter at 40.2 percent with his greatest support coming from the border and upper South states. Regular Northern Democrat Douglas received 13.4 percent of the vote. He did well in the border States, but also received double-digit support in such Deep South states as Louisiana, Alabama, and Georgia. Republican Lincoln was not on the ballot in most of the South, but did receive some support in Missouri and scattered votes in Kentucky and Virginia. Of course, the total percentages would have been quite different if the border states of Missouri and Kentucky had not been included and only the true upper and lower South states tabulated.

In addition to the regular vote count, a "Unionist Index" is calculated for each state to provide some measure of possible unionist-secessionist sentiment at the time of the election. The Index is simply the total percentage of the vote for the Republican, Northern Democrat, and Constitutional Union candidates. By far the most unionist slave state was the border state of Missouri. In fact, Northern Democrat Douglas scored his only electoral college victory in this state, narrowly defeating Unionist Bell. It should be noted that Republican Lincoln received over 17,000 votes, more there than in any other slave state.[39] The Index ranks the other border slave state

TABLE 3-6

1860 U.S. Presidential Election

State	Unionist Index[1]	Rank	Republican (%) (Abraham Lincoln)	Northern Democrat (%) (Stephen Douglas)	Constitutional Unionist (%) (John Bell)	Southern Democrat (%) (John C. Breckinridge)	Total Turnout
Missouri	81.1	1	17,028 (10.3)	58,801 (35.5)	58,372 (35.3)	31,362 (18.9)	165,563
Kentucky	63.7	2	1,364 (0.9)	25,651 (17.5)	66,058 (45.2)	53,143 (36.3)	146,216
Virginia	55.5	3	1,887 (1.1)	16,198 (9.7)	74,481 (44.6)	74,352 (44.5)	166,891
Tennessee	55.4	4		11,281 (7.7)	69,728 (47.7)	65,097 (44.6)	146,106
Louisiana	55.1	5		7,625 (15.1)	20,204 (40.0)	22,681 (44.9)	50,510
Georgia	51.1	6		11,581 (10.9)	42,860 (40.3)	52,176 (48.9)	106,717
North Carolina	49.5	7		2,737 (2.8)	45,129 (46.7)	48,846 (50.5)	96,712
Arkansas	46.9	8		5,357 (9.9)	20,063 (37.1)	28,732 (53.1)	54,152
Alabama	46.0	9		13,618 (15.1)	27,835 (30.9)	48,669 (54)	90,122
Mississippi	41.0	10		3,282 (4.8)	25,045 (36.4)	40,768 (59)	69,095
Florida	37.8	11		223 (1.7)	4,801 (36.1)	8,227 (62.2)	13,301
Texas	24.5	12		18 (0.0)	15,383 (24.5)	47,454 (75.5)	62,855
South Carolina[2]							
Total	50.6[3]		20,279 (1.7)	156,372 (13.4)	470,059 (40.2)	521,530 (44.6)	1,168,240

Source: Congressional Quarterly, *Guide to U.S. Elections* (Washington, D.C.: 1985), p. 335.

[1] Total percent of the vote for Republican, Northern Democrat, and Constitutional Unionist combined.

[2] There was no popular vote for president in South Carolina in all the elections prior to the Civil War. The South Carolina state legislature selected members of the electoral college, and they cast all eight votes for Southern Democrat Breckinridge in 1860.

[3] Index average for the twelve voting southern states.

of Kentucky as the second most unionist state. The upper South states of Virginia and Tennessee rank third and fourth in unionist voting percentage. The highest-ranked Deep South state is Louisiana. Unionist Bell and even northerner Douglas did well in Louisiana, but Breckinridge won with a plurality of 44.9 percent (see Table 3-6).

The two most southern and periphery states, Florida and Texas, recorded the great percentage support for the Southern Democrat candidate. The first and second largest cotton states, Mississippi and Alabama, are ranked next in their support of the Southern Democrat. Unfortunately, a popular presidential vote was not taken in South Carolina, perhaps the most prosecession state. In South Carolina the state legislature elected the members of the electoral college and all eight voted for Breckinridge.

Vote by Congressional District. Map 12 gives a more detailed district by district examination of the 1860 vote. Of course, this election took place several months before the districts were established; nevertheless, they are used here to decipher the political background of these areas in order to better understand the Confederate elections and representative behavior during the Civil War. Map 12 identifies which of the four parties won a majority or plurality in each district. These data were compiled by district in "Confederate Nationalism: Politics and Government in the Confederate South,

1861–1865" by John B. Robbins. An additional source was used to verify, illustrate, and analyze the 1860 election, the county vote map in *The Atlas of Historical Geography of the United States* by C. O. Paullin and John K. Wright.[40]

An overwhelming sixty-four of the 106 districts (60.4 percent) supported the Southern Democrat. Again, Breckinridge support was dominant in the Deep South but lessens in the upper South. Thirty-eight of the districts (35.9 percent) showed strong support for the Unionists.[41] These districts are concentrated in the border states of Kentucky and Missouri, and the upper South states of Virginia, Tennessee and North Carolina.

Missouri. The border state of Missouri was the most politically complex of all the states both North and South. Its geographic location between North and South was further complicated by a mix of physiographic, agricultural, economic, and demographic characteristics. Republican Lincoln received 10.3 percent of the statewide Missouri vote, much of it from Saint Louis, winning the majority in this one county district. Stephen Douglas had strong support in three districts, two in the northern Central Lowland and one along the Mississippi River which bordered his native Illinois. Unionists did well in the other three districts, although Southern Democrat support was strong in many southern Missouri counties.

Kentucky. The Constitutional Unionists gained 45.2 percent of the Kentucky vote and regular Northern Democrat Douglas 17.5 percent. Their support dominated in eight of the twelve districts. Historically the Whig party was partially founded in Kentucky and had dominated presidential and congressional elections in the 1830s, 1840s and early 1850s. This was especially so in the Interior Low Plateau portion of the state. The stance of Unionist Bell was a perfect compromise between northern and southern Democratic candidates. Over 80 percent of the population was free, most nonslaveholding farmers, and the state had strong economic ties with the North. Although much less northern in character than Missouri, the majority of the Kentuckians opposed or were neutral toward secession.

Virginia. The third future Confederate state to border the North also ranked third in the Unionist Index. Unionist Bell won a narrow plurality electoral college victory with 44.6 percent of the vote, with Douglas receiving nearly 10 percent and Lincoln a scattering. This narrow splitting of the vote is reflected in the district count with half dominated by Southern Democrats and the other half with Unionist tendencies. Unionist votes came from all regions of this large and complex state. However, the state had a long history of division between the western Appalachian Plateau counties and the Tidewater east.[42] Although Southern Democrat Breckinridge received support from northwest Virginia, economic ties with the North and pro-Union sentiment were strong, especially in the counties bordering the Ohio River and Pennsylvania. The premier example of this was the northern panhandle of Virginia, which was essentially northern in character with the smallest number of slaves of anywhere in the South.

Tennessee. Tennessee's Whig party heritage was very similar to Kentucky's, and in the last antebellum U.S. congressional election opposition candidates beat Democrats in the majority of the districts. Tennessee's percentage vote was extremely similar to Virginia's and Unionist Bell, a former senator from Tennessee, won the state with 47.7 percent, northerner Douglas taking 7.7 percent. This nearly even split is again reflected in the districts, five voting for the Unionists, four with a slight plurality for the Unionists, and two for Southern Democrats. Again, the Unionist vote came from all regions of the state. However, again, Tennessee was split into two, perhaps three, distinct areas: Appalachia, Middle Tennessee, and the cotton-growing west. As in Virginia the Appalachian portion of Tennessee had a large free white population who did not extensively participate in the cotton slave economy. Antisecessionist sentiment in eastern Tennessee was probably dominant.[43]

Louisiana. Although a Deep South state, Louisiana is complex in its history, religious, ethnic, and racial makeup. Cosmopolitan New Orleans was the most diverse and most commercial of all southern cities, and the Whigs had been strong in the delta parishes. In the parishes on the lower Mississippi River surrounding New Orleans the Unionists ran very strong, and even northerner Douglas received 15.1 percent of the vote statewide, most of it coming from the southeast portion of the state. In fact, this strong Douglas showing pushed the state in the Southern Democrat electoral column with a 44.9 percent plurality.

Georgia. Regular Northern Democrat Douglas also gained a large vote in Georgia with nearly 11 percent. Southern Democrat Breckinridge carried the state with 48.9 percent. Three districts in Georgia registered Unionist tendencies. These regions had voted Whig in previous presidential and congressional elections.

North Carolina. Southern Democrat Breckinridge won a clear majority, 50.5 percent, in North Carolina. The geography of the vote was somewhat consistent, the Coastal Plain districts voting for Breckinridge and the western districts voting for Bell. However, the majority of the counties in the northeastern First District were Unionist, and almost all the counties in the Eighth District were Southern Democrat. Again, the farther west toward Appalachia the more antisecessionist the general sentiment.

Arkansas. The frontier state of Arkansas recorded the second smallest turnout and a 53.1 percent Southern Democrat majority. The Southern Democrats carried almost every county, except a band of wealthier cotton counties along the Mississippi River Valley.

Alabama. Alabama voted Democratic in every presidential election in the Whig-Democrat era. In 1860 Breckinridge won the state with 54 percent. It was one of only three voting states to have every district go Southern Democrat. However, northerner Douglas won 15.1 percent of the vote and actually carried several northern Alabama counties.

Mississippi. The largest cotton-producing state gave Breckinridge a substantial 59 percent majority. Unionist Bell received 30.9 percent, much of this coming from a band of wealthy counties along the Mississippi River Valley making up the Fourth District. These counties gave strong Whig support in previous elections.

Florida. Florida was the least populated of the southern states in 1860. The total voter turnout in the presidential election was 13,301. Nearly two-thirds voted Southern Democrat.

Texas. Frontier Texas gave a enormous three-fourths of the vote to the Southern Democrats. Only three counties did not have a Breckinridge majority.

Conclusion

Map 12 clearly shows an upper South versus lower South division in the 1860 U.S. presidential election. The 1860 election took place in November, and the Confederate districts portrayed on the map were not created until 1861.[44] Notwithstanding, the 1860 vote is projected onto these districts to provide some indication of their political heritage and background and to better understand political events in the Confederacy.[45]

The 1860 vote was not a direct referendum on slavery or secession sentiment in the South, but can be used to give some indication of these feelings, at least at the time of the election. However, once

a northern Republican won the election and South Carolina began secession proceedings, sentiment in the South shifted. Another series of political data directly concerning secession in 1861 has been assembled and mapped in a number of publications.[46] These data include secession referendum votes within the states, elections to secession conventions, and votes by county delegations in the secession conventions. Prosecession and antisecession counties can be discerned by these indicators.[47] This data confirms continuance of some antisecessionist areas, such as northwestern Virginia, eastern Tennessee, and the Mississippi delta of Louisiana and shows different areas of antisecessionist feeling in places like northern Alabama and some counties in Texas. In addition, some previous Constitutional Unionist areas, such as in North Carolina, seem to be more secessionist.

After Fort Sumter, sentiment changed again in many areas of the South, especially in the upper South. Most areas then supported secession. Some areas, like Missouri, Kentucky, and northwestern Virginia, remained unionist and were also lost militarily very quickly. In other areas farther South, like the southern Appalachians, Union sentiment was also strong throughout the war. The southern Appalachians evolved to become so different that they even became Republican after the war in an area of the Deep South in which after the war and Reconstruction the Democrats would again control for the next century.

Federal Occupation and Status of Confederate Congressional Districts

Maps 13 through 24 illustrate the territory of the Confederacy under Federal occupation and the status of Confederate congressional districts on the last day of the six sessions of the First and Second Congresses. The specific criteria used to produce these maps are enumerated and explained in detail in Appendix II. The territory of the South occupied by the North is an important variable in understanding Confederate congressional elections and roll-call voting in the House and Senate. This section analyzes and discusses both the occupied area and congressional district status map for each session and reviews the significant events during the period which affect the changes illustrated.

First Confederate Congress, 1862–1864

First Session

    Intersession: None
    Session: February 18, 1862–April 21, 1862
    Total Period: February 18, 1862–April 21, 1862 [63 days]

Map 13 illustrates in blue the area of Union control in the states represented in the Confederate Congress at the end of the First Ses-

sion of the First Congress, April 21, 1862. At the end of the Fifth Session of the Provisional Congress, February 17, 1862, most of the states of Missouri, Kentucky, and the northwestern portion of Virginia were already substantially controlled by the Union (see Map 5 and discussion in Chapter 2). During the First Session of the First Congress the remainder of southern Missouri and Kentucky were occupied, consolidated, and used as staging areas for advances farther south. Union forces moved into northwestern Arkansas from southern Missouri, fought the Battle of Elkhorn Tavern (March 6), and moved on across the northern portion of the state. Federal forces also moved south down the Mississippi River, capturing Columbus, Kentucky (March 3), New Madrid, Missouri (March 14), and Island Number 10–Tiptonville, Tennessee (April 7). At the same time Gen. Ulysses Grant began to move south from Kentucky along the Tennessee River into Middle Tennessee as part of the Shiloh campaign. The Tennessee capital, Nashville, fell on February 25. The actual Shiloh battle (April 6) took place in southernmost Tennessee near the junction of the Alabama and Mississippi boundaries.[48] After Shiloh, Union forces moved into all the major towns in the Tennessee Valley of northwest Alabama by mid April. Several additional inroads were also made along the Atlantic Coast during this short two-month period: Fernandia and St. Augustine, Florida (March 4 and March 11); New Berne, North Carolina (March 14); and Fort Pulaski, Georgia (April 11).

Map 14 illustrates the status of Confederate congressional districts at the end of the First Session. This map, and all the district status maps in this chapter, are, of course, based upon their counterpart map of Union military control and influence of that Congress and Session. In Map 14 all the districts in Missouri and Kentucky are colored light blue to identify them as Union-occupied. Three districts in northwestern Virginia were also occupied by northern military units. Two districts in Tennessee are also colored blue because of the large Union force moving down the Tennessee River (the Eighth District) and the capture of Nashville (the Fifth District) and the subsequent permanent occupation of these areas. Four other Tennessee districts and the First District of Alabama are colored light blue for disrupted because of the Shiloh campaign. In addition, the Ninth District of Virginia across from Washington, D.C., and the northwest Arkansas district are designated disrupted. Of the 106 districts, twenty-four (22.6 percent) were occupied, six disrupted (5.7 percent), and seventy-six remained Confederate-controlled (71.7 percent).

Second Session

    Intersession: April 22, 1862–August 17, 1862
    Session: August 18, 1862–October 13, 1862
    Total Period: April 22, 1862–October 13, 1862 [175 days]

Map 15 illustrates Union military occupation and territorial gain transpiring during the six months from the end of the First Session to the end of the Second Session of the First Congress. Union forces continued to move south along the Mississippi River capturing Memphis (June 6) and Helena, Arkansas (July 12). After establishing a main garrison at Memphis Federal forces were better able to continue operations in northern Mississippi and northern Alabama. More inroads were made along the Atlantic Coast: Fort Macon–Beaufort (April 26), Hatteras Inlet (August 29), and Norfolk (May 10). The most significant geographic breakthrough during this period was the capture of New Orleans (April 29). This not only gave the Union control over the mouth of the strategic Mississippi River, but also established a large Union-occupied area far distant from the North.[49] General Lee's invasion of Maryland in September 1862 was stopped at Antietam (September 17) and only temporarily slowed Union control of parts of northern Virginia. During this same period Gen. Kirby Smith's invasion of central Kentucky was stopped at Perryville, and this area remained under Federal control.

Map 16, the district status map for the Second Session, reflects the Union movements along the Mississippi River. Along the northern portion of the river six more districts in western Tennessee, northern Mississippi, and northeast Arkansas were removed from Confederate control. Along the southern part of the river the First and Second Districts of Louisiana were occupied and the Third District disrupted. In northern Virginia the Tenth District joined the Ninth as disrupted since both geographically strategic districts bordered the North and had Federal troop movements. At the end of this session twenty-eight districts were occupied (26.4 percent), eleven disrupted (10.4 percent), and sixty-seven remained Confederate-controlled (63.2 percent).

Third Session

  Intersession: October 14, 1862–January 11, 1863

  Session: January 12, 1863–May 1, 1863

  Total Period: October 14, 1862–May 1, 1863   [200 days]

Map 17 shows very little change in Union occupation area in the over six months from the end of the previous session, although major battles were fought at Fredericksburg (December 13) and Chancellorsville (April 26). The most significant movement came with Federal troops attempting to implement the western portion of the Anaconda Plan to divide the Confederacy by controlling the entire Mississippi River. Along the southern portion of the river Baton Rouge was occupied on December 17. In the north Fort Hindeman, on the Arkansas River, was captured on January 11, 1863. These and other actions and river movements laid the groundwork for the siege at Vicksburg, which began in mid May 1863 after the end of the Third Session.

Map 18 also reflects very little change in the status of Confederate congressional districts for the First Congress, Third Session.

The First and Second Districts in Virginia, both along the coastline, were now sufficiently disrupted because of Union consolidation of positions along the coast. Two northern Virginia districts changed designation from disrupted to occupied, as did the Third District in Louisiana (Baton Rouge).

Fourth Session

  Intersession: May 2, 1863–December 6, 1863

  Session: December 7, 1863–February 17, 1864

  Total Period: May 2, 1863–February 17, 1864   [292 days]

Over nine months elapsed between the end of the Third Session and the end of the Fourth Session, the longest period portrayed on the maps. The main geographic change reflected in Map 19 is the Federal control of the Mississippi River highlighted by the surrender of Vicksburg (July 4) followed by the capture of Fort Hudson, Louisiana (July 8). The capture of Vicksburg and the subsequent control of the river allowed Union forays into central Mississippi and the consolidation of Arkansas by the capture of two strategic points, Fort Smith and Little Rock (September 1 and 10). The other significant territorial gain during this period came with the Union movement into eastern Tennessee featuring the capture of Knoxville (September 2) and the final battle for Chattanooga (November 23). Reflecting the above changes, Map 20 illustrates that five districts in the Mississippi River valley and four in eastern Tennessee and northeast Alabama were lost to Confederate control during this period.

The defeat of the southern armies at Gettysburg (July 4) stopped the only significant Confederate invasion north of the Mason-Dixon Line. For the remainder of the war fighting was in the South with a resultant continuous slow disruption and loss of territory. At the end of the First Confederate Congress in early 1864 only a little over one-half (52.8 percent) of the districts were still fully controlled by the Confederacy, while forty-one districts were occupied (38.7 percent) and nine disrupted (8.5 percent).

Second Confederate Congress, 1864–1865

First Session

  Intersession: February 18, 1864–May 1, 1864

  Session: May 2, 1864–June 14, 1864

  Total Period: February 18, 1864–June 14, 1864 [118 days]

Map 21 shows very little additional area occupied by the Union during the short four-month period between February and June 1864. However, two very significant movements began late in this period. Gen. William Sherman began his Atlanta campaign (May 1), and a part of northwestern Georgia (District 10) was abandoned by

the South (Map 22). In Virginia both sides sustained large losses at Cold Harbor (May 12), and the assault and siege of Petersburg (June 15) was about to begin. These and other actions demonstrate that northern forces were able to operate in large parts of northern Virginia (districts One, Two, and Eight) and that the South had further withdrawn to defensive positions. While the South lost control of just three districts in this short period, the North was poised to take over significant additional territory and end the war.

Second Session

  Intersession: June 15, 1864–November 6, 1864

  Session: November 7, 1864–March 18, 1865

  Total Period: June 15, 1864–March 18, 1865   [277 days]

The last session of the Confederate Congress witnessed the military collapse of the Confederacy. Map 23 illustrates the territorial effect of General Sherman's Atlanta campaign (June–August), his March to the Sea (November–December), and Carolinas campaign (January–March). The ten districts in Georgia, South Carolina, and North Carolina affected by these movements are all designated disrupted (see Map 24 and explanation in Appendix II). Activity along the Atlantic coast supported the Carolinas campaign with the capture of Fort Fisher, North Carolina (January 15) and Charleston, South Carolina (February 18).

The other territorial advances by the Union were gained by its relentless pressure in Virginia. In Ridge and Valley Virginia (districts Eleven, Twelve, and Thirteen) cities fell in late 1864 and early 1865 as southern forces were weakened and withdrew to Richmond. A final Union campaign around Richmond and a siege of the city began in the late fall of 1864, and the last session of the Confederate Congress was literally spent within sight and sound of the front lines.

By the end of the Civil War forty-eight congressional districts were occupied (45.3 percent), twenty-two disrupted (20.8 percent), and only thirty-six nominally under Confederate control (33.9 percent). These last unoccupied areas were in three pockets: the Appalachian Piedmont region (fifteen districts); most of Florida and Alabama and the central part of the lower South (thirteen districts), and the Trans-Mississippi West (eight districts).[50]

Conclusion

At the beginning of the Permanent Confederate Congresses Federal forces had already disrupted or occupied a great number of congressional districts. Table 3-7 shows that over a quarter (28.3 percent) of the districts were already lost by the end of the First Session. Although the admission of Missouri and Kentucky account for most of this number, nineteen out of thirty, large areas of Virginia and Tennessee were already captured. In each session of the Permanent

TABLE 3-7

Union-Occupied and Disrupted Confederate Congressional Districts

Congress-Session	Number Occupied	Percentage Occupied	Number Disrupted	Percent Disrupted	Total Number	Total Percentage
1-1	24	22.6	6	5.7	30	28.3
1-2	29	27.4	10	9.4	39	36.8
1-3	32	30.2	9	8.5	41	38.7
1-4	41	38.7	9	8.5	50	47.2
2-1	43	40.6	10	9.4	53	50
2-2	48	45.3	21	19.8	69	65.1

TABLE 3-8

Union-Occupied and Disrupted Confederate Congressional Districts, by State

Districts Occupied/Disrupted/Total Percent

Congress-Session

State (districts)	1-1			1-2			1-3			1-4			2-1			2-2		
	O	D	%	O	D	%	O	D	%	O	D	%	O	D	%	O	D	%
Missouri (7)[1]	7	0	100															
Kentucky (12)[1]	12	0	100															
Tennessee (11)	2	3	46	5	2	64	5	2	64	10	0	91	10	0	91	11	0	100
Virginia (16)	3	1	25	3	2	31	5	2	44	5	2	44	7	1	50	11	1	75
Arkansas (4)	0	1	25	0	2	50	0	2	50	3	0	75	3	0	75	3	0	75
Alabama (9)	0	1	11	0	1	11	0	1	11	0	2	22	0	2	22	0	2	22
Louisiana (6)				2	1	50	3	0	50	3	1	67	3	2	83	3	2	83
Mississippi (7)				0	2	29	0	2	29	1	4	71	1	4	71	1	4	71
Georgia (10)										0	1	10	0	5	50			
South Carolina (6)													0	4	66			
North Carolina (10)													0	3	30			
Florida (2)[2]																		
Texas (6)[2]																		

[1] Most of territory occupied during entire Civil War.

[2] Most of territory unoccupied during entire Civil War.

Congresses the number of occupied and disrupted districts increased, even though some sessions were quite short.

Table 3-8 points out that different states were affected at different periods. Again, Kentucky and Missouri were immediately affected, while Texas and large areas of Florida were basically unoccupied. Tennessee was the only true southern state to be totally occupied during the Civil War, although some rural mountainous areas were untouched. Virginia lost its northwestern districts immediately, and most of the war was fought in its eastern districts. The Mississippi River valley states of Louisiana, Mississippi, and Arkansas were all affected by the Second Session of the First Congress and eventually lost a great amount of territory to Union control because of the Federal operations to control this vital waterway. Georgia (1864) North and South Carolina (1865) were significantly affected only late in the war.

[1] The word *slave* was not used in the U.S. Constitution to describe slaves, but it was specifically used in the Confederate Constitution.

[2] Tables of the apportionment population for the slave-holding states from 1790 through 1860 are found in Laurence F. Schmeckebier, *Congressional Apportionment* (Washington, D.C.: Brookings Institution, 1941), pp. 227–229.

[3] The original Confederate Constitution set the ratio not to exceed one member for every fifty thousand, and the final ratio used to calculate original state delegation size in the Constitution was based upon one member for every ninety thousand. The latter ratio was explicit in all the subsequent Provisional Congress laws (see footnotes in Table 3-2) admitting the remaining states. For a discussion on the background of the apportionment ratio in U.S. history see: Kenneth C. Martis and Gregory Elmes, *The Historical Atlas of State Power in Congress* (Washington, D.C.: Congressional Quarterly Press, 1993), pp. 16–22.

[4] The 1850s apportionment allotted seven U.S. House seats to Missouri. This number and the previous U.S. congressional district boundaries were carried on by the Confederate Missouri government in spite of the thirteen seats allocated. See also the section on the Missouri election to the First House.

[5] For a history of the establishment of the single member congressional district as the method of election in the United States see: Kenneth C. Martis, *The Historical Atlas of United States Congressional Districts 1789–1983* (New York: Free Press, 1983), pp. 2–6.

[6] Note the procedure of the pro-South state legislature of Missouri in the previous paragraph.

[7] The only exception is the mentioning of independent cities within counties in the Virginia statute.

[8] Record Group 69, Documents of the Congressional Vote Analysis Unit, Historical Records Survey, Works Projects Administration, National Archives and Records Service, Washington, D.C. William Thorndale and William Dollarhide, *Map Guide to the U.S. Federal Censuses, 1790–1920* (Baltimore: Genealogical Publishing, 1987). Thomas D. Rabenhorst, ed., *Historical U.S. County Outline Map Collection 1840–1980* (Baltimore: Department of Geography, University of Maryland Baltimore County, 1984).

[9] John B. Robbins, "Confederate Nationalism: Politics and Government in the Confederate South, 1861–1865" (Ph.D. diss., Rice University, 1964), pp. 246–272. Smaller versions of these maps were published later in Thomas B. Alexander and Richard E. Beringer, *The Anatomy of the Confederate Congresses* (Nashville: Vanderbilt University Press, 1972), p. 12 and Ezra J. Warner and W. Buck Yearns, *Biographical Register of the Confederate Congress* (Baton Rouge: Louisiana State University Press, 1975), pp. 303–305.

[10] The matching of members with congressional districts was also compared to a partial list in Alexander and Beringer, *Anatomy*. pp. 354–388 and a full listing in Robbins, "Confederate Nationalism," pp. 238–241.

[11] In the first election the Missouri and Kentucky delegations are matched with their proper districts by newspaper reports, hometown and/or county of the representative, and secondary sources.

[12] For a discussion and list of potential variables see: Martis, *Congressional Districts*, pp. 18–29.

[13] E. C. Pirkle and W. H. Yoho, *Natural Landscapes of the United States* (Dubuque, Iowa: Kendall/Hunt, 1985), pp. 111, 123, and 175. W. D. Thornbury, *Regional Geomorphology of the United States* (New York: Wiley, 1965).

[14] For example, the western portions of the Texas districts extended into the Great Plains region and the separated extreme western portion of Texas District One was in the Basin and Range area of the southern Rocky Mountains region. Pirkle and Yoho, *Natural Landscapes*, pp. 225 and 235.

[15] Sam Bowers Hilliard, *Atlas of Antebellum Southern Agriculture* (Baton Rouge: Louisiana State University Press, 1984), p. 67.

[16] C. O. Paullin and John K. Wright, *Atlas of the Historical Geography of the United States* (New York: Carnegie Institution and American Geographical Society, 1932), p. 136, Plates 142 b–c and 143 e–f. Hilliard, *Antebellum Atlas*, pp. 57–58, 67–71.

[17] For example, in the 1860 census of manufacturing, cotton goods is the first category listed and is given the most extensive discussion. *U.S. Census of Manufacturing, 1860*, pp. ix–xxi.

[18] Intensive cultivation is defined as the production of forty thousand bales (of four hundred pounds each) or more within a congressional district. Calculations were made based upon the production map of 1860 in Hilliard, *Antebellum Atlas*, p. 71, and the state production figures in the 1860 Census (see Table 3-3).

[19] The year of the agricultural census was usually the year before the population census, hence, the 1860 census agricultural statistics were actually taken in 1859. The year of the census publication and general reference identification, here 1860, is used to avoid confusion.

[20] Thornbury, *Regional Geomorphology*, pp. 54–55. Gerald R. Webster and Scott A. Samson, "On Defining the Alabama Black Belt: Historical Changes and Variations," *Southeastern Geographer*, XXXII (November 1992): 163–172.

[21] For a discussion on the geographical spread of tobacco and the social impress of its cultivation see: Frederick F. Siegal, *The Roots of the Southern Distinctiveness: Tobacco and Society in Danville, Virginia, 1780–1865* (Chapel Hill: University of North Carolina Press, 1987).

[22] A heavy-tobacco producing district is defined as one with one county or more producing one million pounds or more. The data and map are based on the tobacco production map in Hilliard, *Antebellum Atlas*, p. 76, and tobacco production statistics in the 1860 census.

[23] Again, the agriculture figures are for 1859, the year previous to the population census. The year of the general census publication and reference are used in this atlas. See footnote 19 above. *U.S. Census*, 1860: Agriculture, pp. 200–201.

[24] For a detailed population geography map see Hilliard, *Antebellum Atlas*, p. 26.

[25] There were a small number of free blacks in the South. See Table 3-1.

[26] Robbins, "Confederate Nationalism," pp. 246–272. Hilliard, *Antebellum Atlas*, p. 34.

[27] In the slave states there were 383,637 slaveholders and of this number only 2,292 held one hundred or more slaves. Richard B. Morris, ed., *Encyclopedia of American History* (New York, Harper & Row, 1976), p. 756.

[28] Stephen S. Birdsall and John W. Florin, *Regional Landscapes of the United States and Canada* (New York: Wiley, 1992), Figure 10-2, p. 235.

[29] Richard F. Bensel, *Yankee Leviathan: The Origins of Central State Authority in America, 1859–1877* (Cambridge: Cambridge University Press, 1990), pp. 42–43, 68–78, 195.

[30] Thomas J. Pressly and William H. Scofield, *Farm Real Estate Values in the United States by Counties, 1850–1959* (Seattle: University of Washington Press, 1965).

[31] Alexander and Beringer, *Anatomy*, pp. 354–389. The map of land values on p. 131 in *Anatomy* is different than the numerical values for four districts, Arkansas First, South Carolina Fourth, Alabama Fourth and Seventh. The numerical values are used in this atlas, and therefore the map in this atlas is different than the *Anatomy* map in these four districts. Two districts appear to be geographic anomalies, Virginia Second and South Carolina Second, but the data in Pressly and Scofield, *Farm Values*, list Virginia Second with a 7.5 median and South Carolina Second, even though composed of Charleston county, has a value of 7. Pressly and Scofield, *Farm Values*, pp. 43–46. Additional information for Map 11 was obtained from Hilliard, *Antebellum Atlas*, map 53, p. 43, "Average Value of Farms."

[32] Hilliard, *Antebellum Atlas*, p. 77.

[33] *Ibid.*, pp. 62, 72–76.

[34] The Seventh District of Tennessee was a cotton growing district in the Tennessee River valley.

[35] Pirkle and Yoho, *Natural Landscapes*, pp. 115, 203–204.

[36] For example, see the party elections to the United States Congress in the late 1840s and early 1850s in Martis, *Political Party Atlas*, pp. 99–107.

[37] *Ibid.*, pp. 109–113.

[38] *Congressional Quarterly's Guide to U.S. Elections* (Washington, D.C.: Congressional Quarterly, 1985), p. 334.

[39] Although in the slave state of Delaware Lincoln received 3,822 votes, 23.7 percent of the total.

[40] Robbins, "Confederate Nationalism," pp. 246–272. Paullin and Wright, *Historical Atlas*, Map C, Plate 105.

[41] Robbins, "Confederate Nationalism," lists seven of these districts as splitting support between the Southern Democrats and Unionists: Tennessee Fourth, Sixth, Eighth and Tenth; and Virginia Ninth, Twelfth, and Fourteenth. According to Paullin and Wright the Unionists won a majority of the counties in these districts, and, therefore, they are designated Unionist.

[42] Robert P. Sutton, *Revolution to Secession: Constitution Making in the Old Dominion* (Charlottesville: University Press of Virginia, 1989).

[43] Tennessee seceded in June 1861 and held its "regular" congressional elections on August 1, 1861. "Loyalists" won in the four most eastern districts and three were actually seated in the 37th U.S. Congress. Martis, *Atlas of Political Parties*, pp. 37 and 115.

[44] See section above, "Vote by Congressional District," for an explanation of data collection.

[45] Daniel W. Crofts, *Reluctant Confederates: Upper South Unionists in the Secession Crisis* (Chapel Hill: University of North Carolina Press, 1989).

[46] Clifford L. Lord and Elizabeth H. Lord, *Historical Atlas of the United States* (New York: Henry Holt, 1953), p. 93. This map is repeated in numerous publications, including *Encyclopedia Britannica*, Vol. 29, p. 229.

[47] This data was not projected on the congressional district map since it comes from three different types of activities occurring at somewhat different times. The presidential vote occurred on one specific date and was uniform throughout the South, except in South Carolina.

[48] The dates given for battles are the first day of the engagement.

[49] The Mississippi River campaign is a good example of the application of the rules designating Union-occupied areas. Although Adm. David Farragut sailed up the Mississippi River and briefly captured Natchez, Mississippi (May 13), and besieged Vicksburg (June), these areas are not indicated on the map since the Union forces withdrew and did not permanently capture these areas until later.

[50] Of course, numerous Union military movements and some engagements occurred in these areas. For example, the Union held three coastal forts in Florida throughout the war and subsequently occupied several others. From these positions they occasionally moved inland, where engagements took place. See map "The Civil War in Florida" and discussion in Edward A. Fernald, ed., *Atlas of Florida* (Tallahassee: Florida State University, 1992).

MAPS FOR CHAPTER 3

Members of the First Confederate Congress[1]

February 18, 1862, to February 17, 1864

First Session: February 18, 1862, to April 21, 1862 / Second Session: August 18, 1862, to October 13, 1862 / Third Session: January 12, 1863, to May 1, 1863 / Fourth Session: December 7, 1863, to February 17, 1864

HOUSE

Alabama
1. Thomas Jefferson Foster
2. William Russell Smith
3. John Perkins Ralls
4. Jabez Lamar Monroe Curry
5. Francis Strother Lyon
6. William Parish Chilton
7. David Clopton
8. James Lawrence Pugh
9. Edmund Strother Dargan

Arkansas
1. Felix Ives Batson
2. Grandison Delaney Royston
3. Augustus Hill Garland[2]
4. Thomas Burton Hanly

Florida
1. James Baird Dawkins[3]
   John Marshall Martin[4]
2. Robert Benjamin Hilton

Georgia
1. Julian Hartridge
2. Charles James Munnerlyn
3. Hines Holt[5]
   Porter Ingram[6]
4. Augustus Holmes Kenan
5. David William Lewis
6. William White Clark
7. Robert Pleasant Trippe
8. Lucius Jeremiah Gartrell
9. Hardy Strickland
10. Augustus Romaldus Wright

Kentucky
1. Willis Benson Machen
2. John Wesley Crockett
3. Henry English Read
4. George Washington Ewing
5. James Stone Chrisman
6. Theodore Legrand Burnett
7. Horatio Washington Bruce
8. George Baird Hodge
9. Eli Metcalfe Bruce
10. James William Moore
11. Robert Jefferson Breckinridge, Jr.
12. John Milton Elliot

Louisiana
1. Charles Jacques Villere
2. Charles Magill Conrad
3. Duncan Farrar Kenner
4. Lucius Jacques Dupre
5. Henry Marshall
6. John Perkins, Jr.

Mississippi
1. Jeremiah Watkins Clapp
2. Reuben Davis[7]
   William Dunbar Holder[8]
3. Israel Victor Welch
4. Henry Cousins Chambers
5. Otho Robards Singleton
6. Ethelbert Barksdale
7. John Jones McRae

Missouri
1. William Mordecai Cooke[9]
2. Thomas Alexander Harris
3. Casper Wistar Bell
4. Aaron H. Conrow
5. George Graham Vest
6. Thomas W. Freeman
7. John Hyer[10]

North Carolina
1. William Nathan Smith
2. Robert Rufus Bridgers
3. Owen Rand Kenan
4. Thomas David Smith McDowell
5. Archibald Hunter Arrington
6. James Robert McLean
7. Thomas Samuel Ashe
8. William Lander
9. Burgess Sidney Gaither
10. Allen Turner Davidson

South Carolina
1. John McQueen
2. William Porcher Miles
3. Lewis Malone Ayer
4. Milledge Luke Bonham[11]
   William Dunlap Simpsom[12]
5. James Farrow
6. William Waters Boyce

Tennessee
1. Joseph Brown Heiskell[13]
2. William Graham Swan
3. William Henry Tibbs
4. Erasmus Lee Gardenhire
5. Henry Stuart Foote
6. Meredith Poindexter Gentry
7. George Washington Jones
8. Thomas Menees
9. John DeWitt Clinton Atkins
10. John Vines Wright
11. David Maney Currin

Texas
1. John Alexander Wilcox
2. Caleb Claiborne Herbert
3. Peter W. Gray
4. Franklin Barlow Sexton
5. Malcolm Duncan Graham
6. William Bacon Wright

Virginia
1. Muscoe Russell Hunter Garnett
2. John Randolph Chambliss
3. John Tyler[14]
   James Lyons[15]
4. Roger Atkinson Pryor[16]
   Charles Fenton Collier[17]
5. Thomas Stanley Bocock
6. John Goode, Jr.
7. James Philemon Holcombe
8. Daniel Coleman De Jarnette
9. William Smith[18]
   David Funsten[19]
10. Alexander Boteler
11. John Brown Baldwin
12. Waller Redd Staples
13. Walter Preston
14. Albert Gallatin Jenkins[20]
    Samuel A. Miller[21]
15. Robert Johnston
16. Charles Wells Russell

SENATE

Alabama
Clement Claiborne Clay
William Lowndes Yancey[22]
Robert Jemison, Jr.[23]

Arkansas
Robert Ward Johnson
Charles Burton Mitchel

Florida
James McNair Baker
Augustus Emmett Maxwell

Georgia
Benjamin Harvey Hill
John W. Lewis[24]
Herschel Johnson[25]

Kentucky
Henry Cornelius Burnett
William Elliott Simms

Louisiana
Thomas Jenkins Semmes
Edward Sparrow

Mississippi
Albert Gallatin Brown
James Phelan

Missouri
John Bullock Clark
Robert Ludwell Yates Peyton[26]
Waldo Porter Johnson[27]

North Carolina
George Davis[28]
Edwin Godwin Reade[29]
William Theophilus Dortch

South Carolina
Robert Woodward Barnwell
James Lawrence Orr

Tennessee
Landon Carter Haynes
Gustavus Adolphus Henry

Texas
Williamson Simpson Oldham
Louis Trezevant Wigfall

Virginia
Robert Mercer Taliaferro Hunter
William Ballard Preston[30]
Allen Taylor Caperton[31]

---

[1] Membership and seating dates from the *Journal of the Confederate States of America* (Washington, D.C.: Government Printing Office, 1904). Confirmed by Ezra J. Warner and W. Buck Yearns, *Biographical Register of the Confederate Congress* (Baton Rouge: Louisiana State University Press, 1975), pp. 293–297. Nonvoting delegates listed in both sources.

[2] Election unsuccessfully contested by Jilson P. Johnson.

[3] Resigned December 8, 1862, and announced in *Confederate Journal*, January 17, 1863.

[4] Elected to fill vacancy caused by resignation of James Baird Dawkins, and took his seat on March 25, 1863.

[5] Resigned his seat after third session. See also *Columbus Weekly Enquirer*, November 10, 1863.

[6] Elected to fill vacancy caused by resignation of Hines Holt, and took his seat on January 12, 1864.

[7] Resigned after third session.

[8] Elected to fill vacancy caused by resignation of Reuben Davis and took his seat on January 21, 1864.

[9] Died April 14, 1863, and his seat remained vacant. Arthur R. Kirkpatrick, "Missouri's Delegation in the Confederate Congress," *Civil War History* 5 (1959): 188–198.

[10] Although appointed, John Hyer never took his seat and the Seventh District was vacant throughout the First Congress.

[11] Resigned after Second Session to become governor of South Carolina January 17, 1863.

[12] Elected to fill vacancy created by resignation of Milledge Luke Bonham and took his seat on February 5, 1863.

[13] Resigned February 6, 1864.

[14] Died January 8, 1862, before taking his seat.

[15] Elected to fill the seat of John Tyler.

[16] Resigned April 5, 1862.

[17] Elected to seat vacated by Roger Atkinson Pryor and took his seat on August 18, 1862.

[18] Resigned April 4, 1863, and announced in *Confederate Journal*, April 6, 1863.

[19] Elected to fill vacancy caused by resignation of William Smith and took his seat on December 7, 1863.

[20] Resigned after First Session.

[21] Elected to fill vacancy caused by resignation of Albert Gallatin Jenkins and took his seat on February 24, 1863.

[22] Died July 23, 1863.

[23] Elected to fill vacancy caused by the death of William Lowndes Yancey and took his seat on December 28, 1863.

[24] Appointed, until the legislature could elect a replacement, to fill vacancy caused by the decline of Robert Toombs of his election to the Senate. Lewis took his seat on April 7, 1862.

[25] Elected to fill vacancy caused by the decline of Robert Toombs of his election to the Senate and Johnson took his seat on January 19, 1863.

[26] Died September 3, 1863.

[27] Appointed to fill vacancy caused by death of Robert Ludwell Yates Peyton and took his seat on December 24, 1863.

[28] Resigned in January of 1864 to become Confederate Attorney General.

[29] Appointed to fill vacancy caused by the resignation of George Davis and took his seat on January 22, 1864.

[30] Died November 16, 1862.

[31] Elected to fill vacancy caused by the death of William Ballard Preston and took his seat on January 26, 1863.

MAP 6

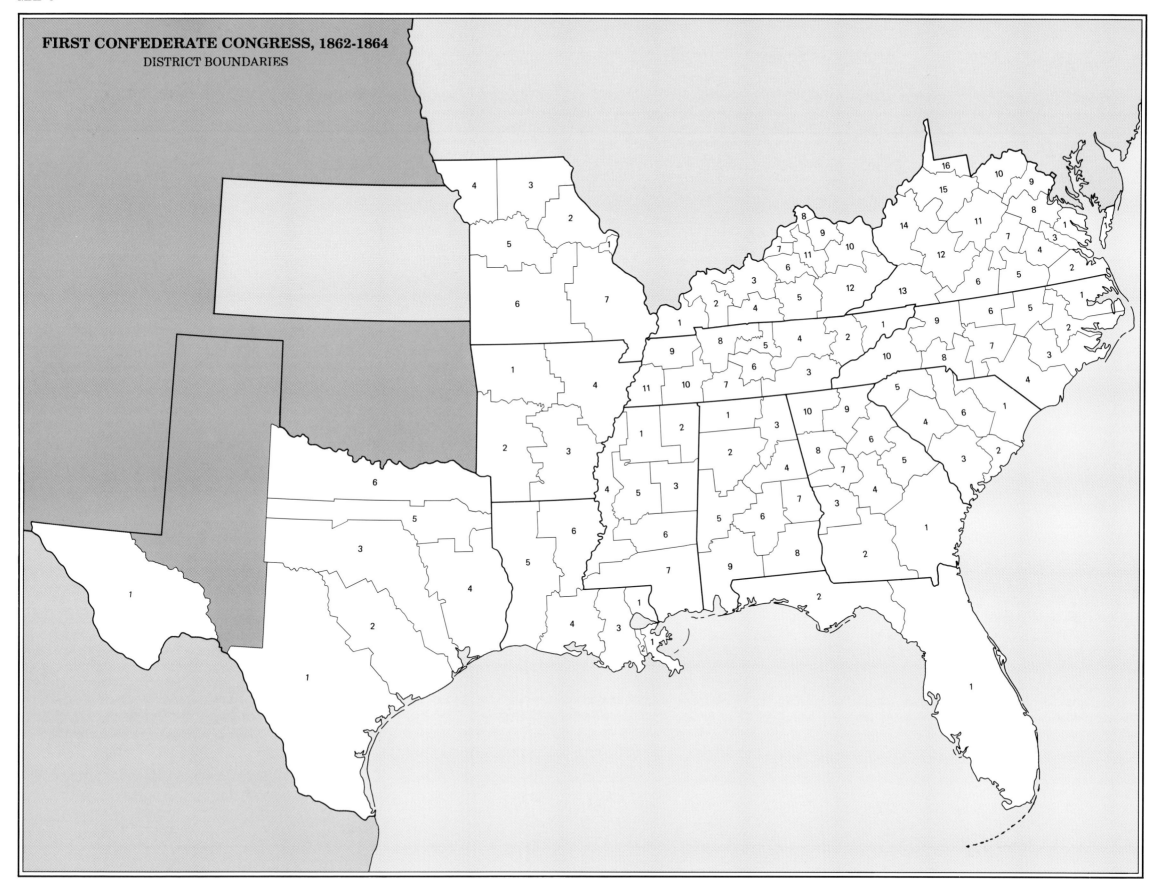

FIRST CONFEDERATE CONGRESS, 1862-1864
DISTRICT BOUNDARIES

Members of the Second Confederate Congress[1]

May 2, 1864, to March 18, 1865

First Session: May 2, 1864, to June 14, 1864 / Second Session: November 7, 1864, to March 18, 1865

HOUSE

Alabama
1 Thomas Jefferson Foster
2 William Russell Smith
3 Williamson Robert Winfield Cobb[2]
4 Marcus Henderson Cruikshank
5 Francis Strother Lyon
6 William Parish Chilton
7 David Clopton
8 James Lawrence Pugh
9 James Shelton Dickinson

Arkansas
1 Felix Ives Batson
2 Rufus King Garland
3 Augustus Hill Garland[3]
  David Williamson Carroll[4]
4 Thomas Burton Hanly

Florida
1 Samuel St. George Rogers
2 Robert Benjamin Hilton

Georgia
1 Julian Hartridge
2 William Ephraim Smith
3 Mark Hardin Blandford
4 Clifford Anderson
5 John Troup Shewmake
6 Joseph Hubbard Echols
7 James Milton Smith
8 George Nelson Lester
9 Hiram Parks Bell
10 Warren Akin

Kentucky
1 Willis Benson Machen
2 George Washington Triplett
3 Henry English Read
4 George Washington Ewing
5 James Stone Chrisman
6 Theodore Legrand Burnett
7 Horatio Washington Bruce
8 Humphrey Marshall
9 Eli Metcalfe Bruce
10 James William Moore
11 Benjamin Franklin Bradley
12 John Milton Elliot

Louisiana
1 Charles J. Villere
2 Charles Magill Conrad
3 Duncan Farrar Kenner
4 Lucius Jacques Dupre
5 Benjamin Louis Hodge[5]
  Henry Gray[6]
6 John Perkins, Jr.

Mississippi
1 Jehu Amaziah Orr
2 William Dunbar Holder
3 Israel Victor Welch
4 Henry Cousins Chambers
5 Otho Robards Singleton
6 Ethelbert Barksdale
7 John Tillman Lamkin

Missouri
1 Thomas Lowndes Snead
2 Nimrod Lindsay Norton
3 John Bullock Clark
4 Aaron H. Conrow
5 George Graham Vest[7]
6 Peter Singleton Wilkes
7 Robert Anthony Hatcher

North Carolina
1 William Nathan Harrell Smith
2 Robert Rufus Bridgers
3 James Thomas Leach
4 Thomas Charles Fuller
5 Josiah Turner, Jr.
6 John Adams Gilmer
7 James Madison Leach
8 James Graham Ramsay
9 Burgess Sidney Gaither
10 George Washington Logan

South Carolina
1 James Hervey Witherspoon
2 William Porcher Miles
3 Lewis Malone Ayer
4 William Dunlap Simpson
5 James Farrow
6 William Waters Boyce

Tennessee
1 Joseph Brown Heiskell
2 William Graham Swan
3 Arthur St. Clair Colyar
4 John Porry Murray
5 Henry Stuart Foote
6 Edwin Augustus Keeble
7 James McCallum
8 Thomas Menees
9 John DeWitt Clinton Atkins
10 John Vines Wright
11 David Maney Currin[8]
  Michael W. Cluskey[9]

Texas
1 Stephen Heard Darden
2 Caleb Claiborne Herbert
3 Anthony Martin Branch
4 Franklin Barlow Sexton
5 John Robert Baylor
6 Simpson Harris Morgan[10]

Virginia
1 Robert Latane Montague
2 Robert Henry Whitfield[11]
3 Williams Carter Wickham
4 Thomas Saunders Gholson
5 Thomas Stanley Bocock
6 John Goode, Jr.
7 William Cabell Rives[12]
8 Daniel Coleman De Jarnette
9 David Funsten
10 Frederick William Mackey Holliday
11 John Brown Baldwin
12 Waller Redd Staples
13 LaFayette McMullin
14 Samuel Augustine Miller
15 Robert Johnston
16 Charles Wells Russell

SENATE

Alabama
Robert Jemison, Jr.
Richard Wilde Walker

Arkansas
Robert Ward Johnson
Charles Burton Mitchel[13]
Augustus Hill Garland[14]

Florida
James McNair Baker
Augustus Emmett Maxwell

Georgia
Benjamin Harvey Hill
Herschel Vespasian Johnson

Kentucky
Henry Cornelius Burnett
William Elliott Simms

Louisiana
Thomas Jenkins Semmes
Edward Sparrow

Mississippi
Albert Gallatin Brown
John William Clark Watson

Missouri
Waldo Porter Johnson
George Graham Vest[15]

North Carolina
William Theophilus Dortch
William Alexander Graham

South Carolina
Robert Woodward Barnwell
James Lawrence Orr

Tennessee
Landon Carter Haynes
Gustavus Adolphus Henry

Texas
Williamson Simpson Oldham
Louis Trezevant Wigfall

Virginia
Robert Mercer Taliaferro Hunter
Allen Taylor Caperton

---

[1] Membership and seating dates are from the *Journal of the Confederate States of America* (Washington, D.C.: Government Printing Office, 1904). Confirmed by Ezra J. Warner and W. Buck Yearns, *Biographical Register of the Confederate Congress* (Baton Rouge: Louisiana State University Press, 1975), pp. 298–302. Nonvoting delegates listed in both sources.

[2] Expelled November 17, 1864. The Third District of Alabama was vacant throughout the Second Congress.

[3] Appointed to the Senate to fill the vacancy caused by the death of Charles Burton Mitchel and took his Senate seat on November 8, 1864.

[4] Elected to fill the vacancy created by Augustus H. Garland's Senate appointment and took his seat on January 11, 1865. See footnote 92, Chapter 4.

[5] Died August 12, 1864.

[6] Elected to fill the vacancy caused by the death of Benjamin Louis Hodge and took his seat on December 28, 1864.

[7] Appointed to the Senate by the governor and Vest took his Senate seat on January 12, 1865. His House seat was vacant the remainder of the Second Congress. Arthur R. Kirkpatrik, "Missouri's Delegation in the Confederate Congress," *Civil War History 5* (1959): 196.

[8] Died on March 25, 1864, before taking his seat.

[9] "After the death of David Maney Currin in March, 1864, Tennessee citizens in army camps all over the country chose Cluskey as his replacement." Warner and Years, *Biographical Register*, p. 55.

[10] Died December 15, 1864.

[11] Resigned March 7, 1865

[12] Resigned March 2, 1865.

[13] Died September 20, 1864.

[14] Appointed to the Senate to fill the vacancy caused by the death of Charles Burton Mitchel and took his Senate seat on November 8, 1864.

[15] Appointed to the Senate by the governor and Vest took his Senate seat on January 12, 1865.

MAP 7

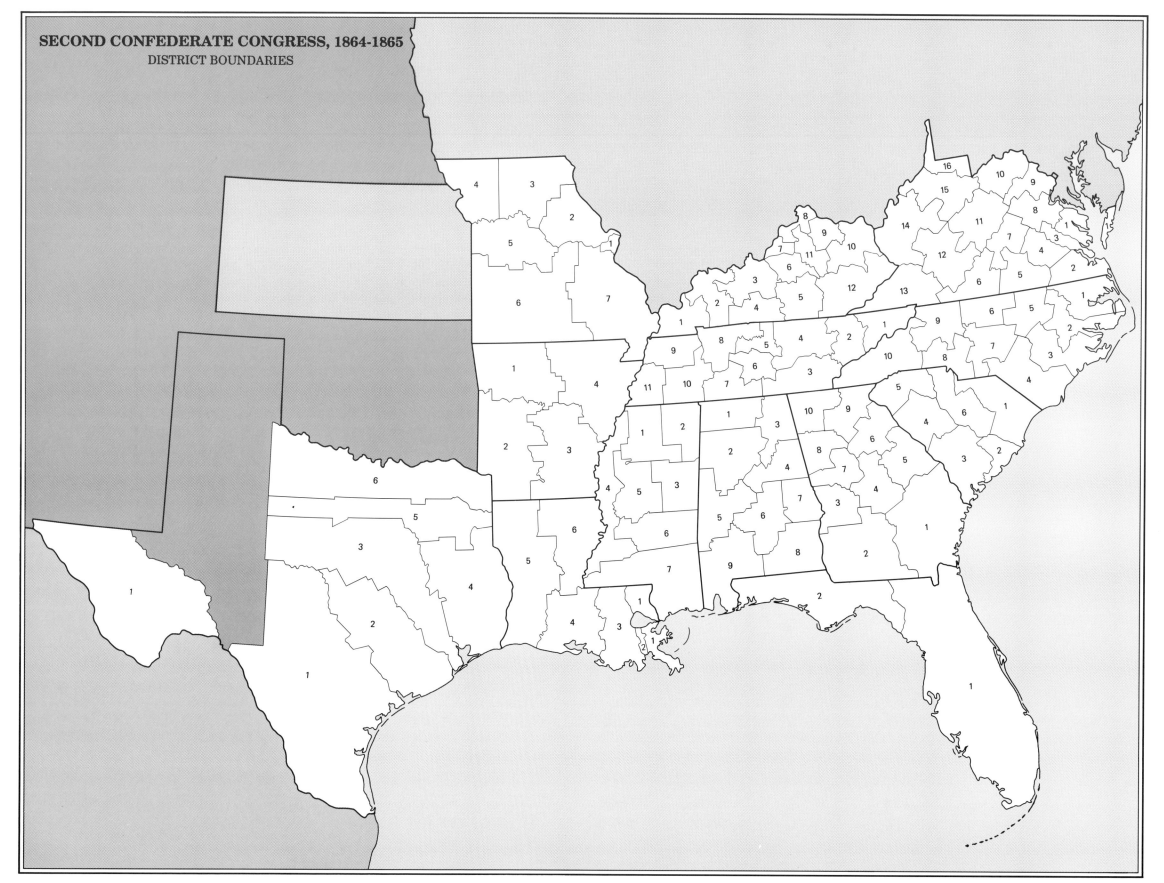

SECOND CONFEDERATE CONGRESS, 1864-1865
DISTRICT BOUNDARIES

MAP 8

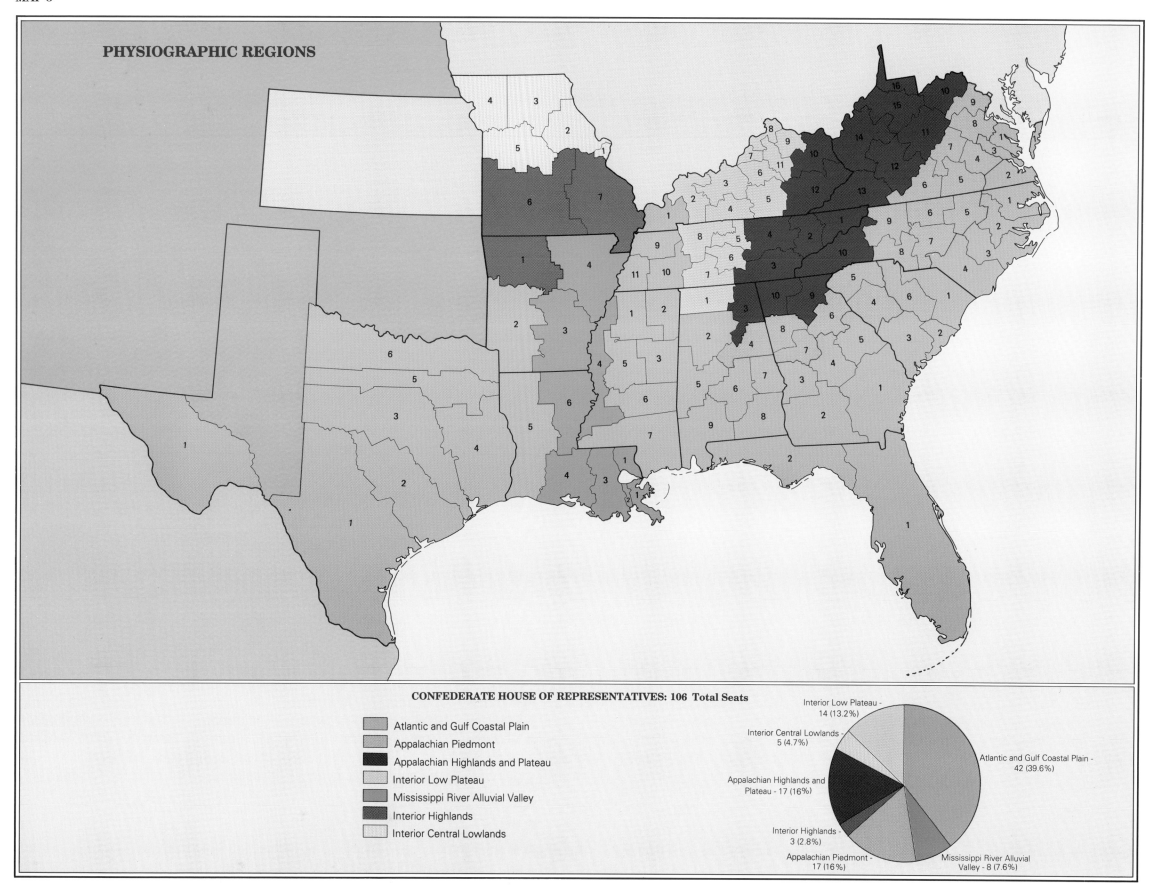

PHYSIOGRAPHIC REGIONS

CONFEDERATE HOUSE OF REPRESENTATIVES: 106 Total Seats

Atlantic and Gulf Coastal Plain
Appalachian Piedmont
Appalachian Highlands and Plateau
Interior Low Plateau
Mississippi River Alluvial Valley
Interior Highlands
Interior Central Lowlands

Interior Low Plateau - 14 (13.2%)
Interior Central Lowlands - 5 (4.7%)
Appalachian Highlands and Plateau - 17 (16%)
Interior Highlands - 3 (2.8%)
Appalachian Piedmont - 17 (16%)
Mississippi River Alluvial Valley - 8 (7.6%)
Atlantic and Gulf Coastal Plain - 42 (39.6%)

37

MAP 9

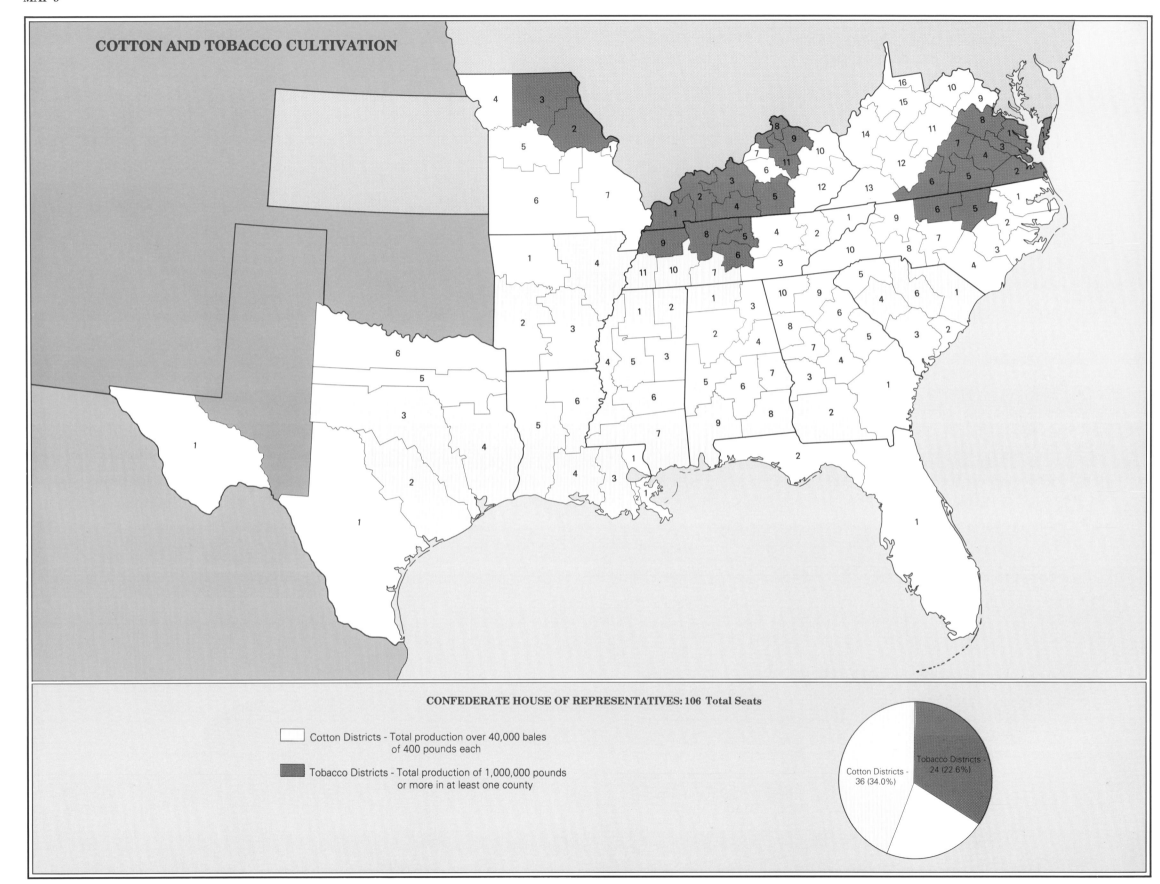

COTTON AND TOBACCO CULTIVATION

CONFEDERATE HOUSE OF REPRESENTATIVES: 106 Total Seats

☐ Cotton Districts - Total production over 40,000 bales
of 400 pounds each

■ Tobacco Districts - Total production of 1,000,000 pounds
or more in at least one county

Cotton Districts -
36 (34.0%)

Tobacco Districts -
24 (22.6%)

MAP 10

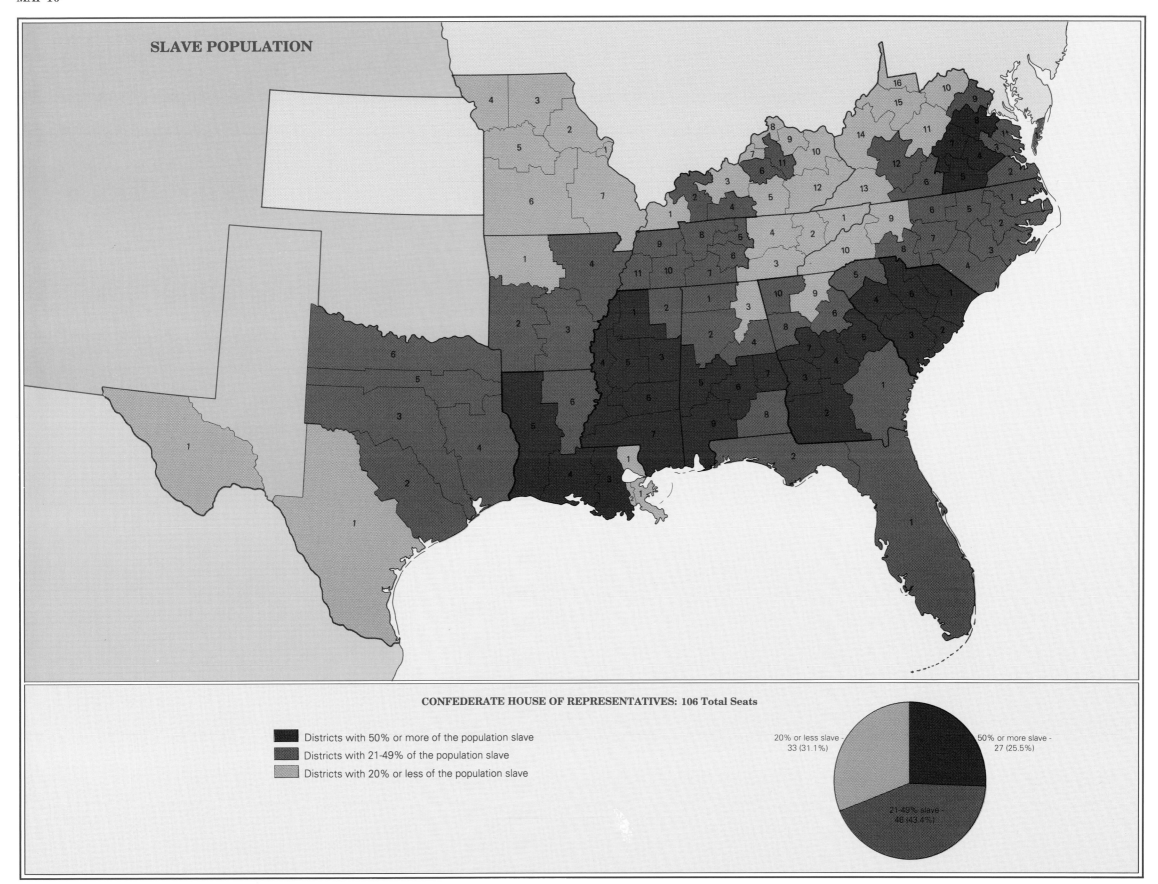

SLAVE POPULATION

CONFEDERATE HOUSE OF REPRESENTATIVES: 106 Total Seats

■ Districts with 50% or more of the population slave

■ Districts with 21-49% of the population slave

■ Districts with 20% or less of the population slave

20% or less slave -
33 (31.1%)

50% or more slave -
27 (25.5%)

21-49% slave -
46 (43.4%)

MAP 11

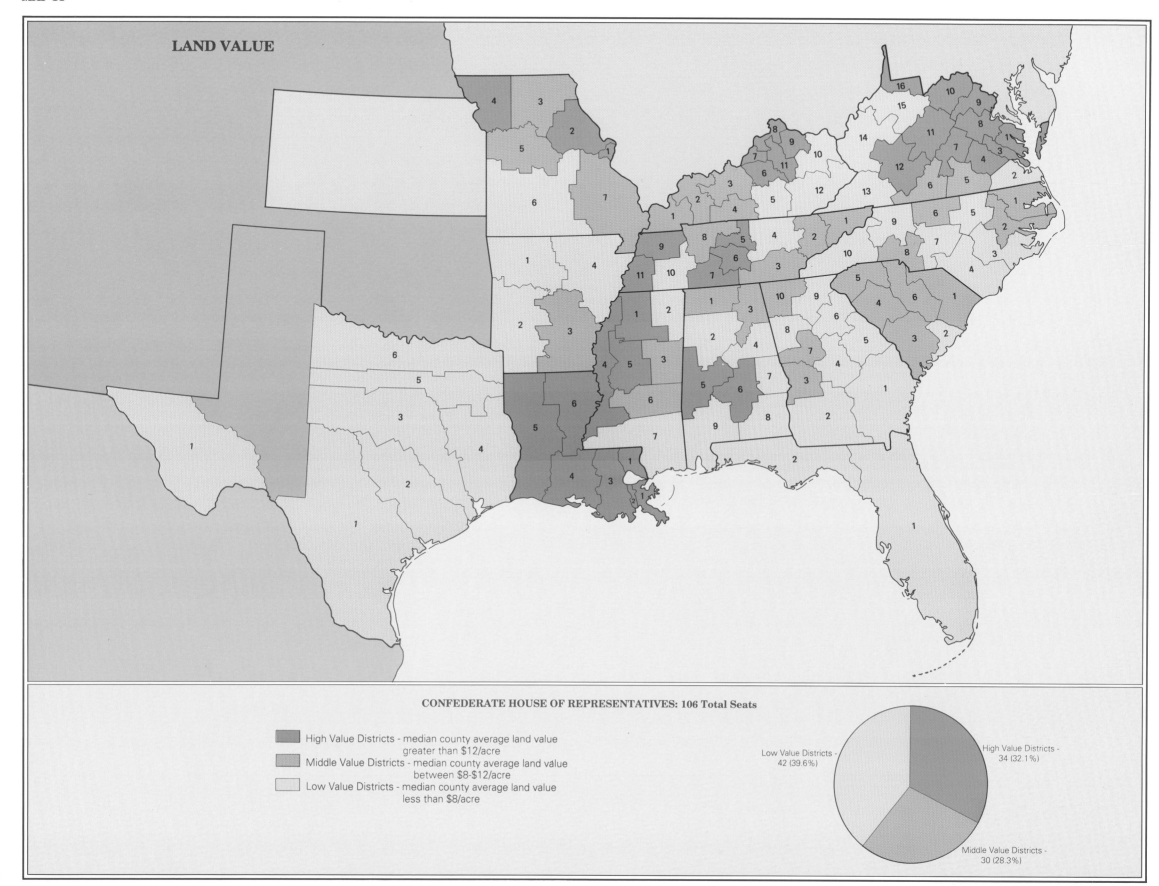

LAND VALUE

CONFEDERATE HOUSE OF REPRESENTATIVES: 106 Total Seats

High Value Districts - median county average land value greater than $12/acre

Middle Value Districts - median county average land value between $8-$12/acre

Low Value Districts - median county average land value less than $8/acre

Low Value Districts - 42 (39.6%)

High Value Districts - 34 (32.1%)

Middle Value Districts - 30 (28.3%)

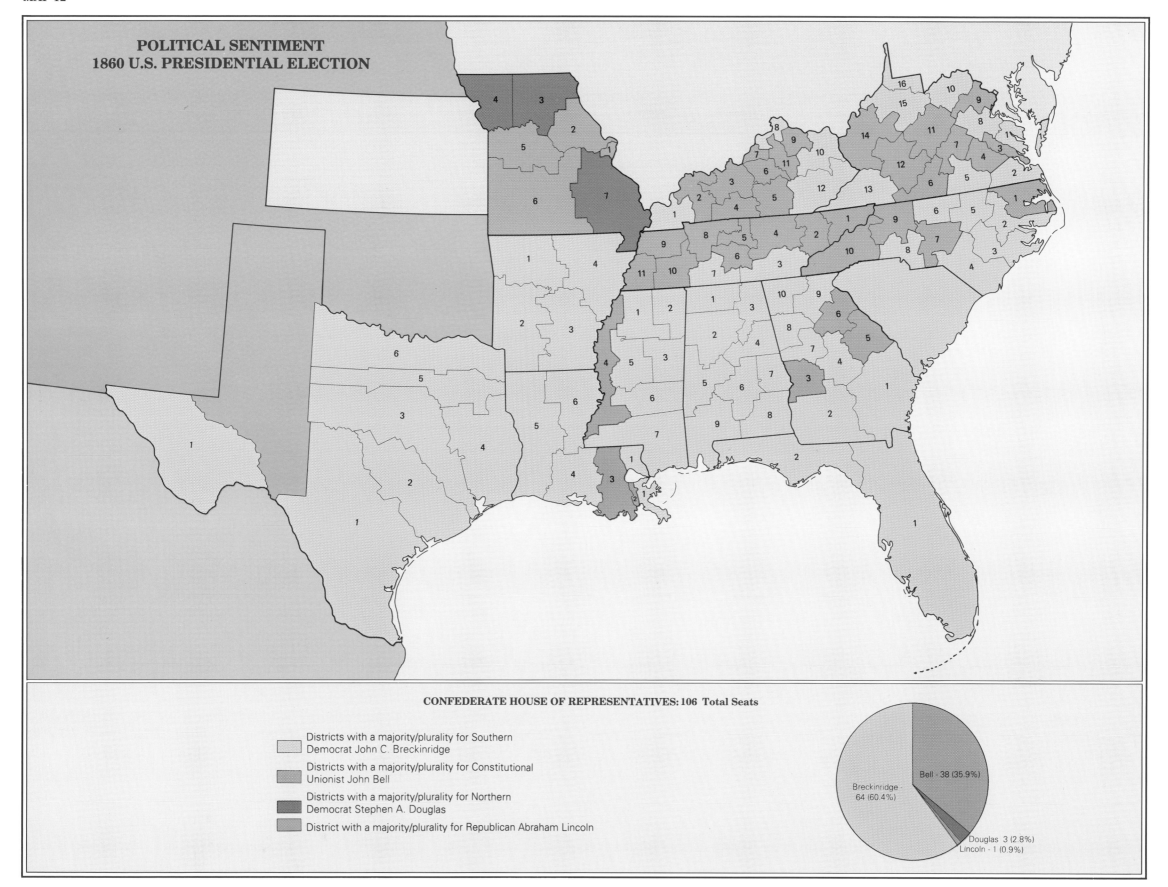

MAP 12

POLITICAL SENTIMENT
1860 U.S. PRESIDENTIAL ELECTION

CONFEDERATE HOUSE OF REPRESENTATIVES: 106 Total Seats

Districts with a majority/plurality for Southern Democrat John C. Breckinridge

Districts with a majority/plurality for Constitutional Unionist John Bell

Districts with a majority/plurality for Northern Democrat Stephen A. Douglas

District with a majority/plurality for Republican Abraham Lincoln

Bell - 38 (35.9%)

Breckinridge - 64 (60.4%)

Douglas 3 (2.8%)
Lincoln - 1 (0.9%)

41

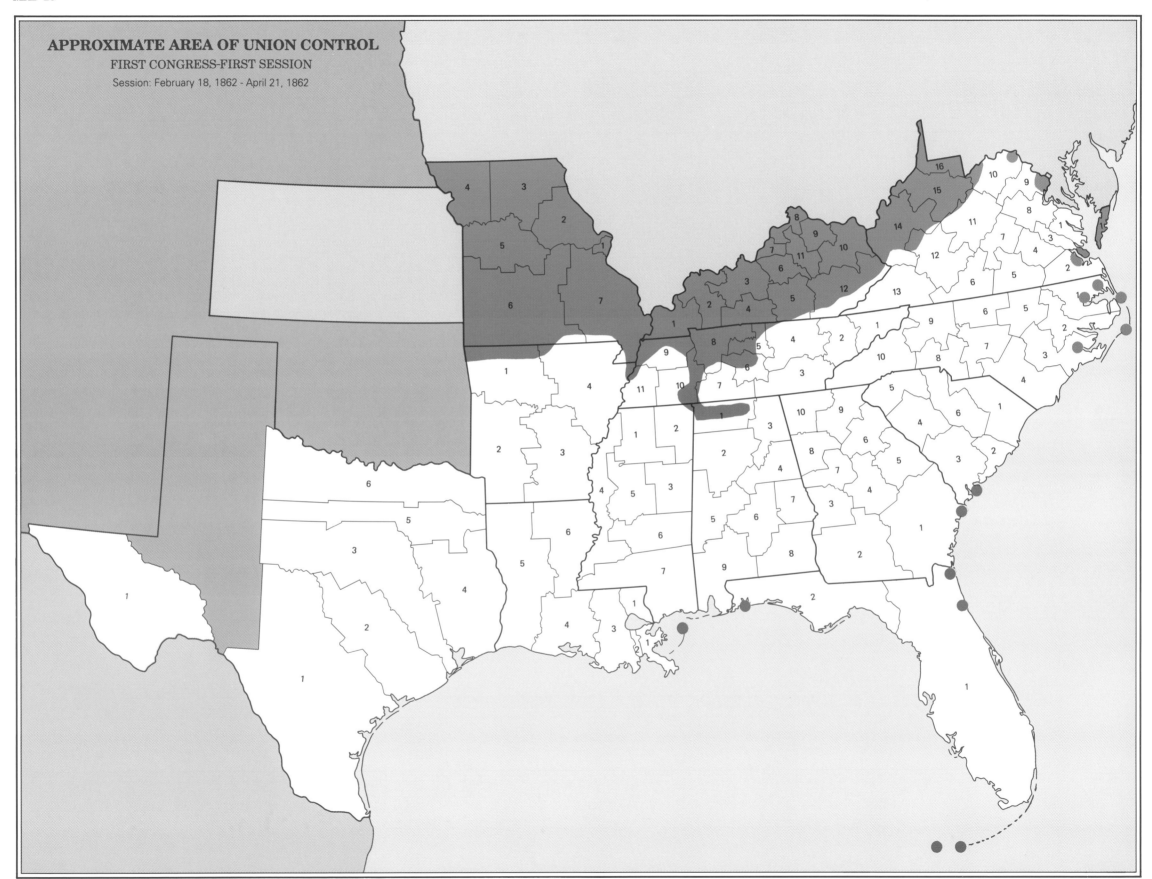

MAP 13

APPROXIMATE AREA OF UNION CONTROL
FIRST CONGRESS-FIRST SESSION
Session: February 18, 1862 - April 21, 1862

MAP 14

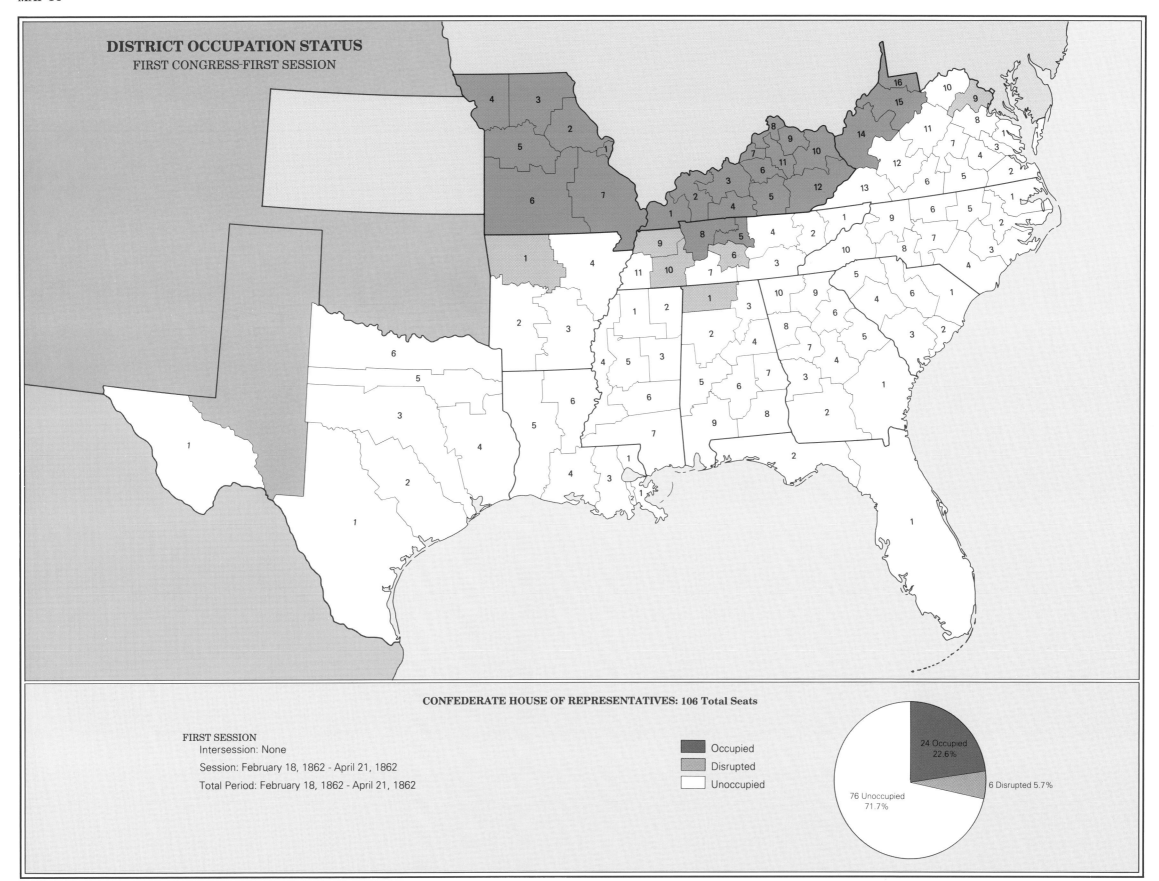

DISTRICT OCCUPATION STATUS
FIRST CONGRESS-FIRST SESSION

CONFEDERATE HOUSE OF REPRESENTATIVES: 106 Total Seats

FIRST SESSION
Intersession: None

Session: February 18, 1862 - April 21, 1862

Total Period: February 18, 1862 - April 21, 1862

Occupied
Disrupted
Unoccupied

24 Occupied
22.6%

6 Disrupted 5.7%

76 Unoccupied
71.7%

MAP 15

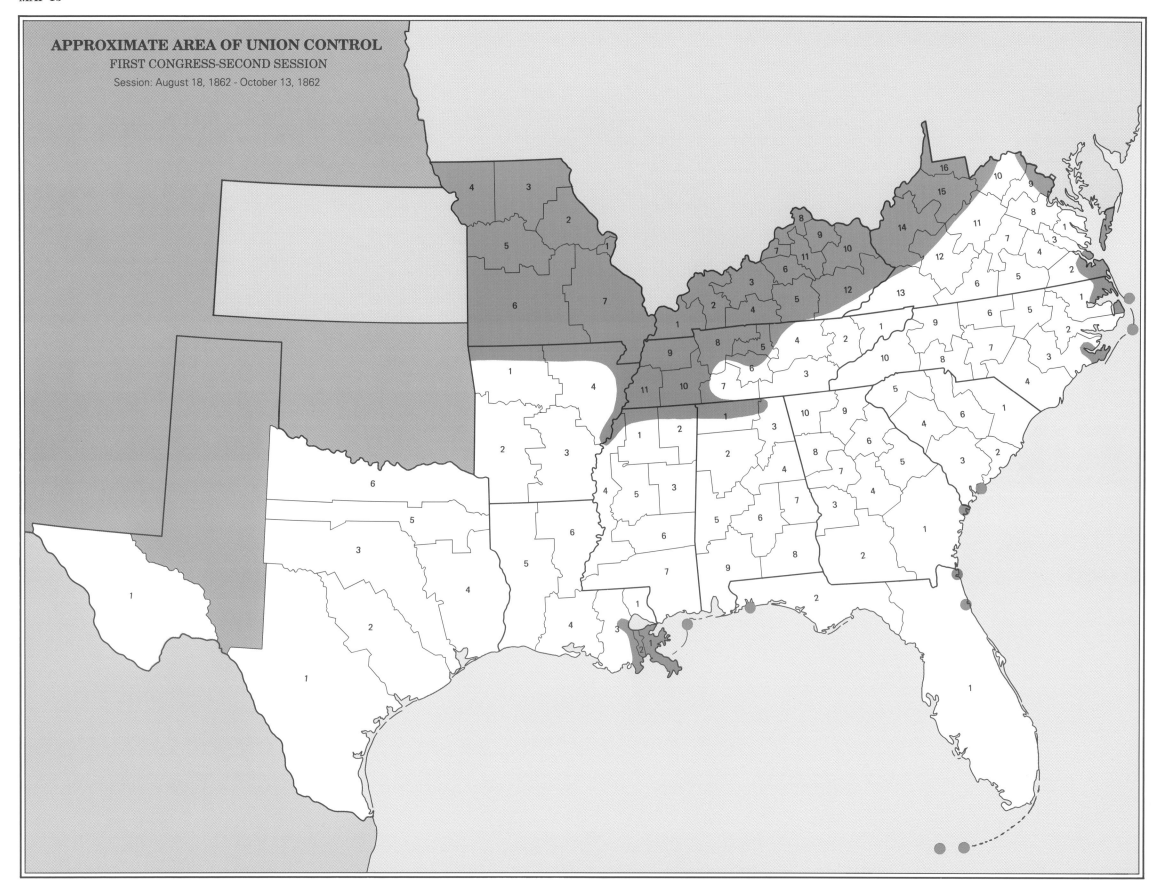

APPROXIMATE AREA OF UNION CONTROL
FIRST CONGRESS-SECOND SESSION
Session: August 18, 1862 - October 13, 1862

MAP 16

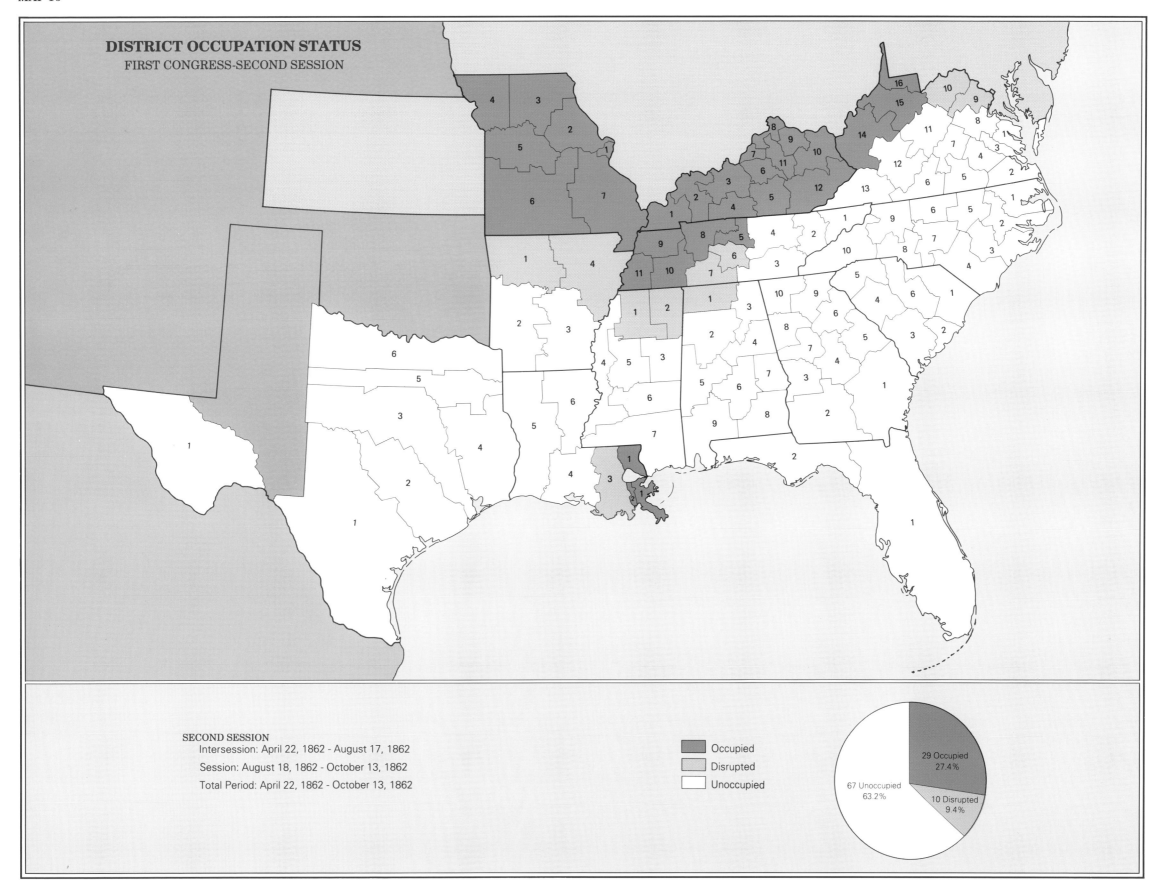

DISTRICT OCCUPATION STATUS
FIRST CONGRESS-SECOND SESSION

SECOND SESSION
Intersession: April 22, 1862 - August 17, 1862
Session: August 18, 1862 - October 13, 1862
Total Period: April 22, 1862 - October 13, 1862

Occupied
Disrupted
Unoccupied

29 Occupied
27.4%

10 Disrupted
9.4%

67 Unoccupied
63.2%

MAP 17

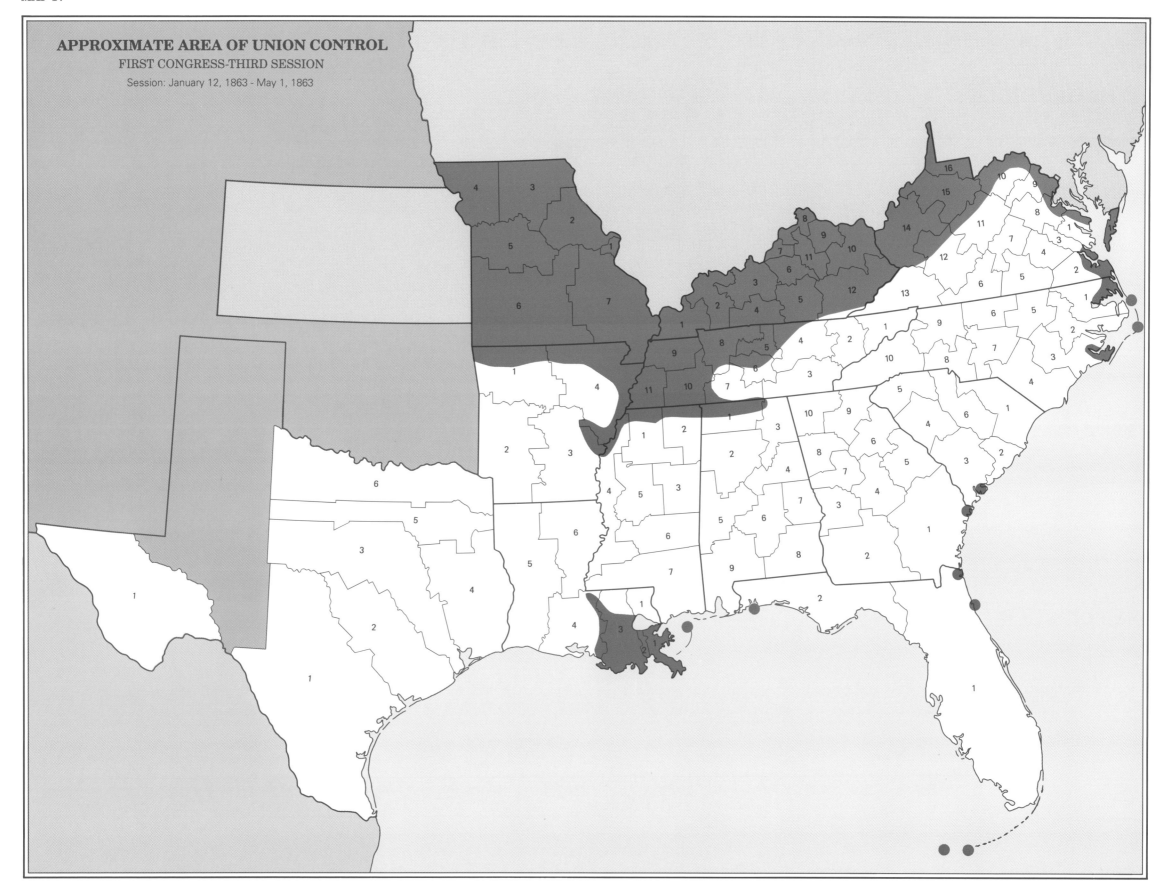

APPROXIMATE AREA OF UNION CONTROL
FIRST CONGRESS-THIRD SESSION
Session: January 12, 1863 - May 1, 1863

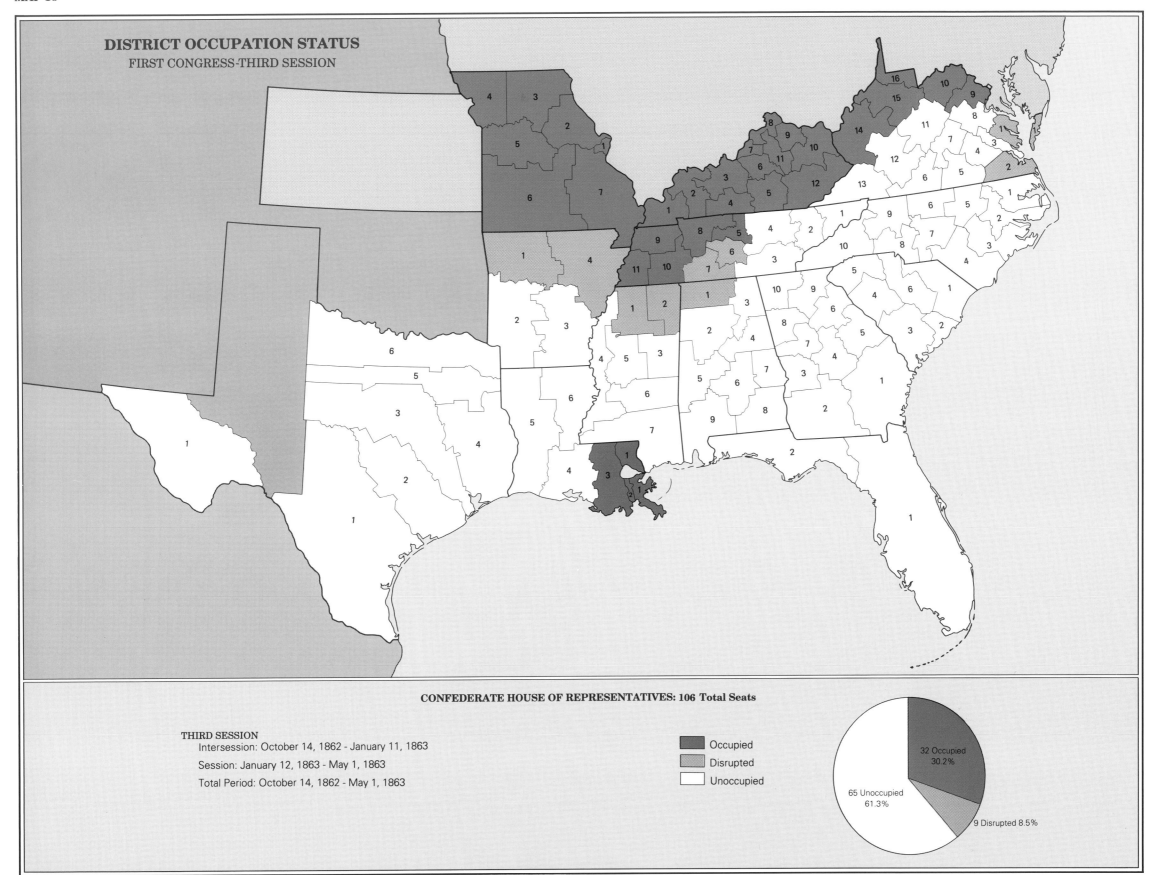

MAP 18

DISTRICT OCCUPATION STATUS
FIRST CONGRESS-THIRD SESSION

CONFEDERATE HOUSE OF REPRESENTATIVES: 106 Total Seats

THIRD SESSION
Intersession: October 14, 1862 - January 11, 1863
Session: January 12, 1863 - May 1, 1863
Total Period: October 14, 1862 - May 1, 1863

Occupied
Disrupted
Unoccupied

32 Occupied
30.2%

9 Disrupted 8.5%

65 Unoccupied
61.3%

MAP 19

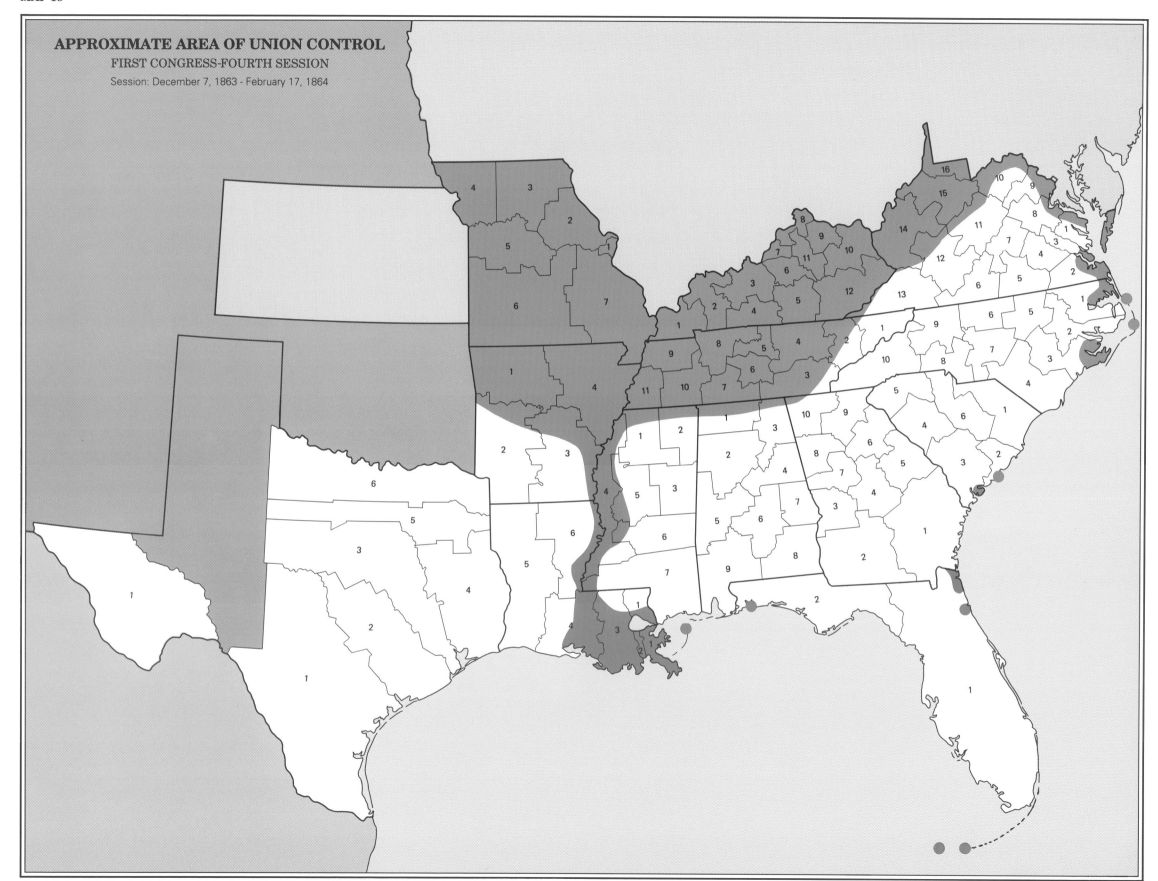

APPROXIMATE AREA OF UNION CONTROL
FIRST CONGRESS-FOURTH SESSION
Session: December 7, 1863 - February 17, 1864

MAP 20

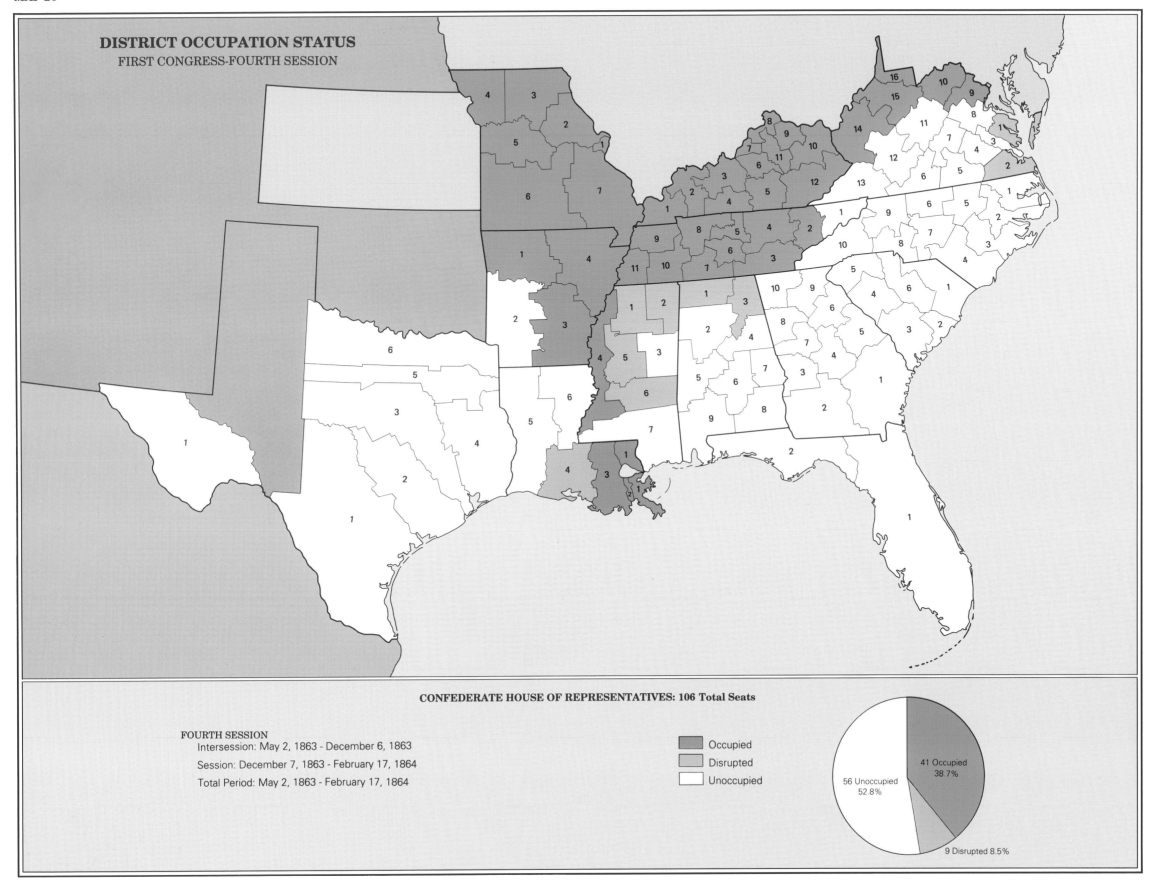

DISTRICT OCCUPATION STATUS
FIRST CONGRESS-FOURTH SESSION

CONFEDERATE HOUSE OF REPRESENTATIVES: 106 Total Seats

FOURTH SESSION
Intersession: May 2, 1863 - December 6, 1863
Session: December 7, 1863 - February 17, 1864
Total Period: May 2, 1863 - February 17, 1864

Occupied
Disrupted
Unoccupied

41 Occupied 38.7%
56 Unoccupied 52.8%
9 Disrupted 8.5%

MAP 21

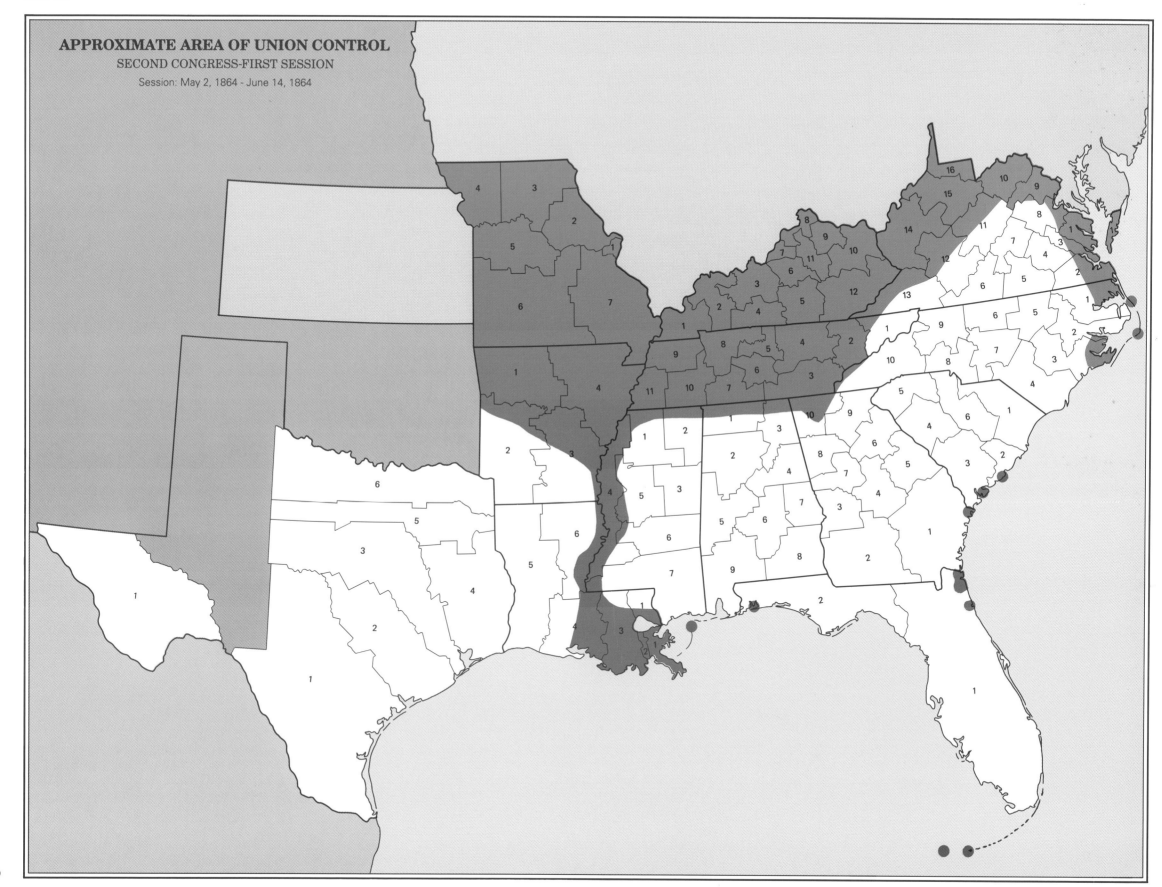

APPROXIMATE AREA OF UNION CONTROL

SECOND CONGRESS-FIRST SESSION

Session: May 2, 1864 - June 14, 1864

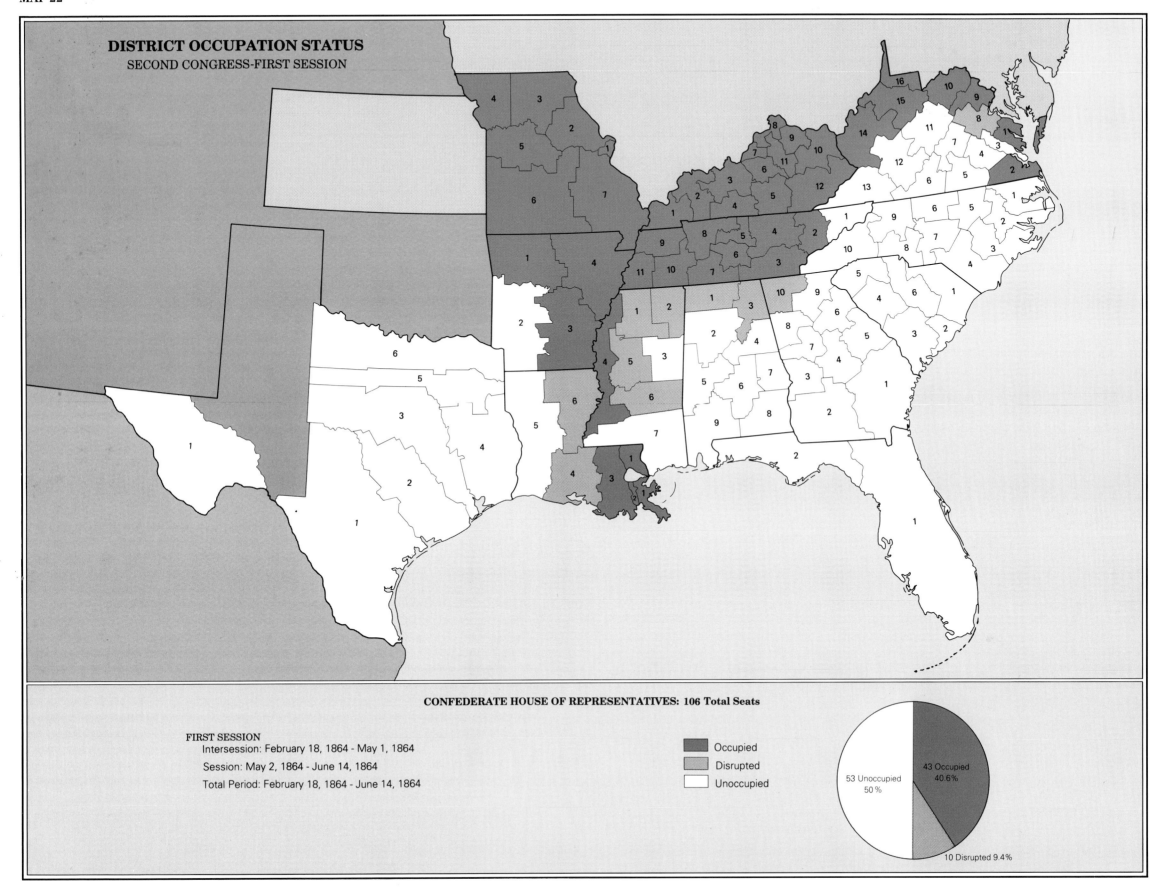

MAP 22

DISTRICT OCCUPATION STATUS
SECOND CONGRESS-FIRST SESSION

CONFEDERATE HOUSE OF REPRESENTATIVES: 106 Total Seats

FIRST SESSION
Intersession: February 18, 1864 - May 1, 1864
Session: May 2, 1864 - June 14, 1864
Total Period: February 18, 1864 - June 14, 1864

Occupied
Disrupted
Unoccupied

53 Unoccupied 50%
43 Occupied 40.6%
10 Disrupted 9.4%

MAP 23

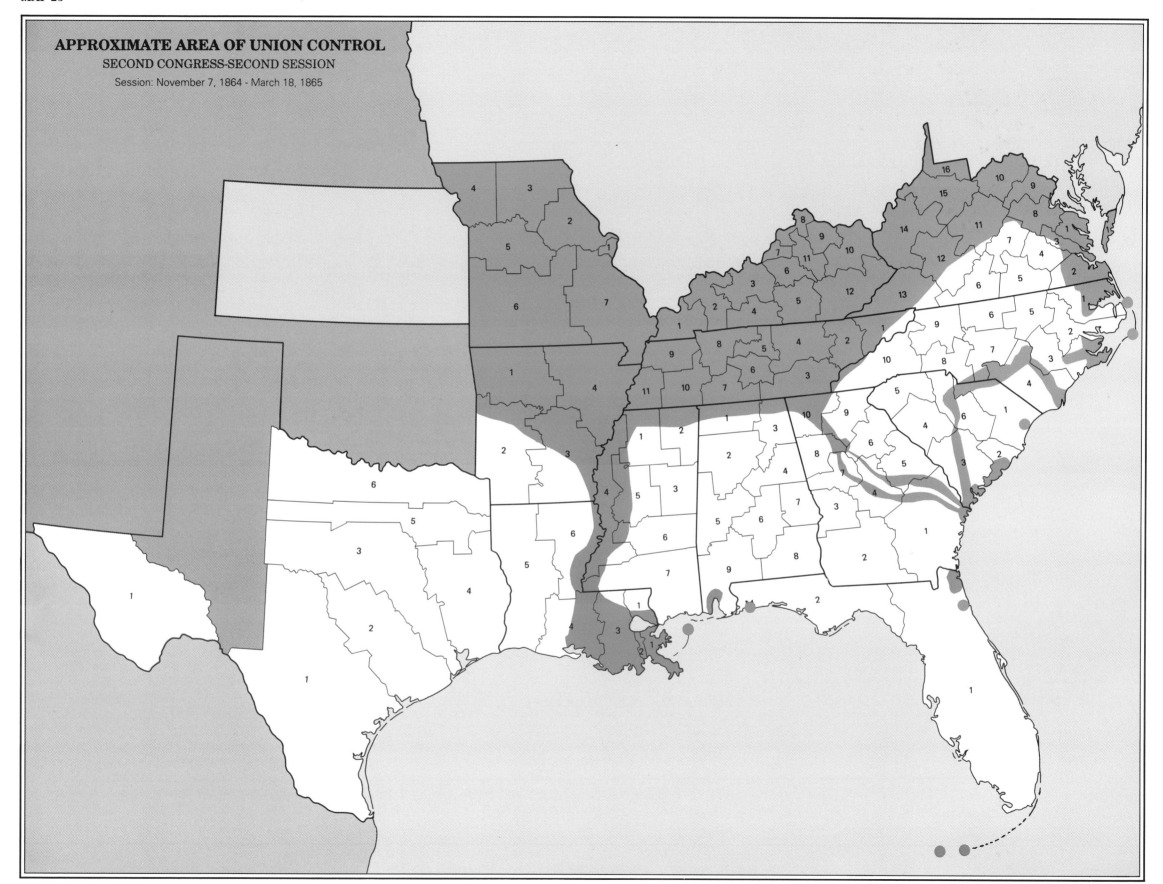

APPROXIMATE AREA OF UNION CONTROL
SECOND CONGRESS-SECOND SESSION
Session: November 7, 1864 - March 18, 1865

MAP 24

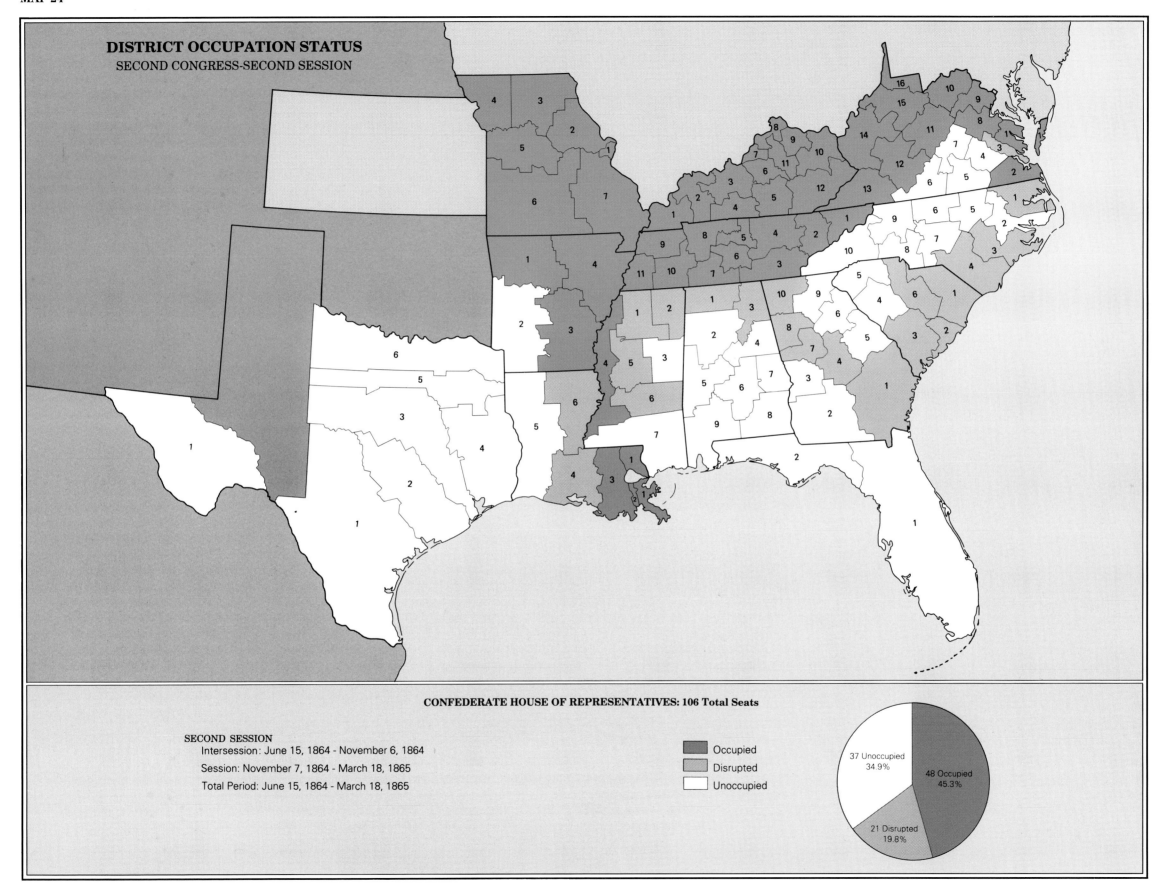

DISTRICT OCCUPATION STATUS
SECOND CONGRESS-SECOND SESSION

CONFEDERATE HOUSE OF REPRESENTATIVES: 106 Total Seats

SECOND SESSION
Intersession: June 15, 1864 - November 6, 1864
Session: November 7, 1864 - March 18, 1865
Total Period: June 15, 1864 - March 18, 1865

Occupied
Disrupted
Unoccupied

37 Unoccupied 34.9%
48 Occupied 45.3%
21 Disrupted 19.8%

4

CONFEDERATE CONGRESSIONAL ELECTIONS

Context of Congressional Elections

Members of the Provisional Congress were selected by the secessionist conventions and the legislatures of the southern states. The unicameral Provisional Congress was the legislative branch of the Confederate government from February 4, 1861, to February 17, 1862. The Permanent Confederate Constitution called for the establishment of a Congress made up of a Senate and House of Representatives. Chapter 4 discusses Senate and House elections and, with respect to House elections, the various characteristics of the electorate and electoral process. The chapter concludes with a examination of the First and Second Congress elections for each state and for the Confederacy as a whole.

Senate

Article I, Section 3, of the Confederate Constitution parallels the U.S. Constitution with respect to the organization of the Senate and election of senators. Each state was allocated two senators irrespective of population. Each state's legislature was given the task of electing these individuals.[1] The term of a senator was six years. To stagger the future election of senators into three somewhat equal groups the initial contingent of Confederate senators was divided into three "classes" of two-, four-, and six-year terms. At the begin-

ning of the First Congress each of the twenty-six senators was assigned by lot to one of these classes.[2] Table 4-1 lists all the original senators by state and their class and term. Those with four- and six-year terms, classes 2 and 3, of course, never stood for reelection. The eight seats in class 1, with two-year terms, had to stand for reelection by the beginning of the Second Congress.

The exact procedure of senatorial election was formulated by each state legislature. In the antebellum era most states elected senators by majority of a joint meeting of the two legislative chambers, while in other states senators needed the majority in each chamber meeting separately. The general philosophy of the time was that senators represented the interests of the states, while House members, who were elected from districts, represented local interests. During the Whig-Democratic era (late 1830s to early 1850s) numerous Whigs served in the U.S. Senate from the South. However, by the 36th Congress (1859–1861), the last prior to the Civil War, the twenty-five of the twenty-six senators from the thirteen future Confederate states were Democrats.[3]

House of Representatives

As with the Senate, Article I, Section 2, of the Confederate Constitution also parallels the U.S. Constitution with respect to the organization of the House and election of representatives. As dis-

cussed above in the section on apportionment in Chapter 3, each state was allocated representatives based upon the size of the apportionment population. The term of representatives was two years. Members of the House were elected by popular vote from single-member districts by citizens who "have the qualifications requisite for electors of the most numerous branch of the State Legislature."[4] The Provisional Congress set a national election date for the First House of Representatives for November 6, 1861.[5] The specific procedure of election of representatives was determined by each state.

Voter Qualifications

The qualifications to vote in Confederate elections were established by each state in its constitution and laws. There was no uniform regulation for the entire Confederacy; however, the states basically allowed most resident free white males twenty-one and over to vote. The qualification of citizenship was the only specific stipulation handed down by the Confederate Constitution. This, in effect, took away the right of voting by aliens that was allowed in certain circumstances in some states. Property-ownership qualifications had generally been eliminated earlier in the century. Appendix I contains the complete voter qualifications section of the Virginia state constitution, revised in 1861. The Virginia law was similar in con-

TABLE 4-1

Class and Terms of Senators
Drawn by Ballot February 21, 1862

State	First Class Two-year Term	Second Class Four-year Term	Third Class Six-year Term
Alabama	Clement C. Clay		William L. Yancey
Arkansas	Robert W. Johnson		Charles B. Mitchel
Florida	James M. Baker	Augustus E. Maxwell	
Georgia	Robert Toombs[1]		Benjamin H. Hill
Kentucky	William E. Simms		Henry C. Burnett
Louisiana		T. J. Semmes	Edward Sparrow
Mississippi	James Phelan	A. G. Brown	
Missouri	John B. Clark	R. L. Y. Peyton	
North Carolina	George Davis	William T. Dortch	
South Carolina		Robert W. Barnwell	James L. Orr
Tennessee		Gustavus A. Henry	Landon C. Haynes
Texas		Louis T. Wigfall	W. S. Oldham
Virginia		William Ballard Preston	R. M. T. Hunter

[1] Robert Toombs declined his election to the Confederate Senate. John W. Lewis was appointed to the position to serve until the seat could be filled by legislative election. Lewis took his seat on April 7, 1862.

tent and style to other state constitutions, statutes, and ordinances of the day.

Table 4-2 lists the approximate number of eligible voters in each state based on the 1860 census. This figure is an extrapolation from the general census data, used to estimate the number of white males twenty-one and over.[6] It should be noted that although the total population of Virginia was larger than Missouri in 1860, the number of eligible voters in Missouri was greater because of the greater proportion of free population (see Tables 3-1 and 4-2).

Electoral System

Times, Places, and Manner of Holding Elections

The Confederate constitution states, "The times, places and Manner of holding Elections for Senators and Representatives, shall be prescribed in each State by the Legislature thereof: but the Congress may at any time by Law make or alter such Regulations, except as to the places of chusing Senators."[7] As noted above the time of the first presidential and House election was set for November 6, 1861, and all states except Missouri and Kentucky held balloting on this date. A national election date for the Second House election was never stipulated by the Confederate Congress, and the states chose numerous times for this election throughout 1863 and early 1864.

Nominations

There were over five months between the law setting the election date and November 6, 1861. Candidates for House elections were nominated during this period in a variety of ways. By far the most common method was self-nomination. Self-nomination for public office goes back to the earliest days of the United States. Beginning in the Jeffersonian era, and especially with the coming of organized political parties in the Whig-Democratic era (late 1830s to early 1850s), public meetings and party caucuses began to play a more formal role in running for public office. In choosing candidates for statewide office, nominating caucuses made up of party members in the state legislature and statewide conventions also grew more common. However, in congressional districts a combination of public meetings, self-nominations, district caucuses, and local political elites, were most often the method of selection.

In the Confederate South the party structure broke down in most states and districts, and self-nomination again became the most common way of running in House races. While the formal party structure may have eroded, informal connections within the elite still existed. Former Whigs and former Unionists all knew the leaders of these movements, as did Democrats, former Democrats, and secession leaders. Although self-nomination may have been the method of announcement, this was usually preceded with discussions among the political elites, town meetings, and precampaign swings through the district. The final formal announcement of can-

didacy normally came in the leading newspaper or newspapers of the district and state, preceded or followed by announcements in large public gatherings. Of course, in some instances, by the time of the final announcement informal organizations of the old party group or the new movement were in place to support the campaign. In the First House election the nomination-campaign process was very open with party labels and structure somewhat discreet or nonexistent. Indeed, many independent or maverick candidates with little political background announced their own candidacies with seemingly little prior thought or preparation. This openness brought a plethora of multicandidate elections. By the time of the Second House election a number of "slates" were drawn up for several districts, many times in conjunction with peace movements or soldiers supporting those favoring the administration and the war. The party structure of the antebellum and Civil War South is discussed further in sections on each state election and in Chapter 5.

Ballots

Balloting procedure also varied in the states. Some states still used the original early American voting method, viva voce, that is, an open, oral, publicly announced vote at the courthouse or polling place. This vote was publicly recorded by name in a poll book. This method was thought to be democratic and to prevent vote fraud.[8] During the Jackson and Whig-Democratic era many states switched to some sort of written paper ballot. The written ballot took many forms: handwritten by the voter and publicly given to the poll worker, handwritten and secretly put in the ballot box, or even a preprinted easily identified political party ballot. Because political parties were not organized and active in the Civil War South, preprinted ballots were never mentioned in the newspapers and literature of the day and probably were not used. Depending upon the state, a form of oral voting or written ballots was used. The modern systematic printed ballot listing all candidates of all parties and secret voting did not become widespread until well after the Civil War.

While the states set the time of election, voter qualifications, and ballot procedure, each county was generally responsible for establishing specific polling places. In the early part of the nineteenth-century the county courthouse many times was the single polling place where voters came to cast their ballot. In fact, the number and size of counties were often based on whether a trip to the courthouse and back was possible in one day. By the eve of the Civil War most counties had set up a system of polling places throughout the county. Larger cities, sometimes at the requirement of the state, divided into wards, each with their own polling place. When the polls closed, ballots were taken to the county seat and a county total tabulated. This task in many states was the duty of the sheriff, clerk of courts, or chief justice. The sheriff or designated official then made a legal written report of the vote to the appropriate state official, most often the secretary of state or governor. The secretary of state or governor then tabulated the total based on the counties making up the congressional district, and an official result was announced. In most cases newspapers reported the local and district results, partial state results, and, after several days, the official results.

Soldier and Refugee Voting

During the Civil War voter participation obviously suffered because of increasing federal occupation and disruption and a large number of voters being away from their home county serving in the army. Dislocation occurred on a scale unequaled in American history. Since approximately 850,000 men served in the Confederate army at one time or another during the Civil War, an extremely large segment of the eligible voters of the South were away from home at any given point in the war. The holding of elections was very important to the national and state Confederate governments. Elections were not only an American democratic tradition, but the Confederate leaders felt they established the legitimacy of the new government. By November 1861 tens of thousands of state militia and volunteers were already with the army. States began to make allowances for soldiers to vote while away, and by the time of the Second House election this was almost a universal right.[9] The process usually entailed assigning one officer in the military unit the responsibility for collecting the vote of men of the state in question. In local and state units this task was easy. The officer then sealed and mailed the final results to the appropriate county or state official. Soldier voting took all the forms mentioned above, oral and written, public and private. Appendix I contains the ordinance passed by the South Carolina state legislature describing the full procedure for voting by soldiers in the Second House election. This South Carolina ordinance is similar to other state and national laws allowing soldier voting.

Allowances were also made for thousands of Confederate citizens to vote in state and congressional elections if they fled their home county because of federal occupation or disruption. If refugees were still in their home state they could usually go to a designated polling place or courthouse, declare their refugee status and home county, and vote. These votes were reported to the appropriate state official as a vote cast for another county or district. If a refugee was in a different state and near an army camp where voting by soldiers took place, the vote sometimes could be cast there and reported with the unit results or reported separately to the appropriate county or state official.

Most Confederate state capitals were permanently or temporarily occupied by the Union at one point or another during the war and the state government permanently or temporarily moved. In these cases the governor and legislature were also refugees. The state government usually moved to a safer part of the state or to a neighboring state well within Confederate lines. Table 4-3 lists the Confederate state capitals, their earliest federal occupation date, and the initial relocation site of state government. All the occupied states continued some semblance of state government to one degree or another, and all held elections, including House elections, with the help of unoccupied counties and soldier and refugee votes.

Of course, soldier and refugee votes became a much larger factor in the Second House election. For example, Appendix V lists the August 6, 1863, Tennessee Confederate House election results. In August 1863 nearly two-thirds of Tennessee was occupied or dis-

TABLE 4-2

Voter Turnout in Antebellum and Confederate Congressional Elections[1]

	Estimated Eligible Electorate[2]	1859 U.S. Congress (%)	1860 U.S. President (%)	1861 Confederate Congress (%)	1863 Confederate Congress (%)
Alabama	114,500	– (51.8)[3]	90,122 (78.7)	41,699 (36.4)	35,251 (30.7)
Arkansas[4]	68,100	59,326 (87.1)	54,152 (79.5)	25,903 (38)	–
Florida[4]	16,700	12,894 (77.1)	13,301 (79.5)	8,365 (50)	6,998 (41.9)
Georgia	125,400	97,559 (77.8)	106,717 (85.1)	47,928 (38.2)	55,644 (44.4)
Kentucky	197,300	141,212 (71.6)	146,216 (74.1)	–	2,094 (1)[5]
Louisiana	86,200	33,435 (38.8)	50,510 (58.6)	31,413 (36.4)	7,198 (8.3)[6]
Mississippi	77,200	32,806 (42.5)[7]	69,095 (89.5)	40,737 (52.7)	–
Missouri[4]	239,600	153,259 (64)	165,563 (69.1)	Appointed	4,583 (1.9)[5]
North Carolina	136,400	81,813 (60)[7]	96,712 (70.9)	–	38,150 (27.9)
South Carolina[4]	64,300[7]	–[3]	–[8]	–	–
Tennessee	180,600	134,018 (74.2)	146,106 (80.9)	43,949 (24.3)	14,070 (7.8)[6]
Texas	93,300	56,706 (60.8)	62,855 (67.4)	38,266 (41)	29,935 (32.1)
Virginia	233,400	– (60.9)[3]	166,891 (71.5)	–	41,648 (17.8)
Total	1,633,000	(65)[9]	1,168,240 (75.4)[10]	(39.6)[9]	

[1] Estimates based upon voter participation tables by Walter Dean Burnham in *Historical Statistics of the United States, Colonial Times to 1970* (Washington, D.C.: Government Printing Office, 1975), pp. 1067–69, 1072. Eligible electorate was calculated using voter participation percentages in *Historical Statistics* and vote totals for the presidential election in *Congressional Quarterly's Guide to U.S. Elections* (Washington, D.C.: Congressional Quarterly, 1985), p. 335. The 1859 congressional vote totals are also from the CQ's *Guide*, pp. 762–764. A dash (–) means complete returns are not available for every district.

[2] Rounded to the nearest one-hundredth to emphasize the status as an estimated figure.

[3] Estimated statewide voter turnout percentage based on available districts, in Alabama 50,799 in six out of seven districts, in Virginia 87,489 in eight out of thirteen districts. Vote totals were not found for any of the six South Carolina districts in 1860.

[4] Congressional election in 1860.

[5] Voting was from soldiers and refugees located outside of the state participating in a general ticket election by district; that is, each voter could select one candidate in each of the districts. See the discussion of Second House election for Kentucky and Missouri.

[6] Voting was from unoccupied counties, soldiers, and refugees located inside and outside of the state participating in a general ticket election by district; that is, each voter could select one candidate in each of the districts. See the discussion of Second House election for Louisiana and Tennessee.

[7] Data provided by Walter Dean Burnham. Personal correspondence January 29, 1993.

[8] South Carolina did not have a popular vote for president. Members of the electoral college were chosen by the state legislature.

[9] Average of the percentages of the states in which full congressional voting data is available.

[10] Percentage calculated on the estimated 1,568,700 voters in the South outside of South Carolina.

rupted by the federals. The 1863 congressional vote came from unoccupied counties, refugees, and Tennessee soldiers in various units in and out of the state. In this case the soldier and refugee ballots made up 42.7 percent of all votes cast. The general impact of such a large soldier vote in southern elections and the specific results of the 1863 Tennessee election and other state results are discussed in detail later in this chapter.

Voter Participation

Voter participation is defined as the proportion of eligible voters who actually cast a ballot in an election. Voter participation in mid-nineteenth-century America was higher than late-twentieth-century America. Voter participation in presidential elections has always been slightly higher than in midterm congressional elections.

For purposes of comparison, voter participation in the immediate antebellum South is measured by two elections: the U.S. House elections of 1859 and the U.S. presidential election of November 1860. *Historical Statistics of the United States* gives the percent voter participation for each presidential election.[10] Table 4-2 lists the state percentages for the 1860 presidential election. The actual vote total is taken from *Congressional Quarterly's Guide to U.S. Elections* as tabulated in Table 3-6.[11] These two figures allow the calculation of the approximate eligible voter figure.

TABLE 4-3

Confederate State Capitals

State	Capital	Initial Occupation	Initial Relocation
Missouri	Jefferson City	June 15, 1861[1]	Neosha-Cassville
Kentucky	Frankfort	September 2, 1861[2]	Bowling Green
Tennessee	Nashville	February 25, 1862	Memphis
Louisiana	Baton Rouge	May 12, 1862	Opelousas
Mississippi	Jackson	May 14, 1863	Columbus
Arkansas	Little Rock	September 10, 1863	Washington
Georgia	Milledgeville	November 21, 1864	–
South Carolina	Columbia	February 17, 1865	–
Virginia	Richmond	April 3, 1865	–
Alabama	Montgomery	April 12, 1865	–
North Carolina	Raleigh	April 13, 1865	–
Florida	Tallahassee	–	
Texas	Austin	–	

[1] Date when federal troops entered the capital. Pro-Confederate governor Claiborne F. Jackson and sympathetic members of the state legislature evacuated the city the day before.

[2] Secessionists were never fully in control of state government. Date when new legislature expressed pro-Union sympathies.

Voting participation in the 1860 presidential election varied greatly over the South, and there is no regional or demographic consistency. The highest participation rates were in Mississippi (89.5 percent) and Georgia (85.1 percent), and the lowest in Louisiana (58.6 percent) and Texas (67.4 percent). The average participation rate for the South in the highly important multicandidate 1860 presidential election was 75.4 percent. The national participation rate in the 1860 presidential election was 81.2 percent, the second highest in U.S. history. This figure and the individual state rates indicate voting participation in the southern states was lower than the average participation rate in the northern states.

Voting participation in the 1859 U.S. House elections also varies greatly, and virtually all states had a lower participation rate than the 1860 presidential election. The vote total for the 1859 congressional races is also tabulated from the data in *Guide to U.S. Elections*.[12] Three states are not included in this tabulation because they have missing data for one or more districts, and therefore a complete statewide congressional vote total is not available. Arkansas had the highest participation at 87.1 percent, and Florida was second at 77.1 percent. These very high rates are generally explained by the fact that these are two of the four southern states that held their congressional election in 1860 rather than in 1859. Louisiana again had the lowest House election turnout rate at 38.8 percent. The average congressional election participation rate was 65 percent, about 10 percent lower than the presidential average. The vote total in the two elections serves as a basis of comparison with voter turnout in the Confederate House elections discussed in this chapter.

Political Parties in the Antebellum South

Knowledge of the political party structure in the antebellum South gives insight into politics and elections in the Confederate South. The mid-1850s witnessed the most significant party realignment in American political history. The 1850s began with two major parties, the Whigs and the Democrats, both drawing electoral support from all regions of the United States. As the 1850s progressed the slavery issue, which had always divided the parties along sectional lines, split both parties. The Whigs not only split but disintegrated: the 1852 presidential and the 1852–1853 congressional elections were their last national participation. In the North the Whigs were first replaced by an antislavery, free soil, anti-Nebraska, opposition that finally coalesced into the strictly northern Republican party. In the South the Whigs were replaced by an anti-Democrat opposition that at first nominally used the American or Know-Nothing party label. By the time of the last U.S. congressional election before the Civil War the southern anti-Democrat forces used various "Opposition" and "Independent Democrat" labels.[13] By 1860 the Democratic party also formally split into two factions, northern and southern. Political party sentiment in the antebellum South is measured by three variables: elections to the 31st (1849–1851) through 36th (1859–1861)

U.S. House of Representatives; party representation in the U.S. Senate from the 31st through 36th Congresses; and the 1860 U.S. presidential election.

Table 4-4 enumerates the political party composition of the southern delegations in the U.S. House of Representatives in the 1850s. Since the Democratic party remained somewhat identifiable throughout this period it is used as the gauge of party composition. The Democrats controlled approximately 70 percent of all southern seats during this period. The Whigs were their major competition in the 31st to 33rd congressional elections and the Americans and Opposition candidates in the remainder. The low point in Democratic strength occurred in the 1850–1851 elections. Throughout the South there was great political turmoil over the Compromise of 1850. Political parties were particularly disrupted in Georgia, Mississippi, and to some extent in Alabama. In these states the normal Whig versus Democrat structure broke down and a new State Rights versus Unionist structure emerged.[14] The State Rightists, mostly Democrats but some Whigs, took an extreme stance with respect to slavery and secession. The Unionists were proslavery but took moderate and compromising views and were staunchly antisecessionist. The Unionists had a strong Whig core group, but were supported by many Union Democrats. This alignment mirrored most of the antebellum South. Most, but not all, Democrats had secessionists learnings, especially as the decade progressed, and most, but not all, Whigs were pro-Union. Although the parties resumed their normal alignment in the 1852–1853 House election, this split heralded the final demise of the Whig party and exposed the continuing divisions within the South over the desirability, propriety, and practicality of secession.

Table 4-4 also indicates state differences in the election of Democrats and opposition candidates. South Carolina and Arkansas had 100 percent Democrat delegations in the 1850s. Virginia ranks third in Democrat strength in this period even though it had areas of anti-secessionist sentiment. After the demise of the Whig party the Democrats eventually totally dominated the Alabama, Florida, and Mississippi elections. The least Democratic states in this period were Missouri and Kentucky, although they both still elected half of their representatives as Democrats. Other states in which opposition was strong were Tennessee, North Carolina, and Georgia.

Table 4-5 enumerates the political party breakdown in the U.S. Senate during the 1850s. There was a slightly larger proportion— an average of three-fourths—of southern Democrats in the Senate than in the House. Five states elected all Democrats during this period: Alabama, Arkansas, Mississippi, South Carolina, and Virginia. At the other extreme was Kentucky, which elected only one Democrat during this period. Tennessee had the next lowest percentage of Democrat senators, 33.3 percent, but even Tennessee had two Democrats in the last prewar Congress. Democratic strength increased steadily during the latter part of the decade, and on the eve of the Civil War twenty-five of the twenty-six southern senators were Democrats. Of the twenty-six southern senators in 1861 twenty-four either resigned, withdrew, or were expelled for supporting

TABLE 4-4

Political Party Strength in the Antebellum South
U.S. House of Representatives

Congress Dates State (Rank)	31st 1849–1851	32nd 1851–1853	33rd 1853–1855	34th 1855–1857	35th 1857–1859	36th 1859–1861	Total Democrat/ Total Seats(%D)
South Carolina 1	6D	6D	6D	6D	6D	6D	36D/36 (100)
Arkansas 2	1D	1D	2D	2D	2D	2D	10D/10 (100)
Virginia 3	14D,1W	13D,2W	13D	12D,1A	13D	8D, 4ID 1Opp	73D/82 (89)
Texas 4	2D	2D	2D	1D,1A	2D	1D 1ID	10D/12 (83.3)
Mississippi 5	4D	3U,1SR	5D	4D,1A	5D	5D	23D/28 (82.1)
Alabama 6	5D,2W	4D,2W 1U	6D,1W	5D,2A	7D	7D	34D/42 (81.0)
Louisiana 7	3D,1W	2D,2W	3D,1W	3D,1A	3D,1A	3D,1A	17D/24 (70.8)
Florida 8	1W	1W	1D	1D	1D	1D	4D/6 (66.6)
Georgia 9	4D,4W	6U,2SR	6D,2W	6D,2A	6D,2A	6D 2Opp	28D/48 (58.3)
North Carolina 10	3D,6W	3D,6W	5D,3W	5D,3A	7D,1A	4D 4Opp	27D/50 (54)
Tennessee 11	7D,4W	6D,4W 1ID	5D,5W	5D,5A	7D,3A	3D 7Opp	33D/62 (53.2)
Kentucky 12	4D,6W	5D,5W	5D,5W	4D,6A	8D,2A	5D 5Opp	31D/60 (51.6)
Missouri 13	5D	2D,3W	3D,4W	1D,6Opp	4D,2A 1ID	4D 1A, 1ID 1R	19D/38 (50)
Total Party	58D, 25W	44D 25W 10U 3SR 1ID	62D 21W	55D 22A 6Opp	71D 11A 1ID	55D 19Opp 6ID 2A 1R	345D/498
(%D)	69.9	53.0	74.7	66.3	85.5	66.3	69.3

D=Democrat, W=Whig, ID=Independent Democrat, Opp=Opposition, SR=States Right, U=Unionist, A=American, R=Republican

Source: Kenneth C. Martis, *The Historical Atlas of Political Parties in the United States Congress 1789–1989* (New York: Macmillan, 1989).

rat Stephen Douglas, and Constitutional Unionist John Bell. Table 3-6 indicates strong Unionist strength still existed in the South in November 1860 and Map 12 indicates much of this strength in the upper South and border states.

Taking all three antebellum indicators into consideration it is clear that the Democratic party dominated South Carolina and Arkansas throughout this period, and eventually dominated Mississippi, Alabama, and Florida. These states probably had the most extreme stance on slavery and secession. Two states clearly stand out as least supportive of the Democrats, Kentucky and Missouri, where the pro-Union sentiment was strongest. Four states stand in a middle group of a noticeable Democrat opposition, Tennessee, Louisiana, North Carolina, and Georgia. Virginia is an anomaly, because before the war the Democratic party dominated the state. Opposition strength in Virginia came from a number of different counties in all areas of the states, but never consistently controlled any area. The Democrat-secessionist and opposition-Unionist correlation is seemingly less consistent in antebellum Virginia than in other parts of the South.

First Confederate Congress Elections

State and District Results

Elections to the First Confederate Congress, with the exception of Kentucky, took place in 1861. According to the stipulations in the Confederate Constitution elections to the Senate were conducted in the various state legislatures. Since this was the First Confederate Congress all the states elected two senators. The Provisional Congress set November 6, 1861, as the date for the first Confederate national election for president and members of the House.[15] This same legislation stipulated the Permanent Congress was to conduct its opening session and organize on February 18, 1862.

This section discusses the results of the first Confederate elections. These results are analyzed primarily with respect to:

1. occupied areas (Maps 13 to 24),
2. competition and method of election (Map 25; Appendix IV),
3. voter turnout (Table 4-2; Appendix IV),
4. former political parties (Map 26),
5. secession stand (Map 27), and
6. incumbency (Maps 28 and 29).

Each southern state had a myriad of state and local political elites, elected officials, and local political intricacies and issues during the Civil War. These intricacies and individuals are discussed only if they had a direct bearing upon the final congressional election results. References to relevant state and local histories, newspapers of the day, and other sources appear in this section, Appendix IV, and the Bibliography. Short state-by-state discussions of Confeder-

secession and the Confederacy. Only Democrats Lazarus Powell of Kentucky and Andrew Johnson of Tennessee remained loyal to the United States and retained their seats.

The U.S. presidential election of 1860 also gives an indication of southern political party structure on the eve of the Civil War. This election is covered in detail in the section above on the characteristics of Confederate congressional districts. In 1860 the party structure had broken down to such an extent that four major presidential candidates contested the election, Republican Abraham Lincoln, Southern Democrat John Breckinridge, Northern Democ-

ate elections appear in Wilfred B. Yearns, *The Confederate Congress*, and John B. Robbins, "Confederate Nationalism."[16] Short biographical sketches of each member of Congress are found in *Biographical Register of the Confederate Congress* by Ezra J. Warner and W. Buck Yearns, *Biographical Dictionary of the Confederacy* by Jon L. Wakelyn, and *Encyclopedia of the Confederacy*, edited by Richard N. Current.[17] This section discusses the results of first Confederate elections state by state and then summarizes national results.

Alabama

Electoral competition in Alabama House races tended to the extreme: in four of the nine districts there was no opposition; in four there were multicandidate races; and only one had a normal two-way race. This is a good example of the fluidity of the new Civil War political system. A total of 49,699 men voted in the 1861 election, 36.4 percent of the estimated eligible electorate. This number was enhanced by soldier voting.[18]

In the election three former Whigs and six former Democrats were selected.[19] Remarkably, all the Whigs were unionists and all the Democrats secessionists. Only in Alabama and South Carolina does this general correlation occur in every case, although this was probably the situation in Mississippi. In the Senate election two secessionist former Democrats were sent to Congress by the Alabama General Assembly. Former Whigs and unionists in the legislature tried to elect a well-known prosouthern former Whig, but he was narrowly defeated, probably because of intrastate regionalism.[20] In the antebellum period Alabama was a Democratic and prosecessionist lower South state, and it demonstrated these characteristics in the 1861 elections.

Arkansas

Although Arkansas was one of the most Democratic states prior to the Civil War, it originally voted not to seceded. After Fort Sumter and the call for Union troops the secession convention reconvened and changed its vote. Eventually Arkansas elected a Confederate congressional delegation with a mixed political background.[21] Two of the four House members were former Democrats, one a former Whig, and one unknown. The Whig was Unionist prior to Fort Sumter, but one Democrat was also a Unionist, one a secessionist, and the other representative a secessionist. Arkansas is an example that shows that those who were Whigs in the early 1850s and unionists prior to the 1860 presidential election, Fort Sumter, and the call for Union troops could be staunch supporters of the Confederacy, the war, and the South after Fort Sumter and after secession of their state.

A total of 25,903 voters participated in the November congressional ballot, 38 percent of the electorate. There were normal two-way races in the First and Fourth Districts, but the other two were multicandidate races, both with five candidates receiving over 5 percent of the vote. In fact, the Third District race was so close it was the

only contested election brought before the First Confederate Congress.[22] In the Senate two former Democrats were elected, one secessionist and one unionist.

Florida

In the early 1850s Florida Whigs had some electoral success, but with the demise of the party the Democrats took firm control of

the state. The November 1861 Confederate House elections were wide-open affairs, the First District having four candidates receiving over 5 percent of the vote and the Second District five candidates. Of the eligible voters 50 percent participated in the election, the second-highest known percentage in Civil War congressional elections. This is partially attributed to absentee soldier voting. Florida was by far the least populous southern state, and the final vote count was only 8,365.

TABLE 4-5

Political Party Strength in the Antebellum South
U.S. Senate

Congress Dates	31st 1849–1851	32nd 1851–1853	33rd 1853–1855	34th 1855–1857	35th 1857–1859	36th 1859–1861	Total Democrat/ Total Seats(%D)
State				Category			
				100%			
Alabama	2D	2D	2D	2D	2D	2D	12D/12 (100)
Arkansas	2D	2D	2D	2D	2D	2D	12D/12 (100)
Mississippi	2D	2D	2D	2D	2D	2D	12D/12 (100)
South Carolina	2D	2D	2D	2D	2D	2D	12D/12 (100)
Virginia	2D	2D	2D	2D	2D	2D	12D/12 (100)
				75–85%			
Louisiana	2D	2D	1D,1W	1D 1Opp	2D	2D	10D/12 (83.3)
Texas	2D	2D	2D	1D,1A	1D,1A	2D	10D/12 (83.3)
Florida	1D,1W	1D,1W	1D,1W	2D	2D	2D	9D/12 (75)
Missouri	2D	1D,1W	1D,1W	1D 1Opp	2D	2D	9D/12 (75)
				50–60%			
North Carolina	2W	2W	1D,1W	2D	2D	2D	7D/12 (58.3)
Georgia	2W	2W	2W	2D	2D	2D	6D/12 (50)
				5–35%			
Tennessee	1D,1W	2W	2W	2Opp	1D,1A	2D	4D/12 (33.3)
Kentucky	2W	2W	2W	2Opp	2A	1D,1A	1D/12 (8.3)
Total	18D	16D	16D	19D	22D	25D	116D/156
Party	8W	10W	10W	6Opp 1A	4A	1A	
(%D)	69.2	61.5	61.5	73.1	84.6	96.2	74.4

D=Democrat, W=Whig, Opp=Opposition, A=American

Source: Kenneth C. Martis, *The Historical Atlas of Political Parties in the United States Congress, 1789–1989* (New York: Macmillan, 1989).

Two secessionist Democrats were elected to the House. The Florida state legislature took over forty ballots to elect their senators.[23] One former Union Whig was elected and one secessionist former Democrat.

Georgia

Georgia had a tradition of strong Democratic opposition in the 1850s. In 1861 five out the ten districts in Confederate Georgia elected former Whigs, three selected former Democrats, and two in districts the party affiliation of the representative is unknown. Four of the Whigs were Unionists while the representatives from five districts were known secessionists and one has an unknown secession stance. The Unionist Whigs were from the area of the state of former Whig strength.

There were spirited contests in all the Georgia districts. Five districts had multicandidate elections and five two-way races. In Georgia 47,928 citizens cast votes in ten districts, the highest number of participants in any First Congress election for which complete figures are available. This number accounts for 38.2 percent of the eligible electorate, about average for the South in this election.

In the state legislature a Unionist Whig was elected senator on the first ballot, 127 to 68.[24] It took five more ballots to elect the other senator, the well-known secessionist former Whig Robert Toombs. Unhappy with the lack of unanimity in his election, Toombs eventually declined, and the governor appointed a secessionist former Democrat to occupy the other Georgia seat. This individual is counted as one of the two first Georgia senators, and his characteristics are depicted on all maps and data tables.

Louisiana

The former political parties of Louisiana Confederate representatives reflect the antebellum political geography of the state. Three former Whigs were elected from the southeast lower Mississippi River area, one of the most antisecessionist regions of the Deep South. In the other three districts two Democrats and one unknown were elected. However, the entire delegation was prosecession except for the New Orleans Second District, which elected a Unionist Whig.

The 36.4 percent turnout, 31,413, is average for the first Confederate elections but good for Louisiana, which had a small participation rate in the antebellum period. The six districts were evenly divided in method of election between no opposition, two-person races, and multicandidate contests.

In the first Confederate Senate elections it was normal for a number of individuals to be nominated and the legislature to vote until one and then two individuals had an absolute majority. This was especially so in states where the legislature met in joint session for the Senate election. In Louisiana there were ten senatorial nominees and a majority vote needed in a joint legislative election.[25] On the second ballot a secessionist former Whig was elected and on the fourth ballot a secessionist former Democrat.

Mississippi

Mississippi registered the highest percent voter turnout, 52.7 percent, of any state in any Confederate congressional election.[26] The 40,737 turnout was actually higher than the 1859 U.S. congressional elections, the only instance in which the count and percentage were higher than the peacetime vote.[27] In 1861 six of the seven districts had two-way races, and one had no opposition.

Mississippi was a heavily Democratic Deep South state, especially after the demise of the Whig party. All the seven representatives were undoubtedly secessionist former Democrats, although documented evidence of one former party and one secessionist stance is unavailable. The Senate elections followed the statewide pattern with the selection of two secessionist former Democrats.

North Carolina

The final vote total is available for only six of the ten 1861 North Carolina House elections. Extensive research was conducted in the state archives, newspapers of the day, writings of historians of the state, and secondary sources for data on the four remaining districts.[28] Three of the unfound districts had uncontested elections. In uncontested situations newspapers had the tendency to publish just the name of the winner of the district with the notation that he had no opposition. Many times the nonreporting of uncontested elections was done in the same election article that carried detailed county-by-county vote results of the districts that had two-way or multicandidate races.[29] While this practice was common, it was by no means consistent. In North Carolina the vote total of two districts with only token opposition, the Second and Eighth, are reported. Newspapers of the day published state results, and even other southern states' results, on an eclectic basis dependent upon the availability of information.

The other district where the actual vote count is not known is an example of another common problem of electoral research in the Civil War South. In the Tenth District of North Carolina the results were reported with respect to the vote *majority* of the winning candidate. In this case Allen T. Davidson beat William H. Thomas by 1,196 votes in an apparent two-way race. County sheriffs or local officials often reported the county results in this manner, especially in two-way races. The belief was that the majority number was all that was needed to calculate the district winner. The majority method of reporting by one or more counties makes it impossible to calculate a complete district vote total.

Since election returns are missing for four North Carolina districts an actual statewide vote count is not possible. The average vote in the six districts that numbers are available for is 4,813. This includes the very low count reported in the Second District. If this average is attributed to the four unknown districts, an estimated forty-five to fifty thousand voters participated in this election. This was approximately 35 percent of the eligible electorate. This is about five percent below the South average, which is consistent with the antebellum North Carolina participation rate.

In North Carolina five of the ten districts had no opposition, and there were three multicandidate contests and two two-way races. Four Unionist former Whigs were elected, three from the western portion of the state. Six former Democrats were elected, five of whom were secessionists before Fort Sumter and one Unionist. As in other states there seems to be no correlation between method of election (no opposition, two-way, or multicandidate) with the former party or secession stance of the winning candidate. In the Senate election two secessionists were chosen, one former Whig and one former Democrat.

South Carolina

South Carolina House elections were the least contested in the South. In three of the six districts there was no opposition, and in the Third District no returns were reported in any discovered source. Although a name of a possible opposition candidate was mentioned, the lack of a return possibly indicates only token or no opposition. As with North Carolina, because of the lack of opposition, final vote totals in one person "elections" were not of special interest to the newspapers or public. Final vote totals are available for two contested South Carolina elections, in the Fourth and Fifth Districts. A total of 3,017 and 3,580 respectively, an average of 3,299, voted in these two contests. A multicandidate replacement election in the Fourth District was held in 1863 for the First Congress, and these results were reported in detail. In the replacement election 2,638 voters participated, probably a normal turnout in a special election with respect to the above district averages and the point in the war at which the election was held.

Voter turnout in the uncontested districts varies from district to district and state to state. Of course, the uncontested Confederate presidential election took place at the same time as did state and local elections in some places. Interest in the uncontested House elections and subsequent voter turnout, in South Carolina at least, was probably summarized accurately by the *Charleston Mercury* newspaper the day after the election: "Yesterday was election day for Mayor and Aldermen of the city of Charleston, and for members of Congress of the Confederate States, for this, the Second District; but, as there was no opposition to the incumbents, and as the public mind was more engrossed with military than civic matters, there was no excitement, and the total number of votes polled was nearly as many as could have been polled in one Ward in a contested election."[30] Within the city limits of Charleston there were at least eight wards in 1861.[31]

Antebellum South Carolina was basically a one-party Democratic state and probably the most single-mindedly secessionist state. The delegation to the First Congress reflects this sentiment. The two senators were secessionist former Democrats, and the entire House delegation was made up of secessionist former Democrats.

Tennessee

A candidate's secession stance and former party affiliation was a significant factor in Tennessee congressional elections. This was expected in this regionally and politically divided upper South state. Five former Whigs and six former Democrats were elected to the House. The former Whigs ran strongest in eastern Tennessee, while the Democrats dominated in the western districts. The sentiment with respect to session stance was also divided with five unionists, five secessionists, and one unknown.

The 24.3 percent participation rate is the lowest known of any southern state. This is also the greatest drop in participation, since antebellum Tennessee rates were well above the southern average.[32] This is even more significant since soldier voting was allowed, and there were contests in ten of the eleven districts. An interesting pattern exists in the Tennessee participation rate. The two districts with the lowest total vote are the First, with 3,244, and Second, with 2,014, in extremely mountainous eastern Tennessee. These Appalachian counties were the stronghold of Union sentiment based on the 1860 presidential election and the June 1861 state secession vote.[33] There is a probable correlation between the lack of enthusiasm for the Confederacy in these districts and the low relative turnout, even well after secession. At the opposite end of the political and geographical spectrum were the two districts with the highest voter count, the Seventh and Eleventh, both with over 5,000. These two districts were both in the western, more prosecession portion of the state.

Not surprisingly, the Senate elections were equally split. Tennessee elected its senators in a slightly different manner within the legislature. Most states met in joint session, nominated a number of individuals, and voted within this one group until one and then two received a majority. Tennessee nominated one set of individuals for one Senate seat and a different group for the second seat. An ultra-secessionist Democrat won on the first ballot for one seat. The other election took thirty-six ballots over three days. A Unionist former Whig eventually won in this election. This philosophically split senatorial delegation was reported by pro-Confederates to be a sign of unity and southern patriotism rather than of internal divisions within the state.[34]

Texas

The Democratic party dominated Texas for most of the 1850s. Texas gave the largest percentage of support by far, 75.5 percent, for Southern Democrat Breckinridge in the 1860 U.S. presidential election. Texas continued this sentiment by electing an entire secessionist Confederate House delegation. Five of these six House members were former Democrats and one a former Whig.

Contested elections were held in all districts, four out of the six having multicandidate contests and two two-way races. The 41 percent turnout, 38,266, is average for the Confederate South. The competition among the prosecessionist candidates hinged upon support of Gov. Francis R. Lubbock, who was elected in August 1861. All candidates aligned with Lubbock won in the November House elections.[35]

In keeping with the House results two secessionist former Democrats were elected by the Texas legislature in mid-November. As in several states in the antebellum period, if the senatorial seats were not split between political parties intrastate regional balances played a role in the choice of individuals. This was also the case in the choice of Texas Confederate senators. Here the division was over representation from the eastern and western portions of the state.[36] Louis T. Wigfall, the eastern candidate, was selected in one ballot. Williamson S. Oldham, supposedly representing the west, won on the third ballot with some opposition.

Virginia

The 1861 Virginia Confederate House election returns could not be located. Extensive research was conducted in the Virginia State Archives, newspapers of the day, writings of historians of the state, and secondary sources for these election returns.[37] This is ironic since Virginia contained the Confederate capital and had the largest number of newspapers, a well-organized state government, and more members of Congress than any other state. Even more ironic, nearly complete official returns in the original handwritten documents are in the Virginia State Archives for the 1863 Second Congress election, which was held at a time when the state was much more occupied and disrupted. The lack of the 1861 Virginia returns is the largest data gap in Confederate congressional elections.

Of the sixteen Virginia districts complete returns are available for the Third District (comprising several counties including the city of Richmond) and partial returns for the neighboring Eighth District. From preelection newspaper articles, partial postelection newspaper accounts, and secondary sources, it is clear that at least four district elections were uncontested, one had a two-way race, and at least two had multicandidate contests. In nine districts there is not even enough information in newspapers or other sources to determine electoral competition definitively, though some names of possible competitors were mentioned.

Virginia is also unique in that part of the state was occupied while the remainder was free to vote in elections. The Fourteenth, Fifteenth, and Sixteenth districts of northwestern Virginia were nearly completely occupied, and voting probably took place by soldier and refugee votes as was the case in the 1863 northwestern Virginia elections. Two, and probably all three, of these districts elected candidates with no serious opposition. Several other smaller areas of the state were also occupied or disrupted including the eastern shore counties, areas around Washington, D.C., and strategic Tidewater locations (see Map 5). The unoccupied areas of these districts held regular elections with some additional soldier and refugee voting.

Although the election results of House members are not known the former party and secession stance of all members are known, except for Robert W. Johnson of the Fifteenth District. Nine former Democrats and six former Whigs were elected. Four of the Whigs come from a string of districts along the Great Valley and Ridge and Valley region, although this was not particularly a Whig area.[38] Six former unionist and nine secessionists were elected. The unionists mostly came from the more Unionist western districts. In the legislature one secessionist former Democrat and one Unionist former Whig were elected to the Confederate Senate.

Missouri—
Appointed November 8, 1861[39]

Missouri gave the least amount of support, 18.9 percent, to Southern Democrat Breckinridge of all the southern states in the 1860 U.S. presidential election and elected the fewest Democratic U.S. representatives in the 1850s. However, after Fort Sumter much of southern Missouri became even more openly prosecession, while Saint Louis and northern Missouri were populated with antislavery immigrants or northern pro-Union migrants. Like other border states, Missouri was divided between Union and Confederate sentiments, and the state legislature reflected these divergent views. Added to all this the sitting governor, Clairborn F. Jackson, was pro-Confederate.

Throughout 1861 prosouthern and pronorthern groups maneuvered politically and eventually militarily for control of the state and state government. Governor Jackson and pro-Confederate legislators fled the Missouri capital, Jefferson City, on June 14, and the next day Union troops occupied the city. Unionists in control of the Missouri government revoked Jackson's authority and in July installed a Union governor. Undaunted, Jackson and the pro-Confederate remnants of the legislature met in a special session on October 21, 1861, at Neosho and October 31 at Cassville in southern Missouri. In order to give support to the pro-Confederate Missourians the Provisional Congress voted conditional admittance and financial aid in August. In response the pro-Confederate legislature voted officially to secede on October 31.

In addition to passing an ordinance of secession, ratifying the Confederate Constitution, and appointing members to the Provisional Congress, the pro-Confederate legislature also provided for holding House elections. However, the bill sent to the governor authorized the appointed Provisional Congress delegates to continue on as the two senators and seven representatives to the First Congress until a House election could be held.[40] Although aware of the potential for problems in this method of selecting representatives Jackson reluctantly signed the bill.[41] The delegation served the remaining term of the Provisional Congress, and, since no general election was held, the Provisional delegates were instructed to continue as First Congress senators and representatives.[42] Although Jackson worried that the method of chosing House members would cause Missouri to be slighted in Congress, "no objection was raised as their names were called by the clerk of the House of Representatives or when they took the oath of office. Their right to seats in the House was never seriously questioned during the life of the First Congress."[43]

Six of the seven Missouri representatives were seated in the House, but the representative appointed to the Seventh District, John Hyer, never came to Richmond. The Seventh District was vacant throughout the First House, the only time this occurred in the First Congress. Of the six Missouri representatives seated, five were former Democrats, one a former Whig, four secessionists, and two unionists. Both Missouri senators were former Democrats, one unionist and one secessionist. The appointment by the pro-Confederate rump legislature and governor of the Missouri House delegation to the First Congress was the only instance in the Confederate Congress where no attempt was made at a general election.

Kentucky— January 22, 1862

Kentucky had the least secessionist sentiment in the South after Missouri. In 1860 only a little over one-third of the electorate voted for Southern Democrat Breckinridge, and in the 1850s they elected by far the fewest number of Democrats to the Senate and House. Two areas of significant Breckinridge support were the extreme eastern and western portions of the state. After Lincoln's election and Fort Sumter the extreme western district along the Mississippi River intensified its prosecessionist sentiment. However, the historically Democratic eastern Appalachian mountain districts turned out to be staunchly pro-Union. Although secessionists came from all areas of Kentucky, the farther south and southwest the more the Confederate support.

In early 1861 Kentucky pushed to be neutral in the Civil War. This continued even after Fort Sumter. Because of the strategic location of Kentucky both the North and the South coveted the state. The Union majority eventually prevailed by controlling the newly elected legislature, which ended neutrality and declared for the Union in September 1861. Angered by the legislature, pro-Confederate Kentuckians called for a sovereignty convention, which met in Russellville in southern Kentucky on November 18, 1861. One hundred fifteen delegates from sixty-eight counties attended the Russellville convention, which declared Kentucky a "free and independent state," requested admission to the Confederacy, and established a provi-

sional government.[44] George W. Johnson was elected provisional governor, several other executive offices were filled, and a ten-man state council was selected.[45] From late November through late January 1862 the provisional government attempted to establish a Confederate civil society behind a southern military defense line stretching through Kentucky from the Cumberland Gap in the eastern mountains to Columbus on the Mississippi River. A provisional capital was established at Bowling Green, the site of a large Confederate encampment.[46]

Kentucky was admitted as the thirteenth and last member of the Confederate States of America on December 10, 1861. The admission of Kentucky and Missouri is one of the most questionable and fateful decisions in the history of the Confederate Congress and one that had significant effects on the Civil War South. The December 10 admission came after the regular Confederate elections. On December 21, 1861, the Provisional Congress apportioned twelve representatives to Kentucky and allowed elections in a manner, time, and place prescribed by the legislature and eventually certified by the governor.[47]

Governor Johnson and the council divided the state into twelve districts and called for elections on January 22, 1862. Since most of Kentucky was in Union hands, the January 22 elections were held by general ticket, the first instance of this type of election in the Civil War South.[48] Voting took place mostly by soldiers and refugees in southern Kentucky and neighboring states, but also by some civilians in secessionist counties within Confederate Kentucky. For example, a week after the election a Memphis paper reported, "The Bowling Green *Courier* says that the polls in Trigg county Ky., were opened on the 22d inst. to within two miles of the camp of the Yankee troops from Cairo and Paducah and that courageous southern men of that neighborhood polled every one of their votes. All honor to them!"[49]

Twelve men were certified by the governor as elected Confederate representatives, but no record has been found in the state or the newspapers of the day of the final vote count or even district competition. Extensive research was conducted in the Kentucky State Archives, State Historical Society, contemporary newspapers, writings of historians of the state, and secondary sources for these election returns.[50] After Virginia, this is the second largest electoral data gap in Confederate congressional history.

The men who eventually served in the Confederate Congress were of mixed or unknown political background. In the First Congress six of the twelve representatives were former Democrats from the Democratic extreme eastern and western portions of the states. Five representatives were former Whigs from the former Whig area of the Bluegrass region and central Kentucky. One representative's party affiliation is unknown. The secession stance of Kentucky representatives is the largest group of unknowns, five out of twelve, of any Confederate state. This gives some indication of the procedure of selection and the resultant obscurity of some of the individuals chosen.

National Results

Occupied Areas

Map 25 indicates eighty-four out of the 106 House districts, 79.2 percent, held free and open elections for the white male electorate on November 6, 1861. The single-member district, nomination, balloting, and vote reporting procedures for each state are outlined at the beginning of this chapter. Union occupation altered the election process in twenty-two districts in three states, Virginia, Missouri, and Kentucky.

In late May 1861 Union forces began the occupation of antisecessionist counties in northwestern Virginia, first along the Ohio River and Pennsylvania border and later away from the river. By the November 1861 elections three districts in northwestern Virginia were for the most part occupied, and voting apparently took place principally by soldiers and refugees. Since the final vote total for these three districts, as well as the rest of Virginia, has not been located the voter turnout is also unknown. A number of other Virginia counties bordering the North in the Ninth and Tenth Districts were also occupied or disrupted, but free voting took place in the other counties in these districts. In the First Congress 2.8 percent of the House, the three northwestern Virginia districts, were occupied and elected their representatives by soldier and refugee votes.

In Missouri the Confederate state government was small and disorganized by the time of its official admission, November 28, 1861. The appointed Provisional Congress members were instructed to continue as First Congress senators and representatives. The acceptance of the appointed Missouri representatives by the Confederate Congress resulted in the only nonelected members of the House. These appointed representatives made up 6.6 percent of the chamber.

Kentucky was admitted as the thirteenth Confederate state in December 1861. The Confederate governor and state council called for a general ticket House election on January 22, 1862. On election day the southern portion of Kentucky was still behind Confederate lines, and an attempt at voting was made with soldiers, refugees, and some unoccupied counties. The disarray and scanty documents of the provisional government, plus its evacuation from the state a little over a week later, led to the apparent permanent loss of any voting records. Newspapers accounts do tell of contests and elections, but the participation rate was undoubtedly limited and, of course, questionable in its representativeness. The twelve general ticket Kentucky representatives made up 11.3 percent of the House.

Competition

The Whig-Democrat two-party era fell apart in the mid 1850s. Nevertheless Table 4-6 shows that in the last regular antebellum U.S. House election in 1859, 78.3 percent of the southern districts still held traditional interparty or intraparty two-way races. The number of two-way races in the 1861 First Confederate House elections was significantly below the 1859 figure at 28.3 percent (Table 4-7). Part of this drop is accounted for by the absence of data for twenty-two districts and the seven appointed House members from Missouri. However, the increase in documented multicandidate elections from 2.4 percent in 1859 to 25.5 percent in 1861 is a strong indication of a change in the political structure of the Confederate South. The rise of the Confederacy further eroded, or even eliminated in some districts, the former political party structure, and for the most part party labels in the campaign and ballot process. The election process was opened to a wide range of individuals. Although nearly a fifth of the House seats were elected with no opposition, this is almost exactly the same as in 1859 and, therefore, is probably not a indicator of a lack of support or interest in Confederate elections.

Voter Turnout

In the eleven unoccupied Confederate states it is estimated that over 400,000 voters participated in the November 6, 1861, congressional balloting.[51] While this number is considerably lower than the immediate previous peacetime elections, it is still a sizable number and indicates some support for and some legitimacy in the process, espe-cially considering the number of men in the army and the general disruption of the war. In the seven states where complete statewide figures are available the participation rate ranges from 52.7 percent to a low of 24.3 percent (see Table 4-2). The average participation rate for these seven states in approximately 40 percent. Voter turnout in contested districts was generally higher than those with no opposition. There is some indication that the participation rates in some Unionist areas is lower than average.

Former Political Party

The political party structure of the antebellum period had completely broken down by the November 1861 Confederate House elections.[52] Since the Democrats dominated in the antebellum period and they tended to support secession it is not surprising that former Democrats were in the majority in the First Confederate Congress (Table 4-8). In the House sixty-four former Democrats were elected, 60.4 percent of the House. This figure is slightly lower than the immediate antebellum percentage (see Table 4-4). Former Whigs constituted approximately a third of the House, 32.1 percent. The political history of seven House members, 6.6 percent, is undocumented, and one House seat was vacant, 0.9 percent. Map 25 illustrates that rep-resentatives with unknown party affiliations come from all states and regions. A large group of former Whigs come from the Appalachian region and a number of former Whig areas such as central Kentucky and Tennessee, central Georgia, and south Louisiana.

In the Senate the majority of former Democrats was even larger. Twenty of the twenty-six senators, 76.9 percent, were former Democrats. This figure is again lower than the immediate antebellum percentage (see Table 4-5). Seven states had both senators former Democrats, including obvious states with little Whig presence such as South Carolina, Arkansas, and Texas. Six states had split delegations including some obvious states with a strong former Whig presence such as Tennessee, Georgia, and North Carolina. No state sent two former Whigs to the First Senate.

The Democratic party not only dominated southern politics in most regions by the time of the Civil War, but also had the most secessionist leaning of any political group. It is not surprising that large numbers of former Democrats were elected to the First Congress, especially in the areas of former strength. However, the House, and especially the Senate, had Democrat percentages below the antebellum rate, and it is tempting to say again that the Confederate political system opened and changed somewhat. Those former Whigs, Opposition candidates, Americans (Know-Nothings), and Constitutional Unionists with pro-Confederate stances were valuable in some states and districts to demonstrate "bipartisan" loyalty to the South. Secession stance was now an important variable in participation and selection in the electoral process.

Secession Stance

Secessionists are defined as those favoring secession prior to Fort Sumter and the call for Union troops by President Lincoln to subdue the rebellion in the lower South. The majority of the House seats, 64 of 106 (60.4 percent) were occupied by secessionists (see Table 4-8). Unionists are defined as those advocating loyalty to the federal Union up to the time of Fort Sumter and the call for troops. Thirty-three districts, 31.1 percent, elected Unionists. Map 27 indicates a predictable political geography of secession stance. Twenty-five of the thirty-three Unionist representatives were from the upper South. The lower South states of South Carolina, Florida, Mississippi, and Texas had total secessionist delegations. Eight districts have representatives with an unknown secessionist stance, and again one district was vacant. Five of the eight unknown secession stances are concentrated in Kentucky, which elected lesser known politicians because of the pro-Confederate minority in the state and the general ticket method of election.

The vast majority of Confederate congressmen taking a Unionist stance before Fort Sumter became supporters of the Confederacy after Fort Sumter or at least when their state seceded. Candidate participation in Confederate elections usually, but not always, indicated support for the Confederacy in some form. Support for the Confederacy did not always mean total support in Congress for all

TABLE 4-6

Election Method and Competition
U.S. House of Representatives Elections
36th Congress

State[1]	Districts	Method	Uncontested Elections[2]	Two-way Races	Multicandidate Elections[3]	Unknown
Alabama	7	District	1	4	1	1
Arkansas	2	District	-	2	-	-
Florida	1	District	-	1	-	-
Georgia	8	District	-	8	-	-
Kentucky	10	District	-	10	-	-
Louisiana	4	District	-	4	-	-
Mississippi	5	District	3	2	-	-
Missouri	7	District	-	6	1	-
North Carolina	8	District	1	7	-	-
South Carolina	6	District	4	2	-	-
Tennessee	10	District	1	9	-	-
Texas	2	District	-	2	-	-
Virginia	13	District	5	8	-	-
Total	83		15	65	2	1
			(18.1%)	(78.3%)	(2.4%)	(1.2%)

[1] Congressional election held in 1859 except Arkansas, Florida, Missouri, and South Carolina, which were held in 1860.

[2] Competition determined by data found in *Congressional Quarterly's Guide to U.S. Elections* (Washington, D.C.: Congressional Quarterly, 1985), pp. 762–64.

[3] Districts with three or more candidates receiving 5 percent or more of the total vote.

TABLE 4-7

Election Method and Competition[1]
First Confederate House of Representatives Elections

State[2]	Districts	Method	Uncontested Elections	Two-way Races	Multicandidate Elections[3]	Unknown
Alabama	9	District	4	1	4	-
Arkansas	4	District	-	2	2	-
Florida	2	District	-	-	2	-
Georgia	10	District	-	5	5	-
Kentucky	12	GT/District[2]	-	-	-	12
Louisiana	6	District	2	2	2	-
Mississippi	7	District	1	6	-	-
Missouri	7	Appointed[2]	-	-	-	-
North Carolina	10	District	5	2	3	-
South Carolina	6	District	3	2	-	1
Tennessee	11	District	1	7	3	-
Texas	6	District	-	2	4	-
Virginia	16	District	4	1	2	9
Total	106		20 (18.9%)	30 (28.3%)	27 (25.5%)	22 (20.7%)

7 Representatives appointed in Missouri
(6.6%)

[1] Competition determined by data found in Appendix IV.

[2] Congressional elections held on November 6, 1861, except in Missouri and Kentucky. The pro-Confederate Missouri governor approved the appointed Missouri congressmen on November 8, 1861. Kentucky held elections on January 22, 1862. Kentucky voters were residents in unoccupied pro-Confederate counties and soldiers, and refugees residing inside and outside of the state. All voters could select one candidate in each district, that is, a general ticket election by district. See the discussion of the Missouri and Kentucky First Congress elections.

[3] Districts with three or more candidates receiving 5 percent or more of the total vote.

TABLE 4-8

Former Political Party and Secession Stance
First Confederate Congress

House of Representatives

	Secessionist	Unionist	Unknown	Vacant	Total Party
Former Democrat	51	8	5	-	64
Former Whig	8	25	1	-	34
Unknown	5	-	2	-	7
Vacant	-	-	-	1	1
Total Secession Stance	64	33	8	1	106

Senate

	Secessionist	Unionist	Unknown	Vacant	Total Party
Former Democrat	16	3	1	-	20
Former Whig	2	4	-	-	6
Unknown	-	-	-	-	-
Vacant	-	-	-	-	-
Total Secession Stance	18	7	1	-	26

aspects of the war or all the policies of the Jefferson Davis Administration. Indeed, there were a few secessionists prior to Fort Sumter who even after Fort Sumter were against war as a means of obtaining southern independence.[53]

Table 4-8 indicates a strong correlation between former Democrats and secessionists and former Whigs and Unionists. Nearly four-fifths, 79.7 percent, of all the secessionists were former Democrats, and three-fourths, 75.6 percent, of all the Unionists were former Whigs. Nevertheless, not all Democrats were secessionists and not all Whigs Unionists. The mix of former party and secession stance is even more complicated when trying to decipher roll-call voting decisions with respect to the war, the Davis Administration, and various issues that came before the Confederate Congress. While the variables effecting elections and roll-call voting are complex, the former party and secession stance give some indications of state and district voting behavior, regional party and secession differences within the South, the general composition of Congress, and a better understanding of legislative actions.

In the Senate eighteen of the twenty-six senators were secessionists, 69.2 percent. Table 4-8 indicates again not only a strong correlation between Democrats and secession and Whigs and Union, but also again that not all Democrats were secessionists and not all Whigs were Unionists. The lower South states tended to have all secessionist senators and all the upper South states, except North Carolina, had split delegations.

Incumbency

Incumbency in the First Confederate Congress is measured in two ways. First, members of the Provisional Congress returned to the First Congress. In the House thirty-five representatives, 33 percent, served in the Provisional Congress (Table 4-9). The Provisional Congress members were elected by secessionist conventions or state legislatures (see Table 2-2), while the First House members were elected by general balloting. In addition, it should be noted the number of delegates allocated to each state for the unicameral Provisional

Congress (109) is less than the total number of seats apportioned to the new House (106) and Senate (26). Nevertheless, one-third is a low incumbency rate, especially with respect to individuals with experience in running the fledgling government.

Map 28 shows that nineteen of the thirty-five Provisional congressmen returned to the First House come from the three northern most states, Missouri, Kentucky, and Virginia. The overall average return rate would even be lower considering that Missouri is counted as returning all members since they were appointed to both congresses and not elected.[54] Only Louisiana and Virginia elected over half of the First House delegation from the members of the Provisional Congress. Florida, Texas, and Mississippi did not return any of their Provisional members. In the more visible and prestigious Senate, elected by the legislatures, the percent of Provisional members returned was somewhat higher, at 50 percent.

Another way of measuring First Congress incumbency is the number of former U.S. congressmen returned to the Confederate Congress. In the First House election 45 out of 106 districts, 42.5

TABLE 4-9

**Members of the Provisional Congress
Elected to the First Congress**

House of Representatives

State	Election Method	Districts	Provisional Members Returned	Percent Returned	Rank[1]
Missouri[2]	Appointed	7	7	100	1
Louisiana	District	6	4	67	2
Virginia	District	16	8	50	3
Kentucky	General Ticket	12	4	33	4
South Carolina	District	6	2	33	5
North Carolina	District	10	3	30	6
Arkansas	District	4	1	25	7
Alabama	District	9	2	22	8
Georgia	District	10	2	20	9
Tennessee	District	11	2	18	10
Florida	District	2	0	0	11
Texas	District	6	0	0	12
Mississippi	District	7	0	0	13
Total		106	35	33	

Senate				
Total		26	13	50

Congress				
Grand Total		132	48	36

[1] When two states are tied in percentage the state with the greater number of returnees is ranked higher.

[2] Delegates appointed to both the Provisional and First Congress. Incumbent member in the Seventh District never took his seat in the First Congress.

percent, elected a man who had served in either the U.S. Senate or House at any time before the Civil War (Table 4-10). This average would be slightly higher if the seven appointed members from Missouri were not counted. The 42.5 percent return rate of the First Confederate House can be contrasted to the incumbency rate of the previous elections for the 36th U.S. House in the South (Table 4-11). In the 1859 antebellum elections 60.2 percent of the incumbents were returned to Congress. In the light of the antebellum return rate the 42.5 percent First Congress return rate is low, but perhaps understandable considering the turmoil of the times. The states with the highest percentage of returned U.S. congressmen to the First Confederate House were South Carolina and Alabama. The lowest elected return rate was in Texas and Florida. In the states with high return rates there seems to have been some continuity between the ante-

bellum politics and politicians and the Confederate electoral system. A case could be made that the states with low federal return rates may have entered a new political era with more change from the past, at least with respect to national elected officials.

Map 29 shows the Appalachian region had a low incumbency rate, possibly showing a significant change from antebellum politics. A new group of Confederate-oriented politicians were now participating in this Unionist region. Kentucky and Missouri had low federal Congress incumbency rate for the same reason. The three trans-Mississippi states—Texas, Louisiana, and Arkansas—also had low incumbency rates. Most of the Coastal Plain-Piedmont Deep South had a high incumbency rate of former U.S. congressmen, indicating some continuity with past political beliefs and systems, at least for the First Confederate Congress. The First Senate again had a slightly higher incumbency rate than the House, 46.2 percent. There is no identifiable regional pattern in Senate incumbency rate. In general, almost half of the First Confederate Congress had previous service in Washington, and these individuals brought a wealth of knowledge and legislative experience.

The U.S. Congress incumbency rate for the First Confederate Congress is neither extremely high nor extremely low. An extremely high rate of incumbency would have indicated a strong continuity with the antebellum system. An extremely low rate would have indicated the Confederate South making a complete break with the past. The mid-range incumbency rate indicates some continuity of elected elites and not a complete break with the past. Of course, the continuity and change rate differs from state to state, and each must be examined regarding its own individual political circumstances.

Second Confederate Congress Elections

State and District Results

The Confederate Constitution and Congress did not specify a national election date for the Second House. As a result the thirteen states conducted House elections over a period from May 1863 through May 1864. Table 4-12 lists the dates of these elections in chronological order along with the method of election and district occupation status. The last three elections were held in 1864, delayed as a direct result of these states, Kentucky, Arkansas, and Missouri, being wholly or nearly completely occupied by federal forces. Five other states had one or more of their districts occupied or seriously disrupted.

The general course of the war not only affected the method of and turnout in House elections, but also the sentiment of the electorate and the characteristics of those elected. All but the Virginia elections took place after the fall of Vicksburg and the southern failure at Gettysburg in July 1863. The First House elections generally lacked contentious political issues and many times were based upon personalities, past records, and general support of secession. The Second

House elections were quite different. The war was not going well for the South. Conscription, impressment, taxes, food supply, and the economy all had significant impact upon virtually every citizen. In addition, the incumbent congressmen now had roll-call voting records to stand on and defend with respect to all the issues of the day.

This section discusses the results of the second Confederate congressional elections state by state and then summarizes the national results. These results are analyzed using the variables applied in the first election, but using a different set of maps and tables. These cartographic and data references are:

1. occupied areas (Maps 21 to 24),
2. date, competition, and method of election (Maps 30 to 32 and Appendix IV),
3. voter turnout (Table 4-2; Appendix IV),
4. former political parties (Map 33),

TABLE 4-10

**Former Members of the United States Congress
Elected to the First Confederate Congress**

House of Representatives

State	Election Method	Districts	United States Congressmen Returned	Percent Returned	Rank[1]
Alabama	District	9	6	66	1
South Carolina	District	6	4	66	2
North Carolina	District	10	6	60	3
Mississippi	District	7	4	57	4
Virginia	District	16	8	50	5
Georgia	District	10	5	50	6
Tennessee	District	11	5	46	7
Louisiana	District	6	2	33	8
Kentucky	General Ticket	12	3	25	9
Arkansas	District	4	1	25	10
Texas	District	6	1	17	11
Florida	District	2	0	0	12
Missouri	Appointed	7	0	0	13
Total		106	45	42	

Senate				
Total		26	13	50

Congress				
Grand Total		132	58	44

[1] When two states are tied in percentage the state with the greater number of returnees is ranked higher.

5. secession stand (Map 34), and
6. incumbency (Map 35).

Each state is discussed in chronological order of the House election, with Virginia first on May 28, 1863, and Missouri last on May 2, 1864. Except for the three elections held in 1864, most southern states scheduled their congressional elections at the time, places, and manner in which the regular state and local elections usually occurred. Again, specific individuals, districts, and issues are not analyzed in detail unless warranted, and additional references are provided for further information.

Virginia—May 28, 1863

Elections were held on May 28, 1863, for the governor of Virginia, several other statewide offices, members of the state House of Delegates and Senate, and the Confederate House of Representatives. At the time of the election five out of the sixteen districts bordering the North were occupied and two districts along the coast seriously disrupted. However, almost all districts reported one or more county returns missing or incomplete as the war in general and Union military operations in particular interfered with normal civil society.

Although large portions of Virginia were either occupied or disrupted, the state government went forward with elections in the regular manner. This was the only state with a very large occupied area that did not hold elections by statewide general ticket voting with the voters choosing one candidate from each district.[55] In totally occupied districts Virginia law allowed elections to take place by soldier and refugee voting. Districts Fourteen, Fifteen, and Sixteen in northwestern Virginia fell into this category. The lowest vote count in the state is in District Sixteen where only 233 votes were cast, according to state records. In districts with one or more counties reporting the election was decided by the unoccupied counties, soldier and refugee votes. Eight districts fit into his category including two, the Ninth and Tenth, designated occupied. Although these two districts were mostly under federal control, several counties still filed partial voting reports. Only four districts in the south central portion of the state were generally free of outside disruption, although the official state returns show that even some counties in this region did not report. Electoral competition was high, with thirteen of the sixteen districts having contested races.

Based on official returns in thirteen districts and partial returns in three districts, over 42,000 men are estimated to have voted in the May congressional elections. This estimate is probably near the mark since the official state results report 51,626 ballots cast for governor, 56.7 percent of these votes coming from country returns and 43.3 percent from military "camps."[56] The turnout for the governor's race was 22.1 percent based on the 1860 census estimate of eligible voters listed in Table 4-2. Based on the low actual count of 41,648,

TABLE 4-11

Incumbents Reelected
U.S. House of Representatives
36th Congress

State[1]	Method	Districts	Incumbents Returned	Percent Returned	Rank[2]
Mississippi	District	5	5	100	1
Florida	District	1	1	100	2
Alabama	District	7	6	86	3
Missouri	District	7	6	86	3
South Carolina	District	6	5	83	5
North Carolina	District	8	6	75	6
Virginia	District	13	8	61	7
Georgia	District	8	4	50	8
Louisiana	District	4	2	50	9
Texas	District	2	1	50	10
Kentucky	District	10	3	30	11
Tennessee	District	10	3	30	11
Arkansas	District	2	0	0	13
Total		83	50	60.2	

Source: Kenneth C. Martis, *The Historical Atlas of Political Parties in the United States Congress 1789–1989* (New York: Macmillan, 1989), pp. 110–112.

[1] House elections held in 1859 except Florida, Missouri, South Carolina, and Arkansas, which were held in 1860.

[2] When two states are tied in percentage the state with the greater number of incumbents is ranked higher.

17.8 percent participated in the House ballot. Obviously the large area of Virginia occupied and disrupted and the large number of her men killed and in arms significantly reduced the election turnout.

The former political party and secessionist alignment in Virginia changed in the second congressional election. The number of former Democrats was reduced from nine to six, and the number of unknown party affiliations rose from one to five. In spite of the former party alignment changing, the number of avowed secessionists was only reduced from ten to nine. Eight members of the sixteen-man delegation were new to the Second Congress. In the Senate the alignment did not change when one Unionist former Whig was replaced by another in the First Congress after secessionist Democrats in the legislature could not agree on a successor. The replacement senator served for the entire Second Congress.

The second Virginia House election demonstrated the growing significance of soldier and refugee voting. In the typical Virginia district the soldier vote was usually well over 95 percent of the absentee vote. Soldier votes had a major influence in the states that allowed the military to participate. Soldiers tended to support congressmen who were friends of the Davis Administration and who supported

a vigorous approach to the war, including issues such as conscription and impressment. Added to this the Virginia civilian voter also generally supported the administration and defense issues since the war was substantially fought on Virginia territory. This support of the war is in contrast to nearby southern states where the war was not so close and where men and supplies were taken to defend Richmond and Virginia. So while the party background of the Virginia delegation changed somewhat, the roll-call voting sentiment remained somewhat the same.[57]

Alabama—August 3, 1863

The northern portion of Alabama incurred Union military disruption very early in the war. After the battle of Shiloh in April 1862, Union troops entered the railroad towns of the Tennessee River valley portion of the state. Most of the rest of Alabama was still untouched by physical destruction, and the regular elections were held for statewide offices and Congress in the normal manner with every county except three in the north reporting at least some votes for one or more races.[58] Competitive elections were held in every district, with six out of the nine contests having multicandidate elections. The turnout of 30.7 percent, 35,251, was somewhat below the 1861 totals, but apparently Alabama did not allow soldier voting in 1863 as it had done in 1861.[59]

The war was the dominant issue in the gubernatorial, legislative, and Confederate House elections in August 1863. A large antiwar sentiment removed the secessionist former Democrat governor and affected the House contests. Although most incumbents won, two secessionist former Democrats were defeated by Unionist former Whigs in the northern Third and Fourth districts. In fact, the winner of the northeastern Third District, William R. W. Cobb, was such an outstanding pro-Union candidate that the Confederate Congress decided to investigate his loyalty in a resolution passed on the second day of the Second Congress.[60] Finding Cobb disloyal and "in friendly terms behind Union lines," they expelled him on November 17, 1864, and declared the seat vacant.[61] Since Cobb never occupied the seat the district is designated vacant, the only instance in the Second Congress. The final makeup of the Alabama delegation was four secessionist Democrats, all from the southern part of the state, and four Unionist former Whigs, all from the northern portion of the state. As in 1861 Alabama had a delegation reflecting perfectly the supposed relationship between former party and secession stance.

The Alabama Senate delegation made the most abrupt turnabout in Confederate congressional history. Alabama went from sending two secessionist former Democrats to the First Congress to two Unionist former Whigs to the Second Congress. The new legislature elected in the 1863 August elections was decidedly Unionist. It was able to replace both senators because one position was a class one seat having an expiring two-year term and the other incurred a vacancy by the death of the senator.

TABLE 4-12

Election Dates and Status of Districts
Second Confederate House of Representatives

State	Districts	Method	Election Date	Status of Districts[1]	
Virginia	16	District	May 28, 1863	5 Occupied	2 Disrupted
Alabama	9	District	August 3, 1863	2 Disrupted	
Texas	6	District	August 3, 1863	Unoccupied	
Tennessee	11	GT/District[2]	August 6, 1863	5 Occupied	3 Disrupted
Florida	2	District	October 5, 1863	Unoccupied	
Mississippi	7	District	October 5, 1863	1 Occupied	4 Disrupted
Georgia	10	District	October 7, 1863	Unoccupied	
South Carolina	6	District	October 20, 1863	Unoccupied	
Arkansas	4	District	November 4, 1863[3]	3 Occupied	
Louisiana	6	GT/District[2]	November 4, 1863	3 Occupied	1 Disrupted
North Carolina	10	District	November 4, 1863	Unoccupied	
Kentucky	12	GT/District[4]	February 10, 1864	12 Occupied	
Missouri	7	GT/District[4]	May 2, 1864	7 Occupied	

[1] Based on status at time of election. See Maps 18 and 20 in Chapter 3.

[2] Voters in Tennessee were from unoccupied counties and soldiers and refugees located inside and outside of the state. Voters in Louisiana were from unoccupied counties and possibly soldiers and refugees located inside and outside of the state. All voters could select one candidate in each district, that is, a general ticket election by district. See the discussion of the Louisiana and Tennessee Second Congress elections.

[3] Special election held for the occupied Fourth District on April 2, 1864. See Arkansas Second Congress election.

[4] Voters in Kentucky and Missouri were soldiers and refugees located outside of the state. All voters could select one candidate in each district, that is, a general ticket election by district. See the discussion of the Kentucky and Missouri Second Congress elections.

Texas—August 3, 1863

Texas was unoccupied at the time of the August 1863 elections and throughout the war.[62] On the first Monday in August elections were held for governor, lieutenant governor, the legislature, and Congress. The elections were held in the regular manner and two-way races occurred in all six districts. The vote total for the Houses races was 29,935, a 32.1 percent turnout. This is slightly less the 31,045 polled in the governor's race.[63] The internal participation rate was probably good, considering Texas soldiers outside of the state were not allowed to vote.

All House incumbents ran for reelection, but only three were victorious. This changed the House composition from five former Democrats and one Whig to two Democrats, one Whig, and three unknown. The delegation went from an unanimous secessionist group to four secessionists, one Unionist, and one unknown. The defeat of the incumbents cannot be definitively attributed to any general cause or issue.[64] Each district had its own characteristics and each candidate his own personality. Texas did not have a two-year-term senator, so the two secessionist former Democrats remained. In general, Texans felt far from the major theater of war,

cut off from the South by Yankee control of the Mississippi River, and saw themselves as a supplier of men and material to the eastern front to the detriment of the western front and the Native American frontier.

Tennessee—August 6, 1863

The regular Tennessee state elections were usually held in August of each odd-numbered year. Most of western and middle Tennessee was occupied in early 1862 by federal movements down the Mississippi and Cumberland rivers prior to the battle of Shiloh. The Tennessee capital at Nashville was occupied on February 25, 1862. By early 1863 Tennesseeans and the Confederate Congress realized that special considerations would have to be made to conduct the upcoming Tennessee state and House elections. On May 1, 1863, the Confederate government approved an electoral system for Tennessee House elections.[65] The statute provided for a general ticket form of election, that is, "each voter shall be entitled to vote one ticket containing the names of one person for each Congressional District in said State; and the persons receiving the greatest num-

ber of votes of the whole of the State, shall be commissioned as Representatives by the Governor." The statute further established the first Thursday in August as election day and established the right of soldiers and refugees to participate.

Three weeks after the statute was passed, Gov. Isham Harris called for a nominating convention for June 17 in the town of Winchester in unoccupied eastern Tennessee. This convention put forward a ticket for the gubernatorial and House elections. In the House elections the final vote revealed two-way contests in six of the eleven districts and no opposition in five. As determined by the official vote returns, 14,070 men participated in the general ticket election. This number is determined by the district election attracting the highest number of individual votes. This district, the Fifth, had a highly contested election featuring the famous incumbent Unionist Henry S. Foote, who was an outspoken personal and political enemy of Jefferson Davis and the Davis Administration. It is important to note that Foote received a majority of the civilian vote and his opponent the majority of the army vote. The other two instances where this occurred was in the Fourth and Seventh Districts where Unionists also won the civilian vote but lost the soldier vote.

The 14,070 figure is a scanty 7.8 percent of the 1860 estimated Tennessee electorate. In the 1863 elections 57.3 percent of all votes came from twenty-nine unoccupied counties concentrated in the eastern portion of the state. Map 30 illustrates the location of these counties in the remaining portion of Confederate Tennessee. The other 42.7 percent of the votes came from military units. Appendix V, a detailed county-by-county and military camp breakdown of the vote in this election, illustrates the unoccupied county and military vote reporting prevalent in the Civil War South. The strong military presence was probably responsible for keeping the Tennessee's delegation with a secessionist and Democratic majority. The former Democrat numbers increased from six to seven and the secessionist numbers increased from three to four. This retention and even increase in secessionist Democrat strength is unlike most other states and the nation as a whole. The same Tennessee senators served in the First and Second Congresses.

Florida—October 5, 1863

Florida is one of the five states classified neither unoccupied nor disrupted for the Second Congress elections, even though Union troops controlled some parts of the coast. The one incumbent won comfortably in a two-way race and an open seat was won by a 31 percent plurality in a four-way race. Both winning candidates were again secessionist former Democrats. The unoccupied statutes of the state and soldier voting from military camps and military precincts put the participation rate at 41.9 percent—the second highest in the 1863 Confederate elections.[66] The split delegation and alignment of the Florida senators also remained the same when the Unionist former Whig was reelected.

Mississippi—October 5, 1863

The Union strategy to control the Mississippi River and divide the Confederacy had a direct impact upon the state of Mississippi. Vicksburg became the main focus of the river campaign, and its final siege began May 18, 1863. As part of the maneuvering for the river and Vicksburg Union general Ulysses Grant temporarily occupied the Mississippi capital at Jackson on May 14. The final surrender of Vicksburg on July 4, 1863, put the major river points in Mississippi in Union hands. At the time of the October elections the river district is classified occupied and four others disrupted by Union action. However, since most of the counties were still functioning, the state government decided to go forward with elections in the usual time, places, and manner.

On October 5, 1863, statewide elections were held for governor, numerous other state offices, the legislature, and Confederate House seats. Research was conducted in the Mississippi Department of Archives and History, newspapers of the day, writings of historians of the state, and secondary sources for these elections returns, but only two of the six House district vote counts were found.[67] The five missing district counts make up the largest piece of missing data in the Second Confederate elections. Detailed county-by-county results for the governor and other statewide offices were found. A total of 23,920 votes were cast in the governor's race, which Charles Clark won in a three-way contest.[68] Surprisingly, only four counties did not report any returns, and only four others had very low counts. In the two House districts where returns were found, an average of 4,000 participated. There were four two-way races, one district with no opposition, and two districts can not be determined without the final vote count. Considering the available district returns and the governor's vote, an estimated twenty to twenty-two thousand participated in the House elections. This is about a quarter of the eligible voters, a rate in contrast with over half of the electorate voting in the 1861 elections, the all-time highest Confederate participation rate.

The results of the House, governor, and other state elections show a movement away from the previous ultra-secessionist sentiment.[69] Two Unionist former Whigs replaced secessionist former Democrats in the Second and Seventh Districts. In the Senate, two-year-term secessionist former Democrat James Phelan withdrew after the thirty-first ballot after being rejected by a Whig-oriented legislature.[70] Unionist former Whig John Watson took Phelan's seat. In 1861 Mississippi was one of the most belligerent Deep South pros-ecessionist states, and the softening of its political resolve in 1863 is noteworthy.[71]

Georgia—October 7, 1863

In 1863 Georgia was still untouched by large-scale Union military destruction. A total of 55,644 civilians and soldiers voted in the House elections, 44.4 percent of the electorate. This was by far the largest participation in the second Confederate congressional elections (see Table 4-2). There was growing discontent in Georgia over the course of the war and its effects upon the state. Georgia was a relatively populous state with numerous available undamaged resources near the major theaters of combat. Conscription, impressment, war casualties, and general economic deprivation all hit Georgia especially hard. There was resentment against the Confederate government as represented by President Davis and Congress. Gov. Joseph E. Brown was a foe of many of the "dictatorial" measures of the Davis Administration and Congress, although he remained steadfastly pro-Confederate and state rights.

On October 7, 1863, statewide elections were held for governor, state offices, and the ten Confederate House seats. The war and the presence of popular antiadministration Governor Brown in the campaign had a role in the election results. Brown won by a large margin, and nine out of ten House incumbents were not returned to Congress. This virtual clean sweep was the largest turnover in the second congressional elections. Interestingly, the state political alignment changed only slightly in spite of this large member turnabout. The party alignment remained similar, with four former Whigs, three Democrats, and three unknowns, but the Unionist group increased from one to five with three secessionists and two unknowns. The contests in each district produced mixed results with respect to the war, support of the Davis Administration, and political background of the winning candidate. In spite of the lessening of enthusiasm for the war, the election has been interpreted as more of an anti-incumbent feeling and a desire to see new faces rather than total abandonment of the Confederacy and the war effort.[72] This interpretation probably has some validity since the Georgia delegation has one of the lowest prowar voting records in the First Congress and they were still defeated.[73]

In the Senate election the class-one seat of incumbent Herschel V. Johnson was up for reelection. Although a Unionist former Democrat, Johnson supported the Davis Administration and measures to press the war effort vigorously. Antiadministration forces in the legislature fought against him, but the legislature finally reelected him. His victory in the face of opposition was another instance of Georgia's ambivalence about the administration and the war.[74]

South Carolina—October 20, 1863

South Carolina was unoccupied in 1863, although the federals captured Port Royal early in the war and controlled a number of sea islands including some near Charleston. The House elections on Tuesday October 20, 1863, were the only contests on the ballot. Five of the six incumbents were reelected, with three incumbents having no opposition. The election was reported in the *Richmond Dispatch* the next day with the following short item "CHARLESTON, Oct. 21st.—The Congressional elections passed off quietly yesterday. There being no opposition to Hon. Wm. Porcher Miles in the 2d dis-trict, he was unanimously re-elected. Affairs as usual at the batteries."[75] Vote totals have been found in all three districts where there were contested races. The turnout in the First and Fifth districts was 2,438 and 4,365 respectively.

There was one congressional race that did not pass quietly, the hotly contested and widely reported race in the Third District.[76] This contest was between incumbent Lewis A. Ayer and the well-known outspoken ultra-secessionist owner and editor of the *Charleston Mercury*, Robert Barnwell Rhett. Rhett was critical of Jefferson Davis's personal competence and the general handling of the war. While also critical of the administration on some issues, Ayer won the election over obstructionist Rhett. The newspapers of the day simply reported the results as a "504 vote majority for Ayer."[77]

South Carolina did not have a two-year class-one senator, and it kept the same two secessionist former Democrats throughout the war; therefore it returned another unanimous secessionist former Democrat House and Senate delegation. South Carolina was the only state to have such an alignment in both the First and Second Congresses. This does not mean that there was no discontent by 1863 in South Carolina or that the congressional delegation was completely supportive of the Davis Administration. The Ayer versus Rhett contest reveals that opposition to the administration's conduct of the war and the status of the economy came from those who believed the war was not waged vigorously enough as well as those who believed war measures too extreme.

Louisiana—November 4, 1863

The capture of New Orleans in April 1862 represented the first large area of the Deep South to fall to Union forces. The Union objective was to control the outlet of the Mississippi River system and to use New Orleans as a base to capture the entire river and thereby divide the South. By mid-May 1862 federal troops occupied the Louisiana capital, Baton Rouge, and the Confederate state government relocated fifty miles westward to Opelousas. By early 1863 the Union forces consolidated their hold on the parishes in the three lower Mississippi River districts and disrupted the Fourth District. The Confederate Congress, realizing the permanent nature of the situation, passed a special election law on May 1, 1863, allowing Louisiana to conduct elections for "members of Congress for any districts… in which an election can not be conveniently held in consequence of the same being occupied wholly or in part by the troops of the enemy, on proclamation of the Governor of said State, be chosen by the qualified voters thereof, in such portions of the State as shall not be so occupied."[78] The wording of this election law is slightly different from the comprehensive general ticket law passed for Tennessee by the Congress on the same day.[79] The Louisiana state legislature confirmed that state elections were to be held in unoccupied territory and set the time and manner of polling.[80] The official final vote returns report that citizens of all parishes voted for all

House candidates in each district. In the end, the November Louisiana House election was held by general ticket in the same manner as the August Tennessee election.

The voter turnout in the 1863 elections was an extremely low 7,198, as determined by the largest vote count in the Third District. This number is similar to the total for the gubernatorial and other state office elections held on the same day.[81] The 8.3 percent congressional turnout is even more scanty considering there were also concurrent state elections and large portions of the state still had functional Confederate civil governments. Map 31 illustrates the parishes that did participate in the November 1863 elections. The low vote count indicates that soldiers may not have participated, although most sources claim that Louisiana provided for soldier voting. No evidence was found in the official returns or newspapers that solders voted, but many times these votes were combined with the appropriate parish (county) returns. Like other occupied states Louisiana had less competition in congressional elections than unoccupied states. Three of the six Louisiana districts had no opposition, and there were only three contested elections.

Although conscription exemptions were an issue in some areas, again the elections were reported as "passing quietly."[82] Those that did vote did not register an antiadministration or antiwar sentiment.[83] Louisiana returned all five incumbents seeking reelection and chose a secessionist former Whig in the other district. This kept the Louisiana delegation again unanimously secessionist with the former party alignment at four Whigs and two Democrats. Of course, the most populous and most antisecessionist portion of the state was the portion occupied by the North, which did not participate in this election. Neither of the senators was up for reelection, and the secessionist Senate delegation remained the same through the war.

North Carolina—November 4, 1863

North Carolina also held congressional elections on November 4, 1863, but the results were much different from those in Louisiana. Unionist sentiment was always strong in North Carolina, and by 1863 a radical and vocal peace movement had developed in the state. The North Carolina secessionists were even further challenged by a growing moderate Conservative party headed by pro-Confederate but anti-Davis Administration governor Zebulon Vance. Like Georgia, North Carolina was a populous unoccupied state with a number of resources available near the main theater of war in Virginia. The degradation of the economy, conscription, war casualties, and impressment gave the peace advocates support among the general populace.

The participation of Unionist-peace candidates in the November election further turned North Carolina away from the Democrats and secessionists. Seven of the ten House members were new to Congress. Nine out of the ten were Unionists prior to Fort Sumter or outright peace candidates.[84] Only one secessionist former Demo-

crat survived the election and he, Robert R. Bridges in the Second District, won by a scant seventeen votes. The campaign and results in North Carolina were the most radical of the Confederate Congress elections. They went beyond discussion of the competence and measures of the Davis Administration and the conduct and fortunes of war. Latent Unionist-peace sentiment, especially in the western portions of the state, had gone public, and at least half of the delegation sent to Richmond were outspoken critics of the war in the Second Congress.

North Carolina was essentially unoccupied except for strategic areas along the coast. Elections were held in the regular manner, and all ten districts had contested elections—six two-way contests and four multicandidate races. However, the civilian and military vote in this hotly contested election was 27.9 percent of the eligible electorate, a total of 38,150. Governor and other statewide office elections were not held in 1863, but in even-numbered years. The 1863 congressional totals were well below the approximately 75,000 voting in the 1862 governor's race and 72,500 in the 1864 governor's race.[85]

The Senate delegation remained split. A secessionist former Democrat held a four-year seat and remained one of the few North Carolinians to support the Davis Administration in Richmond throughout the war. A two-year seat was held by a Unionist former Whig, and in 1862 another Unionist Whig was elected to begin serving in the Second Congress.[86]

Arkansas—November 4, 1863, and April 4, 1864

Two months prior to the scheduled Second Congress elections in Arkansas, a large portion of the state was overrun by federal troops. Previous to the fall of Vicksburg, Arkansas counties were disrupted along the northern border and close by the Mississippi River. After the fall of Vicksburg in July 1863, Union troops moved permanently into interior Arkansas to consolidate their control of the Mississippi River and secure the Arkansas River. The strategic location at Fort Smith in northwest Arkansas was captured on September 1. The Arkansas capital, Little Rock, was occupied on September 10, 1863, and state government relocated to Washington in the southwest portion of the state. Southwest Arkansas was unoccupied for the remainder of the war, and Washington remained the refugee capital.

Within a few days after the relocation Gov. Harris Flanagin defiantly issued a proclamation ordering the regularly scheduled November 4, 1863, congressional elections to be held.[87] This proclamation "commanded" the sheriffs to hold the election "in the manner prescribed by law." According to the refugee capital paper, the *Washington Telegraph*, congressional elections were held in unoccupied counties on November 4. Research was conducted in the Arkansas History Commission, newspapers of the day, historians of the state, and secondary sources for these election returns, but they were not found.[88] This and the Mississippi returns are the only significant set of election data not found for the Second Congress elections.

The *Washington Telegraph* described the elections, the defeat of incumbent Grandison Royston in the Second District, and the election of Rufus K. Garland in the following manner. "CONGRESSIONAL ELECTION.—The election for members of Congress last Wednesday passed off very quietly. There seemed to be no excitement in any quarter, and in some places the greatest apathy was manifested. In this county even, where both candidates reside, the polls in one township were not opened. In a large portion of the district there has been no voting."[89] The paper attributed the apathy of the voters to the similarity of the candidates and the loss of Royston, whom it supported, to "personal and transient considerations." The harsh measures imposed by the Confederate government and war weariness may have also contributed to Royston's defeat.[90]

In spite of the ability to vote in the southwestern portion of the state the northeastern portion apparently could not hold even quasi-legitimate elections. To address this situation legislation was introduced in the Confederate Congress on January 27, 1864, by Rep. Thomas B. Hanly of the occupied northeast Fourth District. This legislation was approved February 15, 1864. The law required that a general ticket election be held in all future congressional elections beginning in 1865. Furthermore, it called for a special election to be held April 4, 1864, "for the districts in which elections were not held, (or if held, returns thereof were not made in pursuance of law,) at the election in November last."[91] The law made the method of the special election very clear—that is, a regular district election by unoccupied counties, soldiers and refugees choosing one person, not a general ticket election. The law did not specify which districts should hold this special election. A special election was held April 4, 1864, probably just for the Fourth District, with the majority of the votes coming from Arkansas regiments in the Army of Tennessee.[92] The final vote returns for the special election also have not been found.

The final results in Arkansas show that three of the four incumbents were returned, and the one defeated came from the part of the state least occupied and having the most civilian voting. The political alignment of the state changed only slightly since Unionist former Whig Garland won over Unionist former Democrat Royston. In the Senate the same delegation began the Second Congress since two-year-term member Robert Johnson was reelected in 1862.[93]

Kentucky—February 10, 1864

Kentucky was completely occupied for two years at the time of the Second Congress elections. The small Kentucky provisional government, that is, Gov. Richard Hawes and the state council, resided with Kentucky troops in the Army of Tennessee for most of the later part of the war.[94] The Confederate Congress passed legislation in 1862 allowing Kentucky to elect House members in a manner they selected, and a general ticket was again used as in the First Congress election. From headquarters at Macon, Georgia, the provisional government called for an election by soldiers and refugees for February 10, 1864.[95] This would be in time for the May 1864 convening of the Second Congress.

Throughout January 1864 nominations were placed in newspapers near army camps, and "conventions" were even held in some units to put forth slates or tickets.[96] Eventually contested elections took place in ten of the twelve districts. Balloting took place on the appointed date with a few refugees and primarily the Kentucky soldiers in the Army of Tennessee, mostly in the state of Georgia.[97] The results were an overwhelming return of the incumbents, nine out of twelve elected. Because of the large number of incumbents returned the political alignment of the delegation remained somewhat the same. However, in spite of their previous party affiliation or secession stance all of the Kentucky members were friends of the Davis Administration, except newly elected Humphery Marshall of the Eighth District. This level support for the war and Jefferson Davis was common in soldier voting.

Official "state" returns have not been found for this election.[98] Newspaper reports of the vote indicate over two thousand men participated in the balloting.[99] This is less than 1 percent of the supposed Kentucky electorate and the lowest number in any Confederate election. This sham election demonstrates not only the lengths to which state governments went to attempt to prove their legitimacy, but also the acceptance by the Confederate Congress and Confederate government of the diminished representativeness of members from Kentucky and Missouri.

Missouri—May 2, 1864

Missouri was the last state to hold elections to the Second Congress. The May 2, 1864, elections were held nearly three years after the Union occupation of the Missouri capital at Jefferson City. The exiled Confederate Missouri government originally retreated to the southern part of the state, then to Arkansas in 1862, and eventually to Marshall, Texas. After the death of Claiborne F. Jackson in late 1862, Gov. Thomas C. Reynolds headed the expatriate government to the end of the war.

Specifically, in preparation for the Second Congress elections and to keep some semblance of a government, in July 1863 Governor Reynolds ordered from the "Executive Department of the State of Missouri, Little Rock, Arkansas, Executive General Orders, No. 6" calling for the registry of Missouri voters in exile and in the army. In spite of announcements in the major newspapers in the unoccupied southwest and mailings to military units only two registrants complied.[100] Since the Second Congress elections were taking place throughout 1863 in other states and the convening of the Second Congress was scheduled for May 1864, Governor Reynolds requested Congress to establish a national Missouri election. On December 10, 1863, Missouri representatives George Vest and Caspar Bell intro-

duced such legislation, and on January 19, 1864, a general ticket election by soldier and refugee votes was approved.[101] The detailed election law set the date of balloting for the first Monday in May 1864 (May 2).

According to the "full official returns" reported in newspapers of the day, approximately 4,500 men participated in this election.[102] The Sixth District had the largest total vote at 4,583, 1.9 percent of the eligible prewar population of Missouri. According to a May 10 letter from Governor Reynolds to Jefferson Davis, seven to ten thousand participated in this election.[103] Since no official records verify this number the votes reported as official in the newspapers, well after the election date, are used.

There were contested elections in all districts, with three of the seven multicandidate races. Only two incumbents were reelected out of five receiving votes, and the Seventh District vacancy was filled. However, the delegation remained decidedly former Democrat, six with one unknown and decidedly secessionist, five with two unionists. As in Kentucky, Tennessee, Louisiana, and other occupied areas the secessionist friends of the administration did well in Missouri. The Missouri Senate delegation completely changed from the First Congress. This is noteworthy since Missouri did not even have a rump legislature to elect these individuals and the provisional government was entirely run by the executive branch. The four-year senator Robert Peyton died in 1863 and Governor Reynolds appointed a friend of the Davis Administration and Unionist former Democrat, Waldo Johnson, to fill the seat. The two-year senator John Clark was not reappointed by the governor because he was not a friend of the administration. Eventually a Missouri representative, secessionist former Democrat George Vest from the Fifth District, was elevated to the Senate. Like the appointment of Missouri representatives to the First Congress, the appointment of the Missouri senators was conducted in a legally questionable manner, and the acceptance of these congressmen demonstrates the delusions of the Confederacy and the lengths it would go to stretch its reach throughout the slaveholding states.

National Results

Occupied Areas

The North occupied large areas of the South between the November 1861 House elections and the various elections in 1863–1864. Because the Second House elections were held on ten different dates, each state is analyzed with respect to the occupied conditions at the date of the election. Six of the thirteen Confederate states were free of major Union occupation at the time of their House elections, two were totally occupied, and five states had one or more districts occupied.[104] Electorally, occupied districts in these five states are further divided into two categories, wholly occupied districts and occupied districts with some counties reporting votes.

Map 32 illustrates the geographic aspects of the electoral method of the Second House elections. Sixty-one congressional districts, 57.6 percent, were substantially unoccupied at the time of the election. Of course, even these districts had a full range of participation and circumstances. Some unoccupied districts had all counties reporting, but there were numerous instances of unoccupied districts with one or more counties not reporting. Some districts designated unoccupied had several counties under various stages of Union disruption, including Union control of strategic parts of the coastline. Of course, unoccupied districts in Texas and parts of the Deep South were relatively free in 1863, while other unoccupied districts bordering the North or occupied South were threatened or previously disrupted.[105]

Forty-five congressional districts, 42.4 percent of the total House, elected representatives under extraordinary circumstances in the Second Congress. Nineteen of these districts were in the only two wholly occupied states Kentucky (twelve districts) and Missouri (seven districts). These two states elected their representatives by general ticket entirely by a small number of soldiers and refugees located wholly outside of the state. Tennessee (eleven districts) and Louisiana (six districts) elected their representatives by statewide general ticket by the votes of unoccupied counties, plus soldier and refugee votes inside and outside of the state. A total of seventeen districts elected their representatives in this manner.

Nine occupied districts were in states that continued to use the regular district method of election. Four of these nine districts were wholly occupied and held elections by soldiers and refugees located entirely outside of the district: the three northwestern Virginia districts and probably the Fourth District of Arkansas. The remaining five districts, Virginia Ninth and Tenth, Mississippi Fourth, and probably Arkansas First and Third, were occupied, but bravely a few counties in the district actually reported civilian votes to go with the soldier and refugee votes of the occupied counties.

Competition

Electoral competition information is available for all but four of the districts in the Second House balloting (Table 4-13). This is a large increase in known districts over the First House in spite of the disruption of the war. Electoral competition continued to be strong in 1863. Table 4-14 indicates that overall uncontested elections were slightly below the 1861 and even prewar levels. Table 4-15 indicates uncontested elections have a tendency to occur more often in occupied districts and in general ticket states. Multicandidate Confederate contests remain at about a quarter of all races, again well above the prewar levels. The number of multicandidate races in the first election were probably actually higher than a quarter because of the number of unknown races. However, the 22.6 percent national figure in 1863 again probably indicates continued fluidity and openness of the Confederate electoral system especially with respect to prewar

TABLE 4-13

Election Method and Competition[1]
Second Confederate House of Representatives Elections

State[2]	Districts	Method	Uncontested Elections	Two-way Races	Multicandidate Elections[3]	Unknown
Alabama	9	District	-	6	3	-
Arkansas	4	District	-	1	1	2
Florida	2	District	-	1	1	-
Georgia	10	District	-	5	5	-
Kentucky	12	GT/District[4]	2	6	4	-
Louisiana	6	GT/District[5]	3	2	1	-
Mississippi	7	District	1	4	-	2
Missouri	7	GT/District[4]	-	4	3	-
North Carolina	10	District	-	6	4	-
South Carolina	6	District	3	3	-	-
Tennessee	11	GT/District[5]	5	6	-	-
Texas	6	District	-	6	-	-
Virginia	16	District	3	11	2	0
Total	106		17	61	24	4
			(16%)	(57.6%)	(22.6%)	(3.8%)

[1] Competition determined by data found in Appendix IV.

[2] Congressional elections held in 1863 except in Kentucky, Missouri, and the Fourth District of Arkansas, which were held in 1864. See Table 4-12.

[3] Districts with three or more candidates receiving 5 percent or more of the total vote.

[4] Voters in Kentucky and Missouri were soldiers and refugees located outside of the state. All voters could select one candidate in each district, that is, a general ticket election by district. See the discussion of the Kentucky and Missouri Second Congress elections.

[5] Voters in Tennessee were from unoccupied counties and soldiers and refugees located inside and outside of the state. Voters in Louisiana were from unoccupied counties and possibly soldiers and refugees located inside and outside of the state. All voters could select one candidate in each district, that is, a general ticket election by district. See the discussion of the Louisiana and Tennessee Second Congress elections.

TABLE 4-14

Election Method and Competition[1]
36th U.S. House of Representatives Elections
First and Second Confederate House of Representatives Elections

Congress	Districts	Uncontested Elections	Two-way Races	Multicandidate Elections[2]	Unknown	Appointed
U.S. 36th (%)	83	15 (18.1)	65 (78.3)	2 (2.4)	1 (1.2)	-
C.S.A. First (%)	106	20 (18.9)	30 (28.3)	27 (25.5)	22 (20.7)	7 (6.6)
C.S.A. Second (%)	106	17 (16)	61 (57.6)	24 (22.6)	4 (3.8)	-

[1] Competition determined by data found in Appendix IV and interpreted in Tables 4-6, 4-7, and 4-12.

[2] Districts with three or more candidates receiving 5 percent or more of the total vote.

Voter Turnout

By 1863 the war devastated Confederate civil society in Missouri, Kentucky, Louisiana, Arkansas, Tennessee, and much of northern and western Virginia. This reduced electoral participation to low and, in the case of Kentucky and Missouri, minuscule numbers (see Table 4-2). The electoral participation in the remaining states dropped from the already low 1861 levels, which were in turn well below prewar levels. Only Georgia had a higher vote count in 1863 than in 1861, in part because of the strong anti-incumbent–antiadministration sentiment in the state. The soldier vote made up much of the total vote in 1863, especially in the five devastated states listed above. The soldier vote supported prowar proadministration candidates at a level greater than comparable civilian vote. In the cases in which detailed tallies of the vote are available the soldier proportion of the absentee soldier and refugee total was consistently in the 95–99 percent range. The number of refugee white males not in the army and voting was always quite small.

Former Political Party

The former political party composition of the House changed as a result of the Second Congress elections (Tables 4-16 and 4-17). The number of former Democrats went down from sixty-four to fifty, 60.4 percent to less than a clear majority of 47.6 percent. The number of former Whigs increased slightly from thirty-four to forty, 32.4 percent to 38.1 percent. Map 33 indicates former Whig strength increased in North Carolina, Georgia, and Alabama, especially in the southern Appalachian areas. North Carolina was the only state in either election nearly to elect an entire former Whig House delegation. The number of unknown affiliations nearly doubled from 7.6 percent to 14.2 percent, eight to fifteen.

There were fifty new members in the Second House. An analysis of just these newly elected members shows a dramatic change in the political alignment formerly dominated by secessionist Democrats (Table 4-18). In the nonincumbent group former Whigs outnumbered former Democrats twenty-three to seventeen and unionists outnumbered secessionists twenty-eight to sixteen. Unionist former Whigs were the largest single group in the newly elected representatives, and they altered the general congressional alignment away from former Democrats-secessionists toward former Whigs-unionists and new faces. This reflects disenchantment over the war, especially in districts in certain states with free voting and a large civilian proportion of the total vote. Table 4-15 shows that former Democrats outpolled Whigs twenty-three to fifteen in general ticket and occupied districts, but Whigs were just about even in unoccupied districts.

The shift in the Senate followed the same trend as the elected House. The number of former Democrats was reduced from twenty to seventeen, 76.9 percent to 65.4 percent (see Table 4-16). The number of former Whigs increased by the three lost above, from six to

levels. The number of known two-way races doubled in 1863. Part of this doubling is clearly because the number of unknown races was reduced to a small number and because Missouri relied on elections rather than appointment. However, the growing number of two-way races may also indicate some stabilization of the electoral system after the turmoil and instability of immediate postsecession period.

TABLE 4-15

Election Method/Status of Districts and Electoral Outcome
Second Confederate House of Representatives

Electoral Competition

Election Method/ Status	Districts	No Opposition (%)	Two-way Races (%)	Multicandidate Elections (%)	Unknown (%)
GT/Occupied	45	12 (26.7)	21 (46.7)	10 (22.2)	2 (4.4)
Regular/ Unoccupied	61	5 (8.2)	40 (65.6)	14 (22.9)[1]	2 (3.3)
Total	106	17 (16)	61 (57.6)	24 (22.6)	4 (3.8)

Former Political Party

Election Method/ Status	Districts	Former Democrat (%)	Former Whig (%)	Unknown(%)	Vacant (%)
GT/Occupied	45	23 (51.1)	15 (33.3)	7 (15.6)	-
Regular/ Unoccupied	61	27 (44.3)1	25 (41)	8 (13.1)	1 (1.6)
Total	106	50 (47.2)	40 (37.7)	15 (14.2)	1 (0.9)

Secession Stance

Election Method/ Status	Districts	Secessionists (%)	Unionists (%)	Unknown (%)	Vacant
GT/Occupied	45	25 (55.6)	14 (31.1)	6 (13.3)	-
Regular/ Unoccupied	61	29 (47.5)	28 (45.9)[1]	3 (4.9)	1 (1.6)
Total	106	54 (50.9)	42 (39.6)	9 (8.5)	1 (0.9)

Incumbency

Election Method/ Status	Districts	Incumbents Returned	Percent
GT/Occupied	45	30	66.7
Regular/ Unoccupied	61	26[1]	42.6
Total	106	56	52.8

[1] In the Third District of Alabama nonincumbent Unionist former Democrat Williamson R. W. Cobb won in a three-way race. He was expelled by the Second Congress for disloyalty and was never seated. The results of the Alabama Third District are known, and for consistency with other tables the results are used to calculate the electoral results, that is, competition and incumbency, but not the characteristics within Congress, that is, former political party and secession stance.

nine, 23.1 percent to 34.6 percent. Two of the three changes came in Alabama, which went from a total Democrat to total Whig delegation, the only state to send two former Whigs to the Senate. The Democrats held their own in previous one-party Democrat states such as South Carolina, Texas, and Arkansas and in the "appointed" states, Kentucky and Missouri, where no legislature existed.

Secession Stance

Secessionists are defined as those favoring secession prior to Fort Sumter and the call for Union troops by President Lincoln. Two years after Fort Sumter this characteristic probably still gives some important information regarding general national trends. Tables 4-16 and 4-19 indicate the number of House secessionists went down from sixty-four to fifty-four, 60.4 percent to a bare majority of 50.9%. Conversely, the number of former Unionists increased approximately 10 percent from 31.1 percent to 39.6 percent, thirty-three to

TABLE 4-16

Former Political Party and Secession Stance
Second Confederate Congress

House of Representatives

	Secessionist	Unionist	Unknown	Vacant	Total Party
Former Democrat	40	7	3	-	50
Former Whig	6	32	2	-	40
Unknown	8	3	4	-	15
Vacant	-	-	-	1	1
Total Secession Stance	54	42	9	1	106

Senate

	Secessionist	Unionist	Unknown	Vacant	Total Party
Former Democrat	13	4	-	-	17
Former Whig	1	8	-	-	9
Unknown	-	-	-	-	-
Vacant	-	-	-	-	-
Total Secession Stance	14	12	-	-	26

TABLE 4-17

Former Political Party
First and Second Confederate Congresses

House of Representatives

	Democrat Former Democrat (%)	Opposition Former Whig (%)	Unknown (%)	Vacancy (%)	Total Seats
36th U.S. Congress	55 (66.3)[1]	28 (33.7)	-	-	83
First Congress	64 (60.4)	34 (32.1)	7 (6.6)	1 (0.9)	106
Second Congress	50 (47.2)	40 (37.7)	15 (14.2)	1 (0.9)	106

Senate

	Former Democrat (%)	Opposition Former Whig (%)	Unknown(%)	Vacancy (%)	Total Seats
36th U.S. Congress	25 (96.2)[1]	1 (3.8)	-	-	26
First Congress	20 (76.9)	6 (23.1)	-	-	26
Second Congress	17 (65.4)	9 (34.6)	-	-	26

[1] Members identified as regular Democrat, Kenneth C. Martis, *The Historical Atlas of Political Parties in the United States Congress 1789–1989* (New York: Macmillan, 1989), p. 113.

TABLE 4-18

Former Political Party and Secession Stance
New Members of the Second House of Representatives

	Secessionist	Unionist	Unknown	Total
Former Democrat	10	6	1	17
Former Whig	3	19	1	23
Unknown	3	3	4	10
Total	16	28	6	50

Tennessee, the incumbents were returned in a higher proportion, 66.7 percent, than incumbents in unoccupied districts, 42.6 percent (Table 4-15). Fifty members of the First House did not return to the Second House. Map 35 shows the largest regular election turnover was in unoccupied Georgia and North Carolina. Missouri had high turnover, which was surprising, especially considering the low turnover in other occupied area elections.

[1] In the 1861 secession-reorganization period the secession conventions served as the legislature for some states until new Confederate legislatures could be elected or the standing legislature could be called into session.

[2] *Journal of the Congress of the Confederate States of America*, Volume 2, First Congress, First Session, February 21, 1862, pp. 10–14.

[3] The only exception was Kentucky, which retained one American party senator, John J. Crittenton. Kenneth C. Martis, *The Historical Atlas of Political Parties in the United States Congress 1789–1989* (New York: Macmillan, 1989), pp. 112-113.

[4] Permanent Confederate Constitution, Article I, Section 2.

[5] *Statutes At Large of the Provisional Government of the Confederate States of America*, Session II, Chapter XXXIV, May 21, 1861.

[6] For an explanation of this procedure and the statistics see: U.S. Department of Commerce, *Historical Statistics of the United States* (Washington, D.C.: Government Printing Office, 1975), pp. 1067–1072.

[7] Permanent Confederate Constitution, Article I, Section 4.

[8] Since both the census records and polling books have names attached to their data, the two data sets can be correlated and analyzed where the polling books are preserved.

[9] Ringold states that only Arkansas and Alabama (1861 only), Georgia, North Carolina, Florida, South Carolina, Mississippi, and Virginia made allowances for soldier and refugee voting. May Spencer Ringold, *The Role of the State Legislatures in the Confederacy* (Athens: University of Georgia Press, 1966), pp. 65–66, 69–70. Added to this list are: specific allowance for soldier and refugee voting from the Confederate Congress for Tennessee in 1863; and all the voting in Kentucky and Missouri (1864) coming from soldier and refugees. *Statutes at Large*, First Congress, Session III, Chapter XCI, May 1, 1863, pp. 164–165. Yearns states "Of the eleven Confederate states in November 1861, Virginia, North Carolina, Alabama, Florida, and Tennessee had provisions for absentee voting by their soldiers." Wilfred Buck Yearns, *The Confederate Congress* (Athens: The University of Georgia Press, 1960), p. 42.

[10] *Historical Statistics*, p. 1068.

[11] *Congressional Quarterly's Guide to U.S. Elections* (Washington, D.C.: Congressional Quarterly, 1985), p. 335.

forty-two. Map 34 indicates that Unionist strength increased in North Carolina, Georgia, and Alabama and was concentrated in many Appalachian districts. Only a few Unionists elected to the Second House actually called for an immediate end of the war and reconstruction with the United States, such as those mentioned in the North Carolina section above. The majority of former Unionists still supported the Confederacy, but many were critical of the Davis Administration and were predisposed to a negotiated honorable settlement of the war.

As Table 4-16 indicates, there is again a strong correlation between former party and former secession stance. Three-quarters of the fifty-four secessionists were Democrats, and three-quarters of the forty-two Unionists were Whigs. There is also a correlation between method of election and secession stance (see Table 4-15). Secessionists ran well ahead of Unionists, twenty-five to fourteen, in general ticket and occupied districts. In unoccupied districts the number of Unionists elected was virtually the same as secessionists. Nevertheless, to better understand the roll-call voting patterns within Congress discussed in the next chapter it is important to note: there were a few Unionist Democrats and secessionist Whigs; and not all secessionist Democrats totally supported the conduct of the war while not all unionist Whigs were against the Davis Admin-

istration. For example, there were secessionist Democrats who were strong state rights advocates and against some of the harsh measures of the Davis Administration as well as a few ultra-secessionists who advocated even more stringent measures and were therefore against certain measures of the Davis Administration.[106]

The Senate, again, displayed the same trend as the elected House. Secessionists went down from eighteen to fourteen, 69.2 percent to 53.8 percent, while the Unionists increased from seven to twelve, 26.9 percent to 46.2 percent. There is the same correlation between former party and secession stance. In the First Senate sixteen of the eighteen secessionists were Democrats and in the Second Senate thirteen of the fourteen. Two states sent two Unionists to the Second Senate, Georgia and Alabama (see Map 34). This did not occur in the First Senate. In the First Senate six Deep South states sent two secessionist senators, while in the Second Senate this was reduced to three, South Carolina, Louisiana, and Texas.

Incumbency

In the Second House elections 53.8 percent of the incumbents were returned (Table 4-20). In the occupied districts in general, and especially in Kentucky, Arkansas, northwestern Virginia, Louisiana, and

TABLE 4-19

Secession Stance
First and Second Confederate Congresses

House of Representatives

	Secessionists (%)	Unionists (%)	Unknown(%)	Vacancy (%)	Total Seats
First Congress	64 (60.4)	33 (31.1)	8 (7.6)	1 (0.9)	106
Second Congress	54 (50.9)	42 (39.6)	9 (8.5)	1 (0.9)	106

Senate

	Secessionists (%)	Unionists (%)	Unknown(%)	Vacancy (%)	Total Seats
First Congress	18 (69.2)	7 (26.9)	1 (3.9)	-	26
Second Congress	14 (53.8)	12 (46.2)	-	-	26

TABLE 4-20

Members of the First House
Reelected to the Second House

State	Method	Districts	Incumbents Returned	Percent Returned	Rank[1]
Louisiana	General Ticket	6	5	83	1
South Carolina	District	6	5	83	1
Kentucky	General Ticket	12	9	75	3
Arkansas	District	4	3	75	4
Alabama	District	9	6	67	5
Tennessee	General Ticket	11	7	64	6
Mississippi	District	7	4	57	7
Virginia	District	16	8	50	8
Texas	District	6	3	50	9
Florida	District	2	1	50	10
North Carolina	District	10	3	30	11
Missouri	General Ticket	7	2	29	12
Georgia	District	10	1	10	13
Total		106	57	53.8	

[1] When two states are tied in percentage the state with the greater number of incumbents is ranked higher.

[12] *Ibid.*, pp. 762–764.

[13] Martis, *Atlas of Parties*, pp. 102–113.

[14] *Ibid.*, pp. 42-43.

[15] *Statutes At Large of the Provisional Government of the Confederate States of America*, Session II, Chapter XXXIV, May 21, 1861.

[16] Yearns, *Confederate Congress*, pp. 42–69. John B. Robbins, "Confederate Nationalism: Politics and Government in the Confederate South, 1861–1865," (Ph.D. diss., Rice University, 1964), First Congress, pp. 37–63 and Second Congress, pp. 191–223.

[17] Ezra J. Warner and W. Buck Yearns, *Biographical Register of the Confederate Congress* (Baton Rouge: Louisiana State University Press, 1975). Jon L. Wakelyn, *Biographical Dictionary of the Confederacy* (Westport, Connecticut: Greenwood Press, 1977). Richard N. Current, et al., eds., *Encyclopedia of the Confederacy* (New York: Simon & Schuster, 1993).

[18] Yearns, *Confederate Congress*, p. 42–43.

[19] The Whig party label became less common in the South by the mid-1850s. The Democratic opposition was replaced eclectically by the American (Know-Nothing) party (sometimes called the South Americans) and then replaced by the Constitutional Unionists and various opposition and Independent Democrat candidates. The term Whig in this chapter is a comprehensive term referring to those who are identified in the 1850s through 1860 with some sort of non-Democratic party affiliation or sentiment.

[20] Malcolm C. McMillan, *The Disintegration of a Confederate State* (Macon, Georgia: Mercer University Press, 1986), pp. 77–78.

[21] James M. Woods, "Devotees and Dissenters: Arkansas in the Confederate Congress, 1861–1865," *Arkansas Historical Quarterly* 38 (Autumn 1979): 227–237.

[22] Eventually the contester withdrew. Michael B. Dougan, *Confederate Arkansas: The People and Politics of a Frontier State in Wartime* (Montgomery: University of Alabama Press, 1976), pp. 81–82. *Encyclopedia of the Confederacy*, 1st ed. (1993), s.v. "Augustus Hill Garland," by Beverly Watkins.

[23] Warner and Yearns, *Biographical Register*, pp. 11–12, 170–171.

[24] T. Conn Bryan, *Confederate Georgia* (Athens: University of Georgia Press, 1953), p. 37.

[25] *New Orleans Bee*, November 30, 1861.

[26] There is an indication that Mississippi soldiers, at least those in the state, were allowed to vote, since John McRae of the Seventh District included army camps in his campaign swings. Yearns, *Confederate Congress*, p. 44. This would have enhanced the Mississippi total. See also footnote 9.

[27] Three of the five 1859 House races were uncontested elections, and this may account for the lower than normal turnout. The 1861 Confederate House election still had almost twenty thousand voters less than the 1860 U.S. presidential election. See Table 4-2.

[28] Wilson Angley, North Carolina Department of Cultural Resources, letter to author, October 4, 1991. Thomas E. Jeffrey, letter to author, January 27, 1992. Paul Escott, letter to author, November 11, 1991.

[29] A specific North Carolina example of this general tendency is the First House election vote results published in the *Fayetteville Observer*, November 18, 1861.

[30] *Charleston Mercury*, November 7, 1861.

[31] *Ibid.*, November 6, 1861, p. 3.

[32] This is not only shown by the 1859 and 1860 elections, but also the June 8, 1861, statewide secession vote. In this vote 104,913 voted for separation and 47,238 against separation, a 152,151 total. This total is slightly above the 1860 presidential vote. James W. Fertig, *The Secession and Reconstruction of Tennessee* (Chicago: University of Chicago Press, 1972), p. 27.

[33] These districts were not only strong Union areas in the 1860 presidential election, but actually elected loyal Unionists in the regularly scheduled August 1, 1861, state congressional vote. *Ibid.*, pp. 28-32. James W. Patton, *Unionism and Reconstruction in Tennessee, 1860–1890* (Chapel Hill: University of North Carolina Press, 1934), pp. 28–29. Three of the four loyalist representatives were actually seated in the U.S. Congress. Martis, *Atlas of Parties*, pp. 37, 115. Since the Confederate apportionment allocated more seats the state was redistricted and Confederate House elections held on November 6, 1861.

[34] *Republican Banner* (Nashville), October 29, 1861, as cited in John H. DeBarry, "Confederate Tennessee," (Ph.D. diss., University of Kentucky, 1967), p. 82.

[35] Dale Baum, "Texas Elections During the Civil War; Continuity or Change," paper delivered before the Social Science History Association, Washington, D.C., November 18, 1989, p. 11.

[36] Nancy Head Bowen, "A Political Labyrinth: Texas in the Civil War—Questions in Continuity," (Ph.D. diss., Rice University, 1974).

[37] Janet B. Schwarz, Virginia Historical Society, letter to author, July 23, 1992. Nelson D. Lankford, Virginia Historical Society, letter to author, October 31, 1991. Fredrick H. Armstrong, West Virginia Division of Culture and History, letter to author, December 19, 1991.

[38] This was a region of great agricultural wealth of the South and an area where destruction of private property and impressment issues became of great concern to the local population. See also the section in Chapter 3 on agricultural geography and the section in Chapter 5 on impressment.

[39] Date when the Confederate governor signed the effective legislation. *Journal of the Senate, Extra Session of the Rebel Legislature, Called by a Proclamation of C. F. Jackson, Begun and Held at Neosho, Newton County, Missouri, on the Twenty-first of October, 1861*, (Jefferson City: Emory S. Foster, 1865)), pp. 31–32.

[40] Two senators and seven representatives were apportioned to Missouri for the U.S. Congress in the 1850s. However, the Confederate apportionment gave thirteen representatives to Missouri (see Table 3-2 and accompanying text in Chapter 3). Seven representatives continued to be used in the elections to the Second Congress.

[41] Arthur R. Kirkpatrick, "Missouri's Delegation in the Confederate Congress," *Civil War History* 5 (1959): 188–198. See also *Journal of the Senate, Extra Session of the Rebel Legislature, Called by a Proclamation of C. F. Jackson, Begun and Held at Neosho, Newton County, Missouri, on the Twenty-first of October, 1861* (Jefferson City: Emory S. Foster, 1865).

[42] Of the seven House members chosen by the legislature, only six were seated. John

Hyer of the Seventh District never appeared in Richmond, and the district was vacant throughout the First Congress.

43 Arthur R. Kirkpatrick, "Missouri, the Twelfth Confederate State," (Ph.D. diss., University of Missouri, 1954), pp. 296–297.

44 Lowell H. Harrison, "Kentucky," in W. Buck Yearns, ed., *The Confederate Governors* (Athens: University of Georgia Press, 1985), p. 86.

45 Each of the ten councilmen "represented" one of the ten former U.S. congressional districts. A. C. Quisenberry, "The Alleged Secession of Kentucky," *Register of the Kentucky State Historical Society* 15 (May 1917): 27.

46 The Confederate government eventually fled Bowling Green on February 1, 1862, and, other than a short period in October 1862, never functioned again inside the state.

47 *Statutes at Large of the Provisional Government of the Confederate States of America*, Chapter XVI, December 21, 1861, pp. 226–227.

48 Lowell H. Harrison, "Kentucky," in Yearns, *Confederate Governors*, p. 86.

49 *Daily Appeal* (Memphis), January 30, 1862, p. 3, col. 3.

50 Ron Bryant, Kentucky Historical Society, letter to author, September 10, 1991. James A. Ramage, letter to author, November 14, 1991. John D. Smith, letter to author, October 29, 1991. Lowell H. Harrison, letter to author, November 26, 1991.

51 Table 4-2 indicates 278,260 voted in the eight states where full results are available. The following estimates were used for the three other states in which voting occurred: 47,500 for North Carolina; 58,000 for Virginia; and 20,000 for South Carolina. These estimates are based on averages in the districts where results are available and the vote for governor if elected at the same time. The total vote estimate is 403,760.

52 For a discussion of this breakdown and possible consequences see: David M. Potter, "Jefferson Davis and Political Factors in Confederate Defeat," in David Donald, ed., *Why the North Won the Civil War* (Baton Rouge: Louisiana State University Press, 1960), pp. 91–114; and Eric L. McKitrick, "Party Politics and the Union and Confederate War Efforts," in William N. Chambers and Walter Dean Burnham, eds., *The American Party Systems: Stages of Political Developments* (New York: Oxford University Press, 1967), pp. 117–151. See also Richard F. Bensel, *Yankee Leviathan: The Origins of Central State Authority in America, 1859–1877* (Cambridge: Cambridge University Press, 1990), pp. 228–230.

53 Richard E. Beringer et. al., *Why the South Lost the Civil War* (Baton Rouge: Louisiana State University Press, 1986), pp. 68–74.

54 See section above on Missouri First Congress elections.

55 Arkansas originally attempted to do this, but later held another soldier and refugee election for the occupied Fourth District. See the section below on the Second Congress elections in Arkansas.

56 Virginia State Archives, Poll Books, MSS., Election Record No. 433.

57 Yearns, *Confederate Congress*, pp. 53–54.

58 Alabama, Secretary of State, Elections and Registration Division, Series: Election Files, State and National, 1860–1866, Container S.G. 2475.

59 Ringold, *State Legislatures*, p. 70.

60 *Confederate Journal*, Volume 7, p. 12.

61 *Confederate Journal*, Volume 7, p. 276.

62 See the definition of unoccupied districts in Appendix II.

63 Bowen, "Labyrinth," p. 150.

64 Baum, "Continuity or Change?" pp. 17–21.

65 *Statutes at Large*, First Congress, Secession III, Chapter XCI, pp. 164–165.

66 *Governor's Proclamation Book*, Florida Archives, Series 21, Carton 51.

67 Mississippi Department of Archives and History, letter to author, August 11, 1992. Ray Skates, letter to author, November 19, 1991.

68 This is the revised vote total written on the official vote register. Mississippi, Department of Archives and History, RG 28, Box 35a, 1863.

69 A general discussion of the election is found in John K. Bettersworth, *Confederate Mississippi* (Philadelphia: Porcupine Press, 1978), pp. 51–55.

70 *Tri-Weekly Citizen*, November 28, 1863, p. 2, col. 1.

71 John Bettersworth provides an analysis of these electoral results: "It would be hardly justifiable to assume from the obviously conservative trend of the elections of 1863 that it was a contest between Fire-Eaters who wanted to continue the war and Unionists who wanted to submit to the North. There were Unionists of course, but there number was doubtless small; and, except in the few cases where they came armed to the polls, they seemed to be squelched by the loyal. What seems to be more likely to have been the case is that, as in other parts of the Confederacy where the chastening of war had been felt, there were in Mississippi those who hoped that an honorable peace could yet be achieved." *Confederate Mississippi*, p. 55.

72 Robbins, "Confederate Nationalism," pp. 201-207.

73 See the discussion of roll-call voting Confederate support scores in Chapter 5.

74 See comments in footnote 71.

75 *Richmond Dispatch*, October 22, 1863.

76 Charles Edward Cauthen, *South Carolina Goes to War 1860–1865* (Chapel Hill: University of North Carolina Press, 1950), pp. 212–214.

77 *Charleston Courier*, October 26, 1863, and November 10, 1863, as cited in Laura A. White, *Robert Barnwell Rhett: Father of Secession* (New York: Century, 1931), p. 234.

78 *Statutes at Large*, First Congress, Session III, Chapter LXXIX, May 1, 1863, pp. 157–158.

79 See the section above on the second Tennessee House election.

80 Louisiana Acts, Extra Session, 1863, pp. 9–10; as cited in Jefferson Davis Bragg, *Louisiana in the Confederacy* (Baton Rouge: Louisiana State University Press, 1941), p. 182.

81 *Ibid.*, p. 185.

82 *Ibid.*, p. 268.

83 This is similar to the vote in the general ticket election in Tennessee.

84 The only unknown House member was Samuel H. Christian in the Seventh District. He was a well-known peace leader in 1863, although his background prior to Fort Sumter is not fully documented.

85 John G. Barrett, *The Civil War in North Carolina* (Chapel Hill: University of North Carolina Press, 1963), pp. 183, 242.

86 Yearns, *Confederate Congress*, p. 54.

87 "Governor's Proclamation" as published in the *Washington Telegraph* (Arkansas) October 28, 1863.

88 John L. Ferguson, Arkansas History Commission, letter to author, June 20, 1991. Michael B. Dougan, letter to author, July 21, 1992.

89 *Washington Telegraph* (Arkansas) November 11, 1863. p. 1.

90 Dougan, *Confederate Arkansas*, pp. 122–123.

91 *Statutes at Large*, First Congress, Session IV, Chapter XXXVII, February 15, 1864, pp. 189–190.

92 The Atlanta *Daily Appeal* reported a candidate nomination for the Arkansas Fourth District special election on March 28, 1864. The *Richmond Sentinel* reported partial vote returns for three candidates in the Fourth District from Army of Tennessee Arkansas regiments on April 14, 1864, p. 2, col. 1. *The Journal of the Congress of the Confederate States of America*, Volume 7, cites legislation to cover the costs of transporting the Arkansas votes called for by the February 18, 1864, legislation.

There is one piece of strong evidence that the Third District did not participate in the special election. A replacement election was held on October 24, 1864, in the Third District for the seat of Augustus H. Garland, who was appointed to the Confederate Senate. In this election five of the thirteen counties were reported on the secretary of state's official returns (although two other counties claimed to vote), plus military units and some refugee votes. *Washington Telegraph*, November 16, 1864, p. 2, col. 3.

93 Yearns, *Confederate Congress*, p. 57.

94 Lowell H. Harrison, "Kentucky," in Yearns, *Confederate Governors*, p. 90.

95 Yearns, *Confederate Congress*, p. 58.

96 See, for example, items in the Atlanta *Southern Confederacy* on the following dates: January 27, 29, 30, 31, 1864.

97 Kentucky soldier voting was reported from Augusta, Dalton, Smith's Camp, Abingdon, Forsythe, Decatur, Marion, Marietta, plus Griffin, Atlanta, Grigsby's Brigade, Rome, and La Grange. Combined information from *The Sentinel* (Richmond) February 16, 1864, p. 2, col. 1 and *Montgomery Daily Mail*, February 27, 1864, p. 2, col. 3.

98 See the discussion of the Kentucky First House election and footnote 50.

99 The vote count in all of the districts except the First, which was one of the two uncontested races, was similar, and 2,094 votes were reported in the highest district, the Tenth.

100 Kirkpatrick, "Missouri," p. 315.

101 *Statutes at Large*, First Congress, Session IV, Chapter X, January 19, 1864, pp. 173–174.

102 *Southern Confederacy*, June 18, 1864. *Selma Morning Reporter*, June 16, 1864, p. 1, col. 5.

103 Reynolds to Jefferson Davis, May 10, 1864, Reynolds LB 4471, as cited in Arthur R. Kirkpatrick, "Missouri Delegation in the Confederate Congress," *Civil War History*, V (1959): 188–198.

104 See Appendix II for the specific criteria used to designate occupied, disrupted, and unoccupied districts.

105 Twelve districts are classified as disrupted at the time of the elections, and virtually all of these had a combination of unoccupied counties, usually the majority of all the counties, soldiers, and refugees making up the electorate. Except those in Tennessee and Louisiana, they are counted in the regular district election category on Map 32.

106 See the discussion on secession stance in the First Congress.

MAP 25

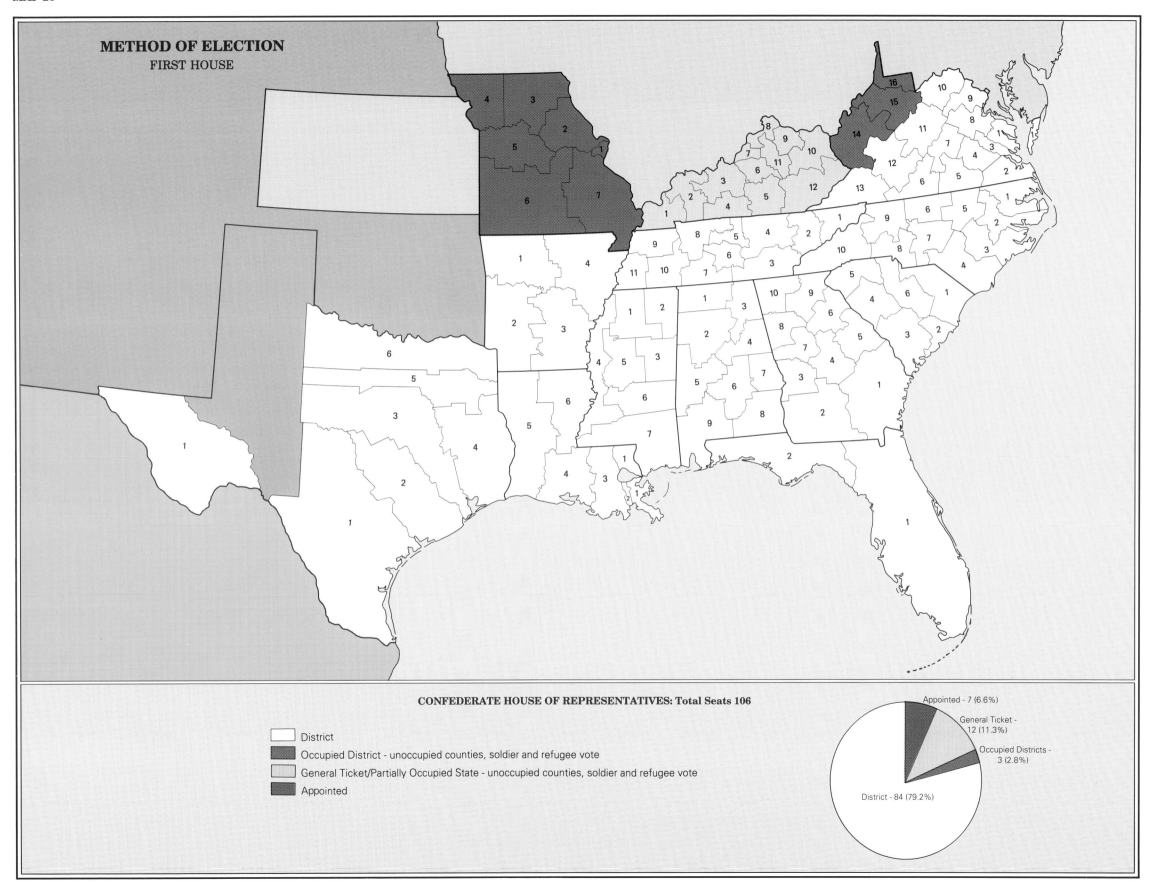

METHOD OF ELECTION
FIRST HOUSE

CONFEDERATE HOUSE OF REPRESENTATIVES: Total Seats 106

District

Occupied District - unoccupied counties, soldier and refugee vote

General Ticket/Partially Occupied State - unoccupied counties, soldier and refugee vote

Appointed

Appointed - 7 (6.6%)

General Ticket - 12 (11.3%)

Occupied Districts - 3 (2.8%)

District - 84 (79.2%)

MAP 26

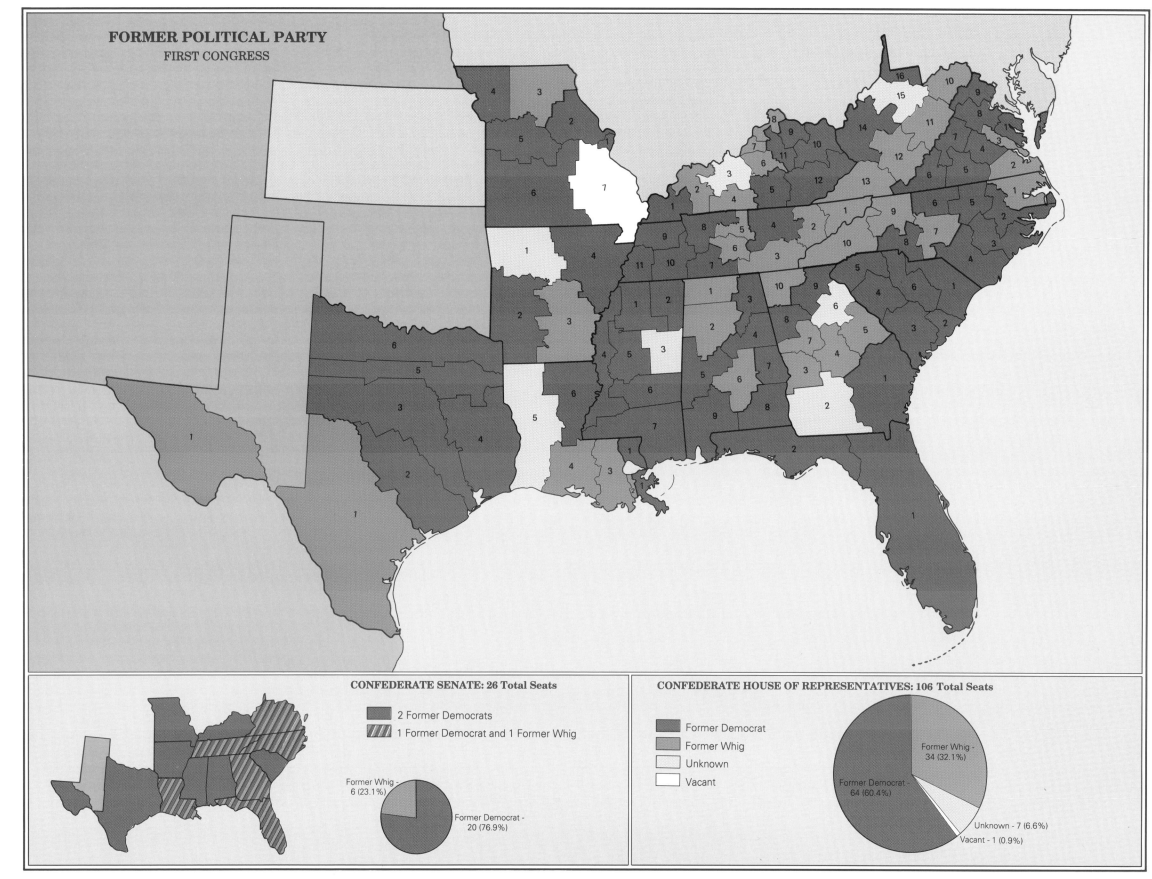

FORMER POLITICAL PARTY
FIRST CONGRESS

CONFEDERATE SENATE: 26 Total Seats

2 Former Democrats

1 Former Democrat and 1 Former Whig

Former Whig - 6 (23.1%)

Former Democrat - 20 (76.9%)

CONFEDERATE HOUSE OF REPRESENTATIVES: 106 Total Seats

Former Democrat

Former Whig

Unknown

Vacant

Former Whig - 34 (32.1%)

Former Democrat - 64 (60.4%)

Unknown - 7 (6.6%)

Vacant - 1 (0.9%)

MAP 27

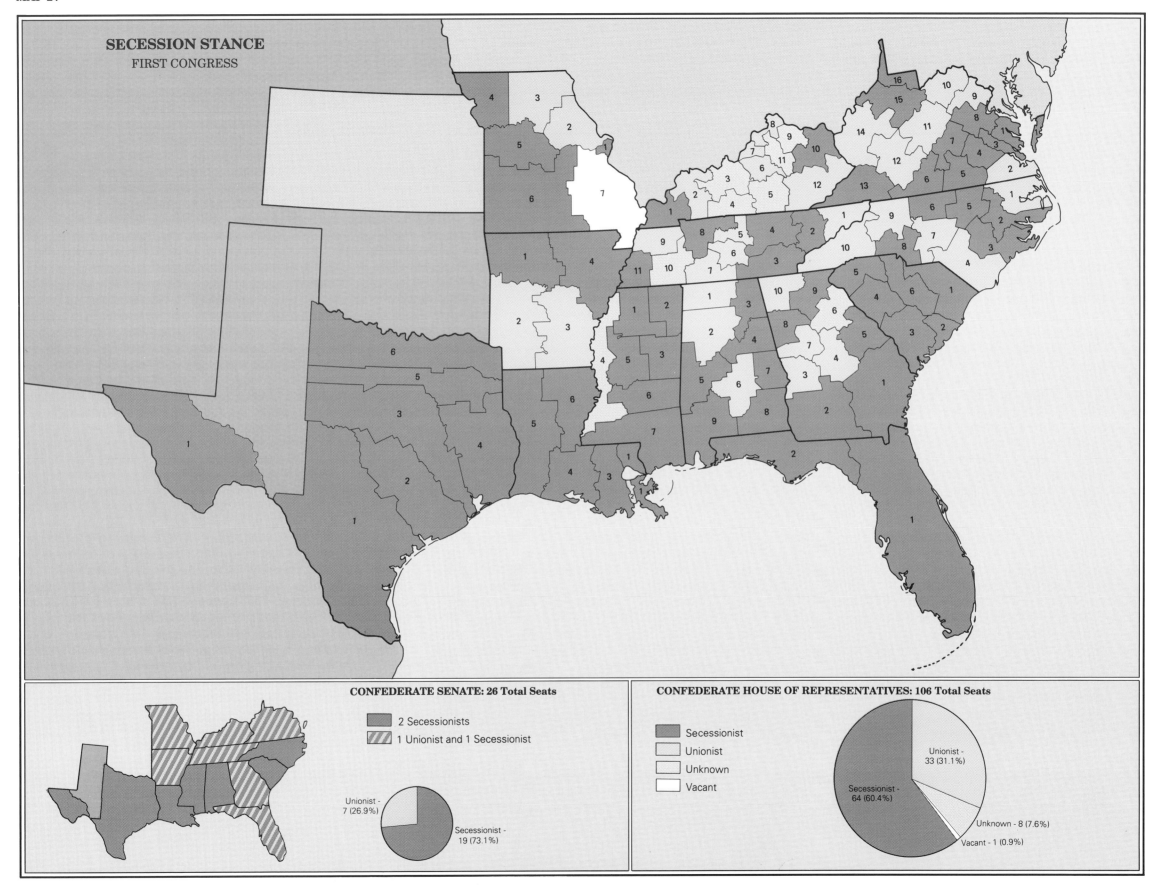

SECESSION STANCE
FIRST CONGRESS

CONFEDERATE SENATE: 26 Total Seats

■ 2 Secessionists
▨ 1 Unionist and 1 Secessionist

Unionist -
7 (26.9%)

Secessionist -
19 (73.1%)

CONFEDERATE HOUSE OF REPRESENTATIVES: 106 Total Seats

■ Secessionist
▢ Unionist
▢ Unknown
□ Vacant

Secessionist -
64 (60.4%)

Unionist -
33 (31.1%)

Unknown - 8 (7.6%)

Vacant - 1 (0.9%)

MAP 28

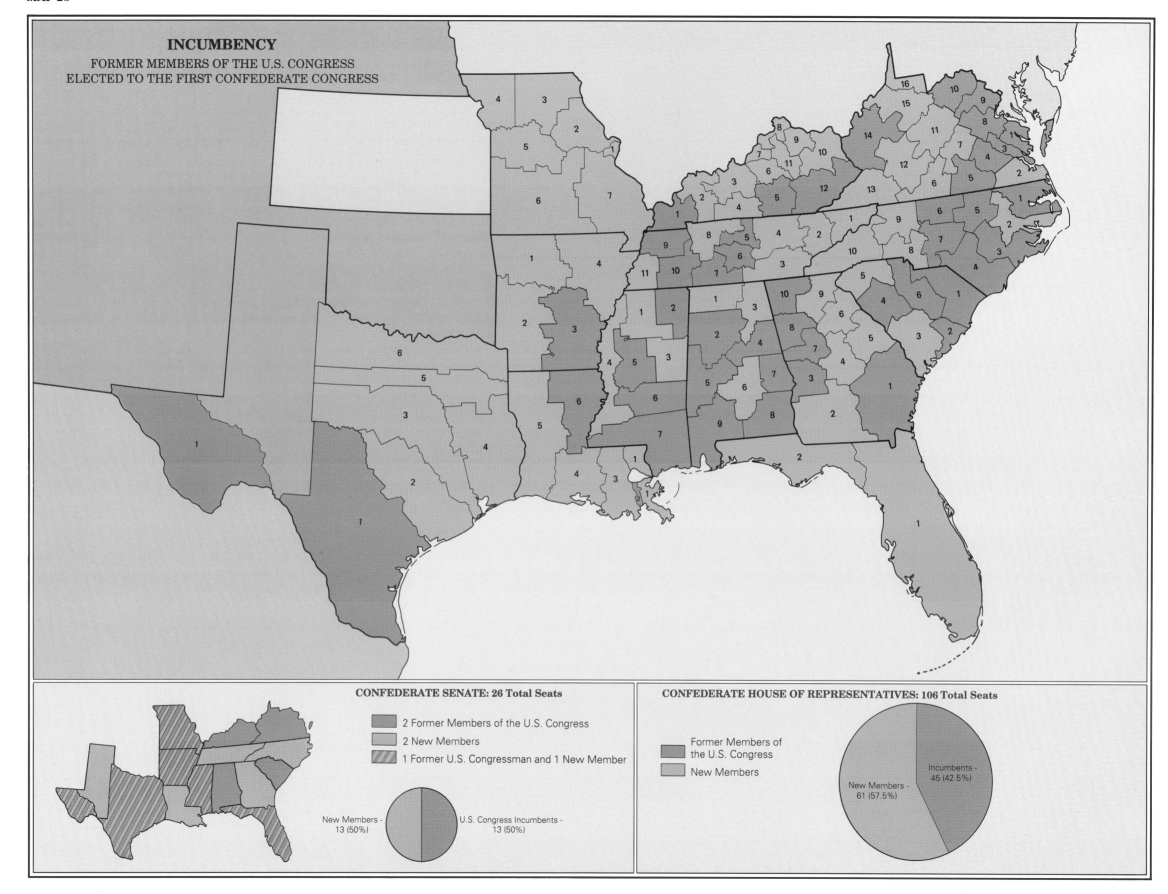

INCUMBENCY

FORMER MEMBERS OF THE U.S. CONGRESS
ELECTED TO THE FIRST CONFEDERATE CONGRESS

CONFEDERATE SENATE: 26 Total Seats

2 Former Members of the U.S. Congress

2 New Members

1 Former U.S. Congressman and 1 New Member

New Members -
13 (50%)

U.S. Congress Incumbents -
13 (50%)

CONFEDERATE HOUSE OF REPRESENTATIVES: 106 Total Seats

Former Members of
the U.S. Congress

New Members

Incumbents -
45 (42.5%)

New Members -
61 (57.5%)

MAP 29

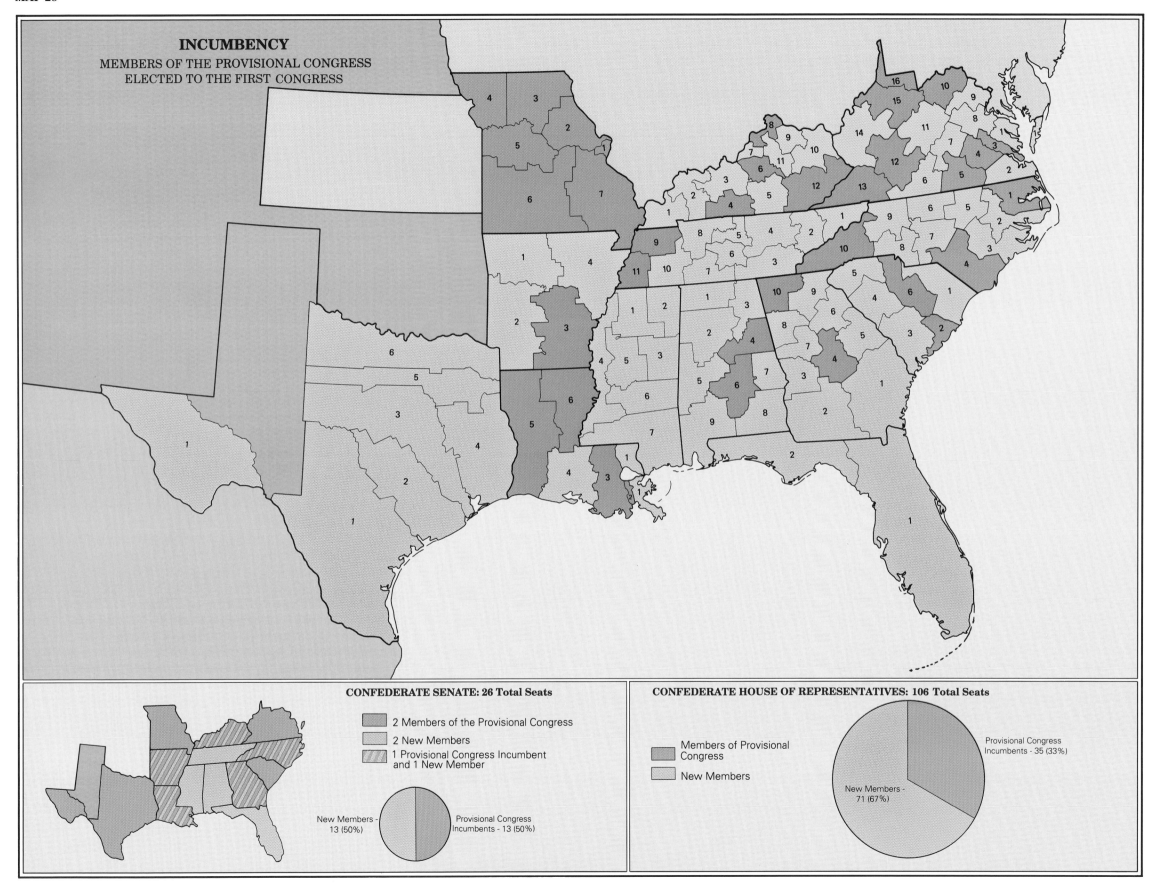

INCUMBENCY
MEMBERS OF THE PROVISIONAL CONGRESS
ELECTED TO THE FIRST CONGRESS

CONFEDERATE SENATE: 26 Total Seats

- 2 Members of the Provisional Congress
- 2 New Members
- 1 Provisional Congress Incumbent and 1 New Member

New Members -
13 (50%)   Provisional Congress
Incumbents - 13 (50%)

CONFEDERATE HOUSE OF REPRESENTATIVES: 106 Total Seats

- Members of Provisional Congress
- New Members

Provisional Congress
Incumbents - 35 (33%)

New Members -
71 (67%)

MAP 30

TENNESSEE CONFEDERATE CONGRESSIONAL ELECTIONS
AUGUST 6, 1863

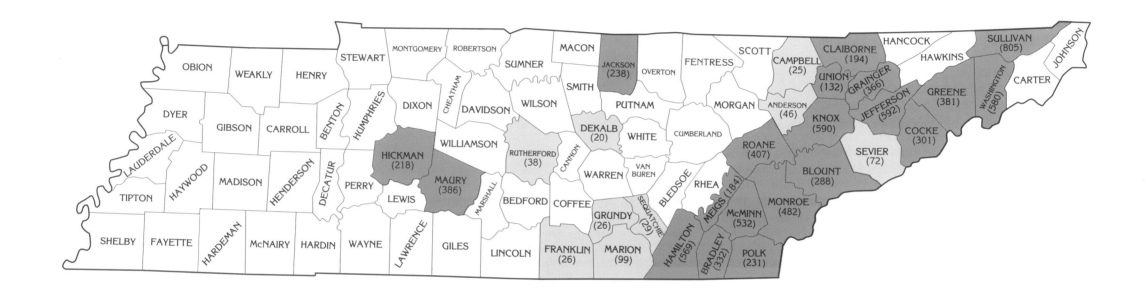

☐ 53 Counties - Occupied and/or No Returns

☐ 9 Counties - Partially Occupied and/or Disrupted

■ 20 Counties - Unoccupied and/or Reporting Returns

Numbers Within Each County Indicate Total Vote

MAP 31

LOUISIANA CONFEDERATE CONGRESSIONAL ELECTIONS
NOVEMBER 3, 1863

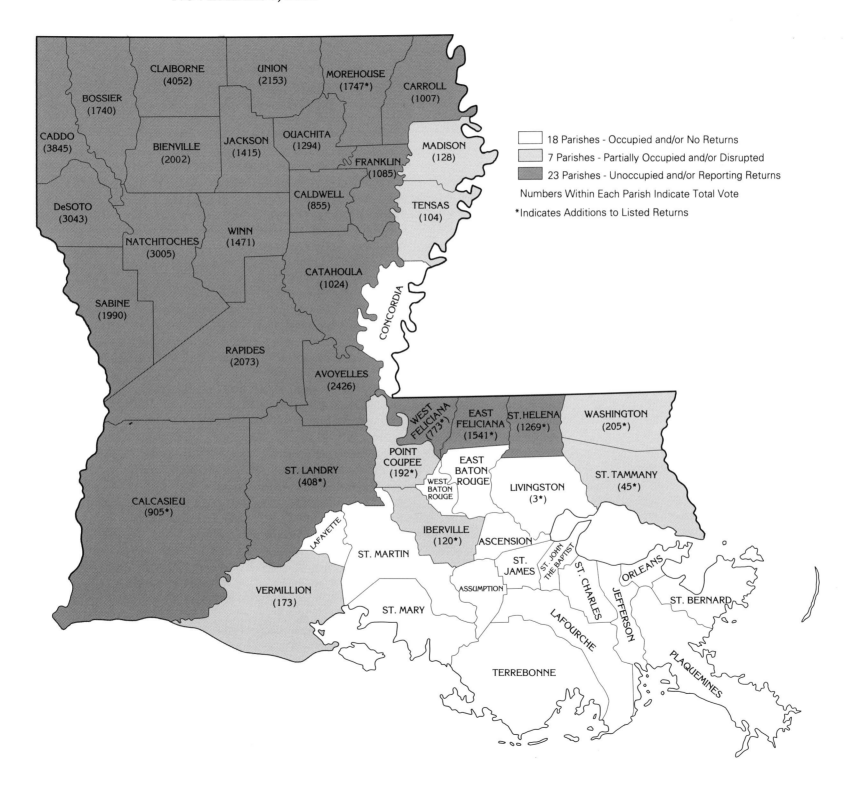

18 Parishes - Occupied and/or No Returns

7 Parishes - Partially Occupied and/or Disrupted

23 Parishes - Unoccupied and/or Reporting Returns

Numbers Within Each Parish Indicate Total Vote

*Indicates Additions to Listed Returns

MAP 32

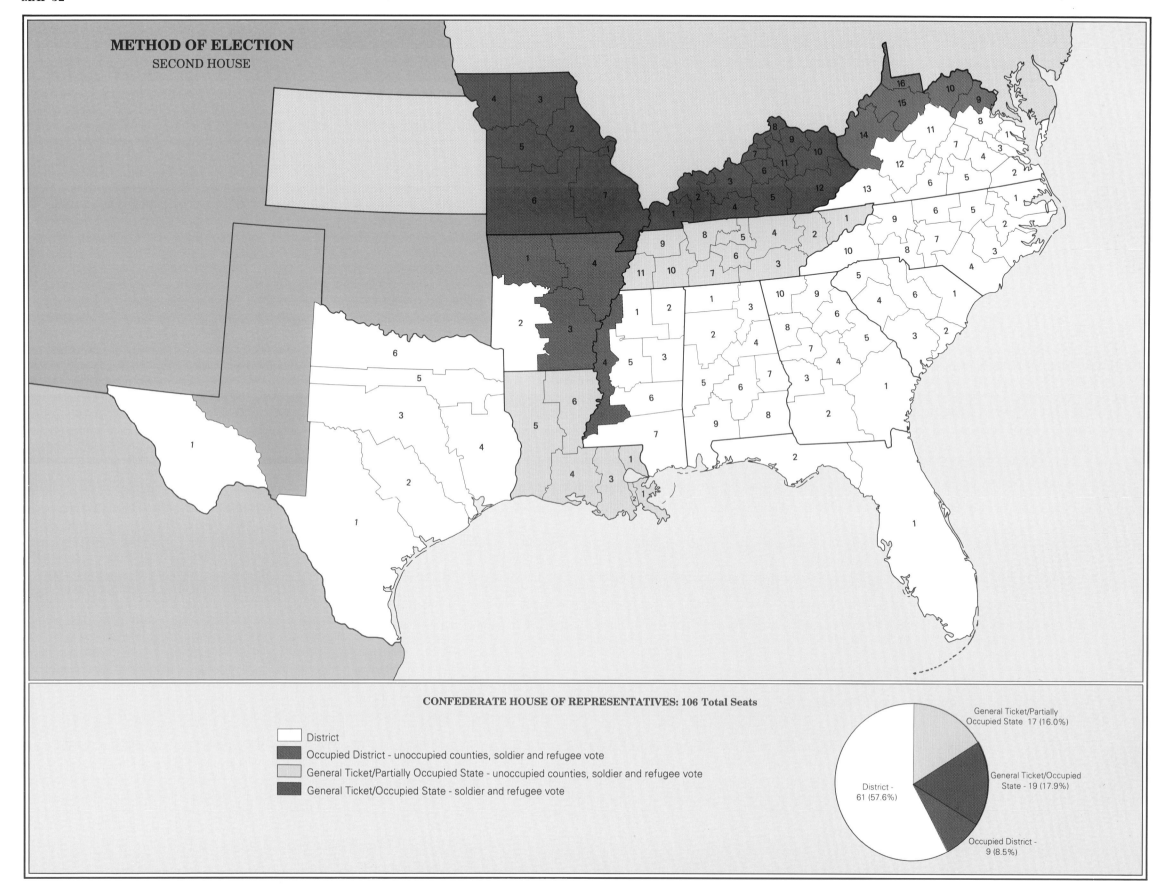

METHOD OF ELECTION
SECOND HOUSE

CONFEDERATE HOUSE OF REPRESENTATIVES: 106 Total Seats

☐ District

■ Occupied District - unoccupied counties, soldier and refugee vote

▢ General Ticket/Partially Occupied State - unoccupied counties, soldier and refugee vote

■ General Ticket/Occupied State - soldier and refugee vote

General Ticket/Partially
Occupied State 17 (16.0%)

General Ticket/Occupied
State - 19 (17.9%)

District -
61 (57.6%)

Occupied District -
9 (8.5%)

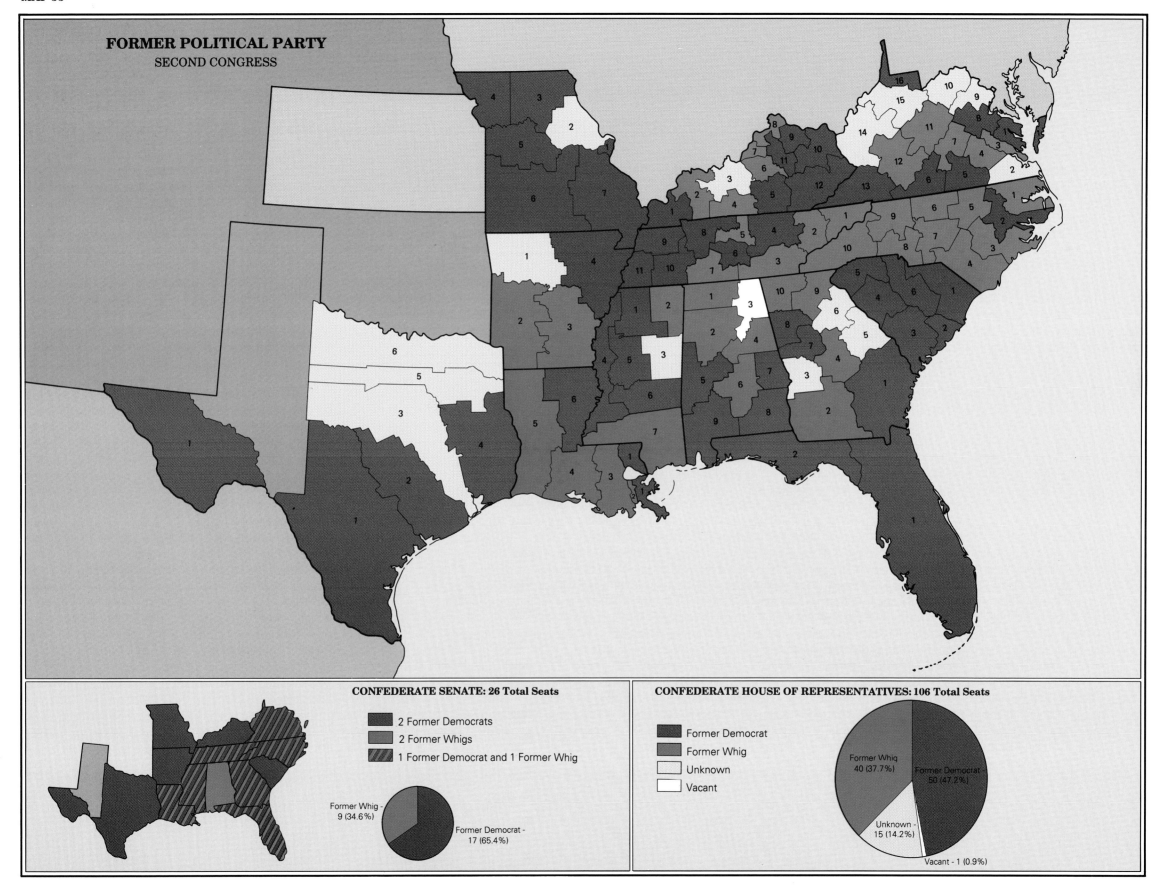

MAP 33

FORMER POLITICAL PARTY
SECOND CONGRESS

CONFEDERATE SENATE: 26 Total Seats

2 Former Democrats
2 Former Whigs
1 Former Democrat and 1 Former Whig

Former Whig - 9 (34.6%)
Former Democrat - 17 (65.4%)

CONFEDERATE HOUSE OF REPRESENTATIVES: 106 Total Seats

Former Democrat
Former Whig
Unknown
Vacant

Former Whig 40 (37.7%)
Former Democrat 50 (47.2%)
Unknown - 15 (14.2%)
Vacant - 1 (0.9%)

MAP 34

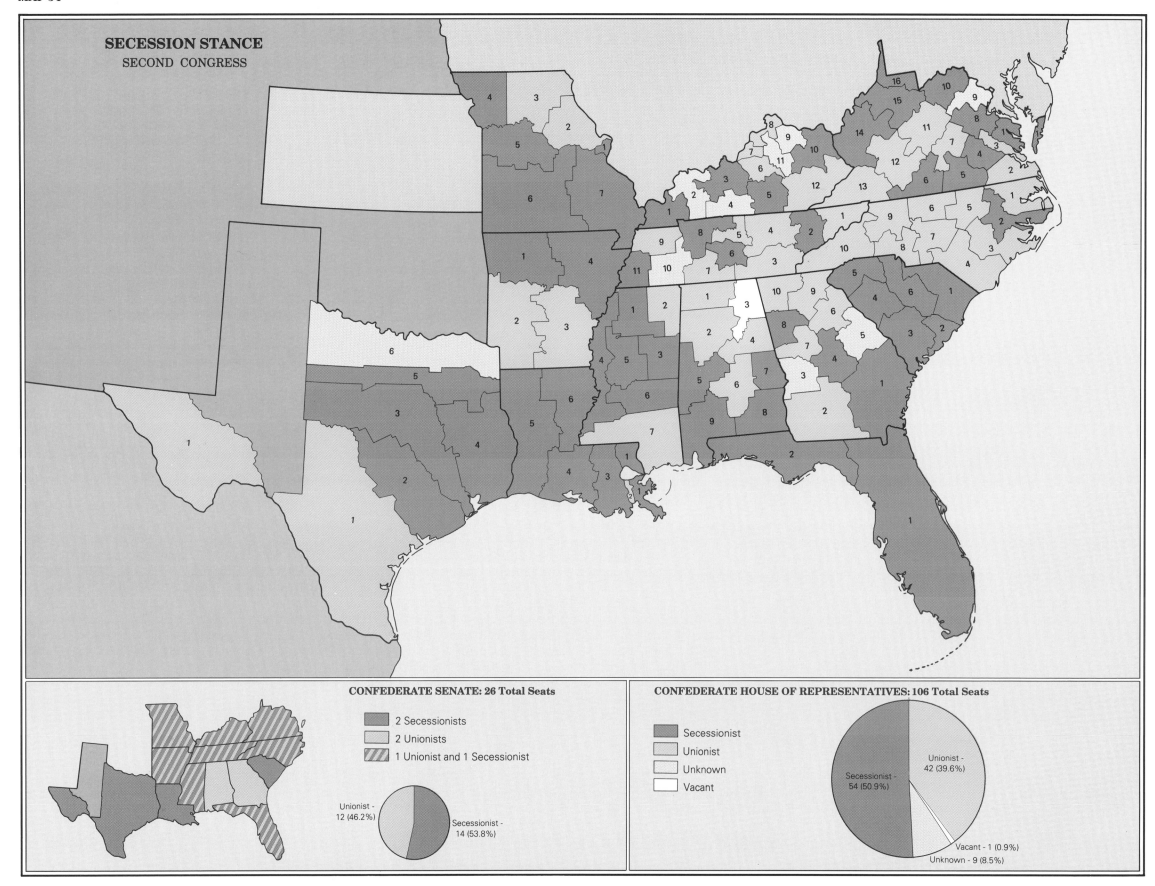

SECESSION STANCE
SECOND CONGRESS

CONFEDERATE SENATE: 26 Total Seats

- 2 Secessionists
- 2 Unionists
- 1 Unionist and 1 Secessionist

Unionist -
12 (46.2%)
Secessionist -
14 (53.8%)

CONFEDERATE HOUSE OF REPRESENTATIVES: 106 Total Seats

- Secessionist
- Unionist
- Unknown
- Vacant

Secessionist -
54 (50.9%)
Unionist -
42 (39.6%)
Vacant - 1 (0.9%)
Unknown - 9 (8.5%)

MAP 35

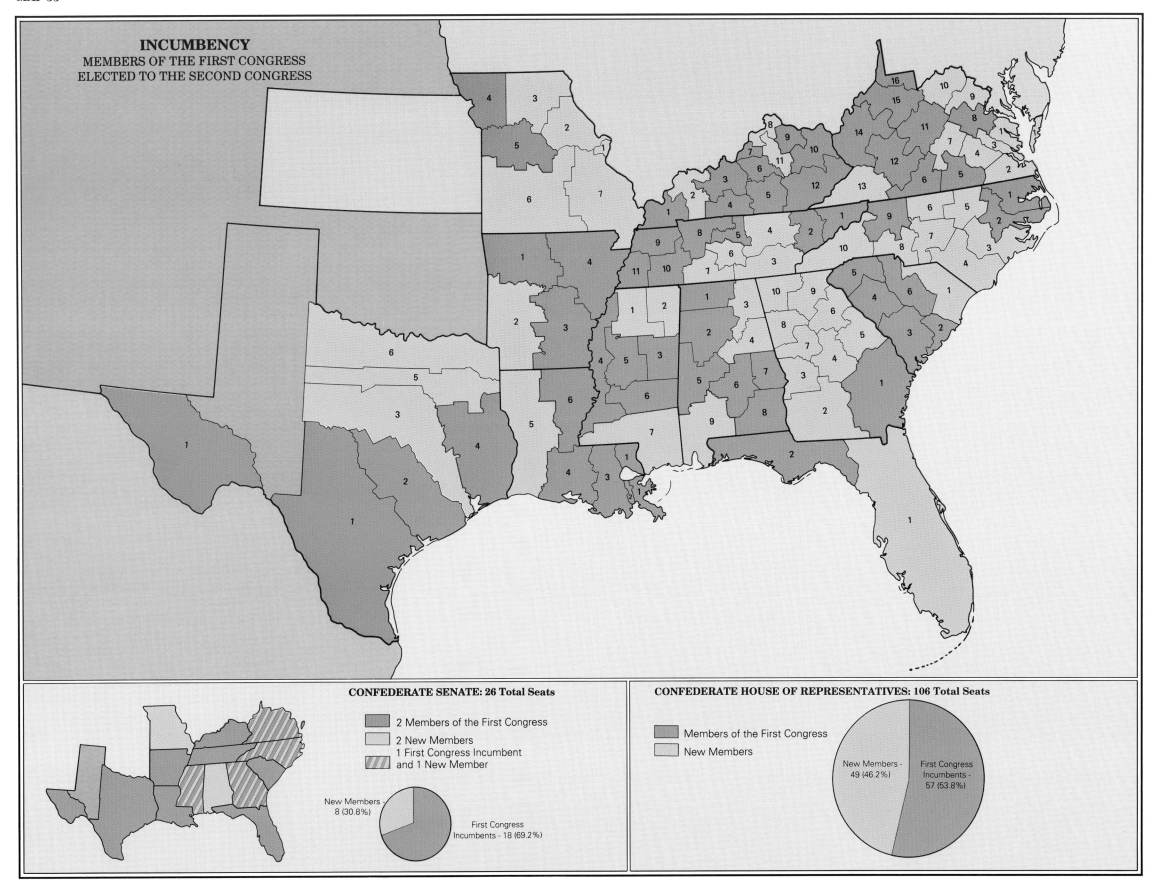

INCUMBENCY
MEMBERS OF THE FIRST CONGRESS
ELECTED TO THE SECOND CONGRESS

CONFEDERATE SENATE: 26 Total Seats

2 Members of the First Congress

2 New Members

1 First Congress Incumbent
and 1 New Member

New Members
8 (30.8%)

First Congress
Incumbents - 18 (69.2%)

CONFEDERATE HOUSE OF REPRESENTATIVES: 106 Total Seats

Members of the First Congress

New Members

New Members -
49 (46.2%)

First Congress
Incumbents -
57 (53.8%)

CHAPTER

5

CONFEDERATE CONGRESSIONAL ROLL-CALL VOTING

Context of Congressional Roll-Call Voting

In the forty-nine-month history of the Confederate Congress, 1,956 roll-call votes were recorded (Table 5-1). In compliance with the Permanent Confederate Constitution "the yeas and nays of the members of either House, on any question, shall, at the desire of one-fifth of those present, be entered on the journal."[1] These yea-nay votes were registered with the name of each member in the *Journal of the Congress of the Confederate States of America*.[2] During the one-year period of the unicameral Provisional Congress, 279 roll-call votes were taken, including twenty votes during the time of the Constitutional Convention. In the First Permanent Congress, 730 recorded votes were taken in the House and 347 in the Senate. In the Second Congress, 440 votes were recorded in the House and 160 in the Senate. These votes are a quantitative treasure of data concerning not only the history and policies of the Confederate Congress, but also the geographical-political differences within the Civil War South. One definitive book-length work treats Confederate roll-call voting, *The Anatomy of the Confederate Congress* by Thomas B. Alexander and Richard E. Beringer.[3] This atlas uses the individual roll-call votes in the *Confederate Journal* and the combined multiple roll-call voting measurements reported in *Anatomy* in the geographical analysis and mapping of Confederate congressional voting behavior.[4]

Voting Procedure in the Provisional Congress

The Provisional Congress assembled in Montgomery, Alabama, on February 4, 1861. On the second day of the unicameral Congress it adopted standing rules, the first one being, "The vote upon all questions in this Congress, except as hereafter otherwise provided, shall be taken by states; each State shall be entitled to one vote."[5] The unicameral Congress and voting procedure were confirmed in the Provisional Constitution. After all thirteen states were admitted, theoretically the closest Provisional Congress vote was seven to six. The vote of each state was determined by balloting within its delegation. Table 2-2 enumerates the number of entitled and seated delegates for each state. This entitled number was calculated by the number of U.S. representatives and senators for each state during the 1850s. For example, Georgia had eight House members and two senators before the Civil War and, therefore, was entitled to ten Provisional Congress delegates. The vote of Georgia within the Provisional Congress was determined by the votes of these delegates. If the delegation voted 6 to 4 in favor of a motion, then the state cast its one vote in favor. If the vote within any state was tied, which was the case on numerous occasions, the state vote was reported as "divided" and it did not count in the final roll-call determination. If the roll-call vote among all the states was tied, for example 6 yea, 6 nay, and 1 divided, the motion did not carry. In

addition to the regular state votes, the Provisional Congress rules allowed at "the motion of any member, seconded by one-fifth of the members present, or at the insistence of any one State, the yeas and nays of the entire body shall be spread upon the Journals upon any question."[6] This recorded vote lists the individual member vote within each state delegation.

Voting Procedures in the First and Second Congresses

Roll-call voting procedures in the Permanent Confederate Congresses followed the precedents established in the U.S. Congress. In the Confederate House each state was allocated representatives based upon population (see Table 3-2), and each member was elected from a district and entitled to one vote in Congress.

Voting in the Permanent Congress usually followed two forms, viva voce (voice vote) and roll-call vote. Rule III of the Confederate House specified:

Questions shall be distinctly put in the following form, viz: "As many as are of opinion that etc. (as the question may be) say Aye," and after the affirmative vote is given, "As many as are of the contrary opinion say No." If the Speaker doubts, or a division is called for, the House shall divide; those in the affirmative of the question rising first from their seats, and afterwards those in the negative.[7]

TABLE 5-1

Recorded Roll-Call Votes in the Confederate Congresses

Provisional Congress			
First Session	33[1]		
Second Session	23		
Third Session	59		
Fifth Session	164		
Total	279		

First Congress	House	Senate	Total
First Session	98	50	148
Second Session	120	83	203
Third Session	295	119	414
Fourth Session	217	95	312
Total	730	347	1,077

Second Congress	House	Senate	Total
First Session	123	51	174
Second Session	317	109	426
Total	440	160	600
Total			1,956

Source: Thomas B. Alexander and Richard E. Beringer, *Roll Call Votes for the Confederate Congresses, 1861–1865* [Machine-readable data file] (Ann Arbor, Michigan: Center for Political Studies - producer, Inter-university Consortium for Political and Social Research - distributor).

[1] Includes twenty votes taken within the convention to frame a permanent constitution.

The division or standing vote as well as a roll-call vote was commonly called for by members. Rule XXXIV of the House stated "In taking the yeas and nays the list of members shall be called alphabetically, except that of the Speaker shall be called last."[8] As the rule indicates, the Speaker of the House participated in roll calls.

In the Senate each state had two members, and each senator had one vote. The Senate also adopted similar voting rules specifying explicitly the constitutional rule, "the yeas and nays shall be called for by one-fifth of the Senators present."[9] The Permanent Confederate Constitution and the Senate rules specify that the Confederate vice president is the president of the Senate and votes to break any ties.

Issues in the Confederate Congresses

The Confederate Congress spent virtually its entire existence while the population was at war. As the national legislative body, Congress dealt with the normal full range of concerns, among them cabinet confirmations, and issues concerning the post office, the judiciary, and public lands; however, the conduct of the war between the states

was its major concern, and the war permeated all issues, even those seemingly indirectly related. Several major issues, policy areas, or "issue dimensions," however, were especially contentious and divided even loyal Confederates.[10] These issues were: conscription, impressment, habeas corpus, economic and fiscal policy, military concerns, and foreign affairs. Table 5-2 outlines these issue dimensions and the subissues and areas of concern within each dimension.[11]

The Confederate Congress debated these major policy areas, and numerous close roll-call votes resulted. The following section briefly discusses each major issue and the significant subissues involved. The subsequent section discusses the numerous variables influencing congressional roll-call voting behavior in general and the major issues in particular. Chapter 5 concludes with an analysis of the geographical aspects of Confederate congressional roll-call voting, including the mapping and discussion of several exemplary individual votes and multiple vote issue dimensions.

Conscription

Conscription is the involuntary drafting of individuals to serve in the armed forces. In the euphoric first months of the Confederacy, volunteers filled the ranks of state and national units in some cases even to the point beyond the ability to arm, clothe, and supply the new units. However, as the North and South organized for a major war the less populous South was the first to face the inevitable manpower shortage. At the behest of the Davis Administration, Congress introduced, debated, and passed America's first conscription bill. The final version of the bill was approved April 16, 1862. Two other major conscription acts were also passed in September 1862 and February 1864, and various aspects of the draft were debated to the last days of Congress.[12]

A number of specific subissues surrounding the conscription legislation were the object of numerous amendments, debates, and votes. The first draft bill targeted men from the ages of eighteen to thirty-five. Eventually this was extended to forty-five and then again to seventeen to fifty. The first draft system had extensive exemption allowances for state officials and other occupations deemed critical to the war effort.[13] The exemption list was expanded but then contracted as the public objected and the need for men increased. One particularly contentious aspect of exemption was the overseer provision or Twenty-slave Law. This allowed every plantation with twenty or more slaves an exemption of one white male. The ownership of twenty slaves indicated some wealth, and this exemption brought great class resentment, especially between upland yeoman farmers and lowland planters. Eventually the overseer requirements were modified. Another aspect of the draft that aroused class suspicion was substitution. This allowed an individual, because of religious or other reasons, to hire or purchase a substitute for money. Substitution was eliminated in late 1863.

Impressment

Impressment is the seizure of private property for support of the army and general war effort.[14] Food (grain, livestock, and so on) was the most often seized item, but a wide variety of other material was impressed during the war, including slaves, horses, mules, wagons, building material, alcohol, cotton, tobacco, firearms, and all types of manufactured goods. The single most contentious issue was the just compensation for impressed material at a fair market price. The procedure of impressment was also uneven with respect to geographic location of seized material, procedure of attachment, and amount paid. The first impressment law (March 1863) established a claims system by which citizens could appeal the compensation received from the impressment officers.

At the beginning of the war a subissue of impressment was widely discussed, the destruction of private property so as to prevent its falling in a useful condition into the hands of the enemy. Most significant were large stocks of cotton, tobacco, and other agricultural and manufactured goods. In 1861 and 1862 the areas of heaviest Union military movements were in northern and northwestern Virginia, western Tennessee, southern Louisiana, and some sea islands. Plantation owners, wholesalers, warehouse owners, manufacturers, and even small farmers in those areas sought compensation from Richmond for lost property.[15]

Habeas Corpus

Habeas corpus literally means, "you should have the body." In common law habeas corpus prevents the arrest, detention, or imprisonment of citizens without a writ or legal document from a properly established civilian judicial authority. Habeas corpus was such a fixture in Western law that it was specifically mentioned in both the original U.S. and Confederate constitutions.

The bold military moves into western Tennessee and the Virginia Tidewater in early 1862 shocked the Confederacy into considering suspension of the writ of habeas corpus in certain areas, and in February 1862 Congress so authorized President Davis. This and other habeas corpus bills had automatic termination dates because of the perceived sacredness of the concept. All told, habeas corpus was suspended for eighteen months of the forty-nine months of the Confederate Congress.[16]

In the places and times the writ was suspended, Confederate military authorities could detain, arrest, and imprison individuals with the mere suspicion of wrongdoing. The most important need for this power was to control suspected espionage in general and protect specific military operations in particular. Conscription laws were also enforced using suspension of habeas corpus as well as detention of suspected deserters. The conscription controversy pitted state and local civilian judges against military authorities with the unavoidable legal questions arising over state sovereignty versus martial law.[17]

Economic and Fiscal Policy

The establishment of the Confederate States of America meant the establishment and organization of an entirely new fiscal and monetary system, a difficult task even without a major war to finance. A vast number of economic problems hit the Confederacy all at once.[18] One of the first needs was the institution and issuance of a Confederate currency. Treasury notes (paper money) were made legal tender, but not backed with precious metal. These notes became the principal method of funding the war and were printed at a rapid pace. The flood of notes resulted in rampant inflation and, along with wartime shortages, the blockade, and other problems, led to the subsequent destabilization of the southern economy. The central government also raised millions by the issuance of Confederate bonds, foreign loans, increases in taxes, and the confiscation of private property (impressment) without compensation.

Besides fiscal matters, a number of other related economic issues came before Congress. The war forced bold action by a heretofore conservative political elite. Measures were brought forward for the government-sponsored building of railroads and improvement and supervision of the telegraph system. Import duties were placed upon luxury and other goods, restrictions placed on the export of cotton and other products, and regulations placed on blockade runners with respect to cargos and tariffs. Although immediate fiscal and monetary concerns were always a matter of consideration for Congress, little legislation addressed relief of economic conditions on the homefront.[19]

Military Concerns

With the power of appropriations, Congress had a direct influence on military affairs in such obvious areas as armaments, provisions, army pay, and coastal and river defenses. Congress also had general oversight over the executive branch and many times voiced its opinion on everything from general long-term strategy, critiquing specific battle plans, winning or ending the war, to officer selection and promotion. Trans-Mississippi congressmen were critical of the neglect of the defense of their area, both from the Yankees and Native Americans. The treatment and governance of state militia were both military and state rights questions. Of course, congressional policy toward conscription and impressment was critical in manning and provisioning the army.[20]

Late in the war one of the most vitriolic and seemingly antithetical debates arose in the administration and Congress—the use of slaves as troops in the Confederate army. From the beginning slave labor was used in all aspects of the war effort, agricultural and industrial, rural and urban, military and civilian. Slaves was impressed to work on fortifications, labor in military camps, and do countless army jobs. As the war progressed the loss of men and the deteriorating military situation forced the Davis Administration and the

generals to go to Congress and request the arming of slaves for the Confederate army. The Confederate government, which was conceived on the premise of racial superiority, was forced to argue that blacks would make good soldiers to fight in the cause of Confederate survival. The slaves who were forced to fight for the Confederacy were undoubtedly to be granted their freedom after the war. The arming and emancipation of southern African-Confederates was hotly debated in the last months of the war.

Foreign Affairs

Congress was least involved with diplomatic relations, the purview of the executive branch. The Confederate States of America was never officially recognized by any nation, but not without numerous solicitations by Confederate commissioners. Most of the congressional involvement with foreign affairs came by way of tariffs, embargos,

loans, and credits. Specifically, the cotton embargo, embargos of other products, and restrictions and taxation of blockade runner cargo all had direct impact upon the Confederacy's foreign commerce.[21]

If civilian relations with the United States are considered "foreign" relations, then a number of issues came before Congress. At the beginning of the war the confiscation of federal property was discussed. As the war progressed, the disposition of Union prisoners of war became an issue. Toward the end of the war the possible peace conference and peace negotiations were debated.

Factors Influencing Roll-Call Voting Behavior

Research concerning representation in legislative bodies has examined a number of diverse topics. One topic receiving significant attention is the analysis of roll-call voting. In the intricate and lengthy

---

TABLE 5-2

Major Roll-Call Voting Issues in the Confederate Congresses

Issue	Subissues and Areas of Concern	Issue	Subissues and Areas of Concern
Conscription	Age Exemptions Overseers Substitution Drafting of Slaves	Military Affairs	Armaments and Provisions, Impressment State Militia, Exemptions Conscription Trans-Mississippi Theater Native American Defense Naval and River Defense Martial Law Slave Labor and Military Units Pay, Rations and Allowances Desertion Black Troops in the Confederate Army arming, emancipation Black Troops in the Union Army White Officers of Black Union Troops
Impressment	Compensation Rate Procedures Claims Destruction of Private Property		
Habeas Corpus	Espionage and Military Operations Conscription Desertion Martial Law State and Local Civilian Judicial Authority		

Economic	Inflation, Price Controls
	Taxation, Tax-in-Kind, Gold Levy
	Currency, Treasury Notes (Paper Money)
	Bonds
	Railroads and Telegraph
	Trading with the "Enemy"
	Loans, Erlanger Loan
	Impressment (Unpaid)
	Congressional/Civil Servant pay, per diem, mileage
	Import Duties, Cotton Embargo, Export Embargo
	Blockade Running
	Pensions, Veteran Homes
	General Appropriations
		Foreign Affairs	Diplomatic Relations
			Foreign Commissioners
			Tariff
			Import Duties, Cotton Embargo, Export Embargo
			Aliens and Naturalization
			Foreign Loans/Credit, Erlanger Loan
			Blockade Running
			Prisoners of War
			Peace Negotiations
			United States
			    property
			    prisoners of war
			    peace negotiations

Military Affairs	Strategy Oversight Officer Selection and Promotion General Staff	Davis Administration	State Rights Nominations and Appointments Presidential Conscription Exemptions Civil Service

legislative process, the final decision point, and the act that defines the end product, is floor voting. For this reason alone the understanding of floor voting is important. In addition, the understanding of roll-call voting gives further insights and understanding to other aspects of the legislative process, such as committee behavior, and to the entire policy-making process.

While the relationship between representatives and their constituency is central to the theory of political representation, research on roll-call voting indicates a number of other variables affecting representatives' behavior. The factors affecting the voting behavior of members of the U.S. Congress in both the past and present have been extensively debated in political science journals and the legislative behavior literature. A number of studies have put forward variables explaining the voting predispositions of members of Congress.[22] Generally, the literature on legislative voting behavior agrees

that a complex interaction of numerous variables is involved in the roll-call decision making process. The most significant of these variables, from a wide range of studies, are listed in Table 5-3.

Understanding legislative behavior in the Confederate Congress is also a complex process. Numerous multifaceted factors influenced Confederate representatives and senators in their final roll-call decisions on the major policy areas discussed above. Table 5-3 also lists the equivalent voting variables believed operating in the Confederate Congresses. This list and the reconstruction of the Confederate legislative environment with respect to voting is derived from antebellum and nineteenth-century U.S. congressional studies, quantitative and historical studies of the Confederate Congress and its members, and modern legislative behavior studies that shed light on voting behavior, some of which can be applied to the Civil War context. Three studies are prominent in the assessment of roll-

call voting in the Confederate Congress: *The Confederate Congress,* by W. Buck Yearns; *The Anatomy of the Confederate Congress,* by Thomas B. Alexander and Richard E. Beringer; and "Southern Leviathan: The Development of Central State Authority in the Confederate States of American," by Richard Bensel.[23] Table 5-4 summaries these studies regarding the major issues identified and variables used to study voting behavior.

The variable most influential in determining a roll-call vote may change from policy area to policy area, subissue to subissue, vote to vote, and Congress to Congress. Nevertheless, the specific studies of the voting behavior in the Confederate Congress suggest the occupied status of a congressional district or state is the most consistent predictor of Confederate roll-call voting behavior. However, the occupied status of the district may be the most critical factor in one vote, state sovereignty in another, and distance from the front line in another. The following discussion identifies several factors that the previous literature suggests are most important in understanding legislative behavior and voting in the Confederate Congress. These factors lay the groundwork for a deeper understanding of the roll-call vote analysis and maps in the next section.

Occupied-Disrupted-Unoccupied District Status

Chapters 2 and 3 define and map the systematic occupation of the South by Union forces. Permanent occupation of a state or district cuts the constituency-representative link that is central in American-style democracy. In the Confederate Congress this link was severed in several ways. First, most obvious, and perhaps foremost, the local constituency was sheltered from the consequences of any roll-call vote, legislative action or law, leaving representatives free to vote for any measure, no matter how extreme, since it would not affect their local areas. The threat of electorate retaliation by ballot was also removed, or, perhaps more accurately in the Confederate Congress, a different electorate-constituency was established, in this case soldiers in the field. In addition, numerous informal linkages were not possible, such as letters from constituents or visits to the local area during recesses and intersessions.

The Confederate Congress provides one of the most interesting cases in the history of legislative behavior since a high percentage of members of Congress represented districts or states that did not specifically elect them. Other areas that did elect representatives were occupied by the enemy during their tenure, and thus the constituency was completely shielded from any effects of legislation representatives voted upon. If constituency concerns and influences are the cornerstones of American-style representative democracy and the constituency is cut off from the representative, then a different array of influences affecting voting behavior can evolve. This situation was especially the case for districts in Missouri, Kentucky, and northwestern Virginia, which were occupied virtually from the beginning of the war. Congressmen from these areas consistently

TABLE 5-3

Determinants of Congressional Roll-Call Voting Behavior

Nineteenth Century and Modern U.S. Congress	Confederate Congress Equivalent	Nineteenth Century and Modern U.S. Congress	Confederate Congress Equivalent
Major Geographical Determinants		Class	Class
			Personal Wealth
District Characteristics	Occupied/Disrupted/Unoccupied District Characteristics		Slaveholding
		Committee Assignment	Committee Assignment
State Delegation	State Delegation		Military Affairs
			Judiciary
Region/Section	Upper South versus Lower South		Ways and Means
	Trans-Mississippi	Fellow Representatives	
	Appalachian-Upland versus Coastal	and Senators	Fellow Congressmen
	Plain-Mississippi River Valley	Campaign Contributions	District Elites
Major Political Determinants		Interest Groups	Lobbyists
Party	Former Political Party	Reading	Reading
Political Ideology	Secession Stance	Seniority	U.S. Congress Incumbency
	State Rights Philosophy	Personal Precedent	Personal Precedent
	Racial/Slavery Ideology	Sociolegislative Groups	Secessionists, Peace groups
Constituency	Constituency	Family	Family
	State Legislature/Governor (Senate)	Personal Friends	Personal Friends
Localism	Localism	Life Experiences	Life Experiences, War Experiences
Other Influences		Personal Characteristics	Personal Characteristics
President	President Davis	Ranking Committee Members	Ranking Committee Members
Administration and		Competitiveness of District	Competitiveness of District
Executive Branch	War Department, Navy Department	Party Leadership	-
	Bureau of Conscription	Staff	-
	Generals and General Staff	Vote Trading/Logrolling	-
	Treasury Department		
Media	Richmond Newspapers		
	Local/State Newspapers		
	War Photographs		

voted for drastic measures to win the war, such as conscription, impressment, suspension of habeas corpus, and stringent economic policies, because they knew these policies would never be imposed in their areas. Elections for the Second Congress even strengthened the voting resolve of representatives from occupied districts since the voters were virtually all soldiers in the field who would benefit most from stringent new legislative measures. As Union occupation spread into Tennessee, northern Virginia, and the lower Mississippi River valley, more and more districts passed into occupied status. In the First Congress unoccupied Tennessee voted differently on a number of issues from occupied Tennessee in the Second Congress. Representatives from the occupied areas of southeast Louisiana voted differently from the unoccupied districts in western Louisiana.

The occupied districts formed the core of support for more and more desperate legislation proposed by the Davis Administration and its supporters. The representatives from unoccupied districts and states were acutely aware of the members from occupied districts and states voting for drastic measures to be applied in their areas.[24] If wartime legislation and the issues of war and peace were left up to only representatives representing free people, the politics of the Confederate government and the entire course of the Civil War could have been quite different.

Constituency

The United State Constitution established the House of Representatives as the guardian of local-district interests.[25] The Confederate Constitution maintained this structure. Most representatives viewed their role as that of national elected officials who were the voice of the local people. Constituency attitudes concerning issues were supposedly reflected by the representatives. As constituent beliefs changed, these new views were supposedly reflected by members of Congress. Indeed, the views on the expediency of the war in 1861 were quite different in most areas in 1863 and 1864.

Studies of congressional roll-call voting in the antebellum period suggest a strong role of party and section in explaining votes, legislative behavior, and national politics.[26] The secession of the South eliminated the stress of classic South/slave state versus North/free state sectionalism in both the federal Congress and the Confederate Congress. In addition, political parties, as they were known in the antebellum decade, were virtually nonexistent in the Confederate elections and Congress (see Chapter 4). The elimination of both party and sectional influences allowed the rise of freedom of roll-call voting to unprecedented levels, and hence the weight of local constituency influence rose beyond its already powerful level.

Constituency influence was manifested not only in the first and second elections, but also in the various issues before Congress. The southern population was more concerned with certain policies such as conscription, impressment, and economic affairs, than it was with others, such as foreign affairs or military strategy. Public

TABLE 5-4

Issues and Possible Factors Influencing Roll-Call Voting Behavior

Study[1]	Major Issues	Possible Determinants of Decision Making[2]
Yearns	Conscription Officer Selection and Promotion Economic Organization Military Strategy Habeas Corpus Foreign Affairs Peace Movement Finance Davis Administration	Opposition to the Administration Constitutionality/State Rights Political Party (former) Generals and General Staff Economic Situation Newspapers Secessionist-Unionist philosophy Slave Philosophy Military Defeats and General Military Situation
Alexander and Beringer	Conscription Impressment Habeas Corpus Economic and Fiscal Problems Nationhood Determination and Defeatism State Rights Race	Former Political Party Secession Stance Personal Slaveholding District Slaveholding Personal vs. District Slaveholding Personal Wealth District Wealth Personal vs. District Wealth Federal Occupation

Bensel	Citizenship
	  conscription
	  impressment
	Centralization
	  officer selection
	  secret sessions
	  judicial questions
	Administrative Capability
	  general staff
	  presidential exemptions
	  civil service
	  Supreme Court
	  presidential appointments / nominations
	  Secret Service
	Control of Property
	  railroads
	  destruction of property
	  impressment / trading with the "enemy"
	  slaves as soldiers
	Client Groups
	  pensions / taxes and bonds
	  price controls / veterans home
	World System
	  foreign commissioners
	  tariff / prisoners of war
	  blockade / peace
		Exterior (occupied) vs. Interior (unoccupied) Districts
		Percentage of Slave Population
		Value Added In Manufacturing (urban-rural Component)
		Committee Membership

[1] Wilfred Buck Yearns, *The Confederate Congress* (Athens: University of Georgia Press, 1960). Thomas B. Alexander and Richard E. Beringer, *The Anatomy of the Confederate Congress* (Nashville: Vanderbilt University Press, 1972). Richard Bensel, "Southern Leviathan: The Development of Central State Authority in the Confederate States of America," in *Studies in American Political Development*, Vol. 2, eds. Karen Orren and Stephen Skowronek (New Haven: Yale University Press, 1987).

[2] In the Alexander and Beringer and Bensel studies these are the initial variables used to examine roll-call voting and they are explicitly stated, while in the Yearns study they are prominently mentioned.

outrage over conscription substitution and the overseer provision eventually led to the reform or elimination of these policies. By the time of the Second Congress elections, constituency influence, by way of elections in the remaining unoccupied regions, made significant changes in the composition of the House and indirectly in the Senate by way of changes in state legislatures. These elections, plus such events as food riots, desertions, and the general course of the war influenced numerous congressmen representing free constituencies to reevaluate their legislative priorities and behavior.

State Sovereignty

Many in the South believed in the sacredness of state rights, that is, the ultimate superiority of state government power over national government power. The use of the doctrine of state sovereignty over the question of slavery was the chief cause of the Civil War. Secession itself was the ultimate expression of state rights. The fifty years of vigorous debate in the United States Congress over the question of state sovereignty carried on in the Confederate Congress. State sovereignty could not be readily jettisoned by some Confederates in spite of the obvious circumstances and practical needs brought about by the Civil War. Some ascribe state sovereignty as one of the major causes of the failure of the Confederacy.[27] The Confederate constitutions are interpreted as explicitly acknowledging state sovereignty and therefore almost inviting state rights concerns over legislation in the Provisional and Permanent Congresses.[28]

The South Carolina delegation in the various Confederate Congresses may be a case in point. No delegation was more secessionist, prosouthern and pro-Confederate. Yet, South Carolina's congressmen and the combined delegation consistently ranked low in voting for drastic legislation needed by the central government and the Confederate military. State sovereignty undoubtedly influenced voting in the South Carolina delegation and other representatives on a number of issues. Perhaps state rights was used in the same way it was used by many in the antebellum U.S. Congress with respect to slavery, that is, as a pretext on issues that affect the constituency or economic welfare of the state or area in question.[29] However, for some congressmen state sovereignty was the basis of the founding of the Confederacy and a philosophy to be staunchly defended.

Former Political Party

Political parties, loose coalitions of like-minded individuals backing a similar political agenda, developed in the United States within Congress in the 1790s. Parties became more like modern-day electoral parties at the beginning of the Whig-Democrat era, the late 1830s and early 1840s. Parties held some roll-call voting influence over representatives and senators because of the advantages of party membership.

Chapters 3 and 4 discuss the political party situation in the antebellum period and the collapse of political parties in the Confederate South. The life of the Confederacy was perhaps too short for the redevelopment of a political party system. Although political parties did not influence Confederate Congress policies former political party affiliation does give information about and insight into voting behavior.[30] In one sense the formation of the Confederacy was a triumph of radical southern Democrats. Former Democrats in the Confederate Congress were wary of former Whigs, Americans (Know-Nothings), and Constitutional Unionists as possible obstructionists. Former Democrats were more likely to come from areas of secessionist sentiment while former opposition members were more likely to come from more Unionist regions (see Maps 26 and 33). Lingering divisions not only caused suspicion but also voting differences in supporting drastic Confederate measures.

Secession Stance

The personal and political decision to separate from the United States was one of great significance for individuals and the nation. An enormous number of complex positions were taken on secession (see Chapter 4). The stance on secession before Fort Sumter gives further insight into voting behavior in the Confederate Congress. Of course, former political party and secession stance are highly correlated. Former Democrats were usually secessionists and former Whigs-Constitutional Unionists were usually antisecessionists (see Tables 4-8 and 4-16 and Maps 26, 27, 33, and 34). Most secessionists, especially at the beginning of the war, tended to support radical measures to assure independence and military victory. Many former Unionists, while loyal to the Confederacy, had lingering doubts about the level of measures needed to fight the Union, especially late in the war. Lingering Union sentiment, like lingering party loyalty, influenced the general political milieu and decisions on certain issues.

District Characteristics

The geographic, demographic, and economic characteristics of an area not only affected constituency interests but also the inherent interests of the district or state. If a district was a large cotton producer then legislation with respect to the cotton trade embargo was of the highest interest. If a region was a tobacco-producing area then the cotton embargo may have been less significant than other agriculture food policy measures. If a region was a large producer of general agricultural food products, such as the Great Valley of Virginia, then food production policy and impressment legislation had a high significance.

Other Influences

Tables 5-3 and 5-4 enumerate many other influences on congressional voting. One of the most outstanding commentaries in the writings of the day was the vitriolic nature of the statements and personal views of some congressmen toward President Jefferson Davis. Anti-Davis sentiment arose for a variety of reasons: his antebellum relationships; caustic personality; presidential policies; and general military conduct of the war. His requests for additional power for the central government were viewed by many as a request for more individual personal power, which many times was indeed the general outcome. Legislation requested by or pushed by the president was viewed unfavorably by his personal political adversaries.

The influence of the generals on military legislation affected the assessment of the situation by some members of Congress. Thought of as war heroes above politics who had intimate knowledge of the daily military situation, they were particularly influential. General Lee was without equal in influencing the populace, administration, and Congress.

One of the most discussed influences within Congress was personal background and characteristics, especially class differences between wealthy slaveholding planters and representatives from mostly poor white, yeoman, mountain districts (see Maps 8 and 10). Poor whites many times criticized secession and the extensive conflict as fighting the rich man's war. Possible Confederate regional differences along these lines were largely eliminated when the core of the poor white area, northwestern Virginia, Kentucky, and Missouri, was occupied early in the war. However, poor white districts in western North Carolina, northern Georgia, and northeast Alabama did display different electorate behavior and subsequent representative voting behavior.

There is no doubt some representatives grew war-weary along with their constituents. Personal experiences in the war or in Richmond and reports of battlefield carnage and losses of families and friends made doubters of many regarding the desirability of continuing the war. These feelings were felt in the North as well as the South, but the South suffered infinitely more. The extreme peace advocates in the second North Carolina delegation, for example, simply wanted the war to end and voted against virtually every drastic measure to continue the struggle. Antiwar sentiment was manifested in one degree or another by numerous other members. While war-weariness and recognition of the "Lost Cause" can be ascribed to other more quantifiable variables, they undoubtedly had an influence on voting, especially in the Second Congress.

Geographical Aspects of Roll-Call Voting Behavior

Representing Places: The Role of Confederate Representatives and Senators

Throughout American history, political representation in the U.S. House of Representatives has been mostly by single-member, geographically defined electoral districts. These representative seats were apportioned to the constituent states on the basis of population, and congressional districts were ideally drawn within each state on somewhat the same basis. This brings about a geography of congressional districts somewhat concomitant on a national scale with the geography of population. As Chapter 3 describes, this was also the case in the Confederate House of Representatives.

Members of the Confederate House were elected from geographically delimited districts and members of the Confederate Senate from the states, and this had tremendous impact upon their interpretation of the concept of representation, and, therefore, their entire legislative behavior. However, as discussed above, theorists of political representation have taken into consideration many variables in determining the relationship between those represented and those acting upon their behalf (see Tables 5-3 and 5-4). An elected legislator represents a geographical area; this does not, however, totally determine his role as a representative. Yet in the United States the representation of places by House and Senate members is intensified by a combination of political, electoral, and legislative circumstances.[31] These circumstances were continued, and perhaps even intensified, in the Confederacy.

Election by single-member, geographically defined districts is the most common form of representation in Western-style democratic national legislatures. However, in most countries, district representation is mitigated by the perception of the role of national legislators in the larger political milieu. In the French, British, and other European traditions, representatives are considered representatives of the entire nation even though elected by department or district. In spite of their French ideological influences and British heritage, most of those who framed the U.S. Constitution took a radically different view of the representative's role in the new U.S. Congress. Replete in the writings of the time was the opinion that representatives were to be agents of their constituencies, dependent upon them, and having intimate knowledge and sympathy with their views.[32] To perpetuate this role for House members, both the federal and Confederate constitutions provided for biennial elections, a radical step that remains, to this day, virtually unique to the United States. The general political sentiment at the time of the framing of the U.S. Constitution was:

> that elected representatives would regard it as their function to promote sectional interests and thought it to be one of the characteristics of good government that a large number of these interests should be represented, so that no one of them would be in a commanding position.[33]

The South in the antebellum period was the champion of local, district and state rights versus the interests of the central government. In general, the framers of the Confederate Constitution carried on the federal system according to which a popularly elected executive contends with national and international affairs and a Congress with inherent interests in local affairs. In the Confederate Congress it was thought normal, right, and just by many to defend state and district interests over national interests, even in time of war.[34]

Another factor that intensifies the representation of place is the tradition of localism in American political history. Both the federal and Confederate constitutions provide that representatives and senators must be residents of the state from which they are elected. Even more important is the rarely broken custom that representatives be inhabitants of the congressional district from where they are elected. This custom was also continued in the Confederacy, especially in unoccupied districts where free and open elections were held. Because representatives were usually long-time residents of the district, they not only had a knowledge and sympathy for area concerns, but usually had some sort of vested financial interest in their region. Even when stringent measures were needed to ensure the survival of the Confederacy, congressmen knew someday they must return to their districts, in victory or defeat, and answer to the local community. Another aspect of localism was the tradition of representatives being nominated by the local residents and backed in the nominating process and general election almost exclusively by local groups rather than national parties. Since representatives were self-nominated or nominated by local elites or organizations, and there were no functioning organized national political parties, members of the Confederate Congress were especially aware of local interests (see Chapter 4).

Those who defend the primacy of constituency influence on representation or defend the existence of local, district, state, or regional influences defend explicitly or implicitly the existence of the district or geographic role of the representative. If the constituency-representative relationship was strong in Confederate politics, certain parallel patterns of voting among similar districts and constituencies should be detected. If contiguous congressional districts have similar geographical and constituency characteristics, representative interests should be similar, and a general regional pattern of voting may emerge.

The Confederate Congress and the Davis Administration were the two significant national policy-making organizations in the Civil War South. Without the influence of party, and with the political heritage of district representation and state rights, Confederate congressmen had a level of voting independence beyond that of members of the U.S. Congress or virtually any other elected national legislature before or since. The electoral procedure and legislative characteristics of members of the Confederate Congress not only allow, but seem to necessitate, the consideration and study of the geographical aspects and mapping of legislative voting behavior in the Confederate Congress. The examination of the spatial patterns and spatial aspects of roll-call voting should in turn aid in the better understanding of Confederate representative behavior in particular, and the policy-making process and political geography of the Civil War South in general.

Mapping Roll-Call Voting

One of the primary goals of this atlas is to provide students, teachers, and researchers in history, political science, and geography readily available Confederate congressional district base maps. These district boundary maps are discussed and presented in Chapter 3. A list accompanying each map assigns every individual who served in the First and Second Confederate Houses to a particular district. This base map and lists provide tools to map not only every roll-call vote, but also a broad range of behavioral and compositional aspects of the Confederate Congress.[35] In Chapter 3, five different district characteristics are mapped along with six Union-occupied district maps. In Chapter 4, a number of electoral variables are mapped, including former political party affiliation and secession stance.

The main objective of Chapter 5 is to study the geographic structure of roll-call voting in the Confederate Congress by way of voting maps. Geographers, political scientists, and historians have long recognized the significance of local, district, state, regional, and sectional influences in policy-making and roll-call voting behavior in the U.S. Congress and the inherent need to examine the geographic aspects of congressional phenomena.[36] The goal of this section is to test these traditional hypotheses with respect to the geographical component in Confederate Congress roll-call voting. The atlas examines the geography of roll-call votes in three ways: single roll-call votes; multiple roll-call votes all relating to one issue, policy area, or issue dimension; and multiple roll-call votes comprising several different issue dimensions, that is, multidimensional votes. The multidimensional vote maps attempt to illustrate and understand a larger stance, ideology, or philosophy regarding a consistent strong support of the Confederacy.

Single Roll-Call Vote Maps

The base maps in this atlas allow the construction of a roll-call map of every vote taken in the Provisional Congress or Permanent Confederate House or Senate. The compilation of a roll-call vote map is essentially the linking of the roll-call data from the *Journal of the Confederate Congress* and the appropriate map and membership list. Three specific votes are mapped in this section to illustrate the geographical aspects of political sentiment in the Confederate Congress and to demonstrate the methodology and research potential of this type of analysis. Two votes are from the House and one from the Senate.[37] The House votes are discussed first since they demonstrate the full potential of the roll-call vote mapping technique. Of course, votes in the Senate are equally important as votes in the House since they determine the exact wording and final passage of legislation. The geographic understanding of Senate votes also aids in the understanding of the politics and behavior of the entire Confederate Congress. However, the Senate vote maps are restricted to the thirteen states admitted to the Confederate Congress. House votes, on the other hand, have over eight times the number of geographic data points, that is, 106 districts. Obviously, the House allows a much more detailed examination of the political variables and geographic variances of any legislative phenomena. Most of the maps in this atlas understandably concentrate on the House, but the Senate is nevertheless important and should be considered in any detailed study of an individual vote, multiple votes, issue, or general policy area.

In the Provisional Congress House or Senate vote map, each state or district is colored depending upon its member's vote. Green indicates a yea vote, taking a certain position concerning the issue under consideration, and red indicates a nay vote, taking an opposite position. Roll-call vote maps attempt to replicate the actual yea-nay response as recorded in the *Confederate Journal* for each member. Because of the complicated procedural nature of many legislative votes, the ballot question is phrased so as to make clear the yea-nay question. The voting maps also indicate any districts vacant at the time of the vote and those representatives absent. The pie chart at the bottom of each map indicates the actual number and percentage of the House or Senate in each of the vote categories. Most Confederate congressional districts were remarkably similar in size, except for some larger ones along the Gulf Coast and the western frontier. This similarity means that the extent of color on a given map approximates numerical support on most issues. The pie chart shows visually the exact area proportion of each vote.

Suspension of Habeas Corpus—House—December 8, 1864. On December 8, 1864, the Confederate House passed a bill, "to suspend the privilege of the writ of habeas corpus in certain cases for a limited time."[38] The vote for final passage was 50 yea and 44 nay, with three districts vacant and only nine representatives absent for the vote. Map 36 illustrates the geographic distribution of the vote on this bill.

There is a clear spatial pattern of support and resistance to the suspension of habeas corpus at this stage of the war. Map 36 shows that support for suspending habeas corpus came mainly from Union-occupied districts, especially in Missouri, Kentucky, northern and northwestern Virginia, and Louisiana. In unoccupied Virginia the threat of federal forces was great, and these Virginia representatives supported suspension as they had other drastic measures throughout the war.[39] Only a few unoccupied Deep South districts in south Alabama and adjacent areas gave widespread support to suspension.

Those resisting suspension of habeas corpus were largely from unoccupied areas, areas where suspension could actually be put into effect by Confederate authorities. The core of resistance was in the Carolinas, Georgia, and westward through northern Alabama and Mississippi. These areas, especially North Carolina and Georgia, were strong areas of antiadministration and antiwar sentiment in the Second Congress elections (see Chapter 4). The Texas delegation, representing an unoccupied state, also resisted suspension. The only large anomaly in the general pattern was the Tennessee

delegation. Although occupied by this time, they resisted, at least in this case, the imposition of military authority over the civilian population. Tennessee's representatives voted this way perhaps because of past precedent in this matter and perhaps because part of their state was specially targeted by President Davis as an example of why he needed the bill.[40]

The congressional debate over the suspension of habeas corpus was almost continuous during the Civil War. The first habeas corpus suspension was approved in February 1862, and the fourth and last renewal ended August 1, 1864. For eighteen months in the above period President Davis had the power to suspend habeas corpus in places and at times deemed necessary. After strong urging by President Davis and General Lee, Congress again debated in November and December 1864 renewing the power of suspension. In early December numerous motions and amendments to the habeas corpus bill were presented and voted on in the House. Unfortunately, because of secret sessions and scanty coverage, the *Proceedings* do not record specific habeas corpus debate during this period; however, lengthy discussions on this issue are found in other volumes of the *Proceedings*, and numerous other sources exist. In spite of the lack of recorded debate, the mapping of over a dozen roll calls of habeas corpus motions and amendments reveal in virtually every case a consistent pattern of weakening amendments supported by unoccupied districts and amendments or procedural actions to strengthen or speed the bill supported by occupied districts and the above coalition. Previous detailed studies of habeas corpus voting and debate show the occupied-unoccupied variable to be the most explanatory, with other characteristics such as former party and secession stance also important.[41] Throughout the war suspension was most often supported by secessionist former Democrats and resisted by Unionist former Whigs. This was more and more consistent as the war continued and as more districts were occupied, especially after the Second House election.

Several other issues were evident in the debate and writings of the day. Strongest among these was state rights. State rightists again asked key questions: Did the central government and President Davis have the right to take away the sacred right of the individual citizen? Did the central government and the military have the right to override state and local civilian judicial authority? Strong state sovereignty utterances by some representatives were a smokescreen covering up personal or constituency interests, but for others they were manifestations of strong long-held beliefs. The South Carolina delegation, virtually all secessionist Democrats, voted against the December 8 passage of suspension. Map 36 indicates unanimous rejection of suspension by both Carolina delegations, even though they come from radically different political backgrounds.

Although the habeas corpus bill passed the House, it never passed the Senate in the exact same language. The debate, and obviously the military need for suspension, went on to the last days of Congress. After August 1, 1864, the habeas corpus statute was never

again suspended, and protection from illegal detention remained the official law of the Confederacy to the end of the war.

Central Government Control over State Militia—House—March 16, 1865. The Confederate Congress met, debated, and voted upon legislation until two weeks before the fall of Richmond. The last day of the Second Session of the Second Congress was March 18, 1865. Confederate troops, President Davis, and the government evacuated Richmond April 2, and federal troops occupied the capital April 3, 1865.

Congress debated many of the issues listed in Table 5-3 literally to its last day. For example, after lengthy debate a bill authorizing the arming of slaves as soldiers was approved March 13, 1865. In addition to normal legislative work, Congress spent much of its last week arguing over another unflattering presidential message to Congress requesting it to stay in session and to pass more stringent laws regarding conscription, impressment, habeas corpus, revenue, and generally to stop blocking action needed at this desperate time.

One of the many pieces of desperate legislation in the last days was the call by President Davis for the central government, in essence President Davis himself, to have the power to assume command of the state militias. In his November 1864 message to the opening of the Second Session, Davis included a request for "A general militia law . . . in the interest of self defense . . . establishing an exact method for calling the militia into Confederate service."[42] On March 13, 1865, Davis, "in bitter words," again asked Congress for power to control the state militia.[43] Both the House and Senate brought bills to the floor authorizing such power. In the House the title of the bill was, "to provide for organizing, arming, and disciplining the militia of the Confederate States, and for governing such part of them as may be employed in the service of the Confederate States, and for calling them forth to execute the laws of the Confederate States, suppress insurrections, and repel invasions."[44] The House Military Affairs Committee had jurisdiction over the legislation and even it reported negatively on the proposal, commenting the militia was generally composed of men not eligible for conscription, boys under seventeen and old men over fifty-five.[45] The critical vote on this bill was a proposal by opponent representative Mark H. Blandford of Georgia to table the bill and not consider the legislation. The vote to table lost by a close 31 yea to 33 nay vote.

Map 37 illustrates the geographic pattern of the sentiment of giving the central government power to assume control of the state militia. The core of support for central government control was from states and areas that had no Confederate militia: Missouri, Kentucky, Tennessee, and northwestern Virginia. A stark regional pattern of opposition to the bill came from the Coastal Plain Deep South, that is, from the states that were only partially occupied and had some state militia under the governor's control. Even secessionist former Democrats in south Alabama, western Louisiana, and Texas voted against losing command of the state militia. The sacredness of state control of its own militia and the thought of forcing boys and old men to fight for a lost cause was virtually unanimously resisted in the unoccupied-disrupted states. Even in the last days of the Confederacy many in Congress resisted drastic measures that thwarted state rights and were deleterious to their districts and states.

The geographical pattern of those supporting and resisting the legislation is interesting in itself, but one additional revealing aspect of the last days of Congress is illustrated by mapping the foregoing vote. This is the number and geographic location of the districts with members who were still present and voting and those members who were absent. In the Second Congress every seat was occupied at least part of the Congress except the Alabama Third District.[46] As the previous December 1864 vote on habeas corpus indicates, there was over 90 percent attendance at the beginning of the Second Session. As the general military situation in northern Virginia and elsewhere deteriorated and the siege of Richmond grew tighter, members of Congress began to flee the capital. The attrition became so great resolutions were introduced for "the Speaker to . . . issue his warrant for the arrest of any member about to absent himself without leave."[47]

The 31 yea to 33 nay vote on the state militias is one of the largest vote totals in the last week of Congress. This is an important consideration in the selection of a vote to map in periods of large absences. A total of thirty-seven representatives (34.9 percent) were absent for this vote, and virtually all of these had officially or unofficially left Richmond. Occupied areas had a great percentage of their congressmen in Richmond to the end. These representatives had no safe home to return to and were wanted by Federal authorities. Only nine of the thirty-seven absent members (24.3 percent) were from occupied districts.[48] The remaining twenty-eight representatives were from unoccupied areas of the Deep South to the south and southwest of Richmond. Another group of congressmen who remained in Richmond were the trans-Mississippi members who were a great distance from home. Only three of the twenty-three trans-Mississippi districts (13.0 percent) were absent.[49]

The vote to table the state militia bill demonstrates that those in favor of granting Administration militia control were in the majority, and the bill passed the House the same day. The Senate vote, however, was a tie, and the legislation never passed Congress.[50] The vote in the House on the state militias again demonstrated the power of the occupied districts in helping to pass extreme administration-sponsored legislation, but also their dominance in the last months of Congress and their role in this period of desperate legislation.

Conscription Exemptions—Senate—February 15, 1865. The first military draft in American history was enacted by the Confederate Congress in April 1862. Conscription was not only one of the major issues in Congress, but perhaps the most contentious and revealing. Table 5-3 indicates conscription had many subissues, one of the most controversial being exemption, that is, individuals excused from military service because of the nature of their position or skill. Exemptions given after the first conscription act included Confederate and state government officials, postal workers, rail-

road and river transportation employees, telegraph operators, ministers, teachers, and workers in important defense industries.[51] Debate about exemption continued throughout the course of the war. As the war progressed the Confederacy needed more men because of casualties, capture, desertions, and the overwhelming numbers of the North. Reducing the number of exemptions and expanding the draft pool was debated to the end of the war. Of course, exemption legislation, like all other legislation, had to pass both the House and Senate to become law; therefore, understanding roll-call voting in the Senate and the geographical pattern of this voting is as important as understanding House voting.

Since the method of election and term of service of Confederate senators is quite different than representatives, this affects the mix of variables influencing roll-call voting behavior (see Table 5-3).[52] In addition, because eighteen of the twenty-six senators drew four- and six-year terms they did not have to stand for reelection, eventually serving for the entire Permanent Confederate Congress (see Table 4-1). All the initial senators were elected in a time of euphoria and high expectations. Many of these senators were chosen because of their prosecessionist, pro-Confederate stance. Most of the four- and six-year senators kept this stance throughout the history of the Confederate Senate in spite of the fortunes of war and changes in most states in the sentiment of the populace, state legislature, or governor. All the two-year senators, and the replacements of the four- and six-year senators, did have to stand for reelection or election in the state legislatures. The state legislatures in many of the unoccupied states changed somewhat over the course of the war, especially after new state elections (see Chapter 4). These newly elected senators usually reflected more closely the changing sentiment of the people, state legislature, and governor during the time they served.

In spite of the numerous possible influences in roll-call voting listed in Table 5-3, Confederate Senate votes many times display clear regional differences. All of the 507 individual Senate roll-call votes can be mapped (see Table 5-1). Map 38 demonstrates one technique of mapping an individual roll-call vote in the Confederate Senate. This vote was on an amendment to legislation reducing conscription exemptions. The vote in question took place February 15, 1865. The specific vote was on an amendment by a supporter of continued exemptions, Sen. James L. Orr of South Carolina. Senator Orr's amendment allowed the continued exemptions of "persons who, upon satisfactory evidence submitted to the Sectary of War, are, or may be, more useful at home to the public by their skill, labor, or services than in the field."[53] Senators voting in favor of the amendment generally desired to keep a higher number of exemptions. Senators opposing the amendment desired to reduce the number of individuals protected from military service. The amendment lost on a roll-call vote of 9 yea, 13 nay, with 4 absent.[54]

Map 38 illustrates the geographical pattern of this exemption vote. States represented by senators voting yea (in favor of the liberal

exemption amendment) are green, and states represented by senators voting nay (for strengthening conscription) are red. States whose senators were absent are colored tan. If a state's two senators both vote nay, the entire state is red; if the state's senators vote differently or one is absent, the state is divided into diagonal strips of different color. Table 5-5 lists the senators serving at the time of this roll-call and their individual vote. This table is provided because in the split vote states it is impossible to determine by the map alone which way senators vote or who is absent.

The geographical pattern of this particular vote is well-defined and similar to some House votes. Senators favoring expanding conscription were from the occupied states of Kentucky, Missouri, and Tennessee, or from the Trans-Mississippi West (Texas, Arkansas, and Louisiana). The Virginia senators split on this conscription vote. In Virginia there was both a need for drastic measures since the war was fought mostly within the state and a desire to protect its citizens since they were most likely to be immediately drafted. Sens. Albert G. Brown of Mississippi and William T. Dortch of North Carolina both voted to reduce conscription exemptions in spite of the change in political sentiment in their states. Both had four-year terms and were elected at the beginning of the war. The nine votes to protect draft exemptions all came from the southeast, the region mostly likely to have previously exempted men called up for service. In addition, many governors, legislators and congressmen from southeastern-Deep South states believed each state had the right to determine the number of government officials and others needed to be exempted from the draft within their particular jurisdiction.[55]

Votes in the Senate were equally important as votes in the House since they determined amendments and the final phraseology of legislation. The geographic understanding of Senate voting is important in the understanding of the politics and behavior of the entire Confederate Congress. Most of the maps in this atlas logically use the House, but the Senate is important as well, and Senate votes should be illustrated in any detailed study of congressional legislation.[56]

Multiple Roll-Call Vote Maps

The previous section discusses and demonstrates the technique of mapping an individual roll-call vote using the congressional district base maps in Chapter 3. Mapping a single critical or illustrative recorded vote is an important tool in understanding the political and geographic aspects of a particular legislative event or an important defining moment. This section discusses the technique of producing one map using the combined data of numerous roll-call votes. Using a number of roll-call votes, that is, multiple roll-call vote mapping, expands the potential understanding of both individual congressional political behavior and the general geographic pattern of that behavior.

Mapping multiple roll-call votes can be done in several ways.[57] A number of votes on one specific bill or specific issue, for example,

TABLE 5-5

Roll-Call Vote
Conscription Exemptions

Second Senate
Second Session
February 15, 1865[1]

Alabama
 Robert Jemison, Jr. - absent
 Richard Wilde Walker - yea

Arkansas
 Robert Ward Johnson - absent
 Augustus Hill Garland - nay

Florida
 James McNair Baker - yea
 Augustus Emmett Maxwell - yea

Georgia
 Benjamin Harvey Hill - absent
 Herschel Vespasian Johnson - yea

Kentucky
 Henry Cornelius Burnett - nay
 William Elliott Simms - nay

Louisiana
 Thomas Jenkins Semmes - yea
 Edward Sparrow - nay

Mississippi
 Albert Gallatin Brown - nay
 John William Clark Watson - yea

Missouri
 Waldo Porter Johnson - nay
 George Graham Vest - nay

North Carolina
 William Theophilus Dortch - nay
 William Alexander Graham - yea

South Carolina
 Robert Woodward Barnwell - absent
 James Lawrence Orr - yea

Tennessee
 Landon Carter Haynes - nay
 Gustavus Adolphus Henry - nay

Texas
 Williamson Simpson Oldham - nay
 Louis Trezevant Wigfall - nay

Virginia
 Robert Mercer Taliaferro Hunter - yea
 Allen Taylor Caperton - nay

[1] *Journal of the Congress of the Confederate States of America, 1861–1865*, (Washington, D.C.: Government Printing Office, 1904), Vol. 4, pp. 561–562.

price controls, can be combined and mapped. One vote on price controls may or may not be typical of a representatives general feeling or behavior on this subject or the general geographic pattern of sentiment. However, two, three, four, or more votes on price controls within one period, session, or Congress give a better picture of congressional behavior and geographic pattern. With a number of votes, an individual representative or senator can be scored or scaled with respect to his support for price controls. For example, if four votes on price controls are recorded in one session, then each congressman can be classified in one of five categories, 0 to 4, with respect to his intensity of support for this policy.

This atlas uses another multiple vote mapping technique, specifically, the combining of a number of roll calls that all pertain to one large issue, policy area, or "issue dimension."[58] For example, price controls are usually thought of as being in the economic policy area. Economic policy was one of the larger issue dimensions in the Confederate Congress. As Table 5-3 indicates, economic policy had numerous subissues in addition to price controls, including currency, trade embargos, railroad construction, and many others.

There are various quantitative and other techniques available to determine if a variety of roll calls are actually within one larger policy area. In *The Anatomy of the Confederate Congress*, Thomas Alexander and Richard Beringer use a number of these techniques to uncover roll-call votes relating to broad policy areas or large issue dimensions operating in the Confederate Congress. Their final roll-call scale scores are used in this atlas to map voting behavior and thereby explore further the geographical aspects of the Confederate Congress. One additional benefit of using multiple roll-call vote mapping in the Confederate Congress is the lessening of problems due to high absenteeism in a large number of individual votes and in certain time periods (see, for example, the single-vote Map 37). Even if a congressman misses several votes, multiple vote analysis reveals, through the votes on in which he does participate, his general tendency and a more complete national roll-call vote map results.

Multiple roll-call voting maps are used in this atlas in two ways. First, to analyze behavior in one dimension or issue area. The important and contentious areas of conscription and impressment are used as examples. Second, multiple vote maps are used to analyze one large multidimensional "Confederate Support Score" by combining a number of issue dimensions. This multidimensional score examines a possible larger all-encompassing ideological, philosophical, or practical dimension operating within the Confederate Congress, thereby exploring a general theory of congressional behavior that the analysis and maps indicate has a strong geographical component.

One Issue Dimension: Conscription. Conscription was one of the most controversial issues in the Confederate Congress.[59] This issue literally meant years of service and life and death for tens of thousands of Southerners. Conscription had many subissues—minimum and maximum age, length of service, exemptions, overseers, substitutes, and drafting of slaves. However, conscription questions

also arose regarding areas such as habeas corpus and, of course, military affairs. Because of the gravity of the issue, questions of equity and fairness were very apparent and obvious to the general populace. Analyzing votes on all the subissues pertaining to the draft gives a larger and more complete picture of this subject.

First House. Map 39 illustrates the geographic pattern of voting on a large number of conscription issues in the First House. Green identifies representatives with a strong and consistent voting behavior supporting not only the establishment of a draft, but also its vigorous enforcement and expansion of its base. These representatives are designated proconscription congressmen. For example, proconscription representatives generally support the draft, including amendments and measures expanding the age of service, increasing the length of service, reducing or eliminating exemptions, and using suspension of habeas corpus to detain possible draft dodgers. Red identifies representatives with a voting record not particularly strong with respect to stringent draft legislation.

Map 39 was constructed using eighty-nine different conscription-related roll-call votes from the First House: fourteen from the First Session, thirty-five from the Second, seventeen from the Third, and twenty-three from the Fourth. *The Anatomy of the Confederate Congress* assigns performance scores of 0 to 9 for each member of Congress for each session based on these combined roll calls.[60] This atlas averages the scores for the four sessions for an aggregate First House score.[61] All representatives averaging 5 to 9 are designated proconscription congressmen and all averaging 0 to 4 are designated as giving less support for conscription.[62] Sixty-one representatives (57.6 percent) scored in the proconscription category and forty-four (41.5 percent) in the lower category. One seat (0.9 percent) was vacant in the First House.

There was a well-defined geographic pattern of conscription roll-call voting in the First House. Strong support for conscription came from three distinct areas. The first was the occupied districts bordering the North in northern Virginia, Kentucky, and Missouri. Obviously, representatives from these districts could support conscription without the consequences befalling the men in their areas. The second region of support was a band of unoccupied districts in the lower South from south Georgia west to the Mississippi River.[63] These representatives were from the region of the South with strong secessionist pro-Confederate sentiment at the beginning of the war. One other possible geographic trend is the tendency for most of the far western frontier districts to support the draft. These areas were farthest from the major theater of war, and the central government conscription apparatus was weakest there. Table 5-6 ranks the ten representatives with the highest proconscription voting scores. The strongest and most consistent support for conscription comes from occupied districts. The first seven ranked conscription supporters all came from occupied Missouri, Virginia, Tennessee, and Kentucky. Two representatives in the top ten came from the Deep South, one from southern Mississippi and one from North Carolina.

There was also a well-defined extensive geographic concentration of districts with weak support for conscription measures. Map 39 clearly shows this area was centered in southern Virginia, North Carolina, and South Carolina. This region had a large manpower pool, was close to the major theater of war, and had an efficient conscription system. Table 5-6 also lists the ten representatives who showed least support of the Confederate draft in the First House.

TABLE 5-6

**Conscription Support
House of Representatives
First Congress**

Highest Ten Representatives and Districts

Rank[1]	Representative	State	District	Conscription Support Score[2]
1	William M. Cooke	MO	1	9
2	Albert Jenkins	VA	14	9
3	William Smith	VA	9	9
4	Aaron Conrow	MO	4	8.5
5	David M. Currin	TN	11	8.33
6	John M. Elloit	KY	12	8.33
7	Thomas W. Freeman	MO	6	8
8	Ethelbert Barksdale	MS	6	7.5
9	William Lander	NC	8	7.5
10	John J. McRae	MS	7	7.25

Lowest Ten Representatives and Districts

Rank	Representative	State	District	Conscription Support Score
96[3]	Thomas McDowell	NC	4	2.5
97	Caleb C. Herbert	TX	2	2.33
98	Robert R. Bridgers	NC	2	2.33
99	John W. Baldwin	VA	11	2.33
100	Allen T. Davidson	NC	10	2.25
101	Thomas S. Ashe	NC	7	2.25
102	Burgess S. Gaither	NC	9	2
103	William N. Smith	NC	1	1.75
104	Henry S. Foote	TN	5	1.75
105[4]	Lewis M. Ayer	SC	3	1.5

[1] If two or more representatives tie in support score they are listed in alphabetical order.

[2] Based on the average of conscription vote scores in the four sessions of the First Congress. A score of 9 indicates strong support for conscription and a score of 0 indicates no support. Thomas B. Alexander and Richard E. Beringer, *The Anatomy of the Confederate Congress* (Nashville: Vanderbilt University Press, 1972), pp. 390–404.

[3] One additional representative scored 2.5 from the Thirteenth District of Virginia.

[4] One district is vacant in the First House.

Nine of these representatives were from unoccupied districts with six of these coming from the state of North Carolina.

Second House. Map 40 illustrates the geographic pattern of voting on multiple conscription votes in the Second House. Green again indicates representatives with a strong and consistent voting behavior supporting conscription and red identifies representatives with a weak conscription-support score. Map 40 was constructed using twenty-one conscription related roll-call votes from the Second Session of the Second House: fourteen from a period at the beginning of the session (November to February); and seven from a period at the end of the session (February to March).[64] Votes were not used from the First Session because the draft was not extensively debated in this period.[65] Again the map uses the average score for the above two periods for an overall Second House score.

In the Second House only forty-nine representatives (46.2 percent) scored in the proconscription category and forty-one (38.7 percent) in the lower category. One seat (0.9 percent) was vacant in the Second House. Because this analysis only considers voting in the Second Session, fifteen representatives (14.2 percent) did not vote often enough for a conscription voting behavior score to be assigned to them accurately. Since the latter portion of the Second Session had a very high absentee rate the combined roll-call score is actually a significant improvement in the analysis and illustration of voting at the end of the Confederate Congress (see, for example, single-vote Map 37).

There was again a well-defined geographic pattern of conscription roll-call voting behavior in the Second House. Strong conscription support was now concentrated in only one area, the occupied districts. The occupied area of the South now included most of the state of Tennessee. In the First House five Tennessee representatives were weak on conscription and in the Second only one.[66] Other proconscription districts were scattered throughout the Deep South, including three in South Carolina which had been invaded by Sherman in his Carolinas campaign. Table 5-7 ranks the ten highest proconscription representatives in the Second Congress. Again, occupied districts dominate the ranking, this time accounting for all the highest conscription support scores. Kentucky, Missouri, and Tennessee each had three congressmen in the highest group.

The Second Congress elections had an effect on conscription voting (see Chapter 4). Anticonscription congressmen were strongest in North Carolina and Georgia, but were also evident in Alabama, Mississippi, and Texas, indicating that the lower South, previously united in enthusiastic support of war measures such as conscription, was now divided on these issues. The congressmen who gave the least support to conscription are listed in Table 5-7. They all represented essentially unoccupied districts, although some of the districts were disrupted at the end of the war. Four North Carolina representatives rank at the bottom of the table with scores of 0, and, all told, North Carolina had six of the ten least supportive members.[67] One other member of the House also has a 0 ranking, William

TABLE 5-7

**Conscription Support
House of Representatives
Second Congress**

Highest Ten Representatives and Districts

Rank[1]	Representative	State	District	Conscription Support Score[2]
1	Rufus K. Garland	AR	3	9
2	Ninrod L. Norton	MO	2	9
3	John B. Clark	MO	3	8.5
4	John M. Elliot	KY	12	8.5
5	Edwin A. Keeble	TN	6	8.5
6	Thomas Menees	TN	8	8.5
7	Henry E. Read	KY	3	8.5
8	Peter S. Wilkes	MO	6	8.5
9	John W. C. Atkins	TN	9	8
10[3]	Theodore L. Burnett	KY	6	8

Lowest Ten Representatives and Districts

Rank	Representative	State	District	Conscription Support Score
81[4]	James T. Leach	NC	3	1
82	Caleb C. Herbert	TX	2	1
83	Julian Hartridge	GA	1	1
84	John A. Gilmer	NC	6	0.5
85	Marcus H. Cruikshank	AL	4	0.5
86	William C. Wickham	VA	3	0
87	James G. Ramsay	NC	8	0
88	George W. Logan	NC	10	0
89	James M. Leach	NC	7	0
90[5]	Thomas C. Fuller	NC	4	0

[1] When two or more representatives have the same support score they are listed in alphabetical order.

[2] Based on votes on conscription in the Second Session of the Second Congress. A score of 9 indicates strong support for conscription and a score of 0 indicates little or no support. Thomas B. Alexander and Richard E. Beringer, *The Anatomy of the Confederate Congress* (Nashville: Vanderbilt University Press, 1972), pp. 390–404.

[3] Seven additional representatives had a conscription support score of 8: Kentucky Fourth and Fifth; Mississippi First; Missouri Fourth; Tennessee Seventh; Virginia Fourteenth and Fifteenth.

[4] One additional representative from the Georgia Eighth District had a conscription support score of 1.

[5] In the Second Congress one seat was vacant, and fifteen representatives were absent often enough that a conscription support score could not be accurately calculated.

C. Wickham, representing the Virginia Third District, which is essentially Richmond at this stage of Congress.[68]

As in any legislative issue, a number of variables are responsible for roll-call voting on conscription. The literature about conscription suggests influences such as state rights, secession stance, and deterioration of the Confederate situation in the war as affecting conscription voting. However, even within subissues of conscription (exemption, for example) variations of intensity of support are manifested by some individual members. Nevertheless, the analysis of the total conscription dimension by combining numerous votes not only gives a general overall picture of voting behavior, but also of the geographic pattern of support. This pattern clearly indicates large regions of support and resistance, with the core of support coming from occupied districts, especially in the Second Congress.

One Issue Dimension: Impressment. The right of private property is sacred in the American economic, legal, and political traditions. The American Revolution was fought to a great extent for the economic freedom of the planter and merchant trader class. The Civil War was fought for the most part over slavery and the right of the southern planter to own and keep his human bondage property. The government confiscation of private property, therefore, was an issue of utmost gravity and had potential personal impacts, perhaps second only to conscription. In times of war, the need for impressment—the confiscation of private property for military purposes—has precedent. However, the times, places, and method of impressment have all been matters of concern. Impressment was a major subject of debate in the Confederate Congress. The impressment subissues include the rights of impressment officers, specific procedures of impoundment, amount, compensation rate, method of payment, right and procedure of appeal of paid compensation, and claims of unpaid impressment. One aspect of impressment debated in the Confederate Congress was the enactment of laws authorizing the destruction of private property (crops, merchandise, agricultural goods, general assets, and so on) so as not to fall in a usable form into the hands of the enemy.

Impressment probably had a distinctive geographical component. Property tends to be commandeered more in areas where large military operations are conducted or near large military encampments. These armies were many times in need of immediate and/or long-term supplies. Areas far from the front lines were less likely to have property destroyed or to have large amounts of goods suddenly confiscated in an emergency. In the Civil War certain areas of the South were more likely to have property seized than others, and these areas change somewhat over the course of the war. Maps 41 and 42 illustrate the geographic pattern of support for impressment legislation in the First and Second Confederate House of Representatives. These maps use the same multiple roll-call vote data analysis and mapping techniques discussed and used in the previous section on conscription.

First House. Map 41 illustrates the geographic pattern of voting on a number of impressment issues in the First House. These impressment votes come from two distinct periods—nine roll-call votes debated in the First Session, First House (February to April 1862), concerning the authorization of private property destruction, and seven roll calls taken in the Third Session, First House (January to May 1863), relating to the passage of the first comprehensive impressment law.[69] During the short First Session an unusually large segment of the South was occupied by the Union, especially parts of northern Virginia, middle and western Tennessee, and New Orleans. In addition, extensive Union military troop movements occurred in northern Alabama and northern Arkansas. Unlike the previous Union consolidation of Kentucky and Missouri, the occupation of these areas raised questions with respect to the obligations of loyal Confederate citizens to destroy their agricultural, commercial, and personal property so as not to allow it to fall into enemy hands and the authorization of the Confederate army or local officials to do the same. The impressment voting behavior scores in these two sessions are similar for most representatives. However, there were some members who were against property destruction in the First Session, but supported general impressment in the Third, and vice versa.[70] This type of voting behavior for some representatives is also present in the various sessions on conscription and other policy areas. Nevertheless, the combination of these two sets of roll-call votes gives a more comprehensive picture of who supported impressment and who were hesitant to do so.

The performance scores of these two groups of roll calls were averaged, and the House membership divided into two groups.[71] Map 41 illustrates the geographic distribution of the supporters and opponents of impressment. Green identifies the fifty-nine House members (55.7 percent) with a voting tendency for stringent impressment policies. Forty-three representatives (40.6 percent) had a low impressment support score and are colored red. Three representatives (2.8 percent) did not vote enough in either session to accurately assign them an impressment score. One seat (0.9 percent) was vacant in the First House.

Support for impressment in the First House was concentrated in the Deep South, the region of the Confederacy farthest away from most military action and having the most strident secessionist sentiment at the beginning of the war. Additional support for impressment came from twelve of the seventeen voting representatives in occupied Kentucky and Missouri. Table 5-8 lists the ten members of the First House most supportive of impressment. Seven of the most proimpressment representatives come from occupied districts, three from Kentucky and Missouri and one from northwest Tennessee. The other three consistent supporters were from the Deep South.

Opposition to impressment legislation also had specific geographic concentrations. First, the Virginia delegation and adjacent areas of northern North Carolina. Virginia was the first true southern state to feel invasion from the North. Property destruction legislation was

particularly sensitive to residents in the northern Virginia districts. As the war progressed through 1861–1862, large southern armies assembled in Virginia, and supplies were needed for their constant care. The Great Valley of Virginia (districts Ten, Eleven, Twelve, and

TABLE 5-8

**Impressment Support
House of Representatives
First Congress**

Highest Ten Representatives and Districts

Rank[1]	Representative	State	District	Impressment Support Score[2]
1	John D. Atkins	TN	9	9
2	Milledge L. Bonham	SC	4	9
3	Aaron H. Conrow	MO	2	9
4	Thomas W. Freeman	MO	6	9
5	Thomas A. Harris	MO	4	9
6	Theodore L. Burnett	KY	6	8.5
7	William P. Chilton	AL	6	8
8	James S. Chrisman	KY	5	8
9	James B. Dawkins	FL	1	8
10[3]	John M. Elliot	KY	12	8

Lowest Ten Representatives and Districts

Rank	Representative	State	District	Impressment Support Score
93[4]	Archibald H. Arrington	NC	5	2
94	Thomas B. Hanly	AK	4	1.5
95	Augustus H. Garland	AK	3	1.5
96	Alexander Boteler	VA	10	1.5
97	William B. Wright	TX	6	1
98	Joseph B. Heiskell	TN	1	1
99	John Goode, Jr.	VA	6	1
100	William Smith	VA	9	0
101	Daniel De Jarnette	VA	8	0
102[5]	John R. Chambliss	VA	2	0

[1] If two or more representatives have the same support score they are listed in alphabetical order.

[2] Based on votes on impressment in the four sessions of the First Congress. A score of 9 indicates strong support for impressment and a score of 0 indicates little or no support. Thomas B. Alexander and Richard E. Beringer, *The Anatomy of the Confederate Congress* (Nashville: Vanderbilt University Press, 1972), pp. 390–404.

[3] One additional representative from the Kentucky Fourth District had an impressment score of 8.

[4] Five additional representatives had an impressment score of 2: Mississippi First; North Carolina Second; South Carolina Second; Tennessee Third and Fourth.

[5] The Seventh District of Missouri was vacant throughout the Congress and three representatives did not vote often enough for an accurate impressment score to be calculated.

Thirteen) was one of the leading agricultural regions of the South in general farming and a storehouse of grain and livestock. Other districts with low impressment support scores were in eastern Tennessee, northern Alabama, northern Mississippi, and northeastern Arkansas, all within or adjacent to major military activity in early 1862. Table 5-8 also lists the ten representatives least supportive of property destruction and impressment in the First House. Three representatives scored zero, all from the most intense war zones in Virginia: the Eighth and Ninth districts between Washington, D.C., and Richmond, and the Second across from Fort Monroe in Tidewater Virginia. All told, five of the most consistent First Congress opponents of impressment were from Virginia.

Second House. Map 42 illustrates the geographic pattern of voting on multiple impressment votes in the Second House. Green again indicates representatives with a strong and consistent voting behavior supporting impressment, and red identifies members with a weak impressment performance score. Map 42 was constructed using twenty-four roll-call votes—eleven impressment related votes from the Second Congress, First Session, and thirteen recorded votes from the Second Session. The average of the scores was used to construct an overall representative voting behavior.

In the Second House fifty-two representatives (49.1 percent) had performance scores above 4.5 on a 0 to 9 scale and are considered proimpressment members.[72] Forty-two members scored 4.5 or below, generally indicating less support for impressment. One seat was vacant in the Second House (0.9 percent) and eleven members (10.4 percent) were absent enough times on this issue to make an accurate assessment of their sentiment impossible. The geographic pattern of impressment support in the Second Congress was not only concentrated and well-defined, but was significantly different from the First Congress. Proimpressment districts were located in an arc on the periphery of the Confederacy comprising the occupied districts of northern Virginia, Kentucky, Missouri, Tennessee, Arkansas, and Louisiana, as well as several districts in the trans-Mississippi West. All these areas, especially the occupied districts, were not likely to be touched by southern impressment agents. In addition, previously unoccupied northern Virginia, Tennessee, and Arkansas changed from substantially opposing impressment legislation in the First Congress to substantially supporting impressment legislation in the Second Congress after occupation (see Maps 41 and 42). Table 5-9 lists the ten highest supporters of impressment in the Second House. Seven of the ten proimpressment representatives were from occupied districts with one additional individual from unoccupied trans-Mississippi Louisiana.

The opposition to impressment was also concentrated geographically and was significantly different from the previous Congress. The opposition congressmen come from an area that is strikingly similar to the unoccupied zone of the Confederacy (see Maps 22 and 24). This area stretches from southern Virginia through the Carolinas and across the Deep South. War-weariness and turnover in the

Second Congress elections transformed large areas of North Carolina, Georgia, and parts of Alabama from supporters of impressment to opponents (see incumbency for the second election, Map 35). In addition, the threat of impressment in these areas was now very real, changing the attitude of many Deep South citizens. Table 5-9 lists those members in the Second House least supportive of impressment. Eight of the ten leading anti-impressment representatives come from the remaining unoccupied zone in the Southeast, with five of these eight from the peace-oriented North Carolina delegation.

Like conscription, the geographic voting patterns with respect to impressment have a strong spatial relationship to occupied and unoccupied districts. In addition, citizens in districts in close proximity to the front lines or encampments, especially those with desirable food stocks, were also wary of impressment.[73] As with all issues in the Confederate Congress, a number of variables must be considered to understand voting on impressment. Some congressmen viewed uncompensated loss of personal property destroyed ahead of the Yankees as different from uncompensated loss of personal property given away to the Confederates. Some held the right of personal property so sacred that they believed it should never be forcibly taken, even with so-called compensation. Some viewed compensation with virtually worthless Confederate treasury notes, or affidavits of future payment, a fraud. A few wealthy plantation owners opposed impressment of slaves, agricultural products, and draft animals because they were most likely to be affected by these particular impressment practices. As the war progressed, some saw the futility of the overall struggle and wanted to end all drastic measures, especially if these measures were to be carried out in their areas. Other representatives, however, took the contrary view that because of the course of the war, drastic measures were needed all the more. As the war progressed, as the area of Union occupation increased, and as the second elections brought new members to Congress, the support for impressment changed; this, as well as all the foregoing factors, resulted in a significant change in the impressment map.

Multidimensional Roll-Call Vote Maps. The previous section discusses and demonstrates the technique of producing one map from a number of roll-call votes concerning one issue, policy area, or issue dimension. This section discusses the production of one map using roll-call data from numerous votes on numerous issue dimensions combined into one large multidimensional analysis.[74] *The Anatomy of the Confederate Congress* assigns each member of the Confederate Congress a multidimensional ranking that reflects an "over-all average performance score or scale position" based on voting on hundreds of roll-call votes in all sessions of Congress in a number of policy areas.[75] These policy areas include conscription, impressment (including property destruction), habeas corpus, economic policy, military affairs, state rights, race, military determination, and defeatism-realism. This multidimensional overall score is called in this atlas the Confederate Support Score.

TABLE 5-9

**Impressment Support
House of Representatives
Second Congress**

Highest Ten Representatives and Districts

Rank[1]	Representative	State	District	Impressment Support Score[2]
1	William W. Boyce	SC	6	9.0
2	Charles M. Conrad	LA	2	9.0
3	Henry Gray	LA	5	9.0
4	Robert A. Hatcher	MO	7	9.0
5	Robert L. Montague	VA	1	9.0
6	William C. Rives	VA	7	9.0
7	William G. Swan	TN	2	9.0
8	Peter S. Wilkes	MO	6	9.0
9	Eli M. Bruce	KY	9	8.5
10[3]	Edwin A. Keeble	TN	6	8.5

Lowest Ten Representatives and Districts

Rank	Representative	State	District	Impressment Support Score
85	Josiah Turner	NC	5	0.5
86	William C. Wickham	VA	3	0
87	William Smith	NC	1	0
88	George W. Logan	NC	10	0
89	James M. Leach	NC	7	0
90	John T. Lamkin	MS	7	0
91	Thomas C. Fuller	NC	4	0
92	Stephen H. Darden	TX	1	0
93	Lewis M. Ayer	SC	3	0
94[4]	John Atkins	TN	9	0

[1] If two or more representatives are tied in support score they are listed in alphabetical order.

[2] Based on votes on impressment in the two sessions of the Second Congress. A score of 9 indicates strong support for impressment and a score of 0 indicates little or no support. Thomas B. Alexander and Richard E. Beringer, *The Anatomy of the Confederate Congress* (Nashville: Vanderbilt University Press, 1972), pp. 390–404.

[3] One additional representative from Alabama Fifth District scored 8.5.

[4] The Third District of Alabama was vacant throughout the Second Congress, and eleven representatives did not vote often enough for an accurate impressment score to be calculated.

The Confederate Support Score suggests a possible all-encompassing ideological, philosophical, or practical dimension operating within the Confederate Congress. This score gauges support for the expansion of Confederate central government power by way of endorsing drastic measures to ensure the survival of the Confederacy irrespective of the impact on the southern population. An extreme supporter of the Confederacy normally took the strongest possible stance on virtually every issue area: expansion and full enforcement of conscription and impressment, permanent suspension of habeas corpus, stringent price controls, a well-enforced cotton embargo, harsh penalties for trading with the enemy, support for central government (Davis Administration) power over the states in such areas as control of the state militia, destruction of private property if needed, use of slaves as soldiers, and not accepting the war as a lost cause even in late 1864 and early 1865. Conversely, a weak supporter of severe measures had a low roll-call vote support score for most of the above issues.

The Confederate Support Score was calculated using hundreds of scalable roll-call votes covering the major issues over the course of the Confederate Congress. Each delegate, representative and senator was assigned an adjusted score in one of ten categories, 0 to 9, depending upon his voting behavior. Each chamber was then divided into two groups, 0 to 4 and 5 to 9, to uncover the general pattern of support and resistance to drastic wartime legislation and to illustrate the geopolitical pattern of this behavior. Green identifies the 5 to 9 group: delegates, representatives, and senators with a strong and consistent voting behavior for measures to strengthen the Confederacy's ability to wage and win the Civil War. Red identifies the 0 to 4 group, congressmen with a lower voting score with respect to backing extraordinary wartime legislation.

Confederate Support Score—Provisional Congress. The Provisional Congress was the governing body of the Confederate States of America in its first year of existence. In this first year many important issues were debated and voted upon and precedents established. Voting in the Provisional Congress was by state with each having one vote. Each member of the state delegation voted yea or nay on each roll call, and the state cast its one vote on this basis.

Since each member's vote was recorded in the *Confederate Journal*, an individual Confederate Support Score was calculated by *The Anatomy of the Confederate Congress* for each delegate. From these individual scores an average support score for each state was calculated for this atlas. For example, the five Provisional Congress delegates from Arkansas had individual support scores of 3, 5, 8, 4, and 4.[76] The average state support score is 4.8. Table 5-10 lists the Provisional Congress support scores for all thirteen states.

Since delegates to the Provisional Congress did not have districts and voting was by state, the geographic pattern of Confederate support in the Provisional Congress is illustrated by state. The average state support score for the Provisional Congress was 4.63. Eight states have a greater than average support score and are designated high Confederate support states.[77] Five states have an average below 4.63 and are designated low Confederate support states. Map 43 illustrates the geographic pattern of the Confederate Support Scores for the Provisional Congress (February 4, 1861, to February 17, 1862). Three geographic patterns are evident: first, in the border-front line states. The border state of Kentucky is by far the

TABLE 5-10

State Confederate Support Scores Provisional Congress

Rank	State	Voting Delegates	Confederate Support Score[1]
1	Kentucky	10	6.5
2	Alabama	9	5.6
3	Missouri	8	5.38
4	Mississippi	7	5.29
4	Texas	7	5.29
6	Louisiana	6	5.17
7	Virginia	15	4.87
8	Arkansas	5	4.8
9	North Carolina	10	4.3
10	Georgia	10	4
11	Tennessee	7	3.29
12	South Carolina	8	3
13	Florida	3	2.70
Total/Average		105	4.63

[1] State average of the adjusted scale position score for each voting member of the state delegation. Replacements of originally seated and voting delegates are not counted in state average. Thomas B. Alexander and Richard E. Beringer, *The Anatomy of the Confederate Congress* (Nashville: Vanderbilt University Press, 1972), Appendix III.

highest-ranking state, with a 6.5 score. By the time of its December 1861 entry into the Provisional Congress, Kentucky was almost totally occupied. Another border state, Missouri, was also almost totally occupied, and it ranks third highest. Virginia also ranks as a supportive state, probably because since the middle of 1861 its western, northern, and Tidewater areas saw military action and were on the front line. A second cluster of support was in the southwest of the Confederacy. Four Deep South states rank after the border states—Alabama, Mississippi, Texas, and Louisiana. The upper South state of Arkansas is last in the high support category.

The five states voting below average are in one geographic concentration in the southeast of the Confederacy. These states were not actually on the front line, but were close enough to feel the demand of stringent wartime legislation. Three of these five states had large unoccupied Unionist areas: North Carolina, Georgia, and Tennessee. Tennessee and North Carolina were adjacent to front line states to their immediate north. Perhaps the most surprising score is South Carolina, the first state to secede and perhaps with the most proslavery, pro-Confederate sentiment. However, even in the euphoric first year of the Confederacy, South Carolina registered its dislike for legislation that made personal and economic demands upon its citizens, built central government power, and undermined state sovereignty.

TABLE 5-11

District Status and Confederate Support[1]

	First Congress			
	High Confederate Support	Low Confederate Support	Vacant	Total Districts
Occupied	30	10	1	41
Disrupted	4	5	-	9
Unoccupied	27	29	-	56
Total	61	44	1	106

	Second Congress			
	High Confederate Support	Low Confederate Support	Vacant	Total Districts
Occupied	35	8	-	43
Disrupted	5	4	1	10
Unoccupied	15	38	-	53
Total	55	50	1	106

[1] District status determined by the situation at the end of the First Congress, Fourth Session, and Second Congress, First Session.

The Provisional Congress map gives an early indication of roll-call vote sentiment in the Confederate Congress. This pattern can be compared to the subsequent two congresses. Confederate Support Scores in the First and Second Houses, however, are able to be mapped with 106 districts and thus give a more detailed geographic analysis of Confederate roll-call voting.

Confederate Support Score—First House and Senate. Map 44 illustrates the geographic pattern of the Confederate support score in the First House and Senate (February 18, 1862, to February 17, 1864). The pattern of support for stringent wartime measures is, not surprisingly, similar to some aspects of the Provisional Congress map and to the patterns of some of the single and multiple roll-call voting maps discussed previously. However, perhaps because it is multidimensional, the patterns on the First House map are not as geographically concentrated as the single vote or single issue maps. In the House, sixty-one representatives (57.6 percent) rank high in multidimensional support of the Confederacy. The most solid areas of support are the occupied districts, specifically northwestern Virginia, Kentucky, Missouri, and the Union-controlled portion of Louisiana. Added to this core are three other pockets of First Congress Confederate support in the unoccupied South: clusters of Deep South districts in southern Mississippi and southern Alabama; the Virginia Piedmont congressmen; and most western frontier districts.[78]

Table 5-11 compares the occupation status of districts and the Confederate support score of their representatives.[79] In the First House thirty of the forty-one occupied districts (73.2 percent) are classified as voting for stringent war legislation. At the beginning of the war, the unoccupied districts were somewhat evenly split between high-scoring representatives (48.2 percent) and low-scoring representatives (51.8 percent). In other words, the highly supportive members were almost evenly divided between occupied and unoccupied areas, while the majority of low-scoring members were from unoccupied areas.

The representatives from occupied districts demonstrated, in virtually all issues before Congress, that they supported drastic measures to win the war, primarily because the consequences did not directly affect their districts and they desired their territory to be eventually liberated and to rejoin the Confederacy. The Virginia delegation also demonstrated support for strong legislation since it continued to be the major battleground for the war. The far western districts were somewhat removed from the most devastating effects of the war and had the tendency to support certain drastic wartime proposals. The Tennessee delegation did not follow the usual political or geographical pattern. Four of the eleven Tennessee representatives scored low. However, the weakest delegates were from the middle and western parts of the state, the most prosecessionist area, occupied early in 1862. The four representatives from eastern Tennessee ranked high in Confederate support even though they were unoccupied for three of the four sessions of Congress. These eastern delegates were elected by a pro-South constituency made up of a small percentage of the total population, but who participated in the First House election (see the discussion of Tennessee elections in Chapter 4).

Table 5-12 lists the top individual representatives in Confederate support in the First House. Six representatives scored 7 with no members scoring 8 or 9. Four of the six top Confederates represented occupied districts, and the other two were from Deep South Georgia. All four representatives from occupied areas won reelection, one from an unoccupied area resigned and one overwhelmingly lost reelection. Twenty-three representatives were in the next highest category, and the majority of these, fourteen, were from occupied districts.

Table 5-13 lists the states in the First Congress in order of their average delegation Confederate Support Score. Three states tied for the highest legislative support of the war with an average of 5.33. The totally occupied border states of Kentucky and Missouri continued to rank high, along with Louisiana. In Louisiana the three districts surrounding New Orleans were occupied early in the First Congress, and the adjacent district was disrupted and on the front line. These occupied and disrupted districts registered very high support scores. Another front line state, Virginia, ranked fourth in Confederate support. Virginia also had high-scoring occupied districts with many other representatives supportive of a vigorous war effort. Although all four of the above states ranked high in the Pro-

visional Congress as the war continued, areas became occupied, and the front line developed, both Louisiana's and Virginia's rank and average score increased. This was also the case with Tennessee.

The pattern of weak support scores in Map 44 is also similar to previously discussed maps, but again not as solid. The core of resistance to stringent wartime measures continued to be in the southeast portion of the Confederacy, the area usually most affected by new legislation. North Carolina, South Carolina, and Georgia constitute the core of this area, along with the Great Valley agricultural districts in Virginia. Table 5-12 also lists the least supportive representatives in the First Congress. Three House members had a score of 2, and nineteen members scored in the next lowest category, with the vast majority of these, sixteen, representing unoccupied districts. The geographical pattern within Louisiana is illustrative of the national pattern. The occupied and disrupted districts, First, Second, Third, and Fourth, have very high support scores of 6, 6, 7, and 6, respectively. The unoccupied western districts, the Fifth and Sixth, have low scores of 3 and 4.

TABLE 5-12

Confederate Support
House of Representatives
First Congress

Representatives and Districts Achieving the Highest Score

Representative	State	District	Confederate Support Score[1]
Aaron H. Conrow	MO	4	7
George W. Ewing	KY	4	7
Hines Holt	GA	3	7
Robert Johnson	VA	15	7
Duncan F. Kenner	LA	3	7
David W. Lewis	GA	5	7

Twenty-three representatives scored in the next highest category (6) and fourteen represent occupied districts.

Representatives and Districts Achieving the Lowest Score

Representative	State	District	Confederate Support Score
William N. Smith	NC	1	2
Caleb C. Herbert	TX	2	2
Henry S. Foote	TN	5	2

Nineteen representatives scored in the next lowest category (3) and sixteen represent unoccupied districts.

[1] Based on votes used to calculate the average adjusted scale position in the four sessions of the First Congress. A score of 9 indicates strong dedication for measures to support Confederate survival and a score of 0 indicates little or no support. Thomas B. Alexander and Richard E. Beringer, *The Anatomy of the Confederate Congress* (Nashville: Vanderbilt University Press, 1972), pp. 390–404.

As Table 5-13 shows, the delegations least supportive of stringent wartime legislation in the First Congress were from the unoccupied states. South and North Carolina rank at the bottom with scores of 3.33 and 3.9 respectively. As in the Provisional Congress, the South Carolina delegation continued to view much of the legislation as either an affront to state sovereignty, a threat to the economy or citizens of the state, giving too much power to Jefferson Davis, or sometimes not drastic enough.

Map 44 indicates the geographic pattern of the Senate Confederate Support Scores was quite similar to the House, even though senators were elected in a different manner and had different lengths of service. In the First Senate eighteen pro-Confederate members (69.2 percent) easily outnumbered the eight (30.8 percent) low-scoring members. The most pro-Confederate senators come from the occupied states, Kentucky, Missouri, Tennessee, Arkansas, and mostly disrupted Mississippi. North Carolina is the only unoccupied state with two high-scoring senators. The remainder of the Deep South had split Senate delegations, except South Carolina, the only state with two low-scoring senators. Interestingly, this is exactly the same as the South Carolina House delegation, the only state to have a unanimous delegation of low-scoring representatives.

The general pattern of strong support for the Confederacy in the First Congress is the reverse of the political history and traditions of the antebellum South. The Deep South was the most secessionist region, and yet it had the majority of the least supportive representatives and senators. South Carolina was the most secessionist state and had the least supportive congressional delegation. State rights philosophy and unoccupied status explain much of this dichotomy. The upper South was the most Unionist region of the South, yet the upper South had the most supportive representatives and senators. The questionable admission of Kentucky and Missouri, the occupied status of districts and states (districts Fourteen, Fifteen, and Sixteen of Virginia, for example), and the upper South's position on the front line with the North explain much of this dichotomy.

Confederate Support Score—Second House and Senate. Map 45 illustrates the geographic pattern of the Confederate Support Score in the Second House and Senate (May 2, 1864, to March 18, 1865). As in the First Congress, the Confederate support score was calculated using numerous roll-call votes covering the major issues of the Civil War. Again, each chamber was divided into two groups, green identifying the pro-Confederate congressmen and red identifying congressmen with a low voting score with respect to authoritarian and restrictive wartime legislation.

The pattern of support for stringent wartime measures was similar to the First Congress, but in the Second Congress is even more geographically concentrated. In the Second House fifty-five representatives (51.9 percent) ranked high in multidimensional support of the Confederacy. The most solid area of support again was the occupied districts—northern Virginia, Kentucky, Missouri, and the Union-controlled portion of Louisiana. Most of the Virginia delega-

TABLE 5-13

State Confederate Support Scores
House of Representatives
First Congress

Rank[1]	State	Districts	Confederate Support Score[2]
1	Kentucky	12	5.33
2	Missouri	7[3]	5.33
3	Louisiana	6	5.33
4	Virginia	16	4.94
5	Georgia	10	4.8
6	Alabama	9	4.77
7	Tennessee	11	4.64
8	Texas	6	4.5
9	Florida	2	4.5
10	Mississippi	7	4.43
11	Arkansas	4	4.25
12	North Carolina	10	3.9
13	South Carolina	6	3.33
Total		106	4.62

[1] If two or more states are tied in support score the state with the greatest number of districts is listed first.

[2] State average of the adjusted scale position score for each member of the state delegation. Thomas B. Alexander and Richard E. Beringer, *The Anatomy of the Confederate Congress* (Nashville, Vanderbilt University Press, 1972), Appendix III.

[3] The Seventh District of Missouri was vacant throughout the First Congress.

tion, outside of the Great Valley, was again solidly in support of drastic war legislation. Only a few other pockets of pro-Confederate representatives remained, mostly in the Deep South and Texas. Although mostly occupied and elected with a large soldier vote, the Tennessee delegation was only slightly pro-Confederate with six out of eleven scoring in the highest category (see the discussion of Tennessee elections in Chapter 4). This was the largest area occupied that was not solidly pro-Confederate.

Table 5-11 also compares the occupation status of districts and the Confederate Support Score of their representatives for the Second Congress.[80] Thirty-five of the forty-three occupied districts (81.2 percent) were classified as voting for stringent war legislation. The unoccupied districts were now mostly voting (71.7 percent) against drastic war legislation. This is a significant change from the voting alignment of the First Congress, mostly caused by turnover in the second elections. In the Second Congress over three-fourths of the low-scoring congressmen come from unoccupied territory, while nearly two-thirds of the high Confederate Support Scores come from occupied territory.

Table 5-14 lists the ten individual representatives ranking highest in Confederate Support Score in the Second House. Ten representatives scored 7, and again no member scored in the highest

categories of 8 or 9. All of the ten highest representatives, except one from central Virginia, represented occupied districts. Members from occupied districts composed the core of consistent support of stringent Confederate war legislation. It should be noted that laws voted on by most occupied representatives did affect their "constituency," that is, the soldiers in the field who participated in Kentucky, Missouri, Tennessee, and Virginia second elections and who needed and desired drastic efforts. Table 5-15 lists the states in the Second Congress in order of the average delegation Confederate support score. The Missouri, Kentucky, Louisiana, and Virginia delegations remain the top four states with the highest composite averages of 6.29, 5.58, 5.5, and 5.25 respectively.[81] Tennessee, now almost fully occupied, jumped two places to fifth position.

The pattern of weak support scores in Map 45 is also similar to the First Congress, but is now more concentrated and solid. The core of resistance to "oppressive" wartime legislation within the Confederate Congress came from the unoccupied Deep South, especially North Carolina, South Carolina, and Georgia. The pattern of weak support from these southeast states was continuous from the Provisional Congress. Table 5-14 also enumerates the least supportive representatives. Two peace-oriented North Carolina representatives scored 0. Eight other representatives scored 1. All ten came from the unoccupied Deep South with North Carolina filling seven of the ten lowest roll-call voting scores.

North and South Carolina were the only states to have unanimous low-scoring delegations, and Table 5-15 indicates they remained at the bottom of the list of state delegation scores. In fact, the composite score of North Carolina, 1.3, is significantly lower than the score of any other state in any Congress. Georgia dropped two places in ranking from the First Congress. The large turnover and antiwar sentiment in the second elections affected both the North Carolina and Georgia scores (see Chapter 4).[82] The average score for the entire Second Congress, 4.26, is only slightly below that of the First Congress, 4.62. But the states at the top of the list grade higher in composite score and the states at the bottom grade lower in composite score. The "political distance" between the occupied and unoccupied districts and states increased in the Second Congress.

Map 45 also illustrates the geographic pattern of the Second Senate Confederate Support Scores and it is again strikingly similar to the House. In the Senate, sixteen members (61.5 percent) are designated pro-Confederate. Although slightly less than the eighteen of the previous Congress, the pro-Confederate senators were now more solidly concentrated in the upper South. Ten senators (38.5 percent) are now ranked in the low support category. All the low-support senators, except one four-year term member from North Carolina, came from the seven original lower South states that first seceded. In the Second Senate, Mississippi changed from two pro-Confederate senators to a split delegation, and Alabama changed from a split delegation to two low-support senators. In an ironic twist of history, South Carolina, the first state to secede, and Alabama, the heart of

Dixie and the home of the first Confederate capital, were now many times acting in an obstructionist role in the Confederate Congress.

The Geography of Roll-Call Voting

There is an important geographical component to roll-call voting in the Confederate Congress. The previous literature on the Confederate Congress suggests a regional component on many issues,

TABLE 5-14

Confederate Support
House of Representatives
Second Congress

Highest Ten Representatives and Districts

Rank	Representative	State	District	Confederate Support Score[1]
1	Aaron H. Conrow	MO	4	7
2	George W. Ewing	KY	4	7
3	David Funsten	VA	9	7
4	Robert A. Hatcher	MO	7	7
5	Robert Johnson	VA	15	7
6	Edwin A. Keeble	TN	6	7
7	Duncan F. Kenner	LA	3	7
8	Samual A. Miller	VA	14	7
9	Robert F. Montague	VA	7	7
10	Peter S. Wilkes	MO	6	7

Lowest Ten Representatives and Districts

Rank	Representative	State	District	Confederate Support Score
96	William C. Wickham	VA	3	1
97	Josiah Turner	NC	5	1
98	George W. Logan	NC	10	1
99	James T. Leach	NC	3	1
100	John T. Lamkin	MS	7	1
101	John A. Gilmer	NC	6	1
102	Thomas C. Fuller	NC	4	1
103	Marcus H. Cruikshank	AL	4	1
104	James G. Ramsay	NC	8	0
105[2]	James M. Leach	NC	7	0

[1] Based on votes used to calculate the average adjusted scale position in the two sessions of the Second Congress. A score of 9 indicates strong dedication for measures to support Confederate survival and a score of 0 indicates little or no support. If two or more representatives are tied in support score they are listed in alphabetical order. Thomas B. Alexander and Richard E. Beringer, *The Anatomy of the Confederate Congress* (Nashville: Vanderbilt University Press, 1972), pp. 390–404.

[2] The Third District of Alabama was vacant throughout the Second Congress.

TABLE 5-15

State Confederate Support Scores
House of Representatives
Second Congress

Rank[1]	State	Districts	Confederate Support Score[2]
1	Missouri	7	6.29
2	Kentucky	12	5.58
3	Louisiana	6	5.5
4	Virginia	16	5.25
5	Tennessee	11	4.73
6	Texas	6	4.5
7	Alabama	93	4.14
8	Florida	2	4
9	Georgia	10	3.6
10	Mississippi	7	3.57
11	South Carolina	6	3.5
12	Arkansas	4	3.5
13	North Carolina	10	1.3
Total/Average		106[3]	4.26

[1] If two or more states are tied in support score the state with the greatest number of districts is listed first.

[2] State average of the adjusted scale position score for each member of the state delegation. Thomas B. Alexander and Richard E. Beringer, *The Anatomy of the Confederate Congress* (Nashville, Vanderbilt University Press, 1972), Appendix III.

[3] The Third District of Alabama was vacant throughout the Second Congress.

especially a relationship between legislative voting and occupied versus unoccupied districts. The maps in this section illustrate for the first time the specific geographic pattern of this voting. In addition, an occupied versus unoccupied pattern is also revealed in Senate voting. Mapping Confederate Congress roll-call votes using the 106 districts as data points reveals detailed information to aid in the understanding of the political process, decision making, and changing sentiment within the Confederacy.

In addition to the occupied verses unoccupied relationship, several other patterns are revealed and illustrated by the roll-call vote maps. A few consistent pockets of support for wartime legislation were located in unoccupied areas, specifically Virginia, regions of the Deep South, and many times the Trans-Mississippi West. One area of the South had a consistent pattern of voting against drastic war measures from the Provisional Congress through the Second Congress, the region comprising North and South Carolina and Georgia. This area had two important geographic characteristics: it was not on the immediate front line in Virginia; but it was in close proximity to the front line, and its transportation, demographic, and economic characteristics were such that it was ideally located to man and supply the war effort.

Over one hundred roll-call vote maps were produced in the preparation of this atlas. Each vote, issue, or policy area had its own particular characteristics and geographic pattern. Indeed, the data on the multiple vote maps can be divided, mapped, and studied in many ways. Nevertheless, a consistent overall voting pattern does emerge in the roll-call vote research and maps, and this is discussed and illustrated in this section. One of the objectives of this atlas is to provide the congressional district base map and membership lists to allow any student, teacher, or researcher to map and analyze any roll-call vote in the history of the Confederate Congress.

[1] Confederate Constitution, Article I, Section 5, Number 4. The yeas and nays were also recorded in the Provisional Congress (see Chapter 2).

[2] *Journal of the Congress of the Confederate States of America, 1861–1865*, Volumes 1–7, (Washington, D.C.: Government Printing Office, 1904).

[3] Thomas B. Alexander and Richard E. Beringer, *The Anatomy of the Confederate Congress: A Study of the Influences of Member Characteristics on Legislative Behavior, 1861–1865* (Nashville: Vanderbilt University Press, 1972). Alexander and Beringer's roll-call data from the *Confederate Journal* as well as additional characteristics of Confederate congressmen are available in machine-readable form from the Inter-university Consortium for Political and Social Research. Thomas B. Alexander and Richard E. Beringer, *Roll Call Votes for the Confederate Congresses, 1861–1865* (Ann Arbor, Michigan: Center for Political Studies—producer, Inter-university Consortium for Political and Social Research—distributor).

[4] One additional recent roll-call analysis is Richard Bensel's "Southern Leviathan." This work was also used in evaluating the major issues debated and voted on in the Confederate Congress and the possible determinants of roll-call behavior. Richard Bensel, "Southern Leviathan: The Development of Central State Authority in the Confederate States of America," in *Studies in American Political Development*, Vol. 2, eds. Karen Orren and Stephen Skowronek (New Haven: Yale University Press, 1987).

[5] *Confederate Journal*, Vol. 1, p. 17.

[6] *Ibid.*

[7] *Ibid.*, Vol. 6, p. 37.

[8] *Ibid.*, p. 41.

[9] *Ibid.*, Vol. 2, p. 17.

[10] The three terms—issue, issue dimension, and policy area—are all used in this atlas to describe the same phenomenon, that is, when a large number of individual roll-call votes are related to one larger area. In the modern era policy areas would include such fields as foreign policy, agriculture, natural resources and the environment. For a discussion of this legislative phenomenon see Aage R. Clausen, *How Congressmen Decide* (New York: St. Martin's, 1973).

[11] Table 5-2 includes the variables initially used in the three major studies on issues and voting in the Confederate Congress. Wilfred Buck Yearns in *The Confederate Congress* highlights nine issue areas: conscription, officer selection and promotion, economic organization, military strategy, habeas corpus, foreign affairs, peace movement, finance, and the Davis Administration. Wilfred Buck Yearns, *The Confederate Congress* (Athens: University of Georgia Press, 1960). Alexander and Beringer in *The Anatomy of the Confederate Congress* report on eight areas in their roll-call vote analysis: conscription, impressment, habeas corpus, economic and fiscal problems, nationhood, determination and defeatism, state rights, and race. In Richard Bensel's article "Southern Leviathan," the focus is on issues of central state authority rather than the full range of topics debated in Congress. The seven issues Bensel deemed important are citizenship (conscription and impressment), centralization (officer selection, secret sessions, and judicial questions), administrative capability (general staff, presidential exemptions, civil service, presidential appointments, and Secret Service), control of property (railroads, destruction of property, impressment, trading with the enemy, and slaves as soldiers), development of client groups (pensions, taxes and bonds, price controls, and veterans home), and world system (foreign commissioners, tariff, prisoners of war, blockade cargo, and peace).

[12] Yearns, *Confederate Congress*, pp. 60–101. Alexander and Beringer, *Anatomy*, pp. 106–164. *Encyclopedia of the Confederacy*, 1st ed. (1993), s.v. "Conscription," by Jennifer Lund. Albert Burton Moore, *Conscription and Conflict in the Confederacy* (New York: Macmillan, 1924).

[13] See also the discussion and maps below on a conscription exemption vote in the Confederate Senate (Map 38) and the multiple conscription votes in the First and Second House (Maps 39 and 40).

[14] Yearns, *Confederate Congress*, pp. 116–125. Alexander and Beringer, *Anatomy*, pp. 139–166. *Encyclopedia of the Confederacy*, 1st ed. (1993), s.v. "Impressment," by Mary A. DeCredico.

[15] See also the discussion and maps below on multiple impressment votes in the First and Second House (Maps 41 and 42).

[16] Yearns, Confederate Congress, pp. 151–160. Alexander and Beringer, *Anatomy*, pp. 166–200. *Encyclopedia of the Confederacy*, 1st ed. (1993), s.v. "Habeas Corpus," by Mark E. Neely, Jr.

[17] See also Map 36 and accompanying discussion on a habeas corpus vote in the Confederate House.

[18] Alexander and Beringer, *Anatomy*, p. 201–235. Yearns, *Confederate Congress*, pp. 116–139. Richard C. Todd, *Confederate Finance* (Athens: University of Georgia Press, 1954). Douglas B. Ball, *Financial Failure and Confederate Defeat* (Urbana: University of Illinois Press, 1991).

[19] For a discussion of this issue see: Mary Elizabeth Massey, *Ersatz in the Confederacy* (Columbia: University of South Carolina Press, 1952), pp. 42–43.

[20] Alexander and Beringer, *Anatomy*, p. 106–165. Yearns, *Confederate Congress*, pp. 60–115.

[21] Yearns, *Confederate Congress*, pp. 161–183.

[22] Clausen, *How Congressmen Decide*. C. H. Cherryholmes and M. J. Shapiro, *Representatives and Roll Calls* (Indianapolis: Bobbs-Merrill, 1969). M. P. Collie, "Voting Behavior in Legislatures," in *Handbook of Legislative Research*, S. C. Loewenberg, et al., eds. (Cambridge, Massachusetts: Harvard University Press, 1985). John W. Kingdon, *Congressmen's Voting Decisions* (New York: Harper and Row, 1973). These studies, and virtually all legislative voting models, incorporate various geographic components, such as constituency, district, state, and regional variables.

[23] See citations in footnotes 3, 4, and 11.

[24] Alexander and Beringer, *Anatomy*, p. 341.

[25] Kenneth C. Martis, *The Historical Atlas of United States Congressional Districts: 1789–1983* (New York: Free Press, 1982), pp. 14–16.

[26] Thomas B. Alexander, *Sectional Stress and Party Strength* (Nashville: Vanderbilt University Press, 1967). Joel H. Silby, *The Shrine of Party* (Pittsburgh: Pittsburgh University Press, 1967).

[27] Frank Lawrence Owsley, *State Rights in the Confederacy* (Chicago: University of Chicago Press, 1925). See also David Donald, *Why the North Won the Civil War* (Baton Rouge: Louisiana State University Press, 1960).

[28] Marshall L. DeRosa, *The Confederate Constitution of 1861* (Columbia: University of Missouri Press, 1991).

[29] See also Map 37 and accompanying discussion on a vote in the Confederate House concerning central government versus state control of the state militias.

[30] Thomas B. Alexander, "Persistent Whiggery in the Confederate South, 1860–1877," *Journal of Southern History* XXVII (1961): 305–329. Richard E. Beringer, "Political Factionalism in the Confederate Congress," (Ph.D. diss., Northwestern University, 1966).

[31] John C. Wahlke, *The Legislative System* (New York: John Wiley, 1962).

[32] A. H. Birch, *Representation* (New York: Praeger, 1971). Hanna F. Pitkin, *The Concept of Representation* (Berkeley: University of California Press, 1967).

[33] Philip Magnus, *Edmund Burke* (London: J. Murry, 1939).

34 This concern over state sovereignty may be more intense in the Senate because of its constitutional and traditional role of representing state interests in Congress while the House in the American tradition represents local and district interests.

35 An extensive enumeration of a number of other possible phenomena that can be mapped is listed in Martis, *Atlas of Districts*, pp. 18–24, for example, committee assignments, personal wealth, and slaveholding.

36 Orin G. Libby, "A Plea for the Study of Votes in Congress," *Annual Report of the American Historical Association* (Washington, D.C.: Government Printing Office, 1896). C. O. Paullin and John K. Wright, *Atlas of the Historical Geography of the United States* (New York: Carnegie Institution and American Geographical Society, 1932). Frederick Jackson Turner, "The Significance of Section in American History," *The Wisconsin Magazine of History* (8): 225–280. Clifford L. Lord, *A Description of the Atlas of Congressional Roll Calls: An Analysis of Yea-Nay Votes* (Newark, New Jersey: Work Projects Administration—Historical Records Survey, 1941). Stanley R. Brunn, *Geography and Politics in America* (New York: Harper and Row, 1974). Richard F. Bensel, *Sectionalism and American Political Development 1880–1980* (Madison: University of Wisconsin Press, 1984). Ruth A. Rowles and Kenneth C. Martis, "Mapping Congress: Developing a Geographic Understanding of American Political History," *Prologue: Journal of the National Archives* 16 (Spring 1984): 5–21. Kenneth C. Martis, "Sectionalism in the United States Congress," *Political Geography Quarterly* 7 (April 1988): 99–109.

37 A Provisional Congress vote map is in the multiple vote section (Map 43). The method of mapping the state by state vote in the Provisional Congress is similar to that of the Senate.

38 *Confederate Journal*, Vol. 7, pp. 346–350.

39 It should be noted the Virginia Third District (Richmond) representative, William C. Wickham, voted against suspension. Richmond was the first area to be put under suspension after the first law, and many citizens claimed martial law was abused and arrogantly enforced in the Confederate capital. Representative Wickham was a Unionist Whig, but he supported Virginia after secession. He served in the Confederate army, was wounded twice, captured, and exchanged. He ran for Congress in May 1863 with known antisecessionist views and reported to the Second Congress only in the Second Session. By this time he believed the war was over and refused to support any additional extraordinary measures to lengthen the conflict. Ezra J. Warner and W. Buck Yearns, *Biographical Register of the Confederate Congress* (Baton Rouge: Louisiana State University Press, 1975), pp. 254–256. Jon L. Wakelyn, *Biographical Dictionary of the Confederacy* (Westport, Connecticut: Greenwood Press, 1977), pp. 436–437.

40 Yearns, *Confederate Congress*, pp. 158–159. In addition, Davis opponent Henry Foote from the Fifth District of Tennessee was an outspoken opponent of this particular bill.

41 In examining determinants of support for suspending habeas corpus Alexander and Beringer in their exhaustive roll-call study found little correlation between suspension and slaveholding or personal wealth. They did find some relationship between former party and secession stance; that is, former Democrats and secessionists tended to support suspension. When the factor of "exterior" (unoccupied) and "interior" (unoccupied) was added to the above a strong explanatory case was found for understanding the vote. These factors became more intense in each session of the Permanent Congresses so that by the last session, the time of this vote, they make a compelling argument. Alexander and Beringer, *Anatomy*, pp. 166–201. Bensel had similar findings, although for an 1862 vote. Bensel also found that membership on the Military Affairs Committee also brought sympathy for suspension, at least in 1862. Bensel, "Southern Leviathan," pp. 85–90.

42 *Confederate Journal*, Vol. 7, p. 253.

43 Yearns, *Confederate Congress*, p. 92.

44 *Confederate Journal*, Vol. 7, p. 776.

45 *War of Rebellion: A Compilation of the Official Records of the Union and Confederate Armies* (Washington, D.C.: Government Printing Office, 1880–1901), Series IV, Vol. III, p. 1145.

46 By the time of the March 16, 1865, vote there were four other vacancies, making a total of five. The additional vacancies were brought about by one death, one promotion to the Senate, and two resignations. The resignations were members from the Second and Seventh Districts of Virginia and occurred in early March 1865; since these seats were technically vacant, they are so designated on Map 37.

47 *Confederate Journal*, Vol. 7, p. 775.

48 Occupied districts are based upon the Second Congress Second Session (see Map 24).

49 In this case the trans-Mississippi districts are defined as all those in Missouri, Arkansas, Louisiana, and Texas.

50 *Confederate Journal*, Vol. 4, p. 720.

51 See Chapter IV, "Statutory Exemptions (1862–1864)," in Albert B. Moore, *Conscription and Conflict in the Confederacy* (New York: Macmillan, 1924).

52 See the section in Chapter 4 on election and terms of senators.

53 *Confederate Journal*, Vol. 4, p. 561.

54 *Confederate Journal*, Vol. 4, pp. 561–562.

55 See also the discussion and maps below on multiple conscription votes in the First House and Senate.

56 See also the section below on the multidimensional "Confederate Support Score." This section provides additional Senate data and maps in parallel with similar House data and maps (see Maps 44 and 45). Note the geographic pattern in the Senate on the Second Congress map (Map 45) is similar, but not exactly so, to the pattern on the individual conscription Senate vote depicted in Map 38.

57 Martis, *Congressional Districts*, pp. 18–23.

58 See explanatory footnote 10.

59 See the section above on issues in the Confederate Congress.

60 The specific methodology and votes used to calculate the performance scores and the final individual scores are listed in Alexander and Beringer, *Anatomy*, pp. 300–313, 390–419.

61 If one or more sessions are missing, a representative's score was calculated using the available sessions.

62 A cutoff of 4.5 was used for several representatives scoring between 4 and 5.

63 This includes the occupied districts of southeast Louisiana.

64 If one or more sessions are missing, a representative's score was calculated using the available sessions. The specific methodology and votes used to calculate the performance scores and the final individual scores are listed in Alexander and Beringer, *Anatomy*, pp. 300–313, 390–419.

65 Alexander and Beringer, *Anatomy*, p. 113.

66 See the section on the second Tennessee election, especially the influence of soldier voting.

67 See the section on the second North Carolina congressional election.

68 See footnote 39.

69 The specific votes used to calculate both the property destruction and impressment are listed in Alexander and Beringer, *Anatomy*, pp. 390–419.

70 There are also some cases where scores could not be calculated for one of the two sessions. In these cases the score for the available session was used as the representative's score.

71 All representatives scored by *Anatomy* in the 5 to 9 category are placed in the highest group and all those in the 0 to 4 category are placed in the lowest group. Again, as in the previous section on conscription, 4.5 was used as a cutoff for representatives having scores between 4 and 5.

72 If one or more sessions are missing, a representative's score was calculated using the available sessions. The specific methodology and votes used to calculate the performance scores and the final individual scores are listed in Alexander and Beringer, *Anatomy*, pp. 300–313, 390–419.

73 Massey, *Ersatz*, p. 25.

74 For example, in the modern U.S. Congresses, multidimensional analysis might combine the votes of representatives and senators on such issue dimensions as economic policy, agriculture, civil rights, foreign affairs, or the environment to determine a broader overriding liberal-conservative stance or score. This liberal-conservative ideological spectrum could then, in turn, aid in the understanding, or even prediction, of roll-call voting.

75 Two sets of multidimensional summary scores are provided: average adjusted scale position, and average adjusted performance score. These two are highly correlated with each other and both are "designed to measure each congressman's total impact upon congressional behavior." The average adjusted scale position is mapped in this atlas. It was calculated using all scale positions of an individual member in all Congresses. See the discussion of the average adjusted scale position and the statistical determination of this number in Alexander and Beringer, *Anatomy*, Chapter 11.

76 Alexander and Beringer, *Anatomy*, pp. 398–405.

77 This division of the states follows the same numerical division of members used below for the First and Second Congresses.

78 A similar pattern is mapped and discussed in Richard F. Bensel, *Yankee Leviathan: The Origins of Central State Authority in America, 1859–1877* (Cambridge: Cambridge University Press, 1990), pp. 221–225. However, Bensel's map pattern is less intense since he used roll-call votes from both the First and Second Congresses. Representatives and roll-call voting behavior changed from the First to the Second Congress, especially in Deep South districts, and the combination of the two Congresses does not take this into consideration.

79 The occupied status of districts was based upon the situation at the end of the First Congress, Fourth Session (see Map 20).

80 The occupied status of districts was based upon the situation at the end of the Second Congress, First Session (see Map 22). The Second Session map and data was not used because of the large number of disrupted districts. If the Second Session occupied numbers were used, the final percentages would be even slightly higher with respect to the relationship between occupied districts and a high Confederate Support Score.

81 Since the adjusted scale position for each representative is one number calculated over his entire period in Congress, a state reelecting a high proportion of its members in the second elections obviously has a tendency to remain stable in its composite score.

82 The geographical pattern within Louisiana again was similar to the general national pattern, that is, the occupied districts supported stringent measures affecting the civilian population and the unoccupied districts usually voted against. This situation occurred again both because of the return of five out of six representatives (therefore having the same scale score) and in spite of the turnover in the Fifth District.

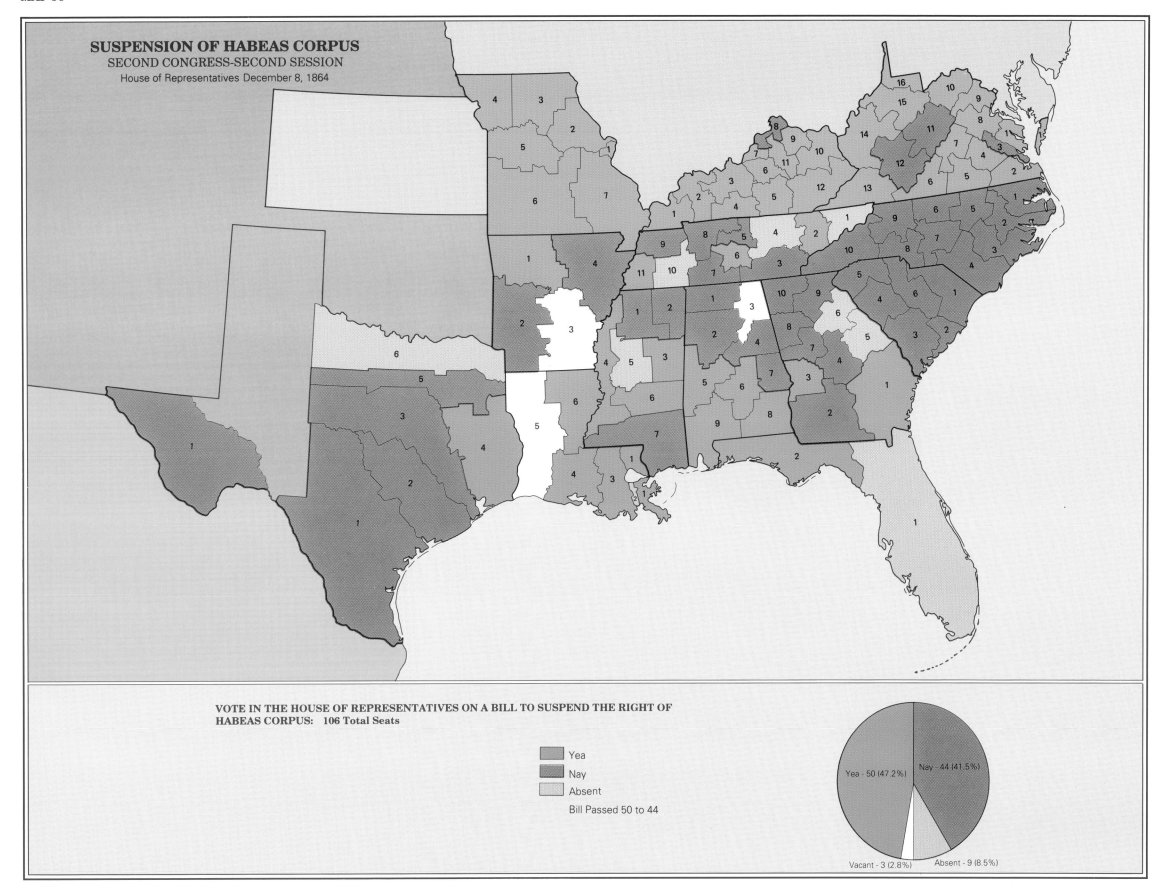

MAP 36

SUSPENSION OF HABEAS CORPUS
SECOND CONGRESS-SECOND SESSION
House of Representatives December 8, 1864

VOTE IN THE HOUSE OF REPRESENTATIVES ON A BILL TO SUSPEND THE RIGHT OF
HABEAS CORPUS: 106 Total Seats

Yea

Nay

Absent

Bill Passed 50 to 44

Yea - 50 (47.2%)

Nay - 44 (41.5%)

Vacant - 3 (2.8%)

Absent - 9 (8.5%)

MAP 37

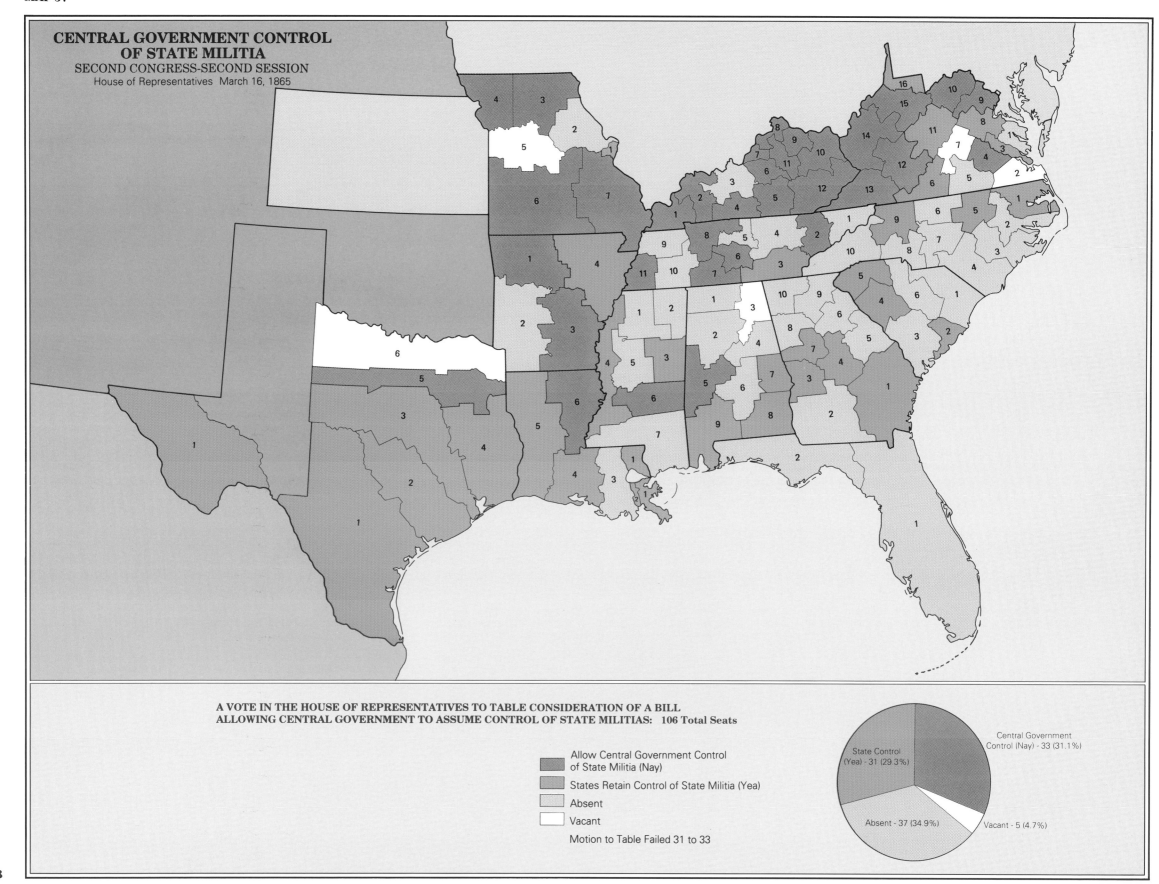

CENTRAL GOVERNMENT CONTROL OF STATE MILITIA

SECOND CONGRESS-SECOND SESSION

House of Representatives March 16, 1865

A VOTE IN THE HOUSE OF REPRESENTATIVES TO TABLE CONSIDERATION OF A BILL
ALLOWING CENTRAL GOVERNMENT TO ASSUME CONTROL OF STATE MILITIAS: 106 Total Seats

Allow Central Government Control
of State Militia (Nay)

States Retain Control of State Militia (Yea)

Absent

Vacant

Motion to Table Failed 31 to 33

Central Government
Control (Nay) - 33 (31.1%)

State Control
(Yea) - 31 (29.3%)

Absent - 37 (34.9%)

Vacant - 5 (4.7%)

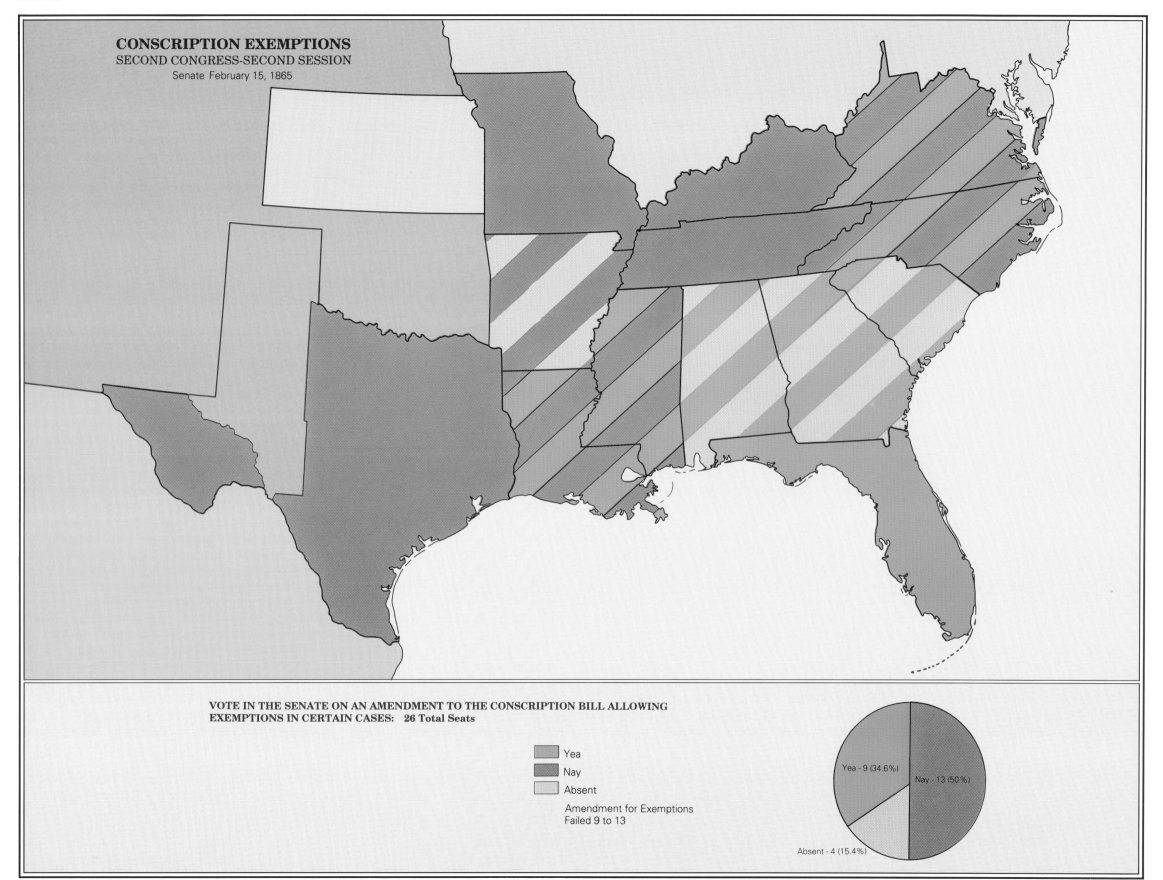

MAP 38

CONSCRIPTION EXEMPTIONS
SECOND CONGRESS-SECOND SESSION
Senate February 15, 1865

VOTE IN THE SENATE ON AN AMENDMENT TO THE CONSCRIPTION BILL ALLOWING
EXEMPTIONS IN CERTAIN CASES: 26 Total Seats

Yea
Nay
Absent

Amendment for Exemptions
Failed 9 to 13

Yea - 9 (34.6%)

Nay - 13 (50%)

Absent - 4 (15.4%)

MAP 39

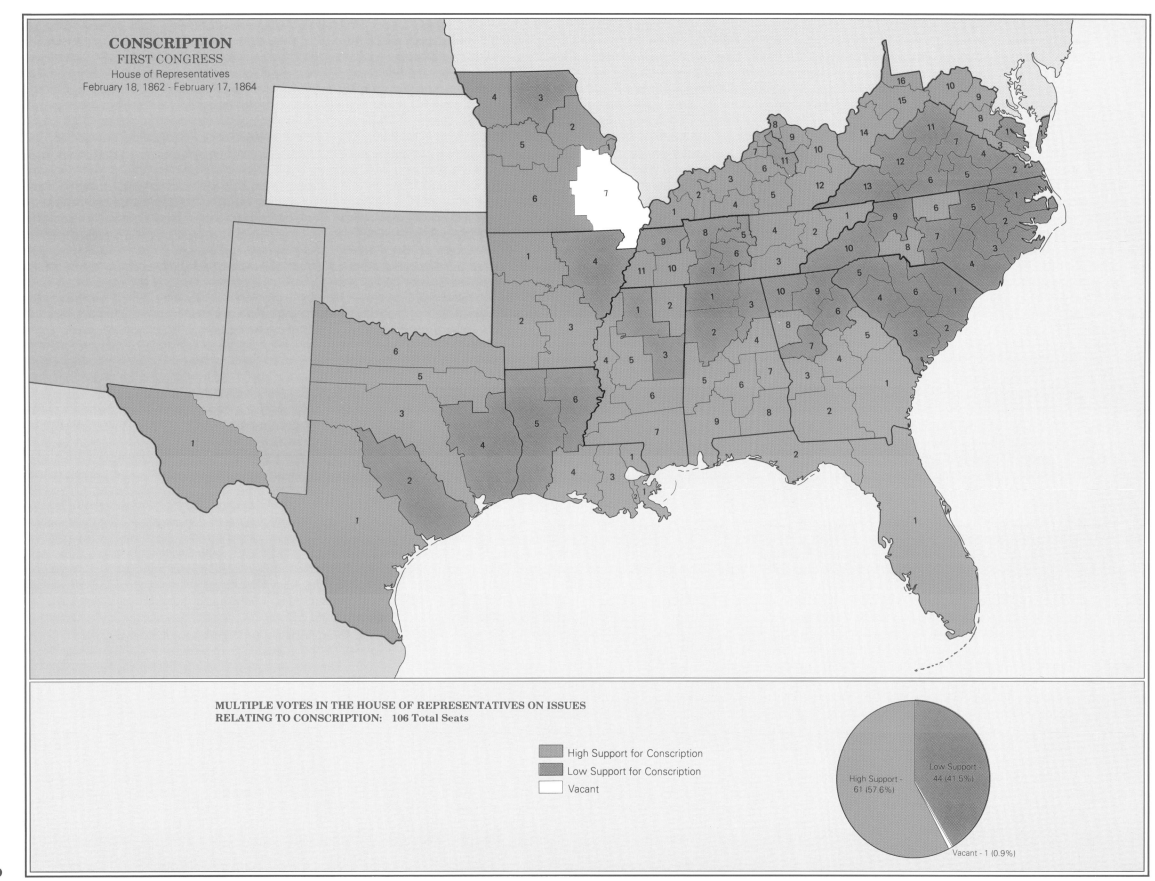

CONSCRIPTION
FIRST CONGRESS
House of Representatives
February 18, 1862 - February 17, 1864

MULTIPLE VOTES IN THE HOUSE OF REPRESENTATIVES ON ISSUES
RELATING TO CONSCRIPTION: 106 Total Seats

High Support for Conscription

Low Support for Conscription

Vacant

High Support -
61 (57.6%)

Low Support -
44 (41.5%)

Vacant - 1 (0.9%)

MAP 40

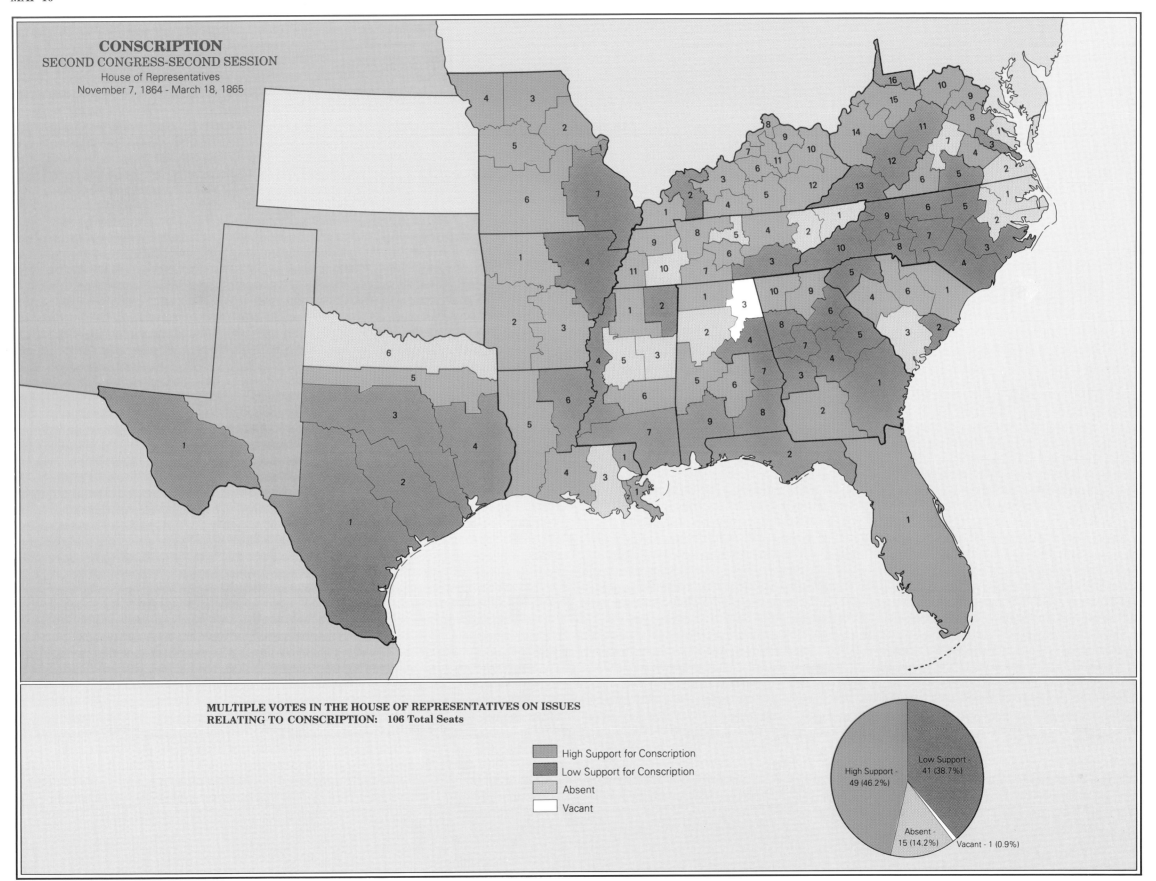

CONSCRIPTION
SECOND CONGRESS-SECOND SESSION
House of Representatives
November 7, 1864 - March 18, 1865

MULTIPLE VOTES IN THE HOUSE OF REPRESENTATIVES ON ISSUES
RELATING TO CONSCRIPTION: 106 Total Seats

High Support for Conscription
Low Support for Conscription
Absent
Vacant

High Support - 49 (46.2%)
Low Support - 41 (38.7%)
Absent - 15 (14.2%)
Vacant - 1 (0.9%)

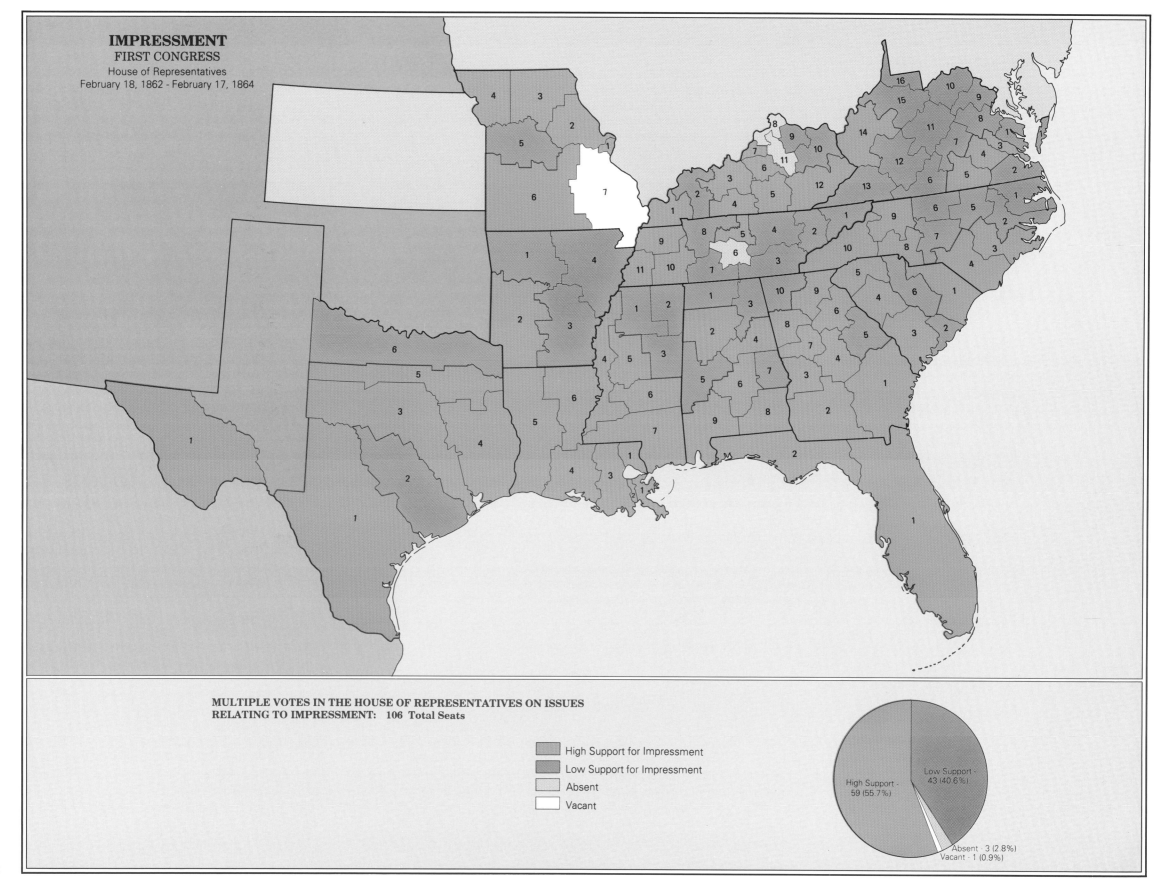

MAP 41

IMPRESSMENT
FIRST CONGRESS
House of Representatives
February 18, 1862 - February 17, 1864

MULTIPLE VOTES IN THE HOUSE OF REPRESENTATIVES ON ISSUES
RELATING TO IMPRESSMENT: 106 Total Seats

High Support for Impressment
Low Support for Impressment
Absent
Vacant

High Support -
59 (55.7%)

Low Support -
43 (40.6%)

Absent - 3 (2.8%)
Vacant - 1 (0.9%)

MAP 42

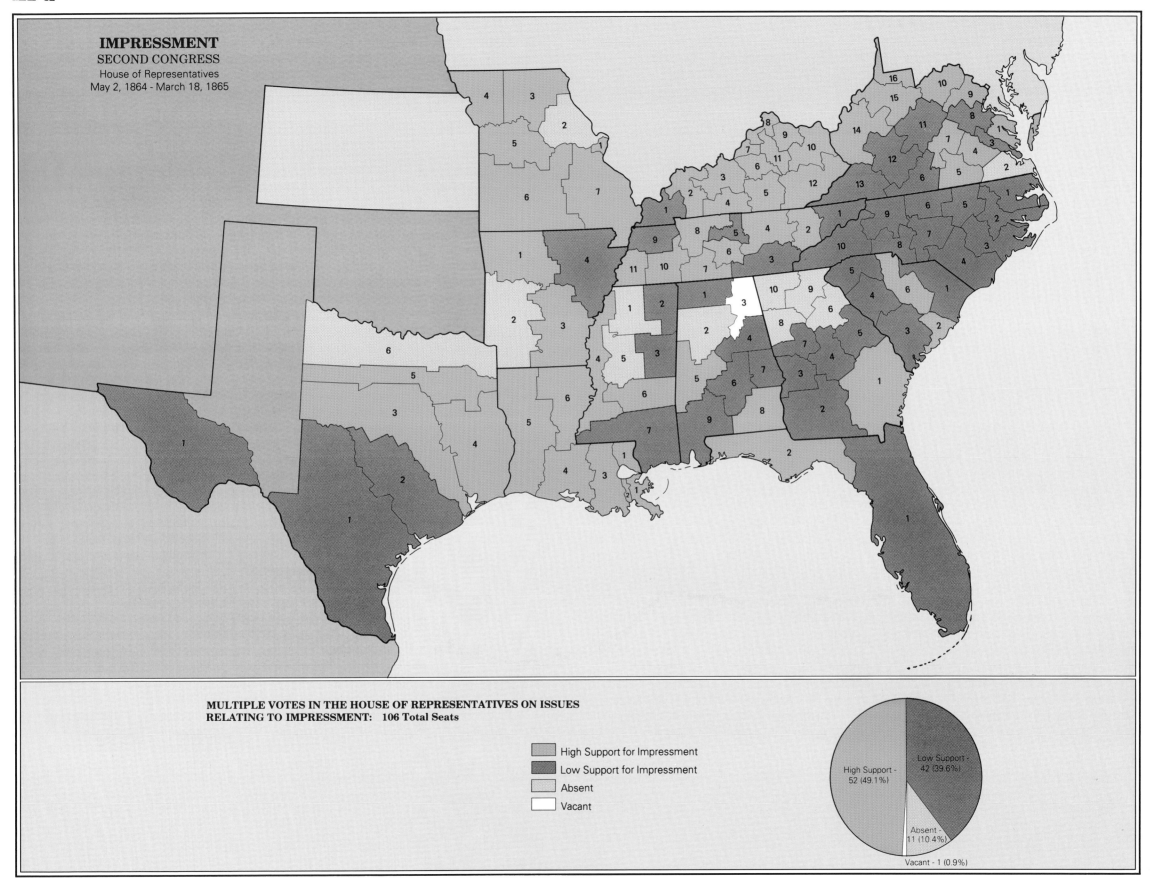

IMPRESSMENT
SECOND CONGRESS
House of Representatives
May 2, 1864 - March 18, 1865

**MULTIPLE VOTES IN THE HOUSE OF REPRESENTATIVES ON ISSUES
RELATING TO IMPRESSMENT: 106 Total Seats**

High Support for Impressment
Low Support for Impressment
Absent
Vacant

High Support - 52 (49.1%)

Low Support - 42 (39.6%)

Absent - 11 (10.4%)

Vacant - 1 (0.9%)

MAP 43

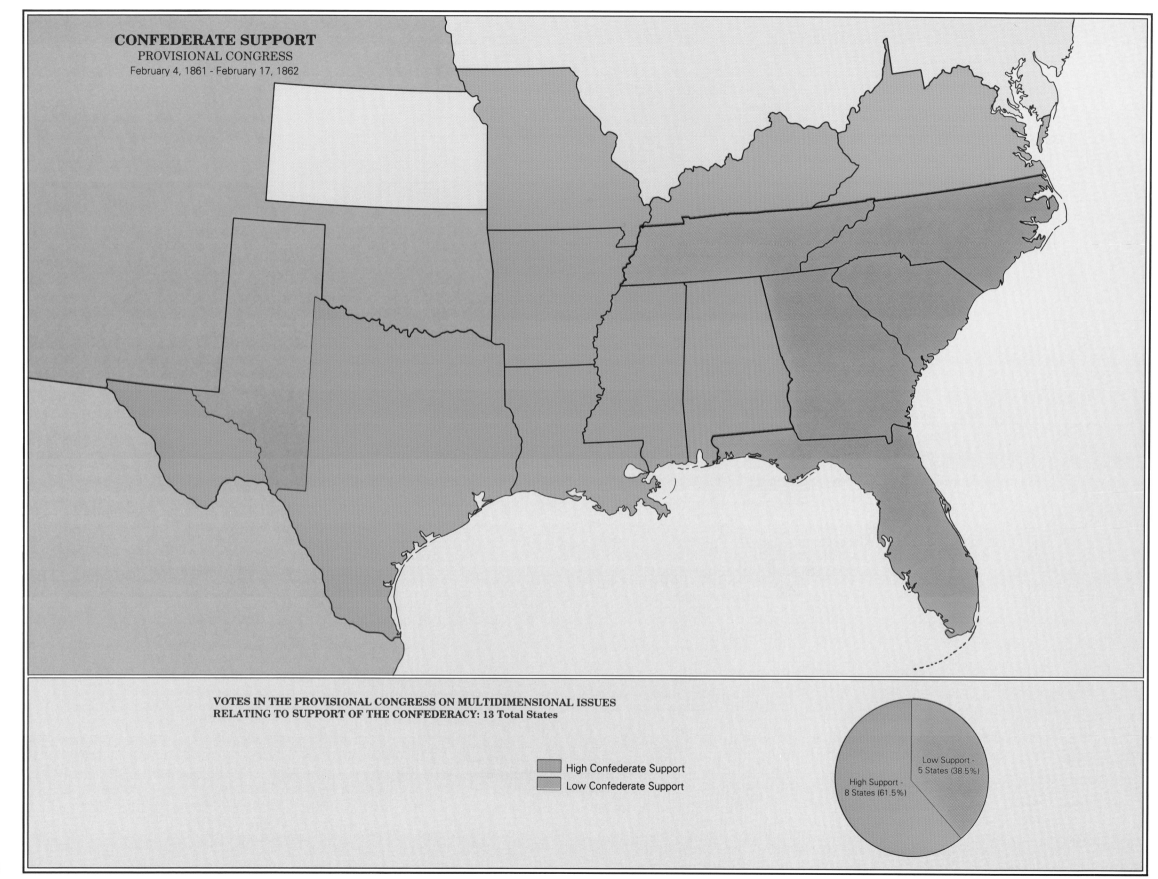

CONFEDERATE SUPPORT
PROVISIONAL CONGRESS
February 4, 1861 - February 17, 1862

VOTES IN THE PROVISIONAL CONGRESS ON MULTIDIMENSIONAL ISSUES
RELATING TO SUPPORT OF THE CONFEDERACY: 13 Total States

High Confederate Support
Low Confederate Support

Low Support -
5 States (38.5%)

High Support -
8 States (61.5%)

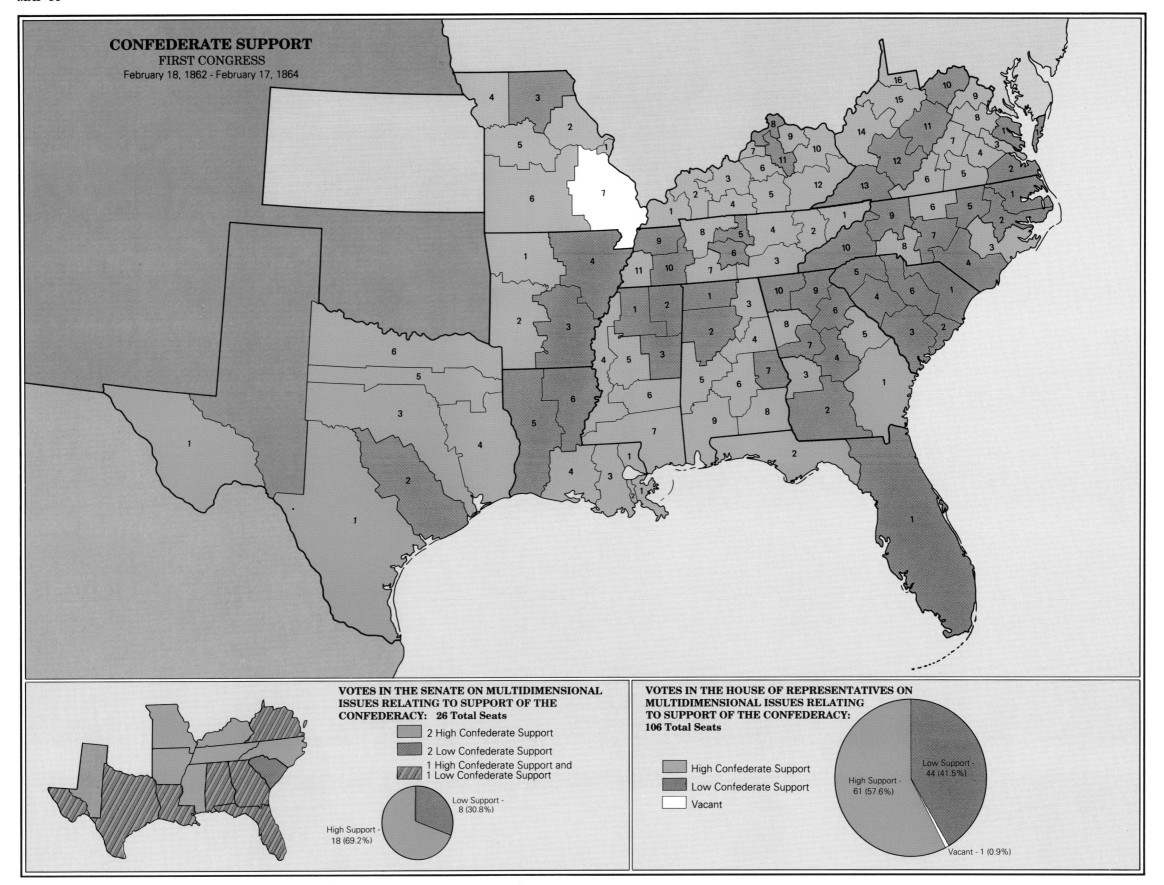

MAP 44

CONFEDERATE SUPPORT
FIRST CONGRESS
February 18, 1862 - February 17, 1864

**VOTES IN THE SENATE ON MULTIDIMENSIONAL
ISSUES RELATING TO SUPPORT OF THE
CONFEDERACY: 26 Total Seats**

2 High Confederate Support

2 Low Confederate Support

1 High Confederate Support and
1 Low Confederate Support

Low Support -
8 (30.8%)

High Support -
18 (69.2%)

**VOTES IN THE HOUSE OF REPRESENTATIVES ON
MULTIDIMENSIONAL ISSUES RELATING
TO SUPPORT OF THE CONFEDERACY:
106 Total Seats**

High Confederate Support

Low Confederate Support

Vacant

Low Support -
44 (41.5%)

High Support -
61 (57.6%)

Vacant - 1 (0.9%)

MAP 45

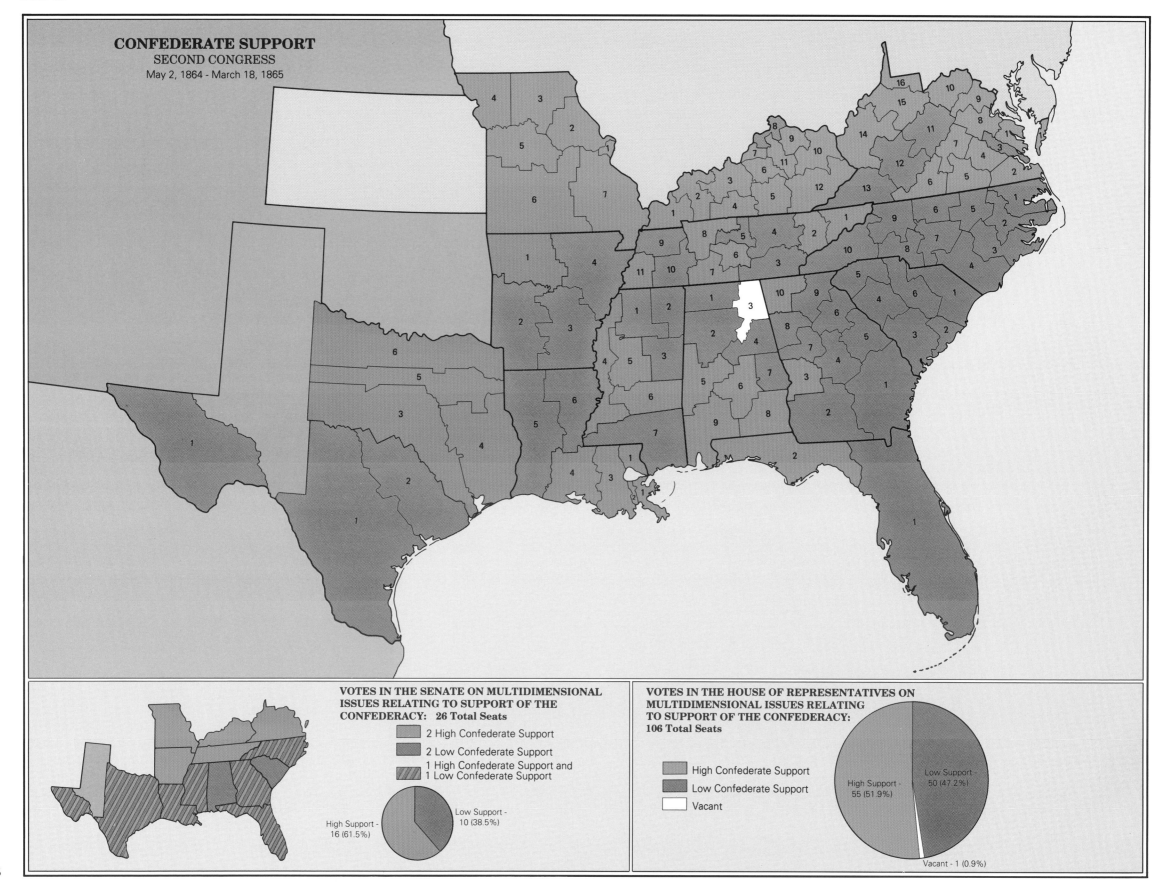

CONFEDERATE SUPPORT
SECOND CONGRESS
May 2, 1864 - March 18, 1865

VOTES IN THE SENATE ON MULTIDIMENSIONAL
ISSUES RELATING TO SUPPORT OF THE
CONFEDERACY: 26 Total Seats

2 High Confederate Support

2 Low Confederate Support

1 High Confederate Support and
1 Low Confederate Support

High Support -
16 (61.5%)

Low Support -
10 (38.5%)

VOTES IN THE HOUSE OF REPRESENTATIVES ON
MULTIDIMENSIONAL ISSUES RELATING
TO SUPPORT OF THE CONFEDERACY:
106 Total Seats

High Confederate Support

Low Confederate Support

Vacant

High Support -
55 (51.9%)

Low Support -
50 (47.2%)

Vacant - 1 (0.9%)

6

CONCLUSION: GEOGRAPHICAL ASPECTS OF THE CONFEDERATE CONGRESSES

This atlas examines the Civil War in a way never before attempted. Maps in the preceding chapters on a wide variety of phenomena in the Confederate Congresses suggest important regional differences in the Civil War South. This conclusion analyzes some of the most important differences and their importance in understanding the South, the Confederate States of America, and the Civil War.

Representation in the Permanent Congresses

In the unicameral Provisional Confederate Congress, each state had one vote irrespective of size or population. This was a radical institutionalization of federalism and state rights. However, the Permanent Confederate Constitution continued the U.S. Constitution legislative organization: a Senate with two members from each state and a House of Representatives apportioned by population. The Confederate founders continued the Senate and House system to lure the upper South slave states into the Confederacy and to validate their contention that the South was the true legacy of the American Revolution and Constitution.

The continuation of the structure of the U.S. Congress prompted the continuation of the established philosophy of American political representation into the Confederacy. Senators were still elected by the state legislatures and, as was the custom, many considered their first role as advocates of their states in Congress. Representatives continued to be elected by congressional districts (Maps 6 and 7), and, as was the custom, many considered their first role as advocates of their local district constituency. In addition, many considered the philosophy of state rights one of the cornerstones of the Confederate Constitution. The continuation of state and local representation and the state rights philosophy was at times incompatible with a national all-out war effort.

Initial Differences in the Upper and Lower South

The South in 1860 was an area of great diversity. The physical geography of the South (Map 8) reflected a wide variety of landscapes. Southern economic development (Map 11) showed pockets of both prosperous agricultural and urban development and lagging regions. However, the geographic distribution of cotton and tobacco cultivation (Map 9) and a corresponding distribution of slave and free population (Map 10) illustrate a significant distinction between the upper and lower South. Antebellum political geography reflected this upper South–lower South difference. This political difference manifested itself in a number of ways, most significantly: antebellum political party strength; the U.S. presidential election of 1860 (Map 12); the seven states that initially seceded (Map 2); and, to some extent, the former political party and secession stance of members chosen in the First Congress elections (Maps 25 and 26). After the admission of the six upper South states, the original seven states had fewer than half (43 percent) of the membership of the Confederate

House of Representatives. Initially, there was fear of sectionalism within the Confederate States of America. However, this large-scale sectionalism never fully evolved because of the rapid Union occupation of Kentucky, Missouri, and northwestern Virginia. Nevertheless, significant resistance to secession and the war continued in several poor white areas with low slaveholding, such as the Appalachian portion of western North Carolina and eastern Tennessee.

Expansion of the Confederacy— Admission of Kentucky and Missouri

One of the most far-reaching and fateful decisions of the Confederate Congress was the admission of Missouri and Kentucky in late 1861. The majority of the population in these states was pro-Union or neutral. The majority of the population in the other eleven southern states was prosecession.

The expansion of the Confederacy to include Missouri and Kentucky had significant repercussions on the Confederate Congress. It gave political power to areas that held slaves but were not secessionist. In the House of Representatives these two states held nineteen out of 106 seats (17.9 percent). Most importantly, Kentucky and Missouri were substantially occupied at the time of their admission (Map 5). Their admission gave early de facto recognition of the right of states and districts to be represented in Congress in spite of being fully occupied by the Union.

Representation of Territory under Union Occupation

In the history of democratically elected national legislatures the Confederate Congress is unique in that it is one of the few examples in which areas not under the control of the nation (Maps 13 to 24) were granted representation. As stated above this precedent was set by the admission of occupied Kentucky and Missouri to the Provisional Congress in late 1861 (Map 5). The precedent continued in February 1862 when the First Permanent Congress seated a Missouri House delegation elected by a rump legislature, a Kentucky delegation elected by a questionable poll of soldiers, refugees, and a few pro-Confederate counties, and three congressmen elected in northwestern Virginia mostly by soldier and refugee votes (Map 25). The seating of these representatives and their full participation in the Confederate House paved the way for the continued acceptance of representatives, and later even election (Map 32), of congressmen from occupied districts. As the war progressed membership from occupied areas became a greater and greater proportion of the total membership. The legislative behavior of representatives and senators from occupied areas was significantly different from the legislative behavior of representatives and senators from the unoccupied Confederacy.

Divisions in Roll-Call Voting

Mapping roll-call votes in the Confederate Congress shows significant geographic concentrations of support and resistance to a wide variety of measures (Maps 36 to 47). Previous studies and this atlas (Maps 25 to 35) suggest many explanatory variables for these regional differences. Of these variables, the occupied status of a state or district (Maps 13 to 24) explains the most about roll-call voting behavior. Representatives from occupied districts tended to support stringent wartime measures since these measures would not affect their constituency. This support increased as the war continued. Representatives from unoccupied districts had the propensity to vote against stringent measures since these laws would be enforced in their districts. This was especially so in South Carolina, North Carolina, and Georgia. This resistance increased as the war continued and the areas of the South supplying men and material grew smaller and smaller.

The continuation of elections and representation from Union-occupied districts on an equal footing with Confederate-controlled districts not only raised questions about democratic representation, but the result was a profoundly different kind of representative speaking for a different kind of constituency. The representatives from occupied districts formed the core of support for the Davis Administration and the continuance of the war. The presence of these congressmen enabled the pro-Confederate congressmen, in essence supporters of the Davis Administration, to have a clear majority in all three Confederate Congresses. Most of the members freely elected from unoccupied districts in the 1863 Second House

election challenged this majority and its strong support of the war. The possibility exists that the American Civil War may have ended substantially sooner, or have taken a different course, if only those Confederate congressmen representing unoccupied districts had the right to vote in Congress. However, since the precedent was set that Confederate elections and representation could take place from federal-occupied areas, the Davis Administration relied on a growing core of congressmen from occupied areas to continue to support the war. The presence and support of congressmen from Union-occupied districts was an important political factor that prolonged the "Lost Cause."

Congressional Elections

Elections for a wide range of congressional, state, and local public offices continued in the South throughout the Civil War. These elections were important to the national and state Confederate governments, continuing the American democratic tradition and proving their legitimacy. In addition, these elections were meaningful to the individual white male voters, giving them a sense that they were carrying on democratic principles and that they had a voice in the decisions of the day.

Elections to the Confederate Congresses were an important part of this electoral tradition. There were two general elections for members of the Confederate House of Representatives, one national election in November 1861 for the First Congress and one for the Second Congress held on different dates in each state in 1863 and early 1864. These elections reveal a number of important aspects of Civil War history, the inner workings of the Confederacy, and the operation of the Confederate government (Maps 25 to 35). Besides illustrating and analyzing the political geography of Confederate congressional elections, this atlas contains the first national compilation of voting data on these important contests (Appendix IV). These data give significant insight into turnout, participation rate, and electoral competition in Confederate political life.

The core South—that is, the area other than Kentucky, Missouri, and northwestern Virginia—was relatively free of Union occupation during the November 1861 elections (Map 5). The occupation of large areas of the Confederacy in 1862 had significant electoral affects. The Union presence in the Deep South and the South's failure to expel the federals demonstrated early the probability of the eventual failure of secession. The Union occupation of Tennessee, parts of the coastal Carolinas, and the Mississippi River valley put a seemingly permanent northern presence in the heart of Dixie. In the 1863–1864 elections to the Second House, forty-five districts (42.5 percent) elected representatives by soldiers, refugees, or by general ticket elections by citizens in the unoccupied portion of a state. The occupation of strategic areas of the core South, plus other military and economic factors, caused a change in sentiment in much of the unoccupied South concerning support for the war. The unoccupied districts had a much higher rate of election of new members

to the Second Congress with antisecessionist and Whig backgrounds.

The political party system of the antebellum South collapsed during the Civil War, at least on the face of it. Nominations, election articles, advertising, and final vote returns in southern newspapers reveal a lack of partisan identification in congressional elections. The demise of the party system opened the political process. The Confederate congressional-election vote data show that ballot competition was keen, especially as evidenced by the increased number of multicandidate contests.

While the *party system* broke down, *partisan sentiment* and the legacy of former political affiliation carried on. Partisan labels were labels the electorate could identify. From the mid 1830s until the Civil War the Democratic party and the Whig party and its southern antebellum descendants dominated southern politics. One additional important variable emerged, the stance on secession taken by individuals in the 1850s and especially in the fall of 1860 and early 1861. Stance on secession as well as former political party were significant electoral identifiers.

The southern political elites led the rebellion, and they participated in the state secession conventions and Provisional Congress. In addition, former U.S. congressmen made up nearly half of the membership of the First Permanent Confederate Congress. In some areas the Confederate electoral system brought great change, as evidenced by low incumbency of U.S. congressmen. This was especially so in the border states of Kentucky and Missouri and most of Appalachia. Some areas, like the Deep South Coastal Plain, had a high incumbency rate of former U.S. congressmen. In the debate over continuity or change in Confederate politics each state seemingly was a separate and distinct entity. Continuity with the old system or change to a new system varied state by state and even by regions within states.

The mere holding of elections in the later years of the Civil War South was an indication of the belief in democratic participation and the tenacity of the governments, soldiers, and the general population. There were instances of counties behind northern lines sending election reports to the regular or refugee Confederate state government. Of course, alternatively, there were instances of counties within the unoccupied Confederacy not reporting returns. Nevertheless, voter turnout under the conditions of war was in the hundreds of thousands, and the voice of the electorate was heard, at least in the districts where free elections took place. Elections were and are a part of the American political culture. The Confederates, who believed they were carrying on the true American tradition, found ways to hold these contests to the point of using votes from soldiers in the field, refugees, and unoccupied state areas to elect representatives. Although the territory the Confederacy governed grew smaller and smaller, the Confederate Congress was intact to the end of the war and continued to play a role in Confederate politics. Throughout the Civil War the Confederate Congress illuminated through southern eyes the causes, issues, inner conflicts, and prolongation of the most important single event in American history.

I

ELECTORAL PROCEDURES

Election of Texas Delegates to the Montgomery Convention and Provisional Congress

We the people of Texas in Convention assembled do declare and resolve, and it is hereby declared and resolved,

1st. That this Convention will forthwith proceed to the election by ballot of seven delegates whose duty it shall be when elected to represent the State of Texas in a convention of those States which have seceded or may hereafter secede from the government formerly known as the United States of America.

3rd. That this Convention accepts the suggestion that each of the States seceding from the government of the late United States, and concurring in the formation of a Southern confederacy by said convention, shall be entitled to one vote in said convention upon all questions which may be voted upon therein, and that each State send as many delegates to said convention as are equal in number to the senators and representatives to which it is entitled in the congress of the United States under the late census.

Nominations being next in order.
Mr. Moore of Burnet nominated Mr. John H. Reagan.
On motion of Mr. Wilcox, Mr. Reagan was elected by acclamation.
On motion of Mr. Herbert, Mr. Wigfall was declared elected by acclamation.

Mr. Stockdale nominated W.R. Scurry.
Mr. Cook nominated Thos. J. Devine.
Mr. Rainey nominated Wm. B. Ochiltree.
Mr. Rogers of Harris nominated W.S. Oldham.
Mr. Locke nominated H.R. Runnels.
Mr. Wilcox nominated T.N. Waul.
Mr. Adams nominated Nat. M. Burford.
Mr. Shepard nominated John Hemphill.
Mr. Hobby nominated John Gregg.
Mr. Anderson of Colorado nominated M.D. Graham.
Mr. Rugeley nominated A.C. Horton.
Mr. Shepard nominated Math. Ward.
Mr. Dean nominated F.B. Sexton.
Mr. Wm. Chambers nominated Jno. A. Wharton, who declined
Mr. Ochiltree nominated Pendleton Murrah.
Mr. Todd nominated Jno. T. Mills.
Mr. Jennings nominated Jos. L. Hogg.
Mr. Hughes nominated Jno. A. Wilcox.
Mr. McCraven nominated Peter W. Gray who declined.
Mr. Anderson of Colorado renominated Mr. Gray.
Mr. Waller nominated A.P. Wiley.
Mr. Wharton nominated Robt. C. Campbell.
Mr. Wier nominated Wm. H. Parsons.

Mr. Campbell nominated Guy M. Bryan and Hugh McLeod.
Mr. Waller nominated Jno. A. Wharton, who again declined.
Mr. Robertson of Washington nominated Geo. W. Crawford.
Mesrs. Robertson of Washington, Norris and Holt were appointed tellers.
On motion of Mr. Wharton the Convention adjourned until 7 1/2 o'clock, P.M.

Monday Feby. 4th/61. 7 1/2 o'clock, P.M.

The Convention met pursuant to adjournment. Roll called. Quorum present.

On motion of Mr. Reagan the vote electing him by acclamation was reconsidered.

On motion the vote electing Louis T. Wigfall by acclamation was also reconsidered.

The Convention then proceeded to ballot with the following result.

On the 1st Ballot.

Mr. Reagan received 113 votes, Mr. Wigfall 119 votes, Mr. Hemphill received 76 votes, Mr. Scurry 45 votes, Mr. Devine 50 votes, Mr. Ochiltree 52, Mr. Oldham 61, Mr. Runnels 48, Mr. Waul 73, Mr. Burford 19, Mr. Gregg 60, Mr. Graham 51, Mr. Horton 12, Mr. Ward 18, Mr. Sexton 22, Mr. Murrah 17, Mr. Mills 12, Mr. Hogg 22, Mr. Wilcox 19, Mr. Gray 40, Mr. Wiley 7, Mr. Campbell 33, Mr. Parsons 14,

Mr. McLeod 6, Mr. Bryan 4, Mr. Wharton 3, Mr. Crawford 10, Mr. Daney 1, Mr. Chilton 2, Mr. Maverick 1, Scattering 1, Sam Houston 1, Mr. Hicks 3, Mr. Flournoy 3, Mr. Stockdale 1, Mr. Roberts 1, Mr. Wheeler 1, Mr. Rainey 1, Mr. Foscue 2, Mr. Bee 1, Mr. Rogers of Marion 1, Mr. Frank Lubbock 1, Mr. T. J. Chambers 2, Mr. Pope 1, and Mr. Scott 1. One hundred and fifty-one votes polled.

Mesrs. Wigfall, Reagan and Hemphill having received a majority of all the votes cast were declared elected as three of the seven delegates, and the Convention proceeded to the 2nd ballot.

The names of Mesrs. Runnels, Mills, Hogg and Wiley having been withdrawn.

On the 2nd ballot Mr. Scurry received 27 votes, Mr. Devine 51, Mr. Ochiltree 47, Mr. Oldham 65, Mr. Waul 77, Mr. Burford 18. Mr. Gregg 71, Mr. Graham 43, Mr. Horton 10, Mr. Ward 10, Mr. Sexton 8, Mr. Murrah 3, Mr. Wilcox 17, Mr. Gray 28, Mr. Campbell 21, Mr. Parsons 12, Mr. McLeod 3, Mr. Bryan 4, Mr. Crawford 12, Mr. Rogers of Harris who was nominated by Mr. Moore of Fayette 22, and Scattering 29. One hundred and forty-eight votes polled.

Mr. Waul having received a majority of all the votes cast was declared elected.

The names of Mesrs. Burford, Horton, Ward, Sexton, Murrah, Wilcox, Gray and Parsons were then withdrawn, when the Convention proceeded to the 3rd ballot, whereupon Mr. Scurry received 33 votes, Mr. Devine 45, Mr. Ochiltree 65, Mr. Oldham 67, Mr. Gregg 77, Mr. Graham 42, Mr. Campbell 12, Mr. McLeod 3, Mr. Bryan 4, Mr. Crawford 4, Mr. Rogers of Harris 10, Scattering 18. One hundred and thirty-three votes polled.

Mesrs. John Gregg and W. S. Oldham having received a majority of all the votes cast were declared elected.

The names of Mesrs. Rogers of Harris, Bryan, McLeod, and Campbell were then withdrawn, when the Convention proceeded to a 4th ballot. Mr. Scurry received 11 votes, Mr. Devine 29, Mr. Ochiltree 57, Mr. Graham 23, Mr. Crawford 3, and Scattering 2. One hundred and twenty-five votes polled. No election.

The names of Mesrs. Graham, Scurry and Crawford were then withdrawn, when the Convention proceeded to a 5th ballot. Mr. Ochiltree received 77 votes, Mr. Devine 39, Scattering 3. One hundred and nineteen votes polled.

Mr. Ochiltree having received a majority of all the votes cast was declared elected.

And the President (was) instructed to commission Mesrs. Louis T. Wigfall, John H. Reagan, John Hemphill, T.N. Waul, John Gregg, W.S. Oldham, and Wm. B. Ochiltree as delegates to the Montgomery convention of slave holding States, from the State of Texas.

Journal of the Secession Convention of Texas 1861

Voter Qualifications in Virginia

1. Every white male citizen of the commonwealth, of the age of twenty-one years, who has been a resident of the state for two years, and of the county, city or town where he offers to vote for twelve months next preceding an election—and no other person—shall be qualified to vote for members of the general assembly and all officers elective by the people: but no person in the military, naval or marine service of the Confederate States shall be deemed a resident of this state, by reason of being stationed therein. And no person shall have the right to vote, who is of unsound mind, or a pauper, or a non-commissioned officer, soldier, seaman or marine in the service of the Confederate States, or who has been convicted of bribery in an election, or of any infamous offence.

2. The general assembly, at its first session after the adoption of this constitution, and afterwards as occasion may require, shall cause every city or town, the white population of which exceeds five thousand, to be laid off into convenient wards, and a separate place of voting to be established in each; and thereafter no inhabitant of such city or town shall be allowed to vote except in the ward in which he resides.

3. No voter, during the time for holding any election at which he is entitled to vote, shall be compelled to perform military service, except in time of war or public danger; to work upon the public roads, or to attend any court as suitor, juror or witness; and no voter shall be subject to arrest under any civil process during his attendance at elections, or in going to and returning from them.

4. In all elections votes shall be given openly, or viva voce, and not by ballot; but dumb persons entitled to suffrage may vote by ballot.

1861 Constitution of Virginia, Article III

Soldier Voting in South Carolina

The time fixed at the late session of the Legislature for the election of members to Congress is the 20th of this present month—being the Tuesday after the third Monday in October.

The following is the law for managing the election among those engaged in military service.—To get the returns from camp in time to count before the election is declared, ten days in advance are allowed to hold the election and send in the returns to the Clerk of the Court of the Judicial District. Any one of these ten days may be selected to open polls at each camp—any day from the 10th October in this election.

An Ordinance to Enable Citizens of This State, Who are Engaged in Military Service, to Exercise the Right of Suffrage.

We, the People of the State of South Carolina, in Convention assembled, do declare and ordain, and it is hereby declared and ordained:

Sec 1. That all citizens of this State, who are engaged in the military service either of this State or of the Confederate States, and on that account are absent from their respective Election Districts at the time of any general or District election, shall be entitled to exercise the right of suffrage in all respects as fully as they could do were they present in their respective Election Districts.

Sec 2. That for the purpose of enabling such persons so to exercise the right of suffrage, it shall be their privilege, when any two or more may be at the same camp, or other place where soldiers are congregated, to have opened at such camp or other place, a poll, to be managed by any two commissioned officers, citizens of this State, who may be by such voters selected to manage the same.

Sec 3. That before entering upon the management of such poll, the Managers shall take the oath prescribed by the laws of this State to be administered to Managers of Election, which oath they are hereby authorized to administer to each other; and they are further empowered to administer to the voters the oath prescribed for that purpose by the laws of this State.

Sec 4. That in the management of such poll, the Managers shall make a schedule containing—

1. A caption, setting forth the place and time such election was held, and the Election District and the office for which it was held.
2. The names of all the voters, enrolled by the Managers, and subscribed by the voters to the oath administered to each; each voter affixing his signature, by his own hand, opposite to his name enrolled by the Managers.
3. An attestation signed by the Managers.

Sec 5. That immediately on closing the poll, the Managers shall proceed to count the ballots, and shall subjoin to the schedule above mentioned, a certificate, under their bands, setting forth the fact of counting and the number of votes cast for each individual. And the Managers shall thereupon enclose the said schedule and certificate, under sealed cover, addressed to the Clerk of the Court of the Judicial District in which such Election District may be situated, and endorsed "Election Return for —— Election District, for office of ——," and transmit the same by mail, or by some messenger to be employed at the expense of the voters. And if the election shall be for a member of Congress, with the said schedule and certificate, shall be enveloped the ballots cast.

Sec 6. That the said poll shall be opened on the day fixed for such election to be had in the Election District to which it pertains, or *on any day with ten days preceding that day (not computing that day), and at such hours as the Managers may designate as the most convenient.*

Sec 7. That it shall be the duty of the Clerk of the Court by whom any such election return may have been received, to deliver or transmit the same to the Managers of Elections for such Election District, *on or before the day on which they may assemble at the Court House or other place appointed by law for declaring such election* And the Managers so assembled shall proceed to aggregate the returns which may be thus received with the returns which shall have been made by them from the District precincts, and shall declare the election as how provided by law; and, if the election be for a member of Congress, shall transmit the schedule, certificate and ballots aforementioned, to the office of the Secretary of State, along with the ballots cast in the Election District.

Sec 8. The Executive authority shall cause to be prepared and sent to the Colonels of the various Regiments of the State engaged in actual service, blank forms for the schedules and certificates above required, which shall contain the oaths of Managers and voters.

Sec 9. That this Ordinance shall continue of force only during the continuance of the existing war between the Confederate States of America and the United States; and shall be, and hereby declared to be, a substitute for the provisions of an Act of the General Assembly of this State, entitled "An Act to enable Volunteers in the Military service to exercise the right of suffrage," ratified the twenty-first day of December, in the year of our Lord one thousand eight hundred and sixty-one: *Provided*, That in any election which may be held for a District officer, before the first day of February next, the said Act shall prevail according to its terms and provisions.

Done at Columbia, on the 6th day of January, in the year of our Lord one thousand eight hundred and sixty-two.

D. F. JAMISON, President

Attest: B. F. ARTHUR, Clerk.

As reprinted in *The Mercury*, Charleston, South Carolina, October 7, 1863.

II

UNION OCCUPATION AND STATUS OF CONGRESSIONAL DISTRICTS

The primary objective of this atlas is to illustrate and analyze the geographical aspects of the Confederate Congress. One of the most critical geographical aspects is the territory controlled by the North and the subsequent occupation or disruption of Confederate congressional districts, states, and southern civil society. There were ten legislative sessions during the Confederate Congresses, four in the Provisional Congress, four in the First Congress, and two in the Second Congress. Sixteen maps in Chapters 2 and 3 show the approximate area of Union military control and influence on the last day of each session. These dates are enumerated on each map and in Chapters 2 and 3. Since each map illustrates the farthest extent of permanent Union influence at the end of each session, a determination can be made of the expansion of Union influence from session to session.

Six maps in Chapter 3 illustrate the status of each of the 106 Confederate congressional districts on the last day of each of the six sessions of the Permanent Confederate Congresses. The six occupied area maps of each session of the First and Second Congress are displayed opposite the six district-status maps for comparative purposes. The two maps together, both using the congressional district boundary lines, illustrate that numerous Confederate congressional districts were only partially occupied by Union forces while Confederate military and/or civilian control existed in the remaining portion of the district. This partial Union occupation

includes numerous coastal fortifications, coastal cities, islands, counties, and towns.

Each map illustrating the status of Confederate congressional districts and areas of the South was determined by events occurring during that particular congressional session and previous intersession. Again, the date determining the final map configuration is the last day of each congressional session. The total time period, then, includes the day after the end of the previous session through the last day of the session in question. For example, the status of congressional districts for the First Congress, Second Session, was determined by the criteria listed below occurring between April 22, 1862 (the first day of the intersession after the First Congress, First Session), and October 13, 1862 (the last day of the First Congress, Second Session). The status of each district and area portrayed on the First Congress, Second Session, map was determined, then, by the general situation on October 13, 1862.

The area of Union control and influence and the status of congressional districts are important since they are significant variables in understanding Confederate congressional elections and in the analysis of congressional roll-call voting behavior of senators and representatives.[1] The following two sections enumerate the criteria used to define, in words, and to delimit, on maps, this controlled territory and congressional district status.

Defining Territory and District Status

All the territory of the states admitted to the Confederate Congress is designated as either Union-controlled and influenced or Confederate-controlled. Union-occupied territory is illustrated on Maps 2 to 5 and 13, 15, 17, 19, 21, and 23, found in Chapters 2 and 3. All the congressional districts for all sessions of the First and Second Congresses are designated as either Union-occupied, Union-disrupted, or Confederate-controlled. This district status is illustrated on Maps 14, 16, 18, 20, 22, and 24 in Chapter 3. The following sections discuss the specific criteria used to determine the Union-occupied, Union-disrupted, and Confederate-controlled categories.

Union-Occupied

An area of the South or a Confederate congressional district is designated Union-occupied according to the following criteria:

1. The entire area, major population center(s), or the majority of the territory of a district is captured and physically occupied by Union military forces.

2. The Union military stations a permanent garrison after capture, or a pro-Union/Unionist civilian government is established.[2]

3. Union raids, expeditions, campaigns, demonstrations, operations, reconnaissance, and scoutings of an occasional or temporary nature do not necessarily qualify as permanent Union control of a geographic area or district.[3]
4. Confederate military operations in or reoccupation of an area or district, if for a short period of time, does not negate a previous designation as Union-occupied.[4]
5. Strategic but small areas of the southern coastline occupied by the Union, or an off-shore naval blockade, are not sufficient conditions to designate an entire district as occupied and lost to Confederate control.[5]
6. Inland occupied areas of the South or congressional districts designated Union-occupied are, usually, geographically contiguous to areas and districts previously designated occupied. These areas and districts are within what was determined the approximate line of the farthest extent of safe Union control and movement.

Union-Disrupted

A Confederate congressional district is designated Union-disrupted according to the following criteria:

1. The major population center(s) or the majority of the territory of a district is temporarily captured by Union military forces. This temporary occupation is long enough to disrupt local Confederate government. Local and county Confederate authorities either flee, are captured and arrested, or are killed. After temporary occupation and eventual Union withdrawal, many areas of the South reinstituted Confederate government. Many areas, however, never firmly returned control to the Confederate local, county, state, or national authorities even though a permanent Union army garrison was not left behind or pro-Union/Unionist government established. In many instances, Confederate control was not reestablished because of the close proximity of a permanent Union garrison and their continuous threat of renewed military operations. In these disrupted areas, Confederate national laws, specifically those passed by the Confederate Congress, were difficult, if not impossible, to enforce. In effect, Confederate civil society was ended or seriously disrupted in these areas by direct Union military operations. Civil society is defined as control of an area or district by Confederate civilian officials as evidenced by such undertakings as civil law enforcement, civil court system, elections and elected officials, tax collection, regular mail delivery, and administration of a school system.[6]
2. Districts that reinstitute Confederate civil society after a temporary Union presence are not designated disrupted.[7]
3. Occasional Union raids, expeditions, campaigns, demonstrations, operations, reconnaissance, and scoutings of a temporary nature are carried out in disrupted congressional districts. However, like the Union army, the Confederate army could also operate in these districts and, under military or martial law conditions, could enforce Confederate

conscription, impressment, or other laws on southern citizens. Confederate military recapture or reoccupation, if for a short period of time, or Confederate raids, expeditions, campaigns, demonstrations, operations, reconnaissance, and scoutings do not negate the Union-disrupted designation.
4. Strategic but small areas of the coastline occupied by the Union, or an off-shore naval blockade, are usually not sufficient conditions to designate the entire district as disrupted.
5. Confederate congressional districts designated disrupted are, usually, geographically contiguous to the North or districts previously designated occupied or disrupted.
6. Because of the particular nature of the military movement and its occurrence near the end of the war, all districts affected by Sherman's march to the sea and subsequent Carolinas campaign are designated disrupted.

Confederate-Controlled

An area or congressional district is designated Confederate-controlled, that is, unoccupied, according to the following criteria:

1. All areas of the thirteen southern and border slave states admitted to the Confederate Congress are initially considered unoccupied, that is, territory of the Confederacy under Confederate control. This status changes only when one of the two above-mentioned conditions occurs, specifically, occupation (permanent capture by Union military forces) or disruption (Union military operations or temporary occupation directly causing a permanent breakdown in Confederate civil society).[8]
2. The major population center(s) or the majority of the territory of a district is under Confederate military or civilian control.
3. Union raids, expeditions, campaigns, demonstrations, operations, reconnaissance, and scoutings of an occasional or temporary nature do not necessarily qualify as a loss of Confederate control of a geographic area or district.
4. An area or district is Confederate-controlled even if a strategic but small area of the coastline is occupied by the Union, or even if there is an off-shore naval blockade.
5. Inland areas of the South or congressional districts designated Confederate-controlled are, usually, geographically contiguous to other Confederate-controlled areas, except the Confederate-controlled Trans-Mississippi West. These areas and districts are within the approximate line of farthest extent of safe Confederate control and movement.

Delimiting Territory and District Status

Defining the military and civilian status of the entire Confederacy, or even a particular district for a specific date during the Civil War, is an exceedingly difficult and sometimes ambiguous task. The problem

of definition is further compounded by the problem of delimiting, that is, drawing the defined occupied and disrupted areas on a map. Many of the thousands of works on the Civil War contain maps illustrating the general military situation or area of federal occupation. However, virtually all these national-scale maps are rough generalizations. Many of these purport to show occupied areas at the end of a specific year or the situation before a particular battle—for example, before the Vicksburg siege or before the march to the sea. Indeed, even these rough estimations usually differ from one another.

As suggested in the above section on defining occupied areas, the military situation throughout the Civil War was extremely fluid. Both the Union and Confederate armies carried out raids, expeditions, campaigns, demonstrations, operations, reconnaissance, and scoutings in the other's territory on a continuing basis. The delimiting of actual controlled areas in this atlas is made even more difficult since the situation must be determined for ten specific dates and since the date of permanent Union occupation or permanent Union disruption must be determined for of all areas of the South. Numerous sources were used in this determination. The primary sources are military maps, local and state election data, day-by-day construction of military operations on both sides from written chronologies, and detailed histories of states, counties, and cities during the war.

Military Maps

Prior to this work, all the atlases dealing with the American Civil War were battlefield-military atlases.[9] Most of these atlases relied upon or redrew maps from the original official maps contained in the *Atlas to Accompany the Official Records of the Union and Confederate Armies*.[10] Most of these maps are battle maps portraying movements of troops over a specific battlefield for a specific period of days. Battlefield maps usually do not help in reconstructing the larger national military-cartographic picture. Some campaigns and theater maps do give larger regional situations during specific periods. Only one national-scale authoritatively documented and well-researched military situation map was found over years of research. This national-scale map is Map 92 in the *West Point Atlas of American Wars*, depicting the general national situation in July 1863 on the eve of the Gettysburg campaign.[11] All the maps in the *Official Atlas* and the *West Point Atlas* were compared with the extensive sheet map and atlas collection of the Library of Congress and many secondary sources to put together an initial cartographic picture of occupied areas as depicted by others.[12] Since these military situation map sources are usually in conflict, several additional methods were used to develop a more accurate map.

Local and State Election Data

The data on Confederate congressional elections in this atlas are the most extensive collected in American history. Some of these election data were obtained on a county-by-county basis. In the course of research additional data were obtained by county on Confederate gubernatorial and other statewide races. Original cartographic research was done for this atlas to determine which counties participated in Confederate elections during the Civil War. In some instances—Texas for example—county election data were complete, but not useful, since the Confederates controlled virtually the entire state for the entire war. In other more problematic states, original maps were produced depicting which counties participated in various statewide elections during the war. These maps helped determine which areas were under Confederate control or (although not permanently occupied by federal forces) which areas were significantly disrupted to the extent that residents did not fully participate in Confederate civil society.

Two maps in Chapter 4 demonstrate this method. These maps depict county patterns of participation in congressional elections in states located in the indeterminate front line between Union-controlled and Confederate-controlled territory. The first map, Map 30, illustrates the counties participating in the Tennessee congressional election of August 6, 1863. Military maps do not agree about the areas of the state occupied by Union forces during this period.[13] Tennessee counties are divided into three categories: participation in the election; small participation; and no participation and no returns. Map 30 indicates that twenty counties still had functioning Confederate civil societies, nine counties were somewhat disputed, and fifty-three counties severely disrupted or occupied, or, in this case, may have had Unionist tendencies. The county participation was determined by election data from the Tennessee State Archives tabulated in Appendix V. Again, these categories helped determine the occupied, disrupted, or controlled status of Tennessee. Two counties, Hickman and Maury in Middle Tennessee, seem to be anomalies. In these and other cases the local and state election maps were scrutinized using detailed secondary sources that analyze the history of the county, region, or state during the Civil War. These counties, in spite of their location, did have functioning Confederate governments until shortly after the congressional election.[14]

The second state map depicts the parishes (counties) participating in the November 3, 1863, Louisiana Confederate congressional election.[15] The area of Union occupation in Louisiana is drawn differently on various secondary-source military maps. Map 31 illustrates the parishes participating in the Confederate election and, therefore, those parishes in which Confederate civil society still operated. The Louisiana parishes are again divided into three categories: participation; small participation; and no participation and no returns. The second category indicates that the parish is disrupted, but that Confederate civil society existed in at least some parts of the parish. Twenty-two parishes fully participated in the election, eight had small returns, and seventeen had no returns. Map 31 graphically illustrates the areas occupied and disrupted by the Union in November 1863.

The information from the election data and map not only aided in the determination of the national maps for the Third and Fourth Sessions of the First Congress, but also helped determine the accuracy and reliability of military maps from various secondary sources. The Louisiana map is used in the atlas because another set of election data verifies the status of the parishes and districts. An election was held on February 22, 1864, by the United States military government for a Union governor and to ratify a reconstructed state constitution. The vote returns for this election were reported in Union military records by parish, city, or polling station. These data give very specific locations and indicate which areas were Union-occupied and participated in the federal election. Indeed, the local Union military commander stated, "The proportion [of the vote] given on 22d of February is nearly equal to the territory covered by our arms."[16] The combined Louisiana data illustrated on Map 31 give a succinct geographic illustration of the status of parishes and districts for this period.

Chronology of Military Operations

Since ten specific dates were used in the construction of the occupation and disruption maps, a chronological accounting of military movements was essential to depict the farthest permanent Union penetration at the end of each session. A time line was constructed of major events during each session, such as the occupation of a coastal area, fall of a major city, capture of a major military installation, or thrust of a major campaign. These events were plotted on the Confederate district map. The reference source *The Civil War Day by Day* helped in cataloging detailed events up to the cutoff date.[17]

Secondary Sources: States, Regions, and Counties

The Confederate military and civilian status maps were compiled using numerous historical sources on the Civil War South. Several well-known Civil War state histories were used to decipher the conditions statewide and make inferences concerning occupation or disruption.[18] When very exact lines had to be drawn in disrupted areas, regional and county histories were consulted to determine the date when a city or county lost its Confederate government and, sometime later, if a Union military or a Unionist government was established. In addition to holding Confederate or federal elections, the criteria stated in the defining territory section give other very specific events to determine the status of an area or district. Secondary sources—such as opening of civil courts and court sessions, collection of taxes and tax records, post office records and regular mail delivery, closing of a Confederate newspaper, or opening of a pro-Union newspaper—were searched for indication of these activities.

Final Determination

The determination of the status of an area in the Civil War South is an imprecise science. The maps in this atlas are presented as, and should be interpreted as, illustrations using specific predetermined criteria to depict and analyze occupied and disrupted areas of the South in order to better understand Confederate congressional elections and roll-call voting. Although the designation Confederate-controlled is perhaps the most easily delimited, there were numerous Union military operations inside Confederate areas during the periods dealt with here. In addition, several well-known areas of Unionist activity and sympathy existed continuously in the South throughout the Civil War. For example, in the August 28, 1862, election for governor in North Carolina, thirteen counties on the Atlantic coast were occupied or so disrupted as not to participate at all or participate fully in the election. In addition, however, five counties in the western North Carolina mountains also did not report returns for this election.[19] While most maps, including the ones in this atlas, depict this mountainous area as within Confederate lines during this period, this and other actions demonstrate the Unionist sentiment of the residents of some counties.

The same can be said about the Union-occupied designation. While the Union controlled vast areas of the South, its actual armies were usually on the move with soldiers concentrated in certain garrison towns, forts, and military staging areas. Many areas depicted on the maps in Federal blue had little or no day-to-day Union military scrutiny. Indeed, southern life continued in many counties, especially in mountainous and rural areas, areas off the main transportation routes, and areas away from cities and strategic locations.

Union-disrupted is the most difficult category to determine. This category is necessary simply because some areas of the South were neither permanently Union-occupied nor under Confederate civil society. Although these disrupted districts are placed adjacent to the occupied districts, pockets of disrupted areas are found throughout the South, in Confederate-controlled areas and behind Union lines.[20] This appendix has put forward meaningful and specific criteria to define a significant geographic phenomenon in order to produce a data set and maps using these criteria.

---

[1] See the section on Confederate congressional roll-call voting behavior.

[2] For example, the capture of New Orleans by Union forces in April 1862 and the establishment of loyalty oaths and a local loyal civilian government structure. This occupation even included the election of two representatives to the United States House of Representatives in December 1862 by the local unionist civilians.

[3] For example, Peninsular Virginia. In the Peninsula campaign, April-July 1862, the Union army obviously occupied a large portion of the Third District of Virginia. This occupation was not permanent because of the Union withdrawal. Confederate control over most of the area was reestablished. Also the major population center of the Third District, Richmond, was not captured and permanently held. Thus, on the congressional district map the Virginia Third District is not designated occupied during this period. Even more significant, the First Congress, Second Session (showing areas of the South under Union control), does not designate the entire peninsula region at the end of the Second Session, October 13, 1862, as being permanently occupied by the Union. Another example is the Gulf Coast of Mississippi. The Gulf

Coast of Mississippi was invaded by Union forces in December 1861. The Union forces eventually withdrew, leaving no permanent occupying garrison.

4 For example, Union forces captured Memphis, Tennessee, on June 6, 1862. The one-day occupation of Memphis by C.S.A. forces on August 21, 1864, or, for example, the reoccupation of Columbia, Tennessee, by the Army of Tennessee on November 28, 1864, does not negate the previous Union-occupied designation or designation date.

5 For example, Port Royal Island and its coastal city, Beaufort, South Carolina, were captured by the Union in early November 1861 and held throughout the war. Port Royal served as an important base for the naval blockade of the South. Although only a short distance from Savannah, Georgia, and the main coastal railroad, the Port Royal occupation did not seriously disrupt either until Sherman's march to the sea and Carolinas campaign in December 1864 and early 1865.

6 For example, the First and Second Districts of northern Mississippi and the First District of northern Alabama. Union armies captured and occupied the railroad and major towns in this region intermittently, beginning with the Shiloh campaign and the occupation of Memphis, April–June, 1862. For example, Decatur, Alabama, was occupied April 13, 1862, and Corinth, Mississippi, June 3, 1862. The large Union garrison at Memphis moved in and out of the territory constantly. Southern Unionists were also active in the area. The area of northern Mississippi has been described as a "no man's land" with little consistent organized civil government/society on either side. John K. Bettersworth, *Confederate Mississippi* (Philadelphia: Porcupine Press, 1978), pp. 202–217. Another example is conscription laws. The Confederate draft laws were obviously impossible to enforce in the Union-occupied areas and nearly impossible to enforce by civilian authorities in the districts where Confederate civil society was destroyed and not reestablished.

7 For example, Tennessee was provisionally admitted to the Confederacy in May 1861 and its congressional delegation seated in August 1861. In early 1862 Union forces invaded Middle Tennessee, moving south along the Cumberland and Tennessee rivers. On February 25, 1862, Nashville, the state capital, was captured and permanently occupied for the remainder of the war. Union troops moved through and disrupted many counties in Middle Tennessee south of Nashville, especially in the maneuvering for the battle of Shiloh in early April 1862. Union troops pulled out of much of the area south of Nashville in the late summer of 1862. A number of counties attempted to reinstate Confederate civil society after this withdrawal. For example, Maury County, Tennessee reopened its court under Confederate control from the summer of 1862 through July, 1863. Maury County participated in the Tennessee Confederate congressional elections in August 1863. In February 1864 the Maury court reopened under federal control and remained that way until the end of the war. The districts in this area can be designated fully disrupted only in late 1863 and fully occupied only in early 1864. Stephen V. Ash, *Middle Tennessee Society Transformed, 1860–1870: War and Peace in the Upper South* (Baton Rouge: Louisiana State University Press, 1988), pp. 97–98. Tennessee State Library and Archives, *Statewide Elections Returns*, August 6, 1863, Record Group 87, series number: 1, subseries letter: A.

8 Unionist areas or districts, for example, those in the eastern Tennessee mountains, are considered Confederate until Union military occupation or disruption. Even the stalwart Unionist Wheeling area in the northern panhandle of Virginia is designated an unoccupied Confederate area until northern military forces physically entered the region during the Third Session of the Provisional Congress.

9 See the section on atlases in the Bibliography.

10 U.S. War Department, *Atlas to Accompany the Official Records of the Union and Confederate Armies* (Washington, D.C.: Government Printing Office, 1891–1895). Also referenced as U.S. Congress, House, Miscellaneous Documents (No. 261), v. 40, 52d Congress, 1st Session.

11 Vincent J. Esposito, ed., *The West Point Atlas of American Wars* (New York: Praeger, 1959), Map 92.

12 Richard W. Stephenson, *Civil War Maps: An Annotated List of Maps and Atlases in the Library of Congress* (Washington, D.C.: Library of Congress, 1989).

13 Because of the Union occupation of a large portion of the state, Tennessee elected its representatives by way of a general ticket—that is, each citizen voting for one candidate in each congressional district. The voters were either in Confederate-controlled counties, soldiers, or refugees. See Appendix V and the section on the Tennessee election for the Second House in Chapter 4.

14 In this case the very detailed history of the area seemed to confirm the election data.

15 *Records of the Louisiana State Government, 1850-1888: War Department Collection of Confederate Records*, Roll 14— Records of the Executive Department, 1860–1865, and Records of the Judicial Department, 1861–1862 (Washington, D.C.: National Archives Microfilm Publications). Since the densely populated New Orleans portion of Louisiana, the Confederate congressional election of 1863 was a general ticket election, with voters in the unoccupied portion of the state voting for one candidate in each congressional district. See the section on the Louisiana election for the Second House in Chapter 4.

16 Correspondence of Gen. N. P. Banks, Headquarters Department of the Gulf, New Orleans, February 25, 1864. *War of the Rebellion: A Compilation of the Official Records of the Union and Confederate Armies*, ser. 3, vol 4, (Washington, D.C.: Government Printing Office, 1900), pp. 133–135.

17 E. B. Long, *The Civil War Day By Day: An Almanac, 1861–1865* (Garden City, New York: Doubleday, 1971).

18 See the state histories listed in the bibliography.

19 North Carolina State Archives, General Assembly, Sessions Records, November–December, 1862, Governor's Election Returns.

20 A cartographic analysis of the counties participating in the November 1864 U.S. presidential election illustrates that fifteen counties in southern West Virginia, seven in eastern Kentucky, and eight in southeastern Missouri did not report returns in this election. W. Dean Burnham, *Presidential Ballots 1836–1892* (Baltimore: Johns Hopkins Press, 1955), pp. 458–486, 570–596, 852–864.

III

CONFEDERATE CONGRESSIONAL DISTRICT STATE LAWS

Appendix III contains the legal description for the congressional districts for each Confederate state. The operative portion of the law is condensed and converted into a standard format. These condensations outline the law, eliminate wordiness, use recognized abbreviations, and substitute arabic numbers for written numbers. All place names are counties (parishes in Louisiana) except cities in Virginia where they are designated. Names are spelled as they appear in the district law.

Alabama

1 Lauderdale, Franklin, Lawrence, Limestone, Madison, Morgan
2 Marion, Winston, Blount, Jefferson, Walker, Tuscaloosa, Fayette
3 Jackson, Marshall, DeKalb, Cherokee, St. Clair
4 Calhoun, Randolph, Talladega, Shelby
5 Bibb, Perry, Marengo, Greene, Pickens, Sumter, Choctaw
6 Dallas, Autauga, Coosa, Lowndes, Butler, Montgomery
7 Tallapoosa, Chambers, Russell, Macon
8 Barbour, Henry, Dale, Coffee, Pike, Covington

9 Conecuh, Monroe, Wilcox, Clarke, Washington, Mobile, Baldwin

Congressional District Law - March 18, 1861 (N. 34)

Ordinances and Constitution of the State of Alabama with the Constitution of the Provisional Government of the Confederate States of America (Montgomery: Barrett, Wimbish, and Co., 1861).

Arkansas

1 Benton, Washington, Madison, Carroll, Newton, Crawford, Franklin, Johnson, Pope, Marion, Searcy, Van Buren, Conway
2 Sebastian, Scott, Polk, Sevier, Yell, Montgomery, Pike, Hempstead, Lafayette, Columbia, Ouachita, Clark, Perry, Hot Spring
3 Pulaski, Saline, Dallas, Calhoun, Union, Jefferson, Bradley, Drew, Ashley, Chicot, Desha, Arkansas, Prairie
4 Fulton, Izard, Randolph, Lawrence, Greene, Independence, White, Jackson, Craighead, Poinsett, St. Francis, Crittenden, Mississippi, Monroe, Phillips

Congressional District Law - 1861 (N. 81)

Journal of Both Sessions of the Convention of the State of Arkansas, which were begun and held in the capitol, in the city of Little Rock (Little Rock: Johnson and Yerkes, 1861).

Florida

1 All parts of the state lying east of the Suwannee River
2 Remaining portions of the state not included in the previous limits

Congressional District Law - April 23, 1861 (N. 29)

Constitution or Form of Government for the People of Florida, as Revised and Amended at a Convention of the People Begun and Holden at the City of Tallahassee on the Third Day of January, 1861, Together with the Ordinances Adopted By Said Convention (Tallahassee: Office of the Floridan and Journal, 1861).

Georgia

1 Appling, Bryan, Bulloch, Chatham, Camden, Charlton, Clinch, Coffee, Effingham, Emanuel, Glynn, Liberty, McIntosh, Montgomery, Pierce, Scriven, Telfair, Tattnall, Ware, Wayne
2 Baker, Berrien, Brooks, Calhoun, Clay, Colquitt, Dooly, Decatur, Dougherty, Early, Echols, Irwin, Lee, Lowndes, Mitchell, Miller, Randolph, Terrell, Thomas, Wilcox, Worth
3 Chattahoochee, Harris, Muscogee, Marion, Macon, Quitman, Stewart, Sumter, Schley, Taylor, Talbot, Webster

4 Baldwin, Bibb, Crawford, Jones, Jasper, Houston, Laurens, Putnam, Pulaski, Twiggs, Wilkinson

5 Burke, Columbia, Glasscock, Hancock, Jefferson, Johnson, Lincoln, Richmond, Warren, Wilkes, Washington

6 Clarke, Elbert, Franklin, Greene, Hart, Madison, Morgan, Newton, Oglethorpe, Taliaferro, Walton, Jackson

7 Butts, Clayton, Fayette, Henry, Merriwether, Monroe, Pike, Spalding, Troup, Upson

8 Campbell, Carroll, Coweta, Cobb, DeKalb, Fulton, Haralson, Heard, Paulding, Polk

9 Banks, Cherokee, Dawson, Forsyth, Gwinnett, Habersham, Hall, Lumpkin, Milton, Pickens, Rabun, Towns, Union, White

10 Cass, Catoosa, Chattooga, Dade, Fannin, Floyd, Gordon, Gilmer, Murray, Walker, Whitfield

Congressional District Law - March 23, 1861 (Unnumbered, pp. 392–93)

Journal of the Public and Secret Proceedings of the Convention of the People of Georgia, Held in Milledgeville and Savannah in 1861, Together With the Ordinances Adopted (Milledgeville, Georgia: Boughton, Nisbet, and Barnes, 1861).

Kentucky

1 Fulton, Hickman, McCracken, Graves, Calloway, Marshall, Livingston, Lyon, Caldwell, Trigg, Ballard

2 Union, Webster, Hopkins, Christian, Todd, Henderson, Daviess, Muhlenburg, Crittenden

3 Hancock, Ohio, Grayson, Breckinridge, Meade, Hardin, Larue, Butler, Hart, McLean

4 Logan, Simpson, Allen, Monroe, Barren, Edmonson, Warren, Metcalf

5 Cumberland, Clinton, Wayne, Pulaski, Casey, Lincoln, Taylor, Green, Adair, Russell

6 Spencer, Bullet, Nelson, Washington, Marion, Mercer, Boyle, Garrard, Anderson

7 Jefferson, Shelby, Oldham

8 Henry, Trimble, Carroll, Gallatin, Boone, Grant, Kenton, Campbell

9 Pendleton, Bracken, Nicholas, Harrison, Bourbon, Fleming, Mason

10 Bath, Lewis, Greenup, Boyd, Carter, Laurence, Montgomery, Powell, Rowan, Morgan, Wolfe, Estill, Magoffin

11 Franklin, Woodford, Jessamine, Fayette, Madison, Clark, Owen, Scott

12 Rockcastle, Knox, Harlan, Laurel, Whitley, Clay, Perry, Owsley, Letcher, Breathitt, Floyd, Pike, Johnson, Jackson

Congressional District Law - December 30, 1861 (Unnumbered, pp. 20–21)

Proceedings of the Convention Establishing Provisional Government of Kentucky (Augusta, Georgia: Steam Press of Chronicle and Sentinel, 1863).

Louisiana

1 Plaquemines, St. Bernard, Orleans, (right bank) the Second and Third Municipal Districts of New Orleans, St. Tammany, Washington

2 First and Fourth Municipal Districts of New Orleans, Jefferson

3 St. Charles, St. John the Baptist, St. James, Ascension, Assumption, Lafourche, Terrebonne, Livingston, East Baton Rouge, East Feliciana, St. Helena

4 West Feliciana, Point Coupee, West Baton Rouge, Iberville, St. Landry, Lafayette, Vermillion, St. Martin, St. Mary

5 Calcasieu, Rapides, Sabine, Natchitoches, Winn, DeSoto, Caddo, Bossier, Bienville, Claiborne

6 Avoyelles, Concordia, Catahoula, Caldwell, Franklin, Tensas, Madison, Ouachita, Jackson, Union, Morehouse, Carroll

Congressional District Law - March 25, 1861 (N. 33)

Official Journal of the Proceedings of the Convention of the State of Louisiana (New Orleans: J.O. Nixon, 1861).

Mississippi

1 Marshall, Lafayette, Yallobusha, Calhoun, Tallahatchie, DeSoto, Panola, Chickasaw

2 Tishomingo, Tippah, Itawamba, Pontotoc, Monroe

3 Lowndes, Oktibbeha, Noxubee, Kemper, Winston, Choctow, Neshoba

4 Tunica, Coahoma, Bolivar, Washington, Issaquena, Warren, Claiborne, Jefferson, Adams, Copiah

5 Sunflower, Carroll, Attala, Holmes, Leake, Madison, Yazoo

6 Hinds, Rankin, Scott, Newton, Lauderdale, Simpson, Smith, Jasper, Clark

7 Franklin, Amite, Wilkinson, Pike, Lawrence, Covington, Jones, Wayne, Green, Perry, Marion, Hancock, Harrison, Jackson

Congressional District Law - August 5, 1861 (C XLII)

Laws of the State of Mississippi Passed at a Called Session of the Mississippi Legislature Held in the City of Jackson, July 1861 (Jackson, Mississippi: E Barksdale, 1861)

Missouri

1 St. Louis

2 Marion, Ralls, Monroe, Pike, Audrain, Boone, Callaway, Montgomery, Warren, Lincoln, St. Charles

3 Lewis, Clark, Scotland, Knox, Shelby, Howard, Randolph, Macon, Adair, Schuyler, Putnam, Dodge, Sullivan, Linn, Chariton, Carroll, Livingston, Grundy, Mercer

4 Ray, Caldwell, Daviess, Harrison, Gentry, DeKalb, Clinton, Clay, Platte, Buchanan, Andrew, Nodaway, Atchinson, Holt

5 Jackson, Cass, Henry, Johnson, Lafayette, Saline, Pettis, Benton, Morgan, Moniteau, Cooper, Cole, Miller

6 Bates, Jasper, Newton, McDonald, Barry, Lawrence, Dade, Cedar, Saint Clair, Hickory, Polk, Greene, Stone, Taney, Ozark, Wright, Dallas, LaClede, Camden, Gasconade, Osage, Pulaski, Texas, Oregon

7 Franklin, Jefferson, Ste. Genevieve, Washington, Crawford, Dent, Shannon, St. Francois, Perry, Madison, Reynolds, Cape Girardeau, Bollinger, Wayne, Scott, Ripley, Mississippi, Butler, Stoddard, New Madrid, Dunklin, Pemiscot

Congressional District Law - On November 8, 1861, pro-Confederate Governor C. F. Jackson approved a bill titled "an act to provide for holding an election for Representatives to the Confederate States of America, and for other purposes." This act adopted by default the seven congressional districts used by Missouri in the 1850s. The 1850s congressional district law is listed below.

Journal of the Senate, Extra Session of the Rebel Legislature, Called by a Proclamation of C. F. Jackson, Begun and Held at Neosho, Newton County, Missouri on the Twenty-first of October 1861 (Appendix) (Jefferson City: Emory S. Foster, Public Printer, 1865-1866).

Congressional District Law - February 19, 1853 (Unnumbered, pp. 98–99)

Laws of the State of Missouri Passed at the First Session of the Seventeenth General Assembly Begun and Held at the City of Jefferson on Monday the Thirteenth of August A.D. 1852 (City of Jefferson: James Lusk, 1853).

North Carolina

1 Martin, Hertford, Gates, Chowan, Perquimons, Pasquotank, Camden, Currituck, Northampton, Washington, Tyrell, Bertie

2 Halifax, Edgecombe, Beaufort, Wilson, Pitt, Greene, Lenoir, Hyde

3 Carteret, Craven, Jones, Onslow, Duplin, Wayne, Johnston, Sampson

4 New Hanover, Brunswick, Columbus, Bladen, Robeson, Cumberland, Richmond, Harnett

5 Warren, Franklin, Granville, Wake, Orange, Nash

6 Alamance, Person, Caswell, Rockingham, Guilford, Stokes, Forsyth

7 Randolph, Davidson, Chatham, Moore, Montgomery, Stanly, Anson

8 Rowan, Cabarrus, Union, Mecklenburg, Gaston, Lincoln, Catawba, Cleveland

9 Ashe, Alleghany, Wilkes, Caldwell, Alexander, Yadkin, Surry, Davie, Iredell, Burke

10 Clay, Cherokee, Macon, Jackson, Madison, Buncombe, Transylvania, Henderson, Polk, Yancey, McDowell, Rutherford, Mitchell, Haywood, Watauga

Congressional District Law - September 4, 1861 (C. 3)

Public Laws of the State of North Carolina Passed by the General Assembly At Its Second Extra Session, 1861 (Raleigh: John Spelman, 1861).

South Carolina

1 Lancaster, Chesterfield, Marlboro, Darlington, Marion, Williamsburg, Horry, Georgetown
2 Charleston, exclusive of the Parish of St. John's, Colleton
3 Beaufort, Barnwell, Orangeburg, Colleton, and the Parish of St. John's
4 Lexington, Edgefield, Newberry, Laurens, Abbeville
5 Anderson, Pickens, Greenville, Spartanburg, Union
6 York, Chester, Fairfield, Richland, Kershaw, Clarendon, Sumter

Congressional District Law - South Carolina did not gain or lose seats in the Confederate apportionment and the state secessionist Constitution provided for the continuation of the congressional districts used in the 1850s. An 1863 district law continued the use of these districts and is cited below.

Congressional District Law - September 30, 1863 (N. 4664)

Acts of the General Assembly of the State of South Carolina Passed in September and December, 1863 (Columbia: Charles P. Pelham, 1864).

Tennessee

1 Johnson, Carter, Sullivan, Washington, Hancock, Hawkins, Greene, Cocke
2 Campbell, Claiborne, Union, Grainger, Jefferson, Knox, Sevier, Blount
3 Monroe, McMinn, Meiggs, Rhea, Polk, Bradley, Hamilton, Marion, Sequatchie, Bledsoe, Grundy, Franklin
4 Anderson, Roane, Cumberland, Morgan, Scott, Fentress, Overton, Jackson, Putnam, White, Van Buren, Warren
5 Macon, Smith, DeKalb, Wilson, Davidson
6 Cannon, Coffee, Bedford, Marshall, Rutherford, Williamson
7 Lincoln, Giles, Lawrence, Wayne, Lewis, Maury
8 Sumner, Robertson, Montgomery, Cheatham, Dixon, Humphries, Hickman, Stewart
9 Henry, Weakly, Obion, Dyer, Gibson, Carroll
10 Madison, Hardeman, Henderson, McNairy, Hardin, Decatur, Benton, Perry
11 Fayette, Shelby, Tipton, Lauderdale, Haywood

Congressional District Law - October 18, 1861 (C. 12)

Public Acts of the State of Tennessee Passed at the First Session of the Thirty-Fourth General Assembly for the Years 1861–62 (Nashville: Griffith, Camp and Co., 1861).

Texas

1 Calhoun, Refugio, Bee, San Patricio, Nueces, Cameron, Hidalgo, Starr, Zapata, Webb, Encinal, Duval, Live Oak, McMullin, La Salle, Dimmit, Maverick, Zavala, Frio, Atascosa, Goliad, Victoria, DeWitt, Karnes, Gonzales, Guadalupe, Wilson, Bexar, Medina, Uvalde, Dawson, Kinney, Bandera, Comal, Hays, Blanco, Kerr, Edwards, Gillespie, Kimble, Llano, Mason, Menard, San Saba, McCulloch, Concho, Presidio, El Paso
2 Caldwell, Jackson, Matagorda, Wharton, Lavaca, Colorado, Fayette, Bastrop, Travis, Burnet, Lampasas, Bell, Brazoria, Fort Bend, Austin, Washington, Burleson, Williamson, Milam
3 Galveston, Harris, Montgomery, Grimes, Walker, Leon, Madison, Brazos, Robertson, Limestone, Freestone, Navarro, Ellis, Falls, McLennan, Coryell, Bosque, Hill, Comanche, Hamilton, Johnson, Erath, Eastland, Brown, Coleman, Runnels, Callahan, Taylor
4 Sabine, Shelby, Panola, Angelina, Nacogdoches, San Augustine, Polk, Tyler, Jasper, Newton, Orange, Hardin, Liberty, Jefferson, Chambers, Cherokee, Trinity, Houston, Anderson
5 Harrison, Upshur, Rusk, Wood, Smith, Van Zandt, Henderson, Kaufman, Dallas, Tarrant, Parker, Palo Pinto, Buchanan, Shackelford, Jones
6 Bowie, Cass, Marion, Red River, Titus, Lamar, Hopkins, Fannin, Hunt, Collin, Grayson, Cook, Denton, Montague, Wise, Clay, Jack, Young, Throckmorton, Haskell, Hardeman, Wilbarger, Wichita, Greer

Congressional District Law - April 6, 1861 (C. XLVI)

General Laws of the Eighth Legislature of the State of Texas (Austin: John Marshall and Company, 1861).

Virginia

1 Middlesex, Accomack, Northampton, King William, Gloucester, Matthews, Lancaster, Westmoreland, Richmond, Essex, King & Queen, Northumberland
2 Norfolk city, Norfolk county, Princess Anne, Nansemond, Isle of Wight, Southampton, Sussex, Surry, Greenesville
3 City of Richmond, Henrico, Hanover, Charles City, New Kent, Elizabeth City, Warwick, James City, Williamsburg, York
4 City of Petersburg, Dinwiddie, Chesterfield, Powhatan, Amelia, Nottoway, Cumberland, Goochland, Prince George
5 Prince Edward, Brunswick, Mecklenburg, Lunenburg, Charlotte, Halifax, Appomattox
6 Pittsylvania, Patrick, Henry, Franklin, Bedford, Carroll
7 Albemarle, Campbell, Lynchburg, Amherst, Nelson, Fluvanna, Buckingham
8 Spotsylvania, Louisa, Orange, Madison, Culpeper, Caroline, King George, Stafford, Greene
9 Fauquier, Rappahannock, Prince William, Fairfax, Alexandria, Loudoun, Warren, Page
10 Frederick, Berkeley, Morgan, Hampshire, Clarke, Jefferson, Shenandoah, Hardy
11 Augusta, Rockingham, Rockbridge, Pendelton, Highland, Bath, Pocahontas, Alleghany
12 Botetourt, Roanoke, Montgomery, Floyd, Pulaski, Giles, Craig, Mercer, Monroe, Greenbrier, Raleigh, Fayette
13 Wythe, Smyth, Grayson, Washington, Scott, Lee, Wise, Buchanan, McDowell, Tazewell, Bland, Russell
14 Kanawha, Logan, Boone, Wayne, Cabell, Putnam, Mason, Jackson, Roane, Clay, Nicholas, Braxton, Wirt, Wyoming
15 Lewis, Wood, Pleasants, Tyler, Ritchie, Doddridge, Upshur, Randolph, Webster, Tucker, Barbour, Harrison, Taylor, Gilmer, Calhoun
16 Ohio, Hancock, Brooke, Marshall, Wetzel, Marion, Monongalia, Preston

Congressional District Law - June 28, 1861 (N. 74)

Acts of the General Assembly of the State of Virginia, Passed in 1861 (Richmond: William F. Ritchie, 1861).

IV

CONFEDERATE CONGRESSIONAL ELECTIONS CANDIDATES AND VOTE TOTALS

Elections to the First Confederate Congress
November 6, 1861[1]

Alabama[2]	Votes	Percentage
District 1		
Thomas J. Foster	2,077	41
Henry C. Jones	1,836	36
Z.P. Davis	926	18
R.R. Lindsay	264	5
District 2		
William R. Smith	1,699	35
N.H. Brown	1,458	30
P. Musgrove	1,274	26
William Earnest	451	9
District 3		
John P. Ralls	3,754	66
Williamson R.W. Cobb	1,917	34
District 4		
Jabez L.M. Curry	3,112	100
no opposition		

Alabama[2]	Votes	Percentage
District 5		
Francis S. Lyon	3,166	53
Jack F. Cocke	1,586	26
Thomas H. Herndon	1,242	21
District 6		
William P. Chilton	4,425	100
no opposition		
District 7		
David Clopton	2,584	100
no opposition		
District 8		
James Lawrence Pugh	4,215	100
no opposition		
District 9		
Edward S. Dargan	2,891	51
J.W. Portis	1,594	28
Percy Walker	1,228	21

Arkansas[3]	Votes	Percentage
District 1		
Felix I. Batson	4,234	69
Hugh F. Thomason	1,879	31
R.F. Colburn	36	—
District 2		
Grandison D. Royston	3,459	49
A.S. Huey	1,323	19
J.T. Bearden	864	12
S.M. Scott	572	8
A.G. Mayers	523	7
Green J. Clark	207	3
John F. Wheeler	139	2
District 3		
Augustus H. Garland	2,157	29
Jilson P. Johnson	2,125	29
B.G. Harley	1,719	24
J.C. Murray	527	7
S.F. Arnett	514	7

Arkansas[3]	Votes	Percentage
W.P. Grace	261	4
Scattering	10	
District 4		
Thomas B. Hanly	3,227	60
James H. Patterson	2,127	40

Florida[4]	Votes	Percentage
District 1		
James B. Dawkins	1,462	36
Philip Dell	1,050	26
A.A. Canova	980	24
James M. Commander	561	14
Replacement Election February 2, 1863		
John M. Martin	1,111	39
James Gettis	583	20
W.M. Ives	571	20
James E. Broome	486	17
George E. Hawes	114	4
District 2		
Robert B. Hilton	1,668	39
James L. Mosely	937	22
F.R. Cotton	774	18
John Tanner	497	12
F.L. Villefrigum[5]	436	10

Georgia[6]	Votes	Percentage
District 1[7]		
Julian Hartridge	[3,348][8]	[74]
Thomas M. Foreman	[1,172]	[26]
District 2[9]		
Charles J. Munnerlyn	3,005	58
Richard H. Clark	1,493	29
Jonathon Davis	649	13
District 3[10]		
Hines Holt	2,493	57
Martin J. Crawford	1,900	43
Replacement Election December 7, 1863[11]		
Porter Ingram	[596][8]	[55]
E.G. Raiford	[294]	[27]
W.H. Robinson	[187]	[17]
Parker	[7]	[1]
District 4		
Augustus H. Kenan	2,318	56
Howell Cobb	1,491	36
James W. Traywick	313	8

Georgia[6]	Votes	Percentage
District 5[12]		
David W. Lewis	1,872	55
M. C. Fulton[13]	1,513	45
District 6		
William W. Clark	2,008	36
M.C.M. Hammond[14]	1,961	35
Thomas P. Saffold	1,612	29
District 7[15]		
Robert P. Trippe	3,040	72
L.T. Doyal[16]	1,154	28
District 8[17]		
Lucius J. Gartrell	3,443	72
John A. Jones	1,319	28
District 9		
Hardy Strickland	2,924	45
Rev. R.W. Bigham[18]	2,499	38
James P. Simmons	1,114	17
District 10		
Augustus R. Wright	2,848	54
Leander W. Crook[19]	2,282	43
Lawson Black	157	3

Kentucky[20] January 22, 1862	Votes	Percentage
District 1		
Willis Benson Machen		
District 2		
John Wesley Crockett		
District 3		
Henry English Read		
District 4		
George Washington Ewing		
District 5		
James Stone Chrisman		
District 6		
Theodore L. Burnett		
District 7		
Horatio Washington Bruce		
District 8		
George Baird Hodge		
District 9		
Eli Metcalf Bruce		
District 10		
James William Moore		

Kentucky January 22, 1862	Votes	Percentage
District 11		
Robert J. Breckinridge Jr.		
District 12		
John Milton Elliot		

Louisiana[21]	Votes	Percentage
District 1		
Charles J. Villere	2,597	51
Charles Deblanc	1,461	28
J.B. Wilkinson	822	16
Rufus Dolbear	248	5
District 2		
Charles M. Conrad	2,767	69
W.R. Adams	844	21
Samuel C. Reid	399	10
District 3		
Duncan Farrar Kenner	5,357	100
no opposition[22]		
District 4		
Lucius Jacques Dupre	5,518	100
no opposition[23]		
District 5		
Henry Marshall	3,133	52
John L. Lewis[24]	2,904	48
District 6		
John Perkins Jr.	4,955	92
John S. Richardson	404	8
Scattering[25]	4	

Mississippi[26]	Votes	Percentage
District 1		
Jeremiah W. Clapp	3,731	51
Jehu A. Orr	3,583	49
District 2		
Reuben Davis[27]	4,204	60
Daniel B. Wright	2,728	39
H.R. Miller	108	1
District 3		
Israel V. Welch	4,031	67
A. Murdock	2,008	33
District 4		
Henry C. Chambers	2,229	51
C. L. Buck	2,131	49

Mississippi[26]	Votes	Percentage
District 5		
Otho R. Singleton	3,623	70
Josiah A.P. Campbell	1,586	30
District 6		
Ethelbert Barksdale	5,443	100
no opposition		
District 7		
John J. McRae	3,333	63
John T. Lamkin	1,999	37

Missouri[28]	Appointed November 8, 1861[29]	
District 1	Appointed	
William M. Cooke		
District 2		
Thomas A. Harris Jr.	Appointed	
District 3		
Casper W. Bell	Appointed	
District 4		
Aaron H. Conrow	Appointed	
District 5		
George G. Vest	Appointed	
District 6		
Thomas W. Freeman	Appointed	
District 7		
John Hyer[30]	Appointed	

North Carolina[31]		
District 1		
William N. H. Smith		
no opposition		
District 2		
Robert R. Bridgers	1,111	97
Scattering	34	3
District 3		
Owen R. Kenan	3,205	61
Thomas Faison	1,132	22
C.R. Thomas	492	9
F.D. Koonce	412	8
District 4		
Thomas D. S. McDowell		
no opposition		

North Carolina[31]	Votes	Percentage
District 5		
Archibald H. Arrington	3,847	57
Josiah Turner Jr.	1,973	29
Abraham W. Veneble	896	13
District 6		
James R. McLean[32]	3,120	56
R.P. Dick	2,412	44
District 7		
Thomas S. Ashe	1,939	36
[Samuel H.] Christian[33]	1,858	34
[Maurice Q.] Waddell	1,276	24
[William J.] Headen	352	6
District 8		
William Lander	4,711	98
Scattering	110	2
District 9		
Burgess S. Gaither		
no opposition		
District 10		
Allen T. Davidson	majority of 1,196[34]	
William H. Thomas		

South Carolina[35]		
District 1		
John McQueen		
no opposition[36]		
District 2		
William P. Miles		
no opposition[37]		
District 3		
Lewis M. Ayer		
David F. Jamison[38]		
District 4[39]		
Milledge L. Bonham	2,191	73
John A. Calhoun	826	27
Replacement Election January 20, 1863[40]		
William D. Simpson[41]	1,826	69
William Fort	362	14
M.C. Butler	159	6
J. H. Williams	97	4
R.C. Griffin	79	3
S. McGovern	51	2
J.C. Hope	40	2
Scattering[42]	24	

South Carolina[35]	Votes	Percentage
District 5[43]		
James Farrow	2,680	75
G.F. Townes	900	25
District 6		
William W. Boyce		
no opposition[44]		

Tennessee[45]		
District 1		
Joseph B. Heiskell	2,790	86
James W. Deadrick	453	14
A.J. Tipton	1	—
District 2		
William G. Swan	1,552	77
John Baxter	404	20
J.T. Carmichael	58	3
District 3		
William H. Tibbs	1,643	37
Alford Caldwell	1,375	31
A.G. Welker	807	18
Mitch Pope	632	14
Arthur S. Colyar	29	—
District 4		
Erasmus L. Gardenhire	2,680	74
Thomas Snodgrass	789	22
H.M. Wetterson	122	3
Scattering	27	1
District 5		
Henry S. Foote	2,453	53
Nathan Green	1,641	35
R.E. Thompson	567	12
DeWitt	3	
District 6		
Merideth P. Gentry	2,409	63
C.Reidy	1,120	29
H.P. Keeble	320	8
Thomas Anderson	10	—
District 7		
George W. Jones	2,805	56
Lee M. Bentley	2,156	43
Thomas M. Jones	82	2
District 8		
Thomas Menees	3,453	79
Charles Faxon	835	19
Scattering[46]	90	2

Tennessee[45]	Votes	Percentage
District 9		
John D.C. Atkins	3,316	100
M.R. Hill	2	—
District 10		
John V. Wright	1,963	49
Micajah Bullock	1,864	47
F.C. Saunders	177	4
Scattering[47]	10	—
District 11		
David M. Currin	4,395	83
B.D. Nabors	916	17

Texas[48]	Votes	Percentage
District 1		
John A. Wilcox	3,448	47
Edward R. Hord	2,470	34
William Stewart	1,403	19
District 2		
Caleb C. Herbert	2,479	38
Fred Tate	2,034	31
A.M. Lewis	1,367	21
F.W. Chandler	633	10
District 3		
Peter W. Gray	4,952	74
A.P. Wiley	1,673	25
W.R. Reagan	21	—
Scattering	5	—
District 4		
Franklin B. Sexton	1,644	32
J.L. Hogg	1,062	21
J.N. Maxey	1,053	21
T.J. Wood	926	18
A.W.O. Hicks	350	7
W.R. Poag	100	2
District 5		
Malcomb D. Graham	2,946	52
R.B. Hubbard	2,686	48
District 6		
William B. Wright	3,444	49
Benjamin H. Epperson	2,777	39
T.J. Rodgers	537	8
R.H. Ward	256	4

Virginia[49]	Votes	Percentage
District 1		
Muscoe R.H. Garnett[50]		
District 2[51]		
John R. Chambliss		
Arthur R. Smith		
John R. Kilby		
John J. Kindred		
District 3[52]		
John Tyler	2,949	56
W.H. MacFarland	1,235	24
James Lyons	838	16
Baker P. Lee	215	4
Replacement Election February 10, 1862[53]		
James Lyons	1,320	45
W.H. MacFarland	1,061	36
John B. Young	218	7
Robert Saunders	202	7
George W. Randolph	118	4
District 4		
Roger A. Pryor		
no opposition[54]		
Replacement Election[55] May 1862		
Charles F. Collier	740	43
James A. Seddon	616	35
Epps	385	22
District 5		
Thomas S. Bocock		
Thomas F. Goode[56]		
District 6[57]		
John Goode Jr.		
William M. Tredway		
William Martin		
Beverly A. Davis		
District 7[58]		
James P. Holcomb		
Shelton F. Leake		
R.G.H. Kean		

Virginia[49]	Votes	Percentage
District 8[59]		
Daniel C. DeJarnette	[1,249][8]	[61]
J. Horace Lacy	[451]	[22]
Jeremiah Morton	[350]	[17]
District 9		
William Smith		
Robert E. Scott[60]		
District 10[61]		
Alexander R. Boteler		
Thomas C. Green		
Andrew Hunter		
District 11		
John B. Baldwin[62]		
District 12		
Waller R. Staples		
John T. Anderson[63]		
District 13		
Walter Preston		
Fayette McMullen		
District 14		
Albert G. Jenkins		
no opposition[64]		
Replacement Election		
Samuel A. Miller		
District 15		
Robert W. Johnston		
no opposition[65]		
District 16		
Charles W. Russell[66]		

Elections to the Second Confederate Congress

Alabama[67] August 5, 1863

	Votes	Percentage
District 1		
Thomas J. Foster	1,857	83
Scattering[68]	377	17
District 2		
William R. Smith	1,756	61
William H. Fowler	1,107	39
District 3		
Williamson R.W. Cobb	2,111	59
John Perkins Ralls	966	27
James Sheffield	482	14
District 4		
Marcus H. Cruikshank	3,236	58
Jabez L.M. Curry	2,299	42
District 5		
Francis S. Lyon	2,508	91
Jack F. Cocke	198	7
Scattering[69]	37	2
District 6		
William P. Chilton	3,005	55
M.C. Lane	2,430	45
District 7		
David Clopton	2,498	57
John H. Cadenhead	1,817	42
Scattering[70]	17	—
District 8		
James Lawrence Pugh	1,566	33
Dr. Joseph Jones	1,373	29
J. McCaleb Wiley	1,362	29
A.W. Starke	386	8
District 9		
James S. Dickinson	1,866	48
Charles C. Langdon	1,660	43
Garrett Hall	274	7
Robert H. Smith	63	2

Arkansas[71] November 4, 1863

	Votes	Percentage
District 1		
Felix I. Batson		
District 2[72]		
Rufus K. Garland		
Grandison Royston		

Arkansas[71] November 4, 1863

	Votes	Percentage
District 3		
Augustus H. Garland		
Replacement Election[73] October 24, 1864		
David W. Carroll	729	52
Joseph Stillwell	671	48
Scattering	8	
District 4 April 4, 1864[74]		
Thomas B. Hanly		
Lemuel O. Bridewell		
John Forbes		

Florida[75] October 5, 1863

	Votes	Percentage
District 1		
Samuel S. Rogers	1,050	32
Lewis G. Pyles	949	28
W.J. Harrison	710	21
W.W. McCall	641	19
District 2		
Robert B. Hilton	2,394	66
J.B. Roulhac	1,214	33
S.Y. Finley	40	1

Georgia[76] October 7, 1863

	Votes	Percentage
District 1		
Julian Hartridge	3,077	46
[John M.] King[77]	2,909	43
Hopkins	766	11
District 2		
William E. Smith	2,825	47
Charles J. Munnerlyn[78]	1,220	20
Seward	1,618	27
Davis	350	6
District 3		
Mark H. Blandford	3,429	60
Hines Holt	2,322	40
District 4		
Clifford Anderson	2,478	56
Augustus H. Kenan	1,932	44
District 5		
John T. Shewmake	1,663	36
Gibson	1,373	30
David W. Lewis	784	17
Robert Toombs	747	17

Georgia[76] October 7, 1863

	Votes	Percentage
District 6		
Joseph H. Echols	2,449	47
William W. Clark	1,593	31
Lewis	1,147	22
District 7		
James M. Smith	3,652	84
E.G. Cabiness[79]	690	16
District 8		
George N. Lester	3,309	60
L.J. Glenn[80]	2,240	40
District 9		
Hiram P. Bell	4,486	58
Col. McMillan[81]	3,193	42
District 10		
Warren Akin	2,562	48
Jackson	1,794	33
Augustus R. Wright	1,036	19

Kentucky[82] February 10, 1864

	Votes	Percentage
District 1		
Willis Benson Machen	998	98
Noble	16	2
District 2		
George W. Triplett		
J.D. Morris		
Dennis		
District 3		
Henry English Read	1,018	53
M.H. Cofer	917	47
District 4		
George Washington Ewing	1,234	71
J.R. Barrick	512	29
District 5		
James Stone Chrisman	943	54
Thomas Napier	818	46
District 6		
Theodore L. Burnett	1,330	67
P.B. Thompson	331	17
Ben Hardin	331	17
District 7		
Horatio Washington Bruce	1,535	91
Cocke	149	9

Kentucky[82] February 10, 1864	Votes	Percentage
District 8		
Humphrey Marshall	1,419	74
J.T. Pickett	498	26
District 9[84]		
Eli Metcalf Bruce	1,301	78
Langhorne	174	10
John L. Marshall	163	10
Pickett	39	2
District 10		
James William Moore	1,787	85
Thomas Johnson	181	9
A.J. May	126	6
District 11		
Benjamin F. Bradley	1,208	72
Robert J. Breckinridge	459	28
District 12		
John Milton Elliot	1,558	100
no opposition		

Louisiana[85] November 4, 1863	Votes	Percentage
District 1		
Charles J. Villere	3,685	51
T.G. Hunt	3,567	49
District 2		
Charles M. Conrad	3,862	55
Robert Mott	3,218	45
District 3		
Duncan Farrar Kenner	7,198	100
no opposition		
District 4		
Lucius Jacques Dupre	3,393	48
A.L. Tucker	2,385	34
E.B. Downes	1,254	18
District 5		
Benjamin L. Hodge	6,549	100
no opposition		
Replacement Election[86] October 17, 1864		
Henry Gray	[1,572][8]	[70]
John L. Lewis	[673]	[30]
District 6		
John Perkins Jr.	7,041	100
no opposition		

Mississippi[87] October 5, 1863	Votes	Percentage
District 1[88]		
Jehu A. Orr	2321	56
Jeremiah W. Clapp[89]	1758	43
Simmons	51	1
District 2[90]		
William D. Holder		
Arthur E. Reynolds		
Cornelius Dowd		
Berry		
Falkner		
District 3		
Israel V. Welch		
William D. Lyles[91]		
District 4		
Henry C. Chambers		
no opposition[92]		
District 5[93]		
Otho R. Singleton		
A.P. Hill		
T.C. Tupper		
Franklin Smith		
District 6[94]		
Ethelbert Barksdale	2,039	52
Con Rea[95]	1,854	48
District 7		
John T. Lamkin		
John J. McRae[96]		

Missouri[97] May 2, 1864	Votes	Percentage
District 1		
Thomas L. Snead	3,986	90
John C. Moore	334	8
Uriel Wright	110	2
Trusten Polk	1	—
District 2		
Nimrod L. Norton	3,654	85
Thomas A. Harris Jr.	623	15
E.B. Hull	4	
District 3		
John B. Clark	1,797	41
Casper W. Bell	914	21
Thomas H. Pierce	560	13
R.S. Bevier	524	12
Jos. L. Moore	478	11

Missouri[97] May 2, 1864	Votes	Percentage
Donald C. Roberts	74	2
James Bradley	1	—
District 4		
Aaron H. Conrow	3,301	78
J.H. Godsey	922	22
B.E. Guthrie	1	
District 5		
George G. Vest	3,148	80
G.R. Ratbun	1,083	17
D.H. Lindsey	196	3
District 6		
Peter S. Wilkes	2,814	62
John T. Coffee	970	21
Thomas W. Freeman	796	17
T.T. Taylor	3	
District 7		
Robert A. Hatcher	1,545	37
M.H. Moore	1,352	32
F.C. Hagan	1,325	31
S.J. Kitchen	15	

North Carolina[98] November 4, 1863	Votes	Percentage
District 1[99]		
William N. H. Smith	1,107	47
Edward Warren	606	26
L.D. Stark	483	20
Peyton T. Henry	164	7
District 2[100]		
Robert R. Bridgers	1,557	50
Edward C. Yellowly	1,540	50
District 3		
James T. Leach	2,074	44
Duncan K. McRae	1,493	31
William S. DeVane	720	15
Thomas I. Faison	466	10
District 4		
Thomas C. Fuller	2,630	61
Robert Strange	1,327	31
O.P. Mears	352	8
District 5		
Josiah Turner Jr.	3,551	60
Archibald H. Arrington	2,393	40

North Carolina[98] November 4, 1863	Votes	Percentage
District 6[101]		
John A. Gilmer	2,234	73
Bedford Brown	832	27
District 7		
Samuel H. Christian[102]	3,631	63
Thomas S. Ashe	2,126	37
Replacement Election[103] April 21, 1864		
James M. Leach	4,058	58
A.G. Foster	2,420	35
N.A. Ramsay	482	7
District 8		
James G. Ramsay	3,536	52
William Lander	3,277	48
District 9[104]		
Burgess S. Gaither	1,294	63
S.P. Smith	757	37
District 10[105]		
George W. Logan		
Marcus Erwin		
John Hyman		
Allen T. Davidson		
William F. Jones		

South Carolina October 20, 1863		
District 1[106]		
James H. Witherspoon	1,289	53
John McQueen	1,149	47
District 2[107]		
William P. Miles		
no opposition		
District 3		
Lewis M. Ayer	504 majority[108]	
Robert B. Rhett Sr.		
District 4[109]		
William D. Simpson		
no opposition		
District 5[110]		
James Farrow	2,755	63
J. P. Boyce	1,610	37
District 6[111]		
William W. Boyce		
no opposition		

Tennessee[112] August 6, 1863	Votes	Percentage
District 1		
Joseph B. Heiskell	12,105	100
no opposition		
District 2		
William G. Swan	7,776	60
William M. Cocke[113]	5,122	40
District 3		
Arthur S. Colyar	12,075	99
Vaughn	156	1
District 4		
John P. Murray	7,157	53
M.R. Hill	6,152	45
Cummings	211	2
District 5		
Henry S. Foote	7,462	53
John H. Savage	6,141	44
James W. Nichols[114]	467	3
District 6		
Edwin A. Keeble	11,631	92
P.G. Stiver Perkins[115]	950	8
District 7		
James McCallum	7,740	58
G.H. Nixon	5,395	40
A.O.P. Nicholson[116]	187	2
District 8		
Thomas Menees	12,133	99
John R. House	74	1
District 9		
John D.C.Atkins	12,516	100
no opposition		
District 10		
John V. Wright	12,090	100
no opposition		
District 11		
David M. Currin[117]	11,632	94
Louis J. Dupree[118]	714	6
Replacement election[119]		
Michael W. Cluskey		

Texas[120] August 3, 1863		
District 1		
John A. Wilcox	2,853	62
J. W. Burton	1,762	38

Texas[120] August 3, 1863	Votes	Percentage
Replacement Election[121] August, 1864		
Stephen H. Darden		
District 2		
Caleb C. Herbert	3,294	58
Eggleston D. Townes[122]	2,396	42
District 3		
Anthony M. Branch	3,706	63
Peter W. Gray	2,166	37
District 4		
Franklin B. Sexton	2,065	52
James Anderson	1,920	48
District 5		
John R. Baylor	2,494	51
Malcomb D. Graham	2,396	49
Crosely	39	
District 6		
Simpson H. Morgan	2,585	53
William B. Wright	2,061	43
J.W. Mosely	198	4

Virginia[123] May 28, 1863		
District 1		
Robert L. Montague	1,012	61
Muscoe R.H. Garnett	653	39
District 2[124]		
Robert H. Whitfield	974	32
William Mahone	627	20
W.A.Parham	617	20
D.J. Godwin	480	16
Thomas Hume	369	12
Scattering[125]	3	—
District 3[126]		
William C. Wickham	2,559	66
James Lyons	1,344	34
District 4		
Thomas S. Gholson	2,145	50
Charles F. Collier	2,116	50
Scattering[127]	7	—
District 5		
Thomas S. Bocock	1,922	100
no opposition[128]		
District 6[129]		
John Goode Jr.	3,561	56
William Martin	2,788	44

Virginia[123]	May 28, 1863	Votes	Percentage
District 7			
William C. Rives		1,271	96
Scattering		50	4
District 8			
Daniel C. DeJarnette		2,316	65
James Barbour		1,238	35
District 9			
David Funsten		1,676	86
J. Y. Menefee		274	14
District 10			
Frederick W.M. Holliday		1,632	72
Alexander R. Boteler		643	28
District 11			
John B. Baldwin		[2,590][8]	[65]
John Letcher[130]		[1,398]	[35]
District 12			
Waller R. Staples		[1,000][8]	[53]
H. A. Edmonson[131]		[876]	[47]
District 13			
Fayette McMullen		[1,594][8]	[63]
Walter Preston[132]		[935]	[37]
District 14[133]			
Samuel A. Miller		740	36
William Stratton		604	30
Henry Fitzhugh		481	24
J.D. Warren		211	10
Scattering		2	—
District 15[134]			
Robert W. Johnston		709	100
no opposition			
District 16			
Charles W. Russell		129	55
Zedekiah Kidwell[135]		104	45

[1] The Provisional Congress of the Confederate States of America set the election date for the House of Representatives, president, and vice-president for the first Wednesday in November 1861 (November 6). James M. Matthews, ed., *The Statutes at Large of the Provisional Government of the Confederate States of America* (R. M. Smith: Richmond, 1864), p. 122. Missouri and Kentucky were not admitted to the Confederacy until after the November 6, 1861, elections (see the discussion of Missouri and Kentucky first elections in Chapter 4 and footnotes in this Appendix for the dates and method of election). The elections for the Second House were held on various dates in 1863–1864 according to state laws (see Table 4-12).

[2] *United States Historical Election Returns 1788–1981* [machine-readable data file], Ann Arbor, Michigan: Inter-University Consortium for Political and Social Research (ICPSR), election returns for 1861. *Florence Gazette*, December 11, 1861, p. 2, col. 1. Ezra J. Warner and W. Buck Yearns, *Biographical Register of the Con-*

federate Congress (Baton Rouge: Louisiana State University Press, 1975). Miriam C. Jones, letter to author, July 23, 1991.

[3] *True Democrat* (Little Rock, Arkansas), December 19, 1861, p. 1, col. 3. ICPSR election returns. John L. Ferguson, State Historian, Little Rock, Arkansas, letter to author, June 20, 1991.

[4] *Governor's Proclamation Book*, Florida State Archives, series 21, carton 51.

[5] Spelling of name as best determined from hand-written returns, possibly Villefrigam.

[6] *Southern Confederacy* (Atlanta), November 24, 1861, p. 2, col. 6. Jane G. Nardy, letter to author, July 15, 1991.

[7] Partial returns reported from fourteen of twenty counties in the district.

[8] Vote returns placed in brackets are believed to be partial returns.

[9] *Southern Federal Union* (Milledgeville), November 26, 1861, p. 3, col. 1.

[10] *Daily Columbus Enquirer*, November 14, 1863, p. 2, col. 1. *Columbus Daily Sun*, November 15, 1861, p. 1, col. 4. Quitman county is not reported in either source.

[11] Ingram was elected to complete the term of Hines Holt and took his seat on January 12, 1864. Since Holt's Second Congress replacement was already chosen in October 1863 Ingram's total time of service in the First Congress was five weeks. Warner and Yearns, *Biographical Register*, p. 129. For election returns of six of twelve counties plus a few military votes, see *Daily Columbus Enquirer*, December 22, 1863, p. 1, col. 1.

[12] Nine of eleven counties reporting.

[13] Full name and information found in John B. Robbins, "Confederate Nationalism: Politics and Government in the Confederate South, 1861–1865," (Ph.D. diss., Rice University, 1964), p. 40.

[14] The first names or initials of Hammond and Saffold found in: *Constitutionalist* (Augusta), October 30, 1861.

[15] The *Southern Confederacy* reported nine of ten counties with a 1,886 vote majority for Trippe. The *Columbus Daily Sun*, November 25, 1861, p. 1, col. 6, reported a majority of 1,843 for Trippe.

[16] The initials of Doyal found in *Macon Daily Telegraph*, November 10, 1861, p. 3, col. 2.

[17] Nine of ten counties reporting. Herbert Fielder is listed as a candidate by the *Savannah Republican* on November 4, 1861, but he does not appear in *Southern Confederacy* (Atlanta) returns.

[18] Full names or initials of Simmons and Bigham found in *Savannah Republican*, November 4, 1861, p. 1 col. 3.

[19] Full name of Black and Crook found in *Savannah Republican*, November 4, 1861 p. 1, col. 3.

[20] According to Warner and Yearns under the entry for R.J. Breckinridge, Jr., "voting places were provided and elections were held in counties within the then Confederate lines." Warner and Yearns, *Biographical Register*, p. 32. Research in Confederate and Kentucky newspapers and Kentucky state archives and records did not find any vote totals or other candidates for this election. Matthew G. Schoenbachler, Research Assistant, Kentucky Department for Libraries and Archives, Frankfort, Kentucky, letter to author, July 15, 1991. Lowell H. Harrison, Professor of History, Western Kentucky University, Bowling Green, Kentucky, letter to author, November 26, 1991. Ron D. Bryant, Kentucky Historical Society, letter to author, September 10, 1991. John David Smith, Professor of History, North Carolina State University, letter to author, October 29, 1991.

Records of the Louisiana State Government, 1850–1888: War Department Collection of Confederate Records, Roll 14—Records of the Executive Department, 1860-1865, and Records of the Judicial Department, 1861–1862 (Washington, D.C.: National Archives Microfilm Publications). *New Orleans Bee*, November 6, 1861.

[22] Warner and Yearns, *Biographical Register*, p. 144. *Records of the Louisiana State Government*, Roll 14.

[23] Warner and Yearns, *Biographical Register*, p. 80. *Records of the Louisiana State Government*, Roll 14.

[24] Full name found in *The South-western* (Shreveport), November 27, 1861.

[25] E.B. Townes and James Tire each received one vote, J.C. Scarborough received two votes. *Records of the Louisiana State Government*, Roll 14.

[26] *Weekly Mississippian* (Jackson), December 11, 1861.

[27] Davis resigned his seat on January 21, 1864. Since the election for the Second Congress had been held, the congressman-elect, William D. Holder, replaced Davis. Warner and Yearns, *Biographical Register*, p. 124.

[28] Missouri's delegation to the first Confederate House was appointed by the pro-Confederate governor and members of the Missouri General Assembly. Arthur R. Kirkpatrick, "Missouri's Delegation in the Confederate Congress," *Civil War History* 5 (June 1959): 188–198. *Journal of the Senate, Extra Session of the Rebel Legislature, Called by a Proclamation of C. F. Jackson, Begun and Held at Neosho, Newton County, Missouri on the Twenty-first Day of October 1861* (Jefferson City: Emory S. Foster, 1865).

[29] This date is taken from the communication of Gov. Claibourne F. Jackson approving the appointment of representatives. *Journal of the Senate, Extra Session of the Rebel Legislature*, Appendix, pp. 31–32.

[30] John Hyer never took his seat. District Seven was vacant in the First Congress.

[31] North Carolina State Archives, Miscellaneous Collection, Compiled Election Returns, Box C.E.R. 2 & 3, Confederate Congress, 1861–1864. *Daily Richmond Examiner*, November 11, 1861. *Fayetteville Observer*, November 18, 1861, and November 28, 1861. Thomas E. Jeffrey, Associate Director, Edison Papers, Rutgers University, letter to author, January 27, 1992. Paul Escott, Professor of History, Wake Forest University, letter to author, November 6, 1991.

[32] "He [McLean] won a seat . . . over two more moderate rivals." Warner and Yearns, *Biographical Register*, p. 160. However, the election returns found in the *Daily Richmond Examiner*, November 11, 1861, and *Fayetteville Observer*, November 18, 1861, list only one opponent, R.P. Dick.

[33] The identity of the candidates in brackets is not definite, but follows the determination made by ICPSR and North Carolina Compiled Election Returns.

[34] *Fayetteville Observer*, November 28, 1861. Warner and Yearns say that Davidson won election over two opponents, but the returns found in the *Daily Richmond Examiner*, November 11, 1861, and in the *Observer* list only one opponent, William H. Thomas.

[35] Congressional election returns are not available in state records. Patrick McCawley, South Carolina Department of Archives and History, letter to author, July 3, 1991.

[36] Warner and Yearns, *Biographical Register*, p. 163.

[37] *Ibid.*, p. 174. *Charleston Mercury*, November 7, 1861.

[38] Full name found in Jon L. Wakelyn, *Biographical Dictionary of the Confederacy* (Westport, Connecticut: Greenwood Press, 1977), p. 82.

[39] *Charleston Mercury*, December 9, 1861, p. 1, col. 2. *Columbus Times*, December 11, 1861, p. 2, col. 2.

[40] South Carolina Department of Archives, General Assembly Papers, Misc. Committees to the General Assembly, 1863, no. 34.

[41] "When Bonham resigned his seat . . . Simpson was elected to the position without his knowledge. He took his seat on February 5, 1863 and that October was reelected without opposition." Warner and Yearns, *Biographical Register*, pp. 220–221.

[42] Thomas G. Bacon received fourteen votes and A. Burt received ten votes.

[43] *Charleston Mercury*, December 9, 1861, p. 1, col. 2. *Columbus Times*, December 11, 1861, p. 2, col. 2.

[44] Warner and Yearns, *Biographical Register*, p. 28.

[45] Tennessee State Library and Archives, Record Group 87, Confederate States of America Representatives to Congress. *Brownlow's Whig*, (Knoxville) October 26, 1861. ICPSR election returns, 1861.

[46] John F. House and James M. Quarles received sixty-six and twenty-four votes respectively.

[47] T.W. Jones and Cox received nine and one votes respectively.

[48] *The State Gazette* (Austin), December 21, 1861. *Texas Republican* (Marshall), January 25, 1862. Dale Baum, Professor of History, Texas A & M University, letters to author, June 17, 1991, and July 10, 1991. Dale Baum, "Texas Elections during the Civil War: Continuity or Change?" paper presented before the Social Science History Association, Washington, D.C., November 18, 1989.

[49] Congressional election returns are not available in state records. Nelson D. Lankford, Virginia Historical Society, letter to author, October 31, 1991. Fredrick H. Armstrong, West Virginia Division of Culture and History, letter to author, December 19, 1991.

[50] "In November he [Garnett] won a close race for the Confederate House of Representatives." Warner and Yearns, *Biographical Register*, p. 98.

[51] On October 30, 1861, a meeting was held in the Second Congressional District. At this meeting all candidates withdrew their bids for the seat in the Confederate Congress by their own request except for Col. J. R. Chambliss. *Daily Richmond Examiner*, November 2, 1861.

[52] *Daily Richmond Examiner*, November 25, 1861, p. 2, col. 4.

[53] John Tyler died on January 18, 1862. There was a special election held between his two closest competitors in the November 1861 election. Warner and Yearns, *Biographical Register*, p. 155. *Richmond Daily Whig*, February 17, 1862, p. 2, col. 1 (Hanover county is missing). See also *Daily Richmond Examiner*, February 17, 1862, p. 3, col. 3 for slightly different totals.

[54] A notice appears in the *Daily Richmond Examiner* of October 12, 1861 in which "James A. *Sedden*" declines the nomination for the Fourth District seat. *Richmond Daily Dispatch*, November 7, 1861, says that Pryor faced "no opposition." The names of Meade and *Seldon* are both found in the ICPSR election returns for 1861 with no vote totals. While ICPSR lists this name as *Seldon*, the *Richmond Daily Dispatch*, November 9, 1861, indicates that *Seddon* received votes but was not actually a candidate.

[55] "When Roger A. Pryor resigned his place . . . Collier won a three man race for the position by a small plurality; one of his opponents was James A. Seddon." Warner and Yearns, *Biographical Register*, pp. 58–59. *Daily Richmond Enquirer*, May 12, 1862, p. 2, col. 4.

[56] Full name found in *Daily Richmond Enquirer*, October 1, 1861.

[57] Full names of opposition found in John Goode, *Recollections of a Lifetime* (New York: Neal Publishing, 1906), p. 76.

[58] Full names and initials of opposition appear in advertisements and returns in *Lynchburg Daily Virginian*, November 12, 1861, p. 3, col. 1.

[59] Four of nine counties and three army camps reported returns. *Daily Richmond Examiner*, November 11, 1861, p. 1, col. 6. James Barbour and William H. Browne are listed as candidates in the *Daily Richmond Enquirer*, October 1, 1861, and in an advertisement in the *Daily Richmond Examiner*, October 24, 1861, but their names do not appear in the election returns.

[60] Full name found in Robbins, "Confederate Nationalism," p. 47.

[61] ICPSR returns for 1861. The *Richmond Daily Dispatch*, November 11, 1861.

[62] "Baldwin was elected over two opponents." Warner and Yearns, *Biographical Register*, p. 12. However, no mention of other candidates is made in newspaper sources.

[63] Full name found in *Lynchburg Daily Virginian*, November 15, 1861, p. 5, col. 1.

[64] *Lynchburg Daily Virginian*, November 15, 1861, p. 3, col. 1.

[65] Wakelyn, *Biographical Dictionary of the Confederacy*, p. 260.

[66] "He [Russell] was in every respect a refugee congressmen." Warner and Yearns, *Biographical Register*, p. 212.

[67] Alabama, Secretary of State, Elections and Registration Division, Series: Election Files, State and National, 1860–1866, Container S.G. 2475.

[68] "He [Foster] won re-election without opposition in 1863." Warner and Yearns, *Biographical Register*, p. 89. However, according to the election returns in the Alabama Election File, Thomas J. Foster only received 337 votes of 478 polled in Lauderdale County, and 389 votes of 625 polled in Lawrence County.

[69] Warner and Yearns, *Biographical Register*, p. 154, says that Lyon had no opposition, but in addition to J.F. Cocke the Alabama Election File shows the following scattering: Reaves 8, Herndon 2, Taylor 1, Benners 1, and Dowdell 1.

[70] Samuel C. Dailey received 13 votes, Baker received 3, and Shorter 1 vote. Alabama Election File.

[71] Congressional election returns are not available in state records. John L. Ferguson, State Historian, Arkansas History Commission, letter to author, June 20, 1991.

[72] *Washington Telegraph*, November 11, 1863. The only returns published reflect the vote for Hempstead county, which were Garland 314 and Royston 293. In an article on the election appearing in this same edition, the *Telegraph* reports "the election . . . passed off very quietly . . . in some places the greatest apathy was manifested."

[73] When Augustus H. Garland was nominated to fill the Senate seat vacated by the death of Charles B. Mitchel, a replacement election was held in the 3rd District. *Washington Telegraph*, December 10, 1864.

[74] See the discussion of the Arkansas Second House election in Chapter 4, especially the section on the Fourth District election held on April 4, 1864. Two examples of reports on this election in southern newspapers are: The *Memphis Daily Appeal* (published in Atlanta at this time), March 28, 1864, "By reference to the appropriate column it will be seen that Maj. L.O. Bridewell is a candidate for Congress from the fourth congressional district of Arkansas. We understand he was placed in nomination by the Arkansas troops, or a portion of them at least, and has accepted;" and the *Richmond Daily Sentinel*, April 14, 1864, "The vote for members of Congress for the Fourth Congressional district of Arkansas, in the Arkansas regiments, Army of Tennessee, was for Thomas B. Hanley of Phillips county 581, Lamuel O. Bridewell of Helena 71, and John Forbes of White county 188."

[75] *Governor's Proclamation Book*, Florida Archives, Series 21, Carton 51.

[76] *Savannah Daily Morning News*, October 28, 1863, p. 1, col. 1. *Daily Columbus Enquirer*, November 4, 1863, p. 1, col. 5. *Memphis Daily Appeal* (Atlanta), October 29, 1863, p. 2, col. 5.

[77] Opponent King is probably John M. King, listed as state senator of Glynn, Camden, and Charlton counties in the *Southern Federal Union* (Milledgeville), November 12, 1861.

[78] Full name found in *Richmond Daily Dispatch*, October 17, 1863.

[79] Notation by Cabiness vote total says, "Cabiness no candidate." *Memphis Daily Appeal* (Atlanta), October 29, 1863, p. 2, col. 5.

[80] Full initials found in advertisement in *Memphis Daily Appeal* (Atlanta), October 7, 1863.

[81] *Ibid.*

[82] *Montgomery Daily Mail*, February 27, 1864, p. 2, col. 3. *Richmond Daily Sentinel*, February 16, 1864, p. 2, col. 1. Partial returns found in *Southern Confederacy* (Atlanta), February 16, 1864. *American Annual Cyclopaedia and Register of Important Events of the Year 1864* (New York: D. Appleton, 1865), p. 454.

[83] Returns recorded in the *Montgomery Daily Mail*, February 27, 1864, list J. D. Morris with 807 votes (49%), George W. Triplett with 750 (46%), and Dennis with 76 (5%). George W. Triplett was sent to the Second Congress by the Kentucky Provisional Government as the representative of the Second District.

[84] John Marshall does not appear in the *Montgomery Daily Mail*, returns, but he is listed in the *Richmond Daily Sentinel* returns as well as the partial returns found in the *Southern Confederacy.*

[85] *Records of the Louisiana State Government, 1850–1888: War Department Collection of Confederate Records*, Roll 14 — Records of the Executive Department, 1860-1865, and Records of the Judicial Department, 1861–1862, National Archives Microfilm Publications. Jefferson Davis Bragg, *Louisiana in the Confederacy* (Baton Rouge: Louisiana State University Press, 1941), pp. 267–268.

[86] *Shreveport News*, November 1, 1864, as cited by Bragg, *Louisiana in the Confederacy*, pp. 268–270.

[87] Congressional election returns are not available in state records. Mississippi Department of Archives and History, letter to author, August 11, 1992. Ray Skates, letter to author, November 19, 1991.

[88] ICPSR election returns for 1863, First District.

[89] Full name found in Warner and Yearns, *Biographical Register*, p. 189.

[90] Candidate names in this district are found in the ICPSR list for 1863, but no vote totals are given.

[91] Full name found in *Memphis Daily Appeal* (Atlanta), October 10, 1863, p. 2, col. 5, with some county returns listed.

[92] Warner and Yearns, *Biographical Register*, p. 44.

[93] Full names or initials found in *Tri-Weekly Citizen* (Canton, Mississippi), December 5, 1863, p. 1, col. 2.

[94] *The American Citizen* (Canton, Mississippi), November 14, 1863, p. 1, col. 1.

[95] *Charleston Daily Courier*, October 9, 1863, p. 1, col. 1.

[96] "The piney-woods vote gave Lamkin the victory over the pro-administration McRae." Warner and Yearns, *Biographical Register*, p. 145.

[97] *Southern Confederacy* (Atlanta) June 18, 1864. *Selma Reporter*, June 16, 1864, p. 1, col. 5. Arthur R. Kirkpatrick, "Missouri's Delegation in the Confederate Congress," *Civil War History* 5 (June 1959): 195.

[98] North Carolina State Archives, Miscellaneous Collection, Compiled Election Returns, Box C.E.R. 2 & 3, Confederate Congress, 1861–1864. ICPSR election returns.

[99] The *Daily Richmond Examiner* election returns of November 11, 1861, show no opposition to Smith, but Warner and Yearns say, "he won re-election twice with but token opposition." Warner and Yearns, *Biographical Register*, p. 227. These names and vote tallies are listed in the ICPSR election returns for 1863.

[100] Full name found in Marc W. Kruman, *Parties and Politics in North Carolina 1836–1865* (Baton Rouge: Louisiana State University Press, 1983), p. 255.

[101] Kruman, *Parties and Politics*, pp. 254–255. ICPSR election returns. However, Warner and Yearns state "Gilmer won an uncontested race as representative." Warner and Yearns, *Biographical Register*, p. 101. *The Milton Chronicle*, November 4, 1863, as cited by the N.C. Compiled Election Returns, reported that Brown was not an active candidate.

[102] Died in March of 1864 before taking his seat.

[103] *Daily Confederate* (Raleigh), May 2, 1864.

[104] District totals include "majority" figures reported for two of the ten counties. North Carolina State Archives, Compiled Election Returns.

[105] County vote totals found for the Tenth District in the N.C. Compiled Returns are incomplete and show a different outcome of the election than what apparently occurred: George W. Logan [799, 30%]; Marcus Erwin [935, 36%]; John Hyman [812, 31%]; Allen T. Davidson [35]; and William F. Jones [16]. George W. Logan occupied the Tenth District seat in the Second Congress. Full names of Hyman and Erwin found in Kruman, *Parties and Politics*, pp. 254–255.

[106] *Charleston Mercury*, November 10, 1863, p. 2, col. 2.

[107] Warner and Yearns, *Biographical Register*, p. 174. *Charleston Mercury*, October 20, 1863.

[108] Complete returns for this election were never published, but majorities were given for each county in the *Charleston Courier* on October 26 and November 10, 1863. Laura A. White, *Robert Barnwell Rhett: Father of Secession* (New York: Century, 1931), p. 234, n. 48.

[109] Warner and Yearns, *Biographical Register*, p. 221. *Charleston Mercury*, October 20, 1863.

[110] *Carolina Spartan* (Spartanburg), November 5, 1863, p. 2, col. 1.

[111] Warner and Yearns, *Biographical Register*, p. 28. *Charleston Mercury*, October 20, 1863.

[112] Vote totals were compiled for the first time in this atlas from county and military returns found in the Tennessee State Library and Archives, Statewide General Election, August 6, 1863, Record Group 87, Series Number: 1, sub-series letter: A.

[113] Full name found in election announcement *Chattanooga Daily Rebel*, July 26, 1863, p. 2, col. 1.

[114] Full name found in election announcement *Chattanooga Daily Rebel*, July 28, 1863, p. 2, col. 1.

[115] *Ibid.*

[116] *Ibid.*

[117] Died on March 25, 1864, before taking his seat. Warner and Yearns, *Biographical Register*, p. 67.

[118] Full name of candidate given in *Chattanooga Daily Rebel*, August 6, 1863, p. 2, col. 1.

[119] "After the death of David M. Currin in March, 1864, Tennessee citizens in army camps all over the country chose Cluskey as his replacement." Warner and Yearns, *Biographical Register*, p. 55.

[120] Dale Baum, Professor of History, Texas A & M University, letters to author, June 17, 1991, and July 10, 1991. Dale Baum, "Texas Elections." ICPSR election returns for 1863. Nancy Head Bowen, "A Political Labyrinth: Texas in the Civil War—Questions of Continuity," (Ph.D. diss., Rice University, 1974).

[121] Darden was elected to fill the unexpired term of Wilcox who died suddenly. Darden took his seat on November 21, 1864. Warner and Yearns, *Biographical Register*, p. 69.

[122] Full name found in Bowen, "Political Labyrinth," p. 141.

[123] Virginia State Archives, Poll Books 1863, MSS. Election Record No. 433. *Daily Richmond Examiner*, June 27, 1863.

[124] Full names or initials for Second District candidates found in Warner and Yearns, *Biographical Register*, p. 254; *Daily Richmond Examiner*, June 1, 1863; *Richmond Daily Dispatch*, June 1, 1863; and Wakelyn, *Biographical Dictionary of the Confederacy*, p. 242.

[125] Henry A. Wise, M. R. H. Garnett, and John Chambliss all received one vote in the poll. Virginia State Archives, Poll Books 1863.

[126] *Daily Richmond Examiner*, June 27, 1863.

[127] W.T. Joynes and John Lyon received one and six votes respectively.

[128] *Daily Richmond Examiner*, June 27, 1863. The newspaper returns have the wrong candidates listed in the Fifth, Sixth, and Seventh District races.

[129] *Richmond Daily Whig*, June 28, 1863. The newspaper returns have the wrong candidates listed in the Fifth, Sixth, and Seventh District races.

[130] See election returns in *Daily Richmond Examiner*, June 27, 1863.

[131] Full initials found in election advertisement in *Lynchburg Daily Virginian*, May 28, 1863. He is listed as Col. H. A. Edmonson. In cross-referencing this name with the *Lynchburg Daily Virginian*, November 5, 1861, Henry A. Edmonson is given as an elector for this district in the Confederate Presidential election of November 1861. See also election returns in *Daily Richmond Examiner*, June 27, 1863.

[132] Full name found in Warner and Yearns, *Biographical Register*, p. 161. See election returns in *Daily Richmond Examiner*, June 27, 1863.

[133] Logan county reported a total of 200 votes; the remaining votes are based on soldier and refugee voting.

[134] This figure is based on soldier and refugee votes, with no counties reporting.

[135] Full name found in Charles H. Ambler, *Francis H. Pierpont* (Chapel Hill: University of North Carolina Press, 1937), p. 90. Election return is based on soldier and refugee votes, with no counties reporting.

V

COUNTY, SOLDIER,
AND REFUGEE VOTE
TENNESSEE
CONFEDERATE
CONGRESSIONAL
ELECTION
AUGUST 6, 1863

Tennessee Election: 1863

COUNTIES	1st District	2nd District		3rd District		4th District			5th District		
	Heiskall	Swann	Cocke	Colyar	Vaughn	Murray	Hill	Cumming	Foote	Savage	Nichols
Anderson	45	9	35	45	0	0	40	6	0	45	0
Benton	0	0	0	0	0	0	0	0	0	0	0
Blount	286	231	45	267	0	255	24	0	255	24	0
Bradley	311	248	80	319	2	250	26	0	217	100	5
Campbell	25	16	9	25	0	0	25	0	0	25	0
Claiborne	187	151	43	187	0	173	14	0	172	16	0
Cocke	281	273	13	284	17	282	4	0	281	4	0
DeKalb	20	20	0	20	0	0	20	0	0	20	0
Franklin	26	26	0	26	0	26	0	0	26	0	0
Grainger	309	104	262	303	3	154	154	0	168	132	0
Greene	369	317	64	372	1	340	40	0	318	63	0
Grundy	22	4	17	26	0	0	24	0	6	20	0
Hamilton	549	232	320	527	19	204	352	3	256	259	54
Henry	0	0	0	0	0	0	0	0	0	0	0
Hickman	103	103	0	103	0	103	0	0	103	0	0
Jackson	188	188	0	181	0	236	2	0	47	174	0
Jefferson	452	302	290	457	0	284	176	0	318	151	0
Knox	578	372	272	565	0	328	249	0	372	211	0
Lincoln	0	0	0	0	0	0	0	0	0	0	0
Marion	97	4	90	99	0	4	88	0	2	95	0
Maury	196	196	0	196	0	196	190	0	196	0	0
McMinn	488	410	93	532	0	401	88	0	432	77	0
Meigs	173	138	30	180	0	171	6	0	156	28	0
Monroe	419	347	100	347	0	191	155	0	170	312	0
Polk	200	135	44	216	15	182	18	0	166	39	0
Roane	386	276	119	380	0	272	129	0	270	147	0
Rutherford	38	38	0	38	0	38	0	0	16	22	0
Sequatchie	29	0	28	28	0	0	29	0	25	0	0
Sevier	66	53	17	60	0	55	7	0	60	12	0
Sullivan	805	332	421	773	14	276	472	0	230	541	0
Union	117	79	53	110	0	62	37	0	80	38	0
Washington	511	330	250	472	0	381	148	0	354	176	0
County Totals	**7,276**	**4,934**	**2,695**	**7,138**	**71**	**4,864**	**2,517**	**9**	**4,696**	**2,731**	**59**
MILITARY UNITS											
Camp Rucker	24	24	0	24	0	24	0	0	24	0	0
Capt. Burrough's	84	63	23	80	4	33	46	0	52	34	0
Capt. Fain's	19	12	8	19	1	18	2	0	7	13	0
Capt. McClug's	31	10	20	31	0	16	11	0	27	4	0
Capt. Scott's	17	17	0	17	0	17	0	0	14	1	3
Allison's Squad	94	2	91	94	0	17	93	0	11	95	0
Headquarters	158	72	0	190	0	47	180	0	36	0	106
Maxson's Co.	15	3	11	14	0	6	11	0	9	4	0

Tennessee Election: 1863

6th District		7th District			8th District		9th District	10th District	11th District		COUNTY
Keeble	Perkins	McCallum	Nixon	Nicholson	Menees	House	Atkins	Wright	Currin	Dupree	TOTALS
45	0	0	45	0	45	0	45	45	0	0	450
0	0	0	0	0	0	0	0	0	0	0	0
278	0	255	23	0	279	0	279	277	285	3	3,066
329	3	262	12	18	315	0	320	314	309	3	3,443
25	0	0	25	0	25	0	25	25	25	0	275
187	0	162	27	0	166	0	187	187	187	0	2,046
261	0	278	4	0	283	0	284	283	280	3	3,115
20	0	16	0	4	20	0	20	20	20	0	220
26	0	26	0	0	26	0	26	26	26	0	286
300	3	154	153	0	303	0	301	305	284	28	3,420
330	0	337	38	0	374	0	374	367	368	10	4,082
22	2	1	21	0	21	0	21	21	21	0	249
495	56	305	244	6	548	8	545	553	543	18	6,096
0	0	0	0	0	0	0	0	0	0	0	0
103	0	93	0	11	196	22	103	103	103	0	1,249
183	0	159	31	0	187	1	188	188	187	0	2,140
450	6	286	174	0	458	0	450	457	453	19	5,183
513	67	400	190	0	569	0	578	578	501	77	6,420
0	0	0	0	0	0	0	0	0	0	0	0
93	0	4	90	0	93	0	94	94	92	1	1,040
196	0	188	27	0	196	0	196	196	196	0	2,365
446	0	375	117	0	496	0	493	496	483	27	5,454
167	5	173	1	0	170	4	173	178	175	0	1,928
419	0	222	196	0	345	0	421	421	300	116	4,481
199	1	168	21	0	200	0	201	201	200	0	2,206
370	37	282	107	1	391	0	398	396	387	8	4,356
38	0	0	38	0	38	0	38	38	38	0	418
28	0	0	28	0	28	0	28	28	28	0	307
60	0	36	5	1	62	0	62	61	60	2	679
784	0	382	374	9	787	0	791	789	772	23	8,575
117	0	80	37	0	117	0	117	117	94	0	1,255
527	0	377	151	0	521	0	524	7	387	143	5,259
7,011	**180**	**5,021**	**2,179**	**50**	**7,259**	**35**	**7,282**	**6,771**	**6,804**	**481**	**80,063**
24	0	24	0	0	24	0	24	24	24	0	264
83	0	66	39	0	84	0	83	84	84	1	943
17	3	18	2	0	19	0	19	19	18	2	216
31	0	23	0	0	29	2	31	31	19	12	328
17	0	17	0	0	17	0	18	18	18	0	191
33	63	2	84	1	91	2	94	94	93	1	1,055
114	117	129	0	0	187	0	226	222	185	0	1,969
9	4	3	11	3	14	0	14	14	14	0	159

(continued on next spread)

Tennessee Election: 1863 (continued)

MILITARY UNITS	1st District Heiskall	2nd District Swann	2nd District Cocke	3rd District Colyar	3rd District Vaughn	4th District Murray	4th District Hill	4th District Cumming	5th District Foote	5th District Savage	5th District Nichols
1st Tenn. Cav. Reg.	41	34	19	43	0	40	0	0	30	10	0
Camp Post Oak	136	90	43	136	0	91	39	0	91	40	0
4th Tenn. Cav. Reg.	126	119	3	129	0	43	80	0	54	77	0
Starne's 4th Tenn. Cav.	166	54	105	171	0	40	132	0	65	118	0
Bainbridge Ferry (Ala.)	117	116	0	116	0	116	0	0	117	0	0
10th Tenn. Cav. Reg.	43	33	8	44	0	34	7	0	39	6	0
11th Tenn. Cav. Reg.	77	64	11	77	0	62	12	0	59	16	0
Camp Ebenezer	190	86	115	169	0	80	97	0	34	171	0
1st Tenn. Inf. Battalio	139	139	0	139	0	0	151	0	0	150	0
2d Tenn. Inf. Reg.	146	97	49	80	16	25	145	0	97	61	4
8th Tenn. Inf. Reg.	82	20	72	95	0	37	103	78	33	125	2
12th & 47th Tenn. Inf.	184	69	184	184	0	81	131	0	87	115	23
15th & 37th Tenn. Inf.	106	29	89	92	0	17	109	0	16	128	0
16th Tenn. Inf. Reg.	135	26	108	164	0	43	175	0	20	245	1
17th Tenn. Inf. Reg.	158	84	64	173	0	64	127	0	93	149	2
19th Tenn. Inf. Reg.	135	65	85	144	3	24	21	113	94	57	7
20th Tenn. Inf. Reg.	156	147	126	149	1	34	134	0	167	30	1
23d Tenn. Inf. Battlion	69	26	48	25	0	18	59	0	30	54	0
23d Tenn. Inf. Reg.	128	72	58	155	0	45	199	0	44	134	45
24th Tenn. Inf. Reg.	87	66	21	87	16	53	48	0	48	68	14
25th Tenn. Inf. Reg.	54	24	57	59	0	138	67	0	56	168	0
26th Tenn. Inf. Reg.	146	71	76	115	0	36	110	2	112	43	0
1st & 27th Tenn. Vol.	158	72	100	190	0	47	180	0	36	195	106
28th Tenn. Inf. Reg.	60	18	54	65	0	64	53	0	24	117	2
29th Tenn. Inf. Reg.	161	73	78	139	0	21	123	0	59	100	1
31st Tenn. Inf. Reg.	87	74	30	74	30	59	47	0	64	63	0
32d Tenn. Inf. Reg.	201	179	26	204	0	187	25	0	210	11	0
33d Tenn. Inf. Reg.	31	13	19	28	0	18	23	0	19	41	12
34th Tenn. Inf. Reg.	96	84	19	64	0	14	101	0	32	92	0
35th Tenn. Inf. Reg.	49	3	79	73	0	20	73	0	33	88	2
38th Tenn. Inf. Reg.	32	17	26	33	0	50	42	0	20	90	2
44th Tenn. Inf. Reg.	149	83	62	194	0	49	155	0	98	134	0
47th Tenn. Inf. Reg.	22	13	9	21	0	13	8	0	8	3	10
48th Tenn. Inf. Reg.	32	24	14	33	0	13	72	0	38	17	6
51st & 52d Tenn. Inf.	110	72	40	105	2	74	34	0	103	30	1
63d Tenn. Inf. Reg.	198	96	234	315	0	106	226	0	149	204	0
24th Sharpshooters	24	18	5	24	0	18	5	0	5	15	3
Capt. Winston's	57	68	14	75	0	77	2	0	81	2	0
64th N.C. & Tenn. Vol.	31	16	28	32	0	32	0	0	33	2	0
154th & 13th Tenn. Inf.	184	102	94	169	12	51	174	0	110	82	55
10th Tenn. Cav. (?)	84	83	2	84	0	81	3	0	78	8	0
Military Unit Totals	**4,829**	**2,842**	**2,427**	**4,937**	**85**	**2,293**	**3,635**	**193**	**2,766**	**3,410**	**408**
Candidate Totals	**12,105**	**7,776**	**5,122**	**12,075**	**156**	**7,157**	**6,152**	**202**	**7,462**	**6,141**	**467**
Candidate Percentage	**100%**	**60%**	**40%**	**99%**	**1%**	**53%**	**46%**	**2%**	**53%**	**44%**	**3%**

Tennessee Election: 1863

6th District		7th District			8th District		9th District	10th District	11th District		MILITARY UNIT
Keeble	Perkins	McCallum	Nixon	Nicholson	Menees	House	Atkins	Wright	Currin	Dupree	TOTALS
40	0	40	0	0	40	0	40	40	40	0	457
131	0	77	151	17	127	3	135	140	134	0	1,581
104	0	121	0	1	131	0	123	130	123	0	1,364
163	7	65	104	0	164	0	172	174	168	0	1,868
116	0	116	2	0	116	0	117	118	116	0	1,283
12	30	40	5	0	43	0	48	44	37	7	480
61	30	72	11	0	76	0	76	71	76	0	851
183	2	81	107	0	186	0	185	184	122	58	2,059
139	0	139	4	0	139	0	139	139	139	0	1,556
111	24	60	69	24	141	1	145	143	131	11	1,580
89	0	31	122	0	80	0	82	90	78	0	1,219
184	21	91	123	0	180	10	206	201	186	11	2,271
90	0	21	84	0	94	0	119	107	109	1	1,211
151	2	15	183	11	131	0	136	147	132	0	1,825
184	29	77	149	0	143	0	152	159	137	13	1,957
128	4	84	64	0	138	0	135	140	133	3	1,577
129	52	54	141	4	154	1	154	162	143	7	1,946
61	7	26	44	4	67	0	70	74	66	5	753
233	0	78	134	6	130	0	134	146	132	3	1,876
78	34	37	71	0	88	0	94	90	54	35	1,089
74	43	26	120	0	46	0	48	51	39	5	1,075
126	5	50	92	1	130	0	133	132	131	1	1,512
114	117	129	150	6	187	7	226	222	185	6	2,433
70	4	13	75	1	59	0	59	60	59	1	858
95	13	42	58	35	112	0	104	109	102	10	1,435
69	14	48	46	16	76	0	107	109	66	13	1,092
191	13	195	37	0	202	0	202	203	201	3	2,290
23	3	13	35	0	37	0	78	56	37	6	492
79	19	11	99	0	92	0	96	98	95	0	1,091
37	32	43	27	0	42	0	50	44	46	0	741
33	2	21	50	0	30	0	44	56	55	0	603
153	34	89	124	1	149	13	164	163	146	6	1,966
14	8	14	7	0	19	0	20	22	22	0	233
29	9	15	82	0	31	0	37	57	35	2	546
104	1	50	85	3	106	0	134	133	123	3	1,313
315	0	83	257	0	301	0	300	311	295	6	3,396
10	14	23	0	0	25	0	25	25	24	0	263
78	0	76	2	0	78	0	78	78	77	1	844
32	0	32	0	0	32	0	32	32	32	0	366
177	7	69	153	2	202	0	240	269	263	0	2,415
82	3	70	13	1	85	0	86	84	84	0	931
4,620	**770**	**2,719**	**3,216**	**137**	**4,874**	**39**	**5,234**	**5,319**	**4,828**	**233**	**59,814**
11,631	**950**	**7,740**	**5,395**	**187**	**12,133**	**74**	**12,516**	**12,090**	**11,632**	**714**	**139,877**
92%	**8%**	**58%**	**40%**	**1%**	**99%**	**1%**	**100%**	**100%**	**94%**	**6%**	

BIBLIOGRAPHY

Civil War Atlases

Bosse, David C. *Civil War Newspaper Maps: A Historical Atlas.* Baltimore: Johns Hopkins University Press, 1993.

Esposito, Vincent, J., ed. *Atlas to Accompany Steele's American Campaigns.* West Point, New York: U.S. Military Academy, Department of Military Art and Engineering, 1941.

Esposito, Vincent, J., ed. *The West Point Atlas of American Wars.* New York: Praeger, 1959.

Griess, Thomas, E. *Atlas for the American Civil War.* Wayne, New Jersey: Avery Publishing, 1986.

Illustrated Atlas of the Civil War. Alexandria, Virginia: Time-Life Books, 1991.

Symonds, Craig L. *A Battlefield Atlas of the Civil War.* Baltimore: Nautical and Aviation Publishing Company of America, 1983.

United States War Department. *Atlas to Accompany the Official Records of the Union and Confederate Armies.* Washington, D.C.: Government Printing Office, 1891-1895.

Yoseloff, Thomas. *Atlas to Accompany Confederate Military History.* New York: A. S. Barnes, 1962.

Confederate Newspapers Used in Election Returns Research (original publication site)

Albany Patriot (Albany, Georgia)

Alexandria Gazette (Alexandria, Virginia)

American Citizen (Canton, Mississippi)

Augusta Daily Chronicle and Sentinel (Augusta, Georgia)

Brownlow's Whig (Knoxville, Tennessee)

Carolina Flag (Concord, North Carolina)

Carolina Spartan (Spartanburg, South Carolina)

Charleston Daily Courier (Charleston, South Carolina)

Charleston Mercury (Charleston, South Carolina)

Chattanooga Daily Rebel (Chattanooga, Tennessee)

Columbus Daily Sun (Columbus, Georgia)

Columbus Times (Columbus, Georgia)

Constitutionalist (Augusta, Georgia)

Daily Atlanta Intelligencer (Atlanta, Georgia)

Daily Columbus Enquirer (Columbus, Georgia)

Daily Confederate (Raleigh, North Carolina)

Daily Constitutionalist (Augusta, Georgia)

Daily Journal (Louisville, Kentucky)

Daily Journal (Wilmington, North Carolina)

Daily Mississippian (Jackson, Mississippi)

Daily Richmond Enquirer (Richmond, Virginia)

Daily Richmond Examiner (Richmond, Virginia)

Fayetteville Observer (Fayetteville, North Carolina)

Florence Gazette (Florence, Alabama)

Hinds County Gazette (Raymond, Mississippi)

Lynchburg Daily Virginian (Lynchburg, Virginia)

Macon Daily Telegraph (Macon, Georgia)

Memphis Daily Appeal (Memphis, Tennessee)

Memphis Daily Avalanche (Memphis, Tennessee)

Mobile Daily Advertiser and Register (Mobile, Alabama)

Montgomery Daily Mail (Montgomery, Alabama)

Natchez Courier (Natchez, Mississippi)

New Orleans Bee (New Orleans, Louisiana)

Richmond Daily Dispatch (Richmond, Virginia)

Richmond Daily Sentinel (Richmond, Virginia)

Richmond Daily Whig (Richmond, Virginia)

Savannah Daily Morning News (Savannah, Georgia)

Savannah Republican (Savannah, Georgia)

Selma Reporter (Selma, Alabama)

South-Western (Shreveport, Louisiana)

Southern Confederacy (Atlanta, Georgia)

Southern Federal Union (Milledgeville, Georgia)

Southern Illustrated News (Richmond, Virginia)

Southern Watchman (Athens, Georgia)

State Gazette (Austin, Texas)

Texas Republican (Marshall, Texas)

Tri-Weekly Citizen (Canton, Mississippi)

True Democrat (Little Rock, Arkansas)

Washington Telegraph (Washington, Arkansas)

Weekly Mississippian (Jackson, Mississippi)

Weekly Sun (Columbus, Georgia)

Yorkville Enquirer (York, South Carolina)

Other Sources

Acts of the General Assembly of the State of South Carolina Passed in September and December, 1863. Columbia: Charles P. Pelham, 1864.

Acts of the General Assembly of the State of Virginia, Passed in 1861. Richmond: William F. Ritchie, 1861.

Adamson, Hans Christian. *Rebellion in Missouri: 1861, Nathaniel Lyon and His Army of the West*. New York: Chilton Company, 1961.

Alabama Secretary of State, Elections and Registrations Division, Series: Election Files, State and National, 1860–1866, Container S.G. 2475.

Alexander, Thomas B. "Persistent Whiggery in the Confederate South, 1860–1877." *Journal of Southern History* 27 (1961): 305–329.

Alexander, Thomas B. *Sectional Stress and Party Strength*. Nashville: Vanderbilt University Press, 1967.

Alexander, Thomas B. and Richard E. Beringer. *The Anatomy of the Confederate Congress: A Study of the Influences of Member Characteristics on Legislative Behavior, 1861–1865*. Nashville: Vanderbilt University Press, 1972.

Alexander, Thomas B., and Richard E. Beringer. *Roll-Call Voting Records for the Confederate Congresses, 1861–1865* [Machine-readable data file]. Ann Arbor, Michigan: Inter-University Consortium for Political and Social Research.

Ambler, Charles H. *Francis H. Pierpont*. Chapel Hill: University of North Carolina Press, 1937.

America: History and Life [Machine-readable data file]. Palo Alto, California: DIALOG Information Services, 1993.

American Annual Cyclopaedia and Register of Important Events of the Year 1864. New York: D. Appleton and Company, 1865.

Amlund, Curtis Arthur. *Federalism in the Southern Confederacy*. Washington, D.C.: Public Affairs Press, 1966.

Andrews, J. Cutler. *The South Reports the Civil War*. Princeton: Princeton University Press, 1970.

Archer, J. Clark, and Fred M. Shelley. *American Electoral Mosaics*. Washington, D.C.: Association of American Geographers, 1986.

Arnold, Louise. *The Era of the Civil War — 1820–1876 Special Bibliography 11*. Carlisle, Pennsylvania: U.S. Army Military History Institute, 1982.

Ash, Stephen V. *Middle Tennessee Society Transformed, 1860–1870: War and Peace in the Upper South*. Baton Rouge: Louisiana State University Press, 1988.

Ball, Douglas B. *Financial Failure and Confederate Defeat*. Urbana, Illinois: University of Illinois Press, 1991.

Barney, William L. *The Secessionist Impulse*. Princeton: Princeton University Press, 1974.

Barrett, John G. *The Civil War in North Carolina*. Chapel Hill: University of North Carolina Press, 1963.

Baum, Dale. "Texas Elections During the Civil War: Continuity or Change?" Paper delivered before the Social Science History Association, Washington D.C., November 18, 1989.

Beers, Henry P. *Guide to the Archives of the Government of the Confederate States of America*. Washington, D.C.: National Archives and Records Service, 1968.

Bensel, Richard F. *Sectionalism and American Political Development 1880–1980*. Madison: University of Wisconsin Press, 1984.

Bensel, Richard F. "Southern Leviathan: The Development of Central State Authority in the Confederate States of America." In *Studies in American Political Development*, vol. 2, edited by Karen Orren and Stephen Skowronek. New Haven: Yale University Press, 1987.

Bensel, Richard F. *Yankee Leviathan: The Origins of Central State Authority in America, 1859–1877*. Cambridge: Cambridge University Press, 1990.

Benton, Josiah Henry. *Voting in the Field: A Forgotten Chapter in the Civil War*. Norwood, Massachusetts: Plimpton Press, 1915.

Beringer, Richard E. "A Profile of the Members of the Confederate Congress." *Journal of Southern History* 33 (4) (1967): 518–541.

Beringer, Richard E. "Political Factionalism in the Confederate Congress." Ph.D. Diss., Northwestern University, 1966.

Beringer, Richard E., et. al. *Why the South Lost the Civil War*. Athens: University of Georgia Press, 1986.

Bettersworth, John K. *Confederate Mississippi*. Philadelphia: Porcupine Press, 1978.

Billington, Ray Allan. *Frederick Jackson Turner: Historian, Scholar, Teacher*. New Haven: Yale University Press, 1973.

Billington, Ray Allan. *The Genesis of the Frontier Thesis*. San Marino, California: Huntington Library, 1971.

Biographical Directory of the United States Congress, 1774–1989. Washington, D.C.: U.S. Government Printing Office, 1989.

Birch, A. H. *Representation*. New York: Praeger, 1971.

Birdsall, Stephen S., and John W. Florin. *Regional Landscapes of the United States and Canada*. New York: Wiley, 1992.

Boatner, Mark M. *The Civil War Dictionary*. New York: David McKay Company, 1989.

Bowen, Nancy Head. "A Political Labyrinth: Texas in the Civil War—Questions in Continuity." Ph.D. Diss., Rice University, 1974.

Bragg, Jefferson Davis. *Louisiana in the Confederacy*. Baton Rouge: Louisiana State University Press, 1941.

Brunn, Stanley R. *Geography and Politics in America*. New York: Harper and Row, 1974.

Bryan, T. Conn. *Confederate Georgia*. Athens: University of Georgia Press, 1953.

Burnham, W. Dean. *Presidential Ballots 1836–1892*. Baltimore: Johns Hopkins Press, 1955.

Caskey, Willie M. *Secession and Restoration of Louisiana*. Baton Rouge: Louisiana State University Press, 1938.

Cauthen, Charles Edward. *South Carolina Goes to War 1860–1865*. Chapel Hill: University of North Carolina Press, 1950.

Channing, Steven A. *Crisis of Fear: Secession in South Carolina.* New York: Simon & Schuster, 1970.

Cherryholmes, C. H., and M. J. Shapiro. *Representatives and Roll Calls.* Indianapolis: Bobbs-Merrill, 1969.

Clausen, Aage R. *How Congressmen Decide.* New York: St. Martin's, 1973.

Cohen, Stan. *The Civil War in West Virginia.* Missoula, Montana: Gateway and Litho., 1976.

Cole, Garold L. *Civil War Eyewitnesses: An Annotated Bibliography of Books and Articles, 1955–1986.* Columbia: University of South Carolina Press, 1988.

Collie, M. P. "Voting Behavior in Legislatures." In *Handbook of Legislative Research*, edited by S. C. Loewenberg, et. al. Cambridge: Harvard University Press, 1985.

Congressional Quarterly's Guide to U.S. Elections. Washington, D.C.: Congressional Quarterly, 1985.

Connelly, Thomas L. *Civil War Tennessee, Battles and Leaders.* Knoxville: University of Tennessee Press, 1979.

Constitution or Form of Government for the People of Florida, as Revised and Amended at a Convention Begun and Holden at the City of Tallahassee on the Third Day of January, 1861, Together with the Ordinances Adopted By Said Convention. Tallahassee: Office of the Floridan and Journal, 1861.

Coulter, E. Merton. *The Civil War and Readjustment in Kentucky.* Chapel Hill: University of North Carolina Press, 1926.

Crofts, Daniel W. *Reluctant Confederates: Upper South Unionists in the Secession Crisis.* Chapel Hill: University of North Carolina Press, 1989.

Current, Richard N., et. al., eds. *Encyclopedia of the Confederacy.* New York: Simon & Schuster, 1993.

Curry, Jabez Lamar Monroe. *Civil History of the Government of the Confederate States.* Richmond, Virginia: B.F. Johnson Publishing Company, 1901.

Daniel, Larry J. "'The Assaults of the Demogues in Congress': General Albert Sidney Johnson and the Politics of Command." *Civil War History* 37 (December 1991): 328–335.

Davis, Jefferson. *The Rise and Fall of the Confederate Government.* Gloucester, Massachusetts: Crowell-Collier Publishing Company, 1971.

DeBerry, John H. "Confederate Tennessee." Ph.D. Diss., University of Kentucky, 1967.

DeRosa, Marshall L. *The Confederate Constitution of 1861.* Columbia: University of Missouri Press, 1991.

Donald, David. *The Nation in Crisis 1861–1877.* New York: Johns Hopkins University Press, 1969.

Donald, David, ed. *Why the North Won the Civil War.* Baton Rouge: Louisiana State University Press, 1960.

Dougan, Michael B. *Confederate Arkansas: The People and Politics of a Frontier State in Wartime.* University, Alabama: University of Alabama Press, 1976.

DuBose, John W. *The Life and Times of William Lowndes Yancey: A History of Political Parties in the United States, from 1834 to 1864, Especially to the Origin of the Confederate States.* 2 vols. New York: Peter Smith, 1892; rev. ed. New York: Peter Smith, 1942.

Dyer, Frederick H. *A Compendium of the War of the Rebellion.* New York: Sagamore Press, 1959.

Escott, Paul D. *After Secession.* Baton Rouge: Louisiana State University Press, 1978.

Ferguson, John L. *Arkansas and the Civil War.* Little Rock: Pioneer Press, 1961.

Fernald, Edward A., ed. *Atlas of Florida.* Tallahassee: Florida State University Press, 1992.

Fertig, James W. *The Secession and Reconstruction of Tennessee.* Chicago: University of Chicago Press, 1972.

Fits, Albert N. "The Confederate Convention." *The Alabama Review* 2 (April 1949).

Fits, Albert N. "The Confederate Convention." *The Alabama Review* 3 (July 1949).

Fleming, Walter L. *Civil War and Reconstruction in Alabama.* New York: Columbia University Press, 1905.

Folmsbee, Stanley J., Robert E. Corlew, and Enoch L. Mitchell. *Tennessee, A Short History.* Knoxville: University of Tennessee Press, 1969.

General Laws of the Eighth Legislature of the State of Texas. Austin: John Marshall and Company, 1861.

Goode, John. *Recollections of a Lifetime.* New York: Neal Publishing, 1906.

Governor's Proclamation Book, Florida State Archives, series 21, carton 51.

Griffith, Elmer C. *The Rise and Development of the Gerrymander.* Chicago: Scott Foresman, 1907.

Guide to the Civil War Records of the North Carolina State Archives. Raleigh: State Department of Archives and History, 1966.

Guide to Cartographic Records in the National Archives. Washington, D.C.: National Archives and Records Service, 1971.

Hanson, Gerald T., and Carl H. Moneyhon. *Historical Atlas of Arkansas.* Norman: University of Oklahoma Press, 1989.

Hardesty's Historical and Geographical Encyclopedia, Illustrated. Chicago: H. H. Hardesty and Co. Publishers, 1883.

Harrison, Lowell H. *The Civil War in Kentucky.* Lexington: University Press of Kentucky, 1975.

Hilliard, Sam Bowers. *Atlas of Antebellum Southern Agriculture.* Baton Rouge: Louisiana State University Press, 1984.

Hodler, Thomas W., and Howard A. Schretter. *The Atlas of Georgia.* Athens: Institute of Community and Area Development, University of Georgia, 1986.

Hopkins, Anne H., and William Lyons. *Tennessee Votes: 1799–1976.* Knoxville: Bureau of Public Administration, University of Tennessee, 1978.

Jensen, Richard. "American Election Analysis." In *Politics and the Social Sciences*, edited by Seymour Lipset. New York: Oxford University Press, 1969.

Johns, John E. *Florida during the Civil War.* Tallahassee: University of Florida Press, 1963.

Johnston, R. J. *Political, Electoral, and Spatial Systems: An Essay in Political Geography.* New York: Oxford University Press, 1979.

Jones, Archer. *Confederate Strategy from Shiloh to Vicksburg.* Baton Rouge: Louisiana State University Press, 1961.

Journal of Both Sessions of the Convention of the State of Arkansas, which were begun and held in the capitol, in the city of Little Rock. Little Rock: Johnson and Yerkes, 1861.

Journal of the Congress of the Confederate States of America, 1861–1865. 7 vols. Washington, D.C.: U.S. Government Printing Office, 1904-1905.

Journal of the People of the State of South Carolina. Columbia: R. W. Gibbes, 1862.

Journal of the Public and Secret Proceedings of the Convention of the People of Georgia, Held in Milledgeville and Savannah in 1861, Together with the Ordinances Adopted. Milledgeville: Boughton, Nisbet, and Barnes, 1861.

Journal of the Secession Convention of Texas. Austin: Texas Library and Historical Commission, 1912.

Journal of the Senate, Extra Session of the Rebel Legislature, Called by a Proclamation of C. F. Jackson, Begun and Held at Neosho, Newton County, Missouri on the Twenty-first Day of October 1861. Jefferson City: Emory S. Foster, Public Printer, 1865.

Kingdon, John W. *Congressmen's Voting Decisions.* New York: Harper and Row, 1973.

Kirkpatrick, Arthur R. "Missouri's Delegation in the Confederate Congress." *Civil War History* 2 (June 1959): 188-198.

Kirkpatrick, Arthur R. "Missouri, the Twelfth Confederate State." Ph.D. Diss., University of Missouri, 1954.

Kruman, Marc W. *Parties and Politics in North Carolina 1836–1865*. Baton Rouge: Louisiana State University Press, 1983.

Laws of the State of Mississippi Passed at a Called Session of the Mississippi Legislature Held in the City of Jackson, July 1861. Jackson: E. Barksdale, 1861.

Laws of the State of Missouri Passed at the First Session of the Seventeenth General Assembly Begun and Held at the City of Jefferson on Monday the Thirteenth of August A.D., 1852. Jefferson: James Lusk, 1853.

Lee, Charles R. Jr. *The Confederate Constitutions*. Chapel Hill: University of North Carolina Press, 1963.

Libby, Orin G. "A Plea for the Study of Votes in Congress." *Annual Report of the American Historical Association*. Washington, D.C.: Government Printing Office, 1897.

Long, E.B. *The Civil War Day by Day: An Almanac, 1861–1865*. Garden City, New York: Doubleday, 1971.

Lord, Clifford L. *A Description of the Atlas of Congressional Roll Calls: An Analysis of Yea-Nay Votes*. Newark, New Jersey: Work Projects Administration—Historical Records Survey, 1941.

Lord, Clifford L. and Elizabeth H. Lord. *Historical Atlas of the United States*. New York: Henry Holt, 1953.

Loewenberg, Gerhand, Samuel C. Patterson, and Malcolm E. Jewell. *Handbook of Legislative Research*. Cambridge: Harvard University Press, 1985.

McCrary, Peyton. *Abraham Lincoln and Reconstruction: The Louisiana Experiment*. Princeton: Princeton University Press, 1978.

McKitrick, Eric L. "Party Politics and the Union and Confederate War Efforts." In *The American Party Systems: Stages of Political Development*, edited by William N. Chambers and Walter Dean Burnham. New York: Oxford University Press, 1967.

McMillan, Malcolm C. *The Disintegration of a Confederate State*. Macon: Mercer University Press, 1986.

McPherson, Edward. *The Political History of the United States of America during the Great Rebellion*. Washington, D.C.: James J. Chapman, 1882.

McPherson, James M. *Battle Cry of Freedom: The Civil War Era*. New York: Ballantine Books, 1988.

Magnus, Philip. *Edmund Burke*. London: J. Murry, 1939.

Makie, T. T., and R. Rose. *The International Almanac of Electoral History*. London: Macmillan, 1974.

Massey, Mary Elizabeth. *Ersatz in the Confederacy*. Columbia: University of South Carolina Press, 1952.

Marten, James. *Texas Divided, Loyalty and Dissent in the Lone Star State 1856–1874*. Lexington: University Press of Kentucky, 1990.

Martis, Kenneth C. "Sectionalism and the United States Congress." *Political Geography Quarterly* 7 (April 1988): 99–109.

Martis, Kenneth C. *The Historical Atlas of Political Parties in the United States Congress 1789–1989*. New York: Macmillan, 1989.

Martis, Kenneth C. *The Historical Atlas of United States Congressional Districts 1789–1983*. New York: Free Press, 1982.

Martis, Kenneth C., and Gregory A. Elmes. *The Historical Atlas of State Power in Congress*. Washington, D.C.: Congressional Quarterly Press, 1993.

Massey, Mary Elizabeth. *Refugee Life in the Confederacy*. Baton Rouge: Louisiana State University Press, 1964.

Matthews, James M., ed. *The Statutes at Large of the Provisional Government of the Confederate States of America*. Richmond: R.M. Smith, 1864.

Monaghan, Jay. *Civil War on the Western Border 1854–1865*. Boston: Little, Brown and Company, 1955.

Moore, Albert Burton. *Conscription and Conflict in the Confederacy*. New York: Macmillan, 1924.

Moore, Frank., ed. *The Rebellion Record*. 11 vols. New York: G. P. Putnam, 1861–1863.

Moore, George Ellis. *A Banner in the Hills: West Virginia's Statehood*. New York: Meredith Publishing Company, 1963.

Morrill, Richard L. *Political Redistricting and Geographic Theory*. Washington, D.C.: Association of American Geographers, 1981.

Morris, Richard B., ed. *Encyclopedia of American History*. New York: Harper and Row, 1976.

Munden, Kenneth W. and Henry P. Beers. *Guide to Federal Archives Relating to the Civil War*. Washington, D.C.: National Archives and Records Service, 1962.

Neagles, James C. *Confederate Research Sources, A Guide to Archive Collections*. Salt Lake City: Ancestry Publishing, 1986.

Nevins, Alan, James I. Robertson, and Bell I. Wiley, eds. *Civil War Books: A Critical Bibliography*. 2 vols. Baton Rouge: Louisiana State University Press, 1967.

Nichols, Roy F. *Blueprints for Leviathan: American Style*. New York: Atheneum, 1963.

North Carolina State Archives, Miscellaneous Collection, Compiled Election Returns, Box C.E.R. 2 & 3, Confederate Congress, 1861–1864.

Norton, Phillip. *Legislatures*. New York: Oxford University Press, 1990.

Norton, Clarence Clifford. *The Democratic Party in Ante-Bellum North Carolina 1835–1861*. Chapel Hill: University of North Carolina Press, 1930.

Online Union Catalog [Machine-readable data file]. Dublin, Ohio: Online Computer Library Center, 1993.

Official Journal of the Proceedings of the Convention of the State of Louisiana. New Orleans: J.O. Nixon, 1861.

Ordinances and Constitution of the State of Alabama with the Constitution of the Provisional Government of the Confederate States of America. Montgomery: Barrett, Wimbish, and Co., 1861.

Owsley, Frank Lawrence. *State Rights in the Confederacy*. University of Chicago Press, 1925.

Parrish, William E. *Turbulent Partnership: Missouri and the Union 1861–1865*. Columbia: University of Missouri Press, 1963.

Paullin, C.O., and John K. Wright. *Atlas of the Historical Geography of the United States*. New York: Carnegie Institution and American Geographical Society, 1932.

Patton, James W. *Unionism and Reconstruction in Tennessee, 1860–1890*. Chapel Hill: University of North Carolina Press, 1934

Pearce, Haywood J. Jr. *Benjamin H. Hill: Secession and Reconstruction*. Chicago: University of Chicago Press, 1928.

Pirkle, E. C., and W. H. Yoho. *Natural Landscapes of the United States*. Dubuque, Iowa: Kendall/Hunt, 1985.

Pitkin, Hanna F. *The Concept of Representation*. Berkeley: University of California Press, 1967.

Public Laws of the State of North Carolina Passed by the General Assembly At Its Second Extra Session, 1861. Raleigh: John Spelman, 1861.

Public Acts of the State of Tennessee Passed at the First Session of the Thirty-Fourth General Assembly for the Years 1861–62. Nashville: Griffith, Camp and Co., 1861.

Pressly, Thomas J., and William H. Scofield. *Farm Real Estate Values in the United States by Counties, 1850–1959*. Seattle: University of Washington Press, 1965.

"Proceedings of the Confederate Congress." *Southern Historical Society Papers* XLIV-LII (1923–1959).

Proceedings of the Convention Establishing Provisional Government of Kentucky. Augusta, Georgia: Steam Press of Chronicle and Sentinel, 1863.

Quisenberry, A. C. "The Alleged Secession of Kentucky." *Register of the Kentucky State Historical Society* 15 (May 1917): 15–32.

Rabenhorst, Thomas D., ed. *Historical U.S. County Outline Map Collection 1840–1980.* Baltimore: Department of Geography, University of Maryland Baltimore County, 1984.

Ramsdell, Charles W., ed. *Laws and Resolutions of the Last Session of the Confederate Congress Together with the Secret Acts of the Previous Congresses.* Durham, North Carolina: Duke University Press, 1941.

Reagan, John H. *Memoirs: With Special Reference to Secession and the Civil War.* Austin: Pemberton Press, 1968.

Records of the Louisiana State Government, 1850–1888. War Department Collection of Confederate Records: Roll 14. Records of the Executive Department, 1860–1865, and Records of the Judicial Department, 1861–1862. Washington, D.C.: National Archives Microfilm Publications, 1961.

Ringold, May Spencer. *The Role of the State Legislatures in the Confederacy.* Athens: University of Georgia Press, 1966.

Robbins, John B. "Confederate Nationalism: Politics and Government in the Confederate South, 1861–1865." Ph.D. Diss., Rice University, 1964.

Robertson, James I., Jr. *Civil War Virginia: Battleground for a Nation.* Charlottesville: University Press of Virginia, 1991.

Rowles, Ruth Anderson, and Kenneth C. Martis. "Mapping Congress: Developing a Geographic Understanding of American Political History." *Prologue: Journal of the National Archives* 16 (Spring 1984): 4–21.

Russel, Robert R. *Critical Studies in Antebellum Sectionalism.* Westport, Connecticut: Greenwood Publishing Company, 1972.

Sallnow, J. *An Electoral Atlas of Europe.* London: Butterworth Scientific, 1982.

Schmeckebier, Laurence F. *Congressional Apportionment.* Washington, D.C.: Brookings Institution, 1941.

Secretary of State, MSS Election Returns, 1861 and 1863, RG 307, Texas State Library, Archives Division, Austin.

Shanks, Henry T. *The Secession Movement in Virginia.* Richmond: Garrett and Massie Publishers, 1934.

Siegal, Frederick F. *The Roots of Southern Distinctiveness: Tobacco and Society in Danville, Virginia, 1780–1865.* Chapel Hill: University of North Carolina Press, 1987.

Silby, Joel H. *The Shrine of Party.* Pittsburgh: Pittsburgh University Press, 1967.

Silver, James W. *Mississippi in the Confederacy as Seen in Retrospect.* Baton Rouge: Louisiana State University Press, 1961.

Simms, Henry H. *Life of Robert M.T. Hunter, A Study of Sectionalism and Secession.* Richmond: William Byrd Press, 1935.

South Carolina Department of Archives, General Assembly Papers, Misc. Committees to the General Assembly, 1863, No. 34.

Stampp, Kenneth M. *The Imperiled Union, Essays on the Background of the Civil War.* New York: Oxford University Press, 1980.

Statutes at Large of the Confederate States of America. Richmond: R. M. Smith, 1862–1864.

Statutes at Large of the Provisional Government of the Confederate States of America. Richmond: R. M. Smith, 1864.

Stephenson, Richard W. *Civil War Maps: An Annotated List of Maps and Atlases in the Library of Congress.* Washington, D.C.: Library of Congress, 1989.

Stephenson, Richard W. *A Guide to Civil War Maps in the National Archives.* Washington, D.C.: National Archives and Records Administration, 1986.

Stephenson, Wendell Holmes, and E. Merton Coulter, eds. *A History of the South.* 10 vols. Baton Rouge: Louisiana State University Press, 1950. Vol. 7: *The Confederate States of America 1861–1865*, by E. Merton Coulter.

Stephens, A. Ray, and William M. Holmes. *Historical Atlas of Texas.* Norman: University of Oklahoma Press, 1989.

Stutler, Boyd B. *West Virginia in the Civil War.* West Virginia: Education Foundation, Inc., 1966.

Sutton, Robert P. *Revolution to Secession: Constitution in the Old Dominion.* Charlottesville: University Press of Virginia, 1989.

Tatum, Georgia Lee. *Disloyalty in the Confederacy.* Chapel Hill: University of North Carolina Press, 1934.

Taylor, Peter J. *Political Geography.* London: Longman, 1985.

Taylor, Peter J. "The Geography of Elections." In *Progress in Political Geography*, edited by M. Pacione. London: Croom Helm, 1985.

Tennessee State Library and Archives, Statewide General Election, August 6, 1863. Record Group 87, Series Number: 1, sub-series letter: A.

Thomas, Emory M. *The Confederate Nation 1861–1865.* New York: Harper and Row, 1979.

Thompson, William Y. *Robert Toombs of Georgia.* Baton Rouge: Louisiana State University Press, 1966.

Thornbury, W. D. *Regional Geomorphology of the United States.* New York: Wiley, 1956.

Thorndale, William, and William Dollarhide. *Map Guide to the Federal Censuses, 1790–1920.* Baltimore: Genealogical Publishing Co., 1987.

Todd, Richard C. *Confederate Finance.* Athens: University of Georgia Press, 1954.

Turner, Frederick Jackson. "The Significance of Section in American History." *Wisconsin Magazine of History* 8 (1925): 225–280.

Turner, George Edgar. *Victory Rode the Rails: The Strategic Place of the Railroads in the Civil War.* New York: Bobbs-Merrill, 1953.

U.S. Department of Commerce. *Historical Statistics of the United States.* Washington, D.C.: U.S. Government Printing Office, 1975.

United States Historical Election Returns 1788–1981 [Machine-readable data file]. Ann Arbor, Michigan: Inter-University Consortium for Political and Social Research.

Vandiver, Frank E. *Basic History of the Confederacy.* Huntington, New York: Robert E. Krieger Publishing Company, 1980.

Vandiver, Frank E. *Their Tattered Flags, The Epic of the Confederacy.* New York: Harper's Magazine Press, 1970.

Virginia State Archives, Poll Books 1863.

Wakelyn, Jon L. *Biographical Dictionary of the Confederacy.* Westport, Connecticut: Greenwood Press, 1977.

Wahlke, John C. *The Legislative System.* New York: John Wiley, 1962.

War of the Rebellion: A Compilation of the Official Records of the Union and Confederate Armies. 128 vols. Washington, D.C.: Government Printing Office, 1880–1901.

Ward, Geoffrey C. *The Civil War.* New York: Alfred A. Knopf, 1990.

Warinner, N. E., comp. *A Register of Military Events in Virginia 1861–1865.* Richmond: Virginia Civil War Commission, 1959.

Warner, Ezra J., and Buck W. Yearns. *Biographical Register of the Confederate Congress.* Baton Rouge: Louisiana State University Press, 1975.

Webster, Gerald R., and Scott A. Samson. "On Defining the Alabama Black Belt: Historical Changes and Variations." *Southeastern Geographer* XXXII (November 1992): 163–172.

White, Laura A. *Robert Barnwell Rhett: Father of Secession.* New York: Century, 1931.

Wiley, Bell Irvin., ed. *Letters of Warren Akin: Confederate Congressman.* Athens: University of Georgia Press, 1959.

Wiley, Bell Irvin, and Hirst D. Milhollen. *Embattled Confederates, An Illustrated History of Southerners at War.* New York: Harper and Row, 1964.

Woods, James M. "Devotees and Dissenters: Arkansas in the Confederate Congress, 1861–1865." *Arkansas Historical Quarterly* 38 (Autumn 1979): 227–237.

Woodward, C. Vann. "What the War Made Us." In *The Civil War* by Geoffrey C. Ward. New York: Alfred A. Knopf, 1990.

Wooster, Ralph A. *The Secession Conventions of the South.* Princeton: Princeton University Press, 1962.

Wright, John H., comp. *Compendium of the Confederacy, An Annotated Bibliography.* 2 vols. Wilmington, North Carolina: Broadfoot Publishing Company, 1989.

Yearns, W. Buck., ed. *The Confederate Governors.* Athens: University of Georgia Press, 1985.

Yearns, Wilfred Buck. *The Confederate Congress.* Athens: University of Georgia Press, 1960.

Yearns, W. Buck, and John G. Barrett. *North Carolina Civil War Documentary.* Chapel Hill: University of North Carolina Press, 1980.

INDEX

Maps are referred to by the letter *m* following a page number; tables by the page number, the letter *t*, and the table number; and notes by the page number, the letter *n*, and the note number.